Volume 4 of Russia and the South Pacific, 1696–1840
THE TUAMOTU ISLANDS AND TAHITI

The final volume in a quartet of books on the naval, scientific, and social activities of the Imperial Russian Navy in the South Pacific, this book focuses on the expeditions to Tahiti and the dangerous atoll chains to its east, known as the Tuamotus. Under the command of Captains Otto von Kotzebue and F.F. Bellingshausen, expedition members were the first to chart several of the Tuamotu islands. Highly educated and perceptive, these Russian scientists and naval officers made many fascinating and accurate observations about coral reef and atoll formation, botanical specimens, and the cultural activities of the inhabitants. Yet, unlike their counterparts from other European nations, the Russians made no territorial claims and took pains not to provoke the hostility of the islanders.

Glynn Barratt has made full use of Russian primary materials in describing the sites and individuals the visitors encountered. Contemporary aquarelles and drawings by the expeditionary artists Ludovik Choris and Pavel N. Mikhailov provide pictorial evidence. These are complemented by descriptions and photographs of many of the artifacts gathered by Russian officers and now accessible to scholars in archives in St. Petersburg and Estonia.

GLYNN BARRATT is a professor of Russian at Carleton University.

University of British Columbia Press
PACIFIC MARITIME STUDIES SERIES

Volume 4 of
Russia and the South Pacific,
1696–1840

THE
TUAMOTU
ISLANDS
AND
TAHITI

Glynn Barratt

UBC Press / Vancouver

ISBN 0-7748-0409-2
ISSN 0847-0529

Canadian Cataloguing in Publication Data

Barratt, Glynn.
   The Tuamotu Islands and Tahiti

   (University of British Columbia Press Pacific maritime studies series; 10)
   (Volume 4 of Russia and the South Pacific, 1696–1840, ISSN 0847-0529)
   Includes bibliographical references and index.

   ISBN 0-7748-0409-2

1. Tuamotu Islands—Discovery and exploration—Russian. 2. Tahiti—Discovery
and exploration—Russian. 3. Scientific expeditions—Tuamotu Islands—History.
4. Scientific expeditions—Tahiti—History. 5. Soviet Union—Exploring expeditions.
6. Soviet Union—History, Naval. I. Title. II. Series: University of British Columbia
Press Pacific maritime studies; 10. III. Series: Barratt, Glynn. Russia and the South
Pacific, 1696–1840; v. 4.

DU890.B37 1992   996.3′2   C92-091421-7

This book has been published with the help of a grant from the Social Science Federation
of Canada, using funds provided by the Social Sciences and Humanities Research Council
of Canada.

Publication of this book was also made possible by ongoing support from The Canada
Council, the Province of British Columbia Cultural Services Branch, and the Department
of Communications of the Government of Canada.

UBC Press
University of British Columbia
6344 Memorial Rd
Vancouver, BC V6T 1Z2
(604) 822-3259
Fax: (604) 822-6083

Contents

Illustrations, Maps, and Tables

ILLUSTRATIONS

Following page 142:

MAPS

TABLES

Preliminary Notes

A few words on the problem of rendering into English Tahitian proper names that have been transcribed in Cyrillic: Russian lacks certain letters, notably "h" and "w," and so one must make allowances on encountering, in Russian texts, such names as Guageine and Mata-Giva (Huaheine and Matahiva in English form), even while bearing in mind that Russians in the early nineteenth century were often rendering into Cyrillic Polynesian place and personal names on the basis of James Cook's or his people's orthography. Thus, the eighteenth-century British form of Otahiti becomes O-taiti or Otaiti. By considering Kotzebue's and Bellingshausen's published sources, which were mostly but not exclusively British, one can easily gloss over such place names as Teporionnuu for Te Poroinu'u, or Tagara Point for Taharaa Point. In this volume, there is no standardization of all forms of Tahitian names found in the Russian texts translated, but Tahiti is substituted for O-taiti, O-taite, etc., after the first one or two occurrences. All Russian, French, and German texts are translated on the basis of first editions *except* for the Kotzebue account of the *Predpriiatie* visit to Tahiti in March 1824. It should not be inferred from this that the London version of Kotzebue's narrative, *A New Voyage Round the World* (1830), is an altogether accurate and adequate translation. In reality, it is so free as to be bordering on paraphrase. The point, however, is that London Missionary Society apologists, James Montgomery especially, responded to the 1830 London text when they rebutted Kotzebue's allegations that the mission in Tahiti had not preached true Christianity and that its version of the Gospel was a libel on the Saviour. I discuss translations, adaptations, and reprintings of the Kotzebue narratives of 1821 and 1830 in *The Russian View of Honolulu, 1809-1826* (Ottawa, 1988), pages 300-2.

With regard to Baltic German surnames: widely recognized anglicized forms have been accepted, especially when bearers of names with a Russian and non-Russian form so signed themselves: hence Bellingshausen and not Bellinsgauzen, except in reference to publications by that name, and Kotzebue rather than the awkward Kotsebu. For professional or other reasons, some distinguished Baltic German officers and scholars identified with Russia so much as to adopt the Slavic version of their name when signing documents or even letters. *Predpriiatie*'s young mineralogist is therefore Ernst K. Gofman, not Hoffmann. On the other hand, the artist Ludovik Andreevich (just Ludwig, by baptism) Khoris wrote and published under French colours, as Choris, and his feelings on the matter are respected.

Acknowledgments

I am grateful to the staffs of many libraries and archives for assistance, and to many individuals for their constructive criticism of the first draft of this survey. The archives and manuscript repositories include the Central State Archive of the Navy (TsGAVMF); the Central State Historical Archive in St. Petersburg (TsGIAL); the Archive of the All-Union Geographical Society (AGO); the Central State Historical Archives of Estonia, Tartu (TsGIAE); the Estonian Museum of History in Tallin; the Public Record Office, London; and the Library, Head Office of the London Missionary Society, also in London.

Among Russian and Baltic scholars to whom I am particularly grateful for help and hospitality are Dr. Toomas Tamla and Inge Tallo of Eesti Ajaloomuuseum, Tallin; Kalju Leib, Assistant Director at TsGIAE, Tartu; Irina Grigor'eva, former head of International Exchanges Division at the N.N. Saltykov-Shchedrin Public Library, St. Petersburg; the late Professor R.F. Its, director of the Peter the Great Museum of Ethnography of the Academy of Sciences, in St. Petersburg; and his colleagues there, Dr. Nikolai A. Butinov and Dr. Tamara K. Shafranovskaia of the Australia and Ocean Division; also Dr. N.N. Goncharova of the State Historical Museum on Red Square and Academy of Arts; Sergei Murav'ev of St. Petersburg; and two members of the charming and erudite Staniukovich family of literary and naval antecedents, Tat'iana Vladimirovna and her daughter Mariia, both of St. Petersburg and MAE.

I also express my thanks to Roger Rose of the Bernice P. Bishop Museum, Honolulu; John Dunmore of Massey University, New Zealand; and Dr. Patricia Polansky, Russian bibliographer at the Hamilton Research Library, University of Hawaii at Manoa. Finally, I thank the Social

Sciences and Humanities Research Council of Canada for research grants; Carleton University, Ottawa, for research and travel assistance over a six-year period; and my friends in St. Petersburg for help and hospitality beyond the call of academic duty.

Introduction

This is the final volume in a series entitled *Russia and the South Pacific, 1696-1840*. The first three surveyed the Russians' early dealings in Australia, in Southern and Eastern Polynesia (New Zealand, the Austral Islands, Easter Island), and in Melanesia and the Western Polynesian fringe (Fiji, Vanuatu, Tuvalu, and Anuta). This instalment offers surveys and discussion of the Russians' social, maritime, and scientific dealings in Tahiti and its nearest westward neighbour, Mo'orea, and among the numerous (and dangerous) low atolls to its east, the Tuamotu Archipelago. Like broken necklaces, these atolls stretch at least a thousand miles on a roughly WNW by ESE axis. Even today, they remain a great impediment to efficient trade and commerce. When Russian ships first entered Polynesia in the early nineteenth century, most were unknown to Europeans, who generally avoided the entire archipelago, then marked on atlases as "Dangerous or Low." It is the proud boast of the Russian Navy to have minimized the danger represented by these little specks of coral, one light sweep of which was enough to rip a hole in a wooden vessel.

Russian records for Tahiti—Otaiti in contemporary Russian logs and journals, which so regularly and deliberately echoed those of Bougainville, Cook, and other eighteenth-century "discoverers" of Otaheite—differ in two respects from Russian evidence for other parts of Polynesia in the Southern Hemisphere. Both those differences reflect the lateness of the Russians' arrival on the Tuamotuan-Tahitian scene (1816-20). First, Tahiti was a kingdom in the full sense of that word: with aid and arms from Europeans, the Pomares had become a dynasty, ruling a centralized, if not yet unified, small Polynesian state much as Kamehameha I of the Hawaiian Islands also ruled a state. Second, the European missionary influence was overwhelmingly apparent, at least at Matavai Bay on the north shore of Tahiti, where the Russians always anchored in the twenties, and in Opunohu (Talu) Bay on Mo'orea where they anchored in the later 1830s. To encounter King Pomare II and his queen Terito (Terimo'emo'e) was inevitably to be conscious of the Reverend Henry Nott, chief representative in 1820 of the London Missionary Society, which had transformed Tahitian mores and society. It was Nott who had converted and instructed King Pomare II, who had first preached in his language, who had given him his bible and his Act of Constitution, and who interpreted for Captain Bellingshausen when *Vostok* came to Tahiti. Did the Russians wish to see the "royal residence" at Venus Point? The solid missionary houses and the missionary church lay between the landing-place and "palace." Did the Russians plan to barter with the islanders for foodstuffs? No such barter could be carried on during the Sabbath. Thus are the Pomares, Teremo'mo'e, Paofai, Tati, and Hitoti introduced, in the missionary framework, in Russian records in the company of Henry Nott, Charles Wilson, and other agents of that missionary society that had abolished Arcady by 1820, swaddled Venus in the robes of decency, and brought Jehovah to the former heathen worshippers of Oro and a local pantheon. Some Russian officers were unenthused about the drastic transformation of Tahitian life and culture that had occurred in a single generation. Kotzebue in particular was unimpressed. Indeed, the joylessness of what the missionaries had brought to Otaheite offended him so deeply that he published his opinion of it, as a libel on the Saviour and a blasphemy against His Joyful Word. This disapproval of the banning of all dance and non-religious music was shared by the companies of Russians who arrived before and after him. No doubt, the Russian narratives concur, the London Missionary Society had done its duty in abolishing such practices as human sacrifice, infanticide, and public incest. But the price was very high. Such contentions were rebutted by apologists of the Society, with heat and indignation, from 1830 onward.

Otto Evstaf'evich von Kotzebue, son of the celebrated playwright, sailed for Polynesia in the brig *Riurik* in August 1815, with a truly international scientific company. With him went the Danish traveller and naturalist Morten Wormskiöld (1783-1845), the young zoologist and surgeon Johann Friedrich Eschscholtz (1793-1831), the Franco-German naturalist-poet Adelbert von Chamisso (1781-1838), and a Russo-German artist named Ludovik (Louis) Andreevich Khoris, or Choris (1795-1828). Rounding Cape Horn in late January 1816, *Riurik* called at Talcaguano in Chile before pressing west towards Easter Island and thence, in early April, to the Tuamotu clusters. On this voyage, Kotzebue began the Russian Navy's hydrographic effort, in the course of which ten atolls were discovered and correctly charted.

Surveys are offered here of the botany, zoology, ethnography, surveying, and geodesy that the Russians, and the Germans in their service, undertook in the Tuamotus from 1816 to 1824. Marine astronomy is included under hydrography, which, in the Polynesian context, is properly connected with the name of Kruzenshtern, distinguished author of the *Atlas of the South Pacific Ocean* (*Atlas Iuzhnago moria*, 1823-26). Botanical and zoological materials collected in the Tuamotu Islands by Kotzebue's or by Bellingshausen's people were submitted to St. Petersburg officialdom. Some specimens then went with Chamisso or Eschscholtz to Berlin or Estonia. The great majority, however, went to the Academy of Sciences; and today some remain in the possession of the post-Soviet descendants of that Petrine institution, the Komarov Institute of Botany (BIAN) and the Main Ornithological Division of the Zoological Institute. Having unearthed many such specimens in recent years, I offer comments on the fates and present whereabouts of birds, herbaria, rock samples, and, above all, native artefacts brought from the Tuamotu atolls to St. Petersburg in 1821-26 (see Chapter 3, "Russian Science in the Tuamotu Archipelago").

Riurik was the last vessel to sail from the Baltic to the North Pacific Ocean's frozen rim without provoking the political unease in London that had always been expected of Madrid. The aims of science and of empire were soon to be united in another age of peace and national rivalries. No one, observed Sir John Barrow, indefatigable Secretary to the Admiralty Board in London, could reasonably argue that *Riurik*'s find of Kotzebue Sound on the extreme northwestern tip of North America had no strategic or political significance. Had Kotzebue found the navigable passage that his patron, Count Rumiantsev, and the officers of *Riurik* believed in, whatever purely scientific aims he might have had would have been quite beside the point. The search for Arctic passages was on again, and it was clear that the Russians were not standing idle. At the urging of Barrow and his colleagues, Parliament promised large rewards for the discoverers of any passages if they were British subjects. Thus began for Britain the golden age of Arctic exploration—the age of Scoresby, Franklin, Parry, and the Rosses. These efforts in turn provoked an even grander Russian Arctic undertaking, which was to benefit Polynesian studies, particularly the study of Tahiti.

It was time, the Russian Admiralty felt, for Russians to win laurels and political advantage from a scientific voyage of discovery in the tradition of Cook and Bougainville. Better yet, Russia would launch a double polar expedition. Two ships, *Vostok* and *Mirnyi*, would investigate the furthest south, Antarctica; two more, *Otkrytie* (*Discovery*) and *Blagonamerennyi* (*Well-Intentioned*) would press north in Kotzebue's wake, seeking some navigable passage between North Atlantic and Pacific waters. Thus began the planning of the Bellingshausen-Lazarev Antarctic expedition (1819-21), in the course of which the Russians passed six days (22-27 July 1820) in Matavai Bay, Tahiti, and completed thorough surveys of its human population, flora, fauna, and resources.

Bellingshausen and his people were received with hospitality and warmth by King Pomare II and his court. *Vostok* and *Mirnyi* dropped anchor in Matavai Bay close to the spot where HMS *Dolphin* (Captain Wallis) had stood fifty-three years before in June 1767, and where Cook's vessels had stood. Within minutes, the Russians were encircled by dozens of canoes, carrying hundreds of Tahitians. All was gay and very noisy. Even so, the Russians swiftly understood that what had once been Elysium, La Nouvelle Cythère, had been changed in fundamental ways. One of the agents of that change, the Reverend Henry Nott, was soon at hand.

The Russian evidence for life and culture in Tahiti at the height of the London Missionary Society's success is, in both quality and scope, quite different from that for material and social culture in the Tuamotu atolls, where the European influence was either very faint or non-existent. And it differs fundamentally from contemporaneous accounts of life and culture in the Rangitane-Ngatikuia country of Queen Charlotte Sound, New Zealand, and from 1804 accounts of Nukuhiva in the Washington-Marquesas Islands. For the Russian naval visitors to Taio-hae Bay on Nukuhiva had deliberately used the European castaways they found there, Edward Robarts and the Frenchman Le Cabri, and thereby managed their relations with a Polynesian group whose ancient customs and beliefs remained intact despite the European presence. The Russians took advantage of the presence of assorted English-speaking castaways or settlers in the Hawaiian Islands with equal success. In New Zealand, only weeks before his coming to Tahiti, Bellingshausen had found ample evidence of ways in which potato cultivation, an important legacy of Cook's, had changed the local way of life, migration, diet, and even attitudes toward the future. Conversely, in their dress, decoration, beliefs, customs, and skills, the Maoris encountered in Queen Charlotte Sound still lived the labour-filled, traditional life of their people. It was a different matter in Tahiti, where English missionaries had been toiling with conspicuous success for more than twenty years. Bellingshausen and his people were obliged to gain the missionaries' favour, or at least their understanding, before dealing with representatives of local monarchy.

Still, as required by their orders from the Naval Ministry, the Russian visitors of 1820 deliberately and conscientiously recorded those features of traditional Tahitian life and culture that they saw. Around the bay and in the adjoining districts of Pare and Arue, they examined what remained of local mores and traditional Tahitian crafts after a quarter-century of missionary work. Woven objects, specimens of tapa clothing, wooden figures, weaponry, musical instruments, and small utensils were collected for St. Petersburg. Officers fully described in notes and journals the events and circumstances that indicate not only the provenance of items now in St. Petersburg's Peter the Great Museum of Ethnography but also their value. As for illustrative records for Tahiti, such as the ink-and-pencil drawings and the aquarelles of Pavel N. Mikhailov, *Vostok*'s artist on secondment from St. Petersburg's Academy of Arts, they have an ethnographic value that does not need explanation. Three such drawings, from Mikhailov's original portfolio, are published here for the first time in a scientific context. They are complemented by, and lend additional significance to, detailed photographs of artefacts that went from Matavai Bay to St. Petersburg in 1821-26 or arrived earlier at the Imperial Academy of Sciences by other routes. The Russian narratives, here translated into English for the first time save in Chamisso's, Bellingshausen's, and Kotzebue's cases, are considered in conjunction with pictorial and physical evidence found today in St. Petersburg or Tartu, Estonia. They form the basis for a survey of the botany, zoology, ethnography, hydrography, geology, and meteorology that Russians undertook on Otaheite. If I insist on, so to speak, non-naval sciences, it is because neither Soviet nor Western specialists (Vucinich, Vorob'ev, Pasetskii, Heidemaa) give them more than fleeting glances. If I emphasize the fact that Russian sources, left by trained, objective men, may be of value to the student of Tahiti and other islands, it is because the very fact that they exist is largely ignored throughout the West.

Part One

THE TUAMOTU ARCHIPELAGO

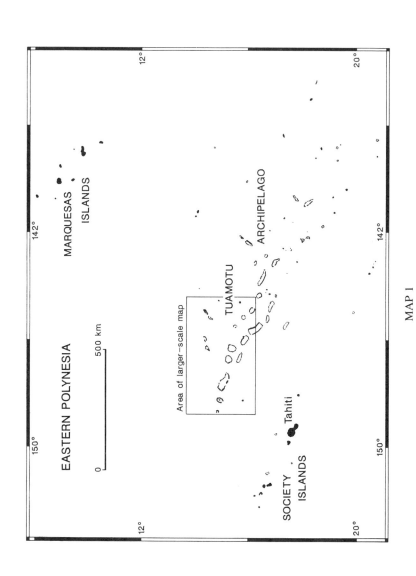

MAP 1

The Tuamotu Archipelago in relation to other Pacific Island groups

1

A SURVEY

GENERAL OBSERVATIONS ON RUSSIAN HYDROGRAPHY IN MID-PACIFIC

The Russian hydrographic record in Central Polynesia in the post-Napoleonic era (1816-26) is a proud one, equal to that of the British and superior to that of the United States and France. Within that record, exploration and surveying in the scattered coral islands that comprise the Tuamotu Archipelago east of Tahiti represent the brightest page of all. Kruzenshtern's two protégés, Otto von Kotzebue and Faddei F. Bellingshausen, brought three dozen coral islands into focus for the first time, for the benefit of international science and cartography; accurately placed them in relation to each other and to Venus Point, Tahiti, in the west; collected careful ethnographical, botanical, and zoological materials relating to specific islands; and discovered ten islands or clusters that had been unknown to Europeans. These were Tikahau, Angatau, Nihiru, the Raevskii cluster, Katiu, Fakarava, Niau, Matahiva, Fangahina, and Aratika.[1] Tikahau was sighted and described by Kotzebue on his voyage in *Riurik* (April 1816), Fangahina and Aratika on his second South Pacific expedition, but third Polynesian visit, in the armed sloop *Predpriiatie* (March 1824). The rest were sighted and described by Bellingshausen in the sloop *Vostok* (July 1820). Using the latest astronomical and other instruments, including telescopes by Troughton and Tully, six thermometers, camera lucidas by Thomas Jones, pocket chronometers by Hardy and Barraud, sounding machines by Massey, and the very finest sextants then available in London or St. Petersburg,[2] the Russians strove to remove the many layered errors adhering, like so many barnacles, to European knowledge of the archipelago. They took their ships along the same westerly routes among the low-lying and dangerous small islands that the Dutch captains Jacob Le Maire and Jacob Roggeveen had followed in 1616 and 1722.[3] Scanning the maps of Purdy, Arrowsmith, and Horsburgh, all issued by the Russian Admiralty, they examined foreign histories of navigation in the Great South Sea from Charles de Brosses's *Histoire des navigations aux Terres Australes* (1756) to James Burney's *Discoveries in the South Sea* (1803-17) in hopes of tracing even older Spanish routes across those islands. It was not the Russian Admiralty's fault that Kotzebue did not know which of the Tuamotus had been seen in 1606 by Pedro de Quiros and his people,[4] or that cautious Bellingshausen should in 1820 follow *San Pablo*'s route of 1606 to Amanu, Raroia, and Takume, ignorant that he was doing so. In short, the Russians did their best to maximize the cartographic benefits of every sweep across the Tuamotu Archipelago, first checking ancient data from the charts, then plugging the inter-island gaps. Zigzagging purposefully north and south and east and west, *Riurik*, *Vostok*, and *Predpriiatie* covered the ocean between 17° and 15°S between longitudes 136° and 146°W. To what effect the heirs of Kruzenshtern had studied all available accounts of other voyages in those same waters is plain when one considers the comparatively few and insignificant discoveries that Louis Isidor Duperrey (*Coquille*, 1823-24) and Frederick William Beechey (*Blossom*, 1826) were to make among the Tuamotu Archipelago's southeastern outliers. For Duperrey there was Reao; for the British Vanavana, Fangataufa, and Ahunui. Beechey reckoned the position of this "Byam Martin's Island" (Ahunui) to be 19°40'S, 140°29'W.[5] Captain-Lieutenant Mikhail Staniukovich of *Moller* was on the spot by April 1827 and, by longer sets of reckonings than had been managed from *Blossom*, gave a different, more accurate position for the island's western tip (19°38' 40"S, 140°25' 35"W).[6] If there was any part of Oceania where Russian officers of scientific bent felt at home and comfortable, it was the region of the Tuamotu Archipelago and the neighbouring Marquesas group. Not only had Staniukovich as good a chart of Central Polynesia as could be had; he also drew support from an awareness of the proximity of two well-known revictualling stations: Matavai, in Tahiti, and the Russian-charted Hakaui Bay (Port Chichagov), in Nukuhiva.[7] Psychologically and practically, the Nukuhiva visit of *Nadezhda* and *Neva* in 1804 was significant for later Russian vessels moving on the great arc, west-by-north, from South America to Petropavlovsk-in-Kamchatka or the Russian Northwest Coast.

Cook and Bougainville had been pursuing national interests in the Pacific, where they vainly sought a vast Terra Australis. Yet the scientific value of their work was obvious. So, too, the Russians, in the first era of European peace for thirty years, strove for both political and academic gain. *Riurik* was built expressly for discovery and scientific work; and *Suvorov* had been modified for trading purposes. Neither ship had heavy armament, yet both were politically significant in North Pacific waters. In the post-Napoleonic age, as in the time of *Resolution* and *Discovery*, "the aims of science and of empire were essentially one and the same."[8] It was some measure of the difference between imperialist outlooks in St. Petersburg and London in the early 1820s, and between the Royal Navy's and the Russian Navy's muscle and perceived needs in the later nineteenth century, that, in the justifiably proud words of L.S. Berg, "neither then nor subsequently did Russia evince the least intention of annexing to her possessions those numerous islands to which, by right of first discovery, she could have laid claim."[9]

It is to Kruzenshtern's and his subordinates' credit that they consciously elected to insist upon the scientific aspect of the Russian Navy's North Pacific enterprise throughout the post-Napoleonic period. Late on the scene, as Kruzenshtern himself observed, the Russians fully recognized the pointlessness of questioning Cook's triumphs in the South Pacific Ocean. Before him, the "notion of a Southern Continent . . . sunk to the bottom of the ocean."[10] In themselves, conversely, Cook's achievements opened up important tasks for Russian seamen. First, there was the matter of an ice-bound continent near the South Pole: Cook himself had not dismissed the possibility of its existence but believed that it would never be observed, still less described. Second, there were the scattered islands that remained, once the idea of the Southern Continent had been exploded. They were numerous and wretchedly charted, bore varieties of names and were a hazard to the shipping of the world. In particular, those due south of the Marquesas, which straddled routes that Russian vessels would most probably be taking in the future on the anticlockwise, westward passage from Chile, called for scrutiny.

Kruzenshtern of course accepted that the *Riurik*'s main task was in the Arctic. As Count Rumiantsev's maritime and naval adviser, he planned the venture in the North.[11] Nevertheless he kept the islands of the Great South Sea in mind. As the discoverer of Hakaui Bay in Nukuhiva, the moving spirit of the first Russian naval expedition into Polynesia, and the heir to Lieutenant James Trevenen, it was inevitable that he should.[12] "Some little islands," as Trevenen had observed in his North Pacific Project of 1787, might well "remain undiscovered within the immense extent of the South Seas. . . ." Why should not Russia "have the glory of putting the finishing stroke to the so much celebrated discoveries of the maritime nations, and rendering the geography of the globe perfect?"[13] Long nourished by Kruzenshtern, such aims were fully realized by Kotzebue.

Supposing [wrote Kruzenshtern of *Riurik*'s impending voyage] that the wished-for discovery of a connection between the two seas should not be made . . . yet many important advantages would accrue from it to the sciences, and especially to navigation. . . . The crossing of the whole South Sea twice, in quite different directions, would certainly not a little contribute to enlarge our knowledge of this great ocean, as well as of the inhabitants of the numerous islands scattered over it; and a rich harvest of objects of natural history was to be expected, as the count had appointed, besides the ship's surgeon [Eschscholtz], an able naturalist [Chamisso].[14]

Kotzebue was in perfect sympathy with Kruzenshtern where South Pacific Islands were concerned; indeed, his ill-wishers later suggested that he beat a swift retreat from Arctic pack-ice, having little stomach for that trial and preferring sunny climes.[15] Slander apart, Kotzebue unabashedly enjoyed his mid-Pacific survey work, expunging non-existent islands from the map, correcting old coordinates, and incidentally permitting Chamisso and Eschscholtz to pursue natural sciences in a distinguished way. "Mr. von Chamisso, of Berlin," writes Kruzenshtern in this connection, "was recommended to the chancellor [Rumiantsev] by Professors Rudolph and Lichtenstein, as a thoroughly well-informed man, passionately devoted to his department of science; how well merited this recommendation was . . . is manifest from the work before us."[16] As the value of the *Riurik*'s tropical cruises was enhanced by Chamisso, so was the scientific value of *Vostok*'s by I.M. Simonov.[17] In management and in scientific method and technique, the Russian sweeps across the Tuamotu Archipelago of 1816-24 represented not a quantum leap, perhaps, but an enormous forward step from the time of Wallis, Cook, and Bougainville.

RIURIK'S ARRIVAL IN THE ARCHIPELAGO, 1816

Crossing the Tuamotu Archipelago a half a century before *Riurik* arrived, Samuel Wallis of *Dolphin* wrongly reckoned the positions of six islands: Pinaki, Nukutavake, Vairaatea, Paraoa, Manuhangi, and Nengonengo. Errors of latitude were slight, but those of longitude were serious. When accuracy *was* obtained, such as at Venus Point, it redounded to the credit not of Wallis or his second-in-command but rather to John Harrison, *Dolphin*'s purser-cum-astronomer. Harrison had a taste for mathematics and, unlike Wallis, understood "Dr. Masculine's Method," that is, Charles Maskelyne's favoured technique for making lunar observations.[18] (When compared with corresponding positions predicted for Greenwich in the new *Nautical Almanac*, such observations gave the number of degrees away from Greenwich.) By such means, wrote Wallis frankly, it proved possible to reckon longitude with more precision than his predecessors ever managed. Even so, it was "a Method which we did not understand."[19]

Kotzebue's science was a world removed from Wallis's bluff ignorance. In fifty years, chronometers and other instruments by which positions of a ship at sea might be determined and refined had been introduced.[20] In addition, the Russian Navy had taken lessons in marine astronomy, with the aid of the Academy of Sciences and the observatory at Tartu (Dorpat) University.[21] *Riurik*'s young mates, Petrov and Khromchenko, were recent graduates from an efficient Russian Navigators' School, in whose curriculum astronomy loomed large. And Gleb Semenovich Shishmarev, Kotzebue's first lieutenant, was adept at using sextants and chronometers. It was unthinkable that any of the new and delicate equipment carried by *Riurik*, from dipping-needles to hygrometers, barometers to sextants, should remain unused or be abused by the ship's company. Thus was Russia's late arrival on the hydrographic scene transformed into a virtue.

Riurik was efficiently designed internally: space was not wanting for bulky ethnographical, botanical, and even zoological collections, yet the crew did not, it seems, suffer discomfort.[22] They were youthful and literate and only twenty-four in number, hand-picked in the Baltic for their loyalty and competence.[23] Fate seemed to smile on *Riurik* as she headed west from Easter Island on 29 March 1816.

Kotzebue's sailing orders of June 1815 called for a pause at Pitcairn Island. Fletcher Christian's long-lost hide-out, equidistant from Tahiti and Easter Island, had exerted as powerful a pull on Russian readers as on Englishmen since the announcement in the *Quarterly Review* (March 1810) that a New England whaler, Captain Mayhew Folger, had discovered the survivors and descendants of *Bounty* mutineers.[24] Kruzenshtern's and Kotzebue's interest in Pitcairn was bequeathed to Russian voyagers of other generations and survived into the present century. Among the educated travellers who called there and described its English-speaking colony were Kiril T. Khlebnikov (with *Amerika*, Captain-Lieutenant Khromchenko, in February 1833) and Nikolai Mikhlukho-Maklai, the ethnologist, in 1876.[25] Nor have Russian historians lost all interest in it yet.[26] From Pitcairn, *Riurik*'s original instructions called for westward probings to 137°W, in seas south of the Mangareva group spotted from Captain James Wilson's *Duff* on her way out to Tahiti. The group was practically unknown.[27] Time pressed, however, and *Riurik* was behind schedule thanks to her stays at Talcaguano and Easter Island, and her long and fruitless searching in the area where Arrowsmith showed "Davis Land" and

"Wareham's Rocks."[28] (In Kotzebue's opinion, both were non-existent
and the latter had for decades been confused with remote Sala-y-Gomez.
He was right.) Disregarding sailing orders, which in any case allowed him
an unusual degree of latitude in choosing routes up to the Arctic, Kotzebue steered NW toward Tahiti. On 8 April, in latitude 18°6′S, longitude
125°16′W, there was a false sighting of land. What was supposed to be an
island soon dissolved into a low black cloud. On the 13th, other places
eluded scrutiny. The island of San Pablo, plainly mapped by Arrowsmith,
could not be found. At this juncture, in latitude 15°S, longitude 133°W,
Kotzebue started consciously looking for islands that the Dutch had
claimed to see in other times. "I steered my course due west to follow,
according to my instructions, the parallel of 15°. Schouten and Le Maire
have several islands that have never since been seen."[29]

It is impossible to follow Kotzebue's westward route into the Tuamotu
Archipelago and not be struck by Kruzenshtern's knowledge of Pacific
exploration in preceding centuries. What did the admiral, who drafted
Kotzebue's orders at his chancellor's behest, know of the voyage of the
Dutch ship *Eendracht* in 1616? More, certainly, than was reflected on a
dozen eighteenth-century French, Dutch, and British charts. Almost alone
among the Russians of his time, he was familiar with the account of
Eendracht's movements that, attributed to J. Le Maire, had been printed
twice in Dutch in 1618 and 1622.[30] Almost alone among contemporary
mariners of any nationality, he had collated that account with later atlases
that showed the whereabouts of Honden Eylandt (Dog Island or Pukapuka), Sonder Grondt (Takaroa-Takapoto), Waterlandt (perhaps Manihi),
and Vlieghen Eylandt (Fly Island or Rangiroa).[31] Cautiously superimpos-
ing Jacob Roggeveen's subsequent track in *Arend*, *Thienhoven*, and *Africaansche Galey* (1722) on Le Maire's and Schouten's data of a century
before, he drew a number of conclusions. First, Roggeveen had not observed Le Maire's islands even though he had been following the same
degree of latitude or one extremely close to it. Hence it was reasonable to
suppose that there were many coral islands close together in the area. Second, the "smooth water" of which Le Maire and Schouten wrote, and
which the Dutch had seen again south of the so-called Sonder Grondt,[32]
seemed to be marked by chains of islands running more or less along a
SE-NW axis. Low and dangerous, these coral chains no doubt incorpo-
rated islands seen by Spanish navigators long before, of which, regrettably, official information had traditionally been withheld by the authorities
in Spain. Finally, various non-native names had been attached to single
islands, so that charts were cluttered with duplications and chimeras. It
was time that Russian seamen under Kotzebue made a full investigation
of an archipelago of which too little had been seen in recent times, producing full, accurate charts.[33]

Kotzebue was not loath to look for islands where the chances of discovering a few appeared high. He saw the pleasant implications of the "smooth water" in question. Since it stretched several hundred miles to the west of Sonder Grondt, he could suppose that there were islands or perhaps a larger land mass further south, by which the smooth water was sheltered from the great Pacific swell.[34] Hence, it was probable that there were undiscovered islands to the west and south of Sonder Grondt. On 15 April, Kotzebue noted signs that land was near: pelicans and man-o-war birds, gusts of wind from the northwest in a locality where easterlies prevailed week by week, a sudden squall. Land was sighted from the masthead at 3:00 pm the next day on the horizon to the NNW:

> The island seemed to us so small and low, that the grove which we could plainly discern seemed to us to rise from the surface of the water. . . . We now doubled the north point, at the distance of a mile and a half; we found the whole island covered with thick bushes, in the middle of which a small lake had a pleasing effect; the shore was surrounded with coral reefs, and the surface appeared so violent that it seemed impossible to effect a landing.[35]

It was Le Maire's "Honden Eylandt" (Pukapuka), first reported on 10 April 1616 and so named because the Dutch had seen no natives, but three dogs, ashore.[36] Understandably delighted, Kotzebue stood off with reefed sails, meaning to take a closer look the next day. The night was passed in preparation. Johann Caspar Hörner's notes on the procedures to be followed in surveying coasts and reckoning coordinates were carefully re-read. ("The ship's way along the coast serves as the basis of the triangle. First, then, let the ship's place for a fixed time be determined by astronomical observations. . . . Latitude . . . by Douwe's well-known method, for which Mendoza's tables afford the best calculations. . . . Use Mercator's projection. . . . ")[37] Kotzebue, Shishmarev, and Khromchenko made extensive use of Hörner's notes (drawn up at Kruzenshtern's request and sent from Zürich, where *Nadezhda*'s ex-astronomer had settled)[38] till *Riurik* returned to Russia. They were models of their kind, offering lucid explanations of involved but necessary mathematical procedures, such as trigonometry, in estimating height; the use of magnetized, vibrating dipping-needles; estimation of magnetic variation; and simple calculus.[39] Suddenly everyone aboard was working hard. Even the night did not impede Eschscholtz and Chamisso in their examination of the sea birds now at hand.[40] With the return of daylight, Kotzebue reached the northern and western points of Pukapuka, sketched its shores, and fixed its length at seven miles.

Kotzebue checked Le Maire's brief description of this empty Honden

Eylandt and compared it with what he saw. The lake and bushes, outline, and dimensions corresponded. Even so, Le Maire's island had been reckoned to lie in 15°12′S, and *Riurik* was not in 14°50′S.[41] Eschscholtz especially was disappointed by the failure to land here, since he had hoped to gather specimens of insect life and fauna. Still, the birds had been preserved, the island properly surveyed, and its coordinates again determined by two noon observations. Land came into sight again within three days, on 20 April.

Only three miles long, this new island to the southwest lacked Doubtful Island's central lake but boasted tall coconut palms, which made a pleasant spectacle. It was Tikei. Paradoxically, the Russians had departed from *their* Doubtful Island to arrive at Roggeveen's! Reaching Tikei on 18 May 1722, Roggeveen had first mistaken it for Honden Eylandt, then, uncertainly, renamed it Doubtful or Deceptive (Bedrieglyke).[42] Kotzebue deepened the paradox by not equating Roggeveen's Doubtful Island with the one he saw ahead. And so, mistakenly, he claimed Tikei as a discovery.

RIURIK AMONG THE CORAL ISLANDS: TIKEI, TAKAPOTO, ARATUA, TIKAHAU

Twenty-three days had passed since *Riurik*'s men had last spent time ashore, on Easter Island; and the very fact of making a discovery produced an urge to land again. Accordingly, the ship was brought under the unknown island's lee while Second Lieutenant Ivan Zakharin went with a boat to take a close look at the surf breaking against the reef. It proved impossible to take the boat across the surf. Two youthful seamen, on the other hand, whom curiosity and a determination not to be deprived of time ashore drove onward, made it safely through the boiling foam. Both walked around a little, "but did not venture far, as there were many traces of the island being inhabited."[43] To prove that they had landed, the pair brought back coconuts and a "braided cord . . . tied to a pole." Such limited success inflamed the *Riurik*'s company. It was decided to construct a little pram, just large enough to carry one man, on the quarterdeck. Boards, nails, ropes, and poles were brought together and the carpenters worked through the night despite a brisk north wind and rain.

Riurik returned to Tikei's reef at seven the next morning, and Kotzebue, Shishmarev, Eschscholtz, Chamisso, and a group of seamen put off in two boats, with the pram. The two former discoverers repeated their performance of landing, then pulled the pram along a rope attached ashore. Thus the Russians landed, wet and bruised,[44] on the island's northwest shore. Natives had called there intermittently for many years, as was indicated by footpaths on the coral that had an almost shiny look. Subsistence was possible during these periodic visits because rainwater collected in specially dug pits or reservoirs. The Russians took some water from these pits, together with six artefacts and a herbarium.[45]

Wine was drunk to celebrate the day, the whole crew was given double rations, and a salvo was fired. Spirits were high. Tikei's centre was reckoned to lie in latitude 14°57′20″S, longitude 144°28′30″W.

Land was sighted again on 22 April. This time it was Takapoto. The visitors, not recognizing it as the "Schadelijk Eylandt" on which Roggeveen's *Africaansche Galey* had been wrecked in May 1722,[46] named it "Spiridov" after an admiral who had been kind to Kotzebue. Visiting the place in 1765, Commodore Byron's men had found the relics of a Dutch longboat. The Russians saw no signs of habitation and, mindful of the surf, merely described and measured Takapoto (three miles by eleven, with a central lake, treeless, in latitude 14°41′S).[47] From here, *Riurik* moved WSW in the direction of Cook's Palliser group. Land was again sighted, from port and starboard bows, within a day.

Kotzebue knew his Cook. Moving southwest from Takapoto, he expected to see the islets now commonly known as Apataki and, five miles south of it, Kaukura and Toau. Apataki duly came in sight, ahead and on the port side. On the starboard side, however, land appeared where British charts showed nothing, even though Cook *had* spotted the place. It was the low, circular isle of Arutua, which Roggeveen had seen and called Meerder Zorg, "More Trouble Island," fifty-two years before Cook's *Resolution* came. The Dutch had reckoned it to lie in latitude 15°10′S.[49] Again the Russians, pardonably but mistakenly, believed that they had found an island unknown to Europeans. Coasting half a mile offshore, they trained their telescopes between the bent coconut palms in search of people. They saw none. As *Riurik* sped west, it grew apparent that she was passing not one single island but a dozen tiny islands in an oval. None was more than two miles long or more than half a mile broad; and none was wholly disconnected from the interlocking reef by open water. All supported palms. Kotzebue named the low circular cluster "Riurik's Chain."[50] Next day, having rapidly passed Arrowsmith's Dean's Island, he approached what turned out to be his first true discovery in the Pacific: Tikahau.[51]

Moving through Palliser's Isles in April 1774, Cook had sailed westward from the south of Apataki; he had seen no island west of Kaukura.[52] Yet the Tuamotu chains plainly extended on a SE-NW axis. Islands stretched a hundred miles to the ESE and/or SE of Kaukura, so that land might reasonably have been expected in the area NW of it. Only the Dutch, it seems, had been in that direction, Le Maire having observed his Vlieghen Eylandt (Rangiora) in 15°20′S.[53] The Russians had intersected Cook's route of April 1774 at Aratua. They were conscious of the approx-

imate coordinates for Vlieghen Eylandt. Kotzebue steered deliberately
west from Aratua. Bearing the above factors in mind, one must conclude
that Kotzebue *sought* the island that he sighted, Tikahau, on the basis of
the data available to him. The sighting, far from being accidental, was the
fruit of a well considered search.[54] Tikahau was reckoned to lie in latitude
15°00′00″S, longitude 148°41′W. Like most of Kotzebue's 1816 reckonings, it was correct enough to be of use to navigators for the next hundred
years.

In the course of his ten-day crossing (16-25 April 1816) of the archipelago, Kotzebue sighted, described, and determined the locations of
Pukapuka, Tikei, Takapoto, Aratua, Rangiroa, and Tikahau (Map 2).
Magnetic needle variations were from 5°E to 6°16′E. All latitudes were
estimated by noon observations of the sun; longitudes, by the readings of
three chronometers. Landings were made on Tikei on 20-21 April. The
only real discovery was Tikahau (25 April). No contact was made with
Tuamotu Islanders. Cook's coordinates for Apataki and Takapoto were
slightly corrected, by inference from Kotzebue's own for Takapoto and
Aratua. The islands of San Pablo and Baumann or Bouman, indicated on
Arrowsmith's chart as lying in 15°02′S, 154°38′W, were shown to be
non-existent there. Sketches and running surveys were made of all six islands or clusters sighted. These were used by Kruzenshtern, together with
Kotzebue's and Bellingshausen's later Tuamotuan findings, in his *Atlas
of the South Sea* (1823-26). Kruzenshtern's significant decision to collate
sightings from *Riurik* with those from early Dutch and British vessels was
acclaimed by Chamisso.[56] It led to identification of Spiridov (Takapoto)
with *Eendracht*'s Sonder Grondt despite discrepancies between Le
Maire's and Kotzebue's narratives.

Sailing north-by-west from Tikahau, *Riurik* was too far from Matahiva
for a sighting to be possible. The honours of discovery were thus reserved
for Bellingshausen. Kotzebue sighted Penrhyn Island, or Tongareva in the
Northern Cooks, five days after leaving Tikahau, 30 April.[57] There, too,
spirits rose, all the more because water was now rationed on *Riurik*'s long
haul to Petropavlovsk-in-Kamchatka.

SUVOROV AT CARYSFORT'S ISLAND, APRIL 1818

In company with *Kutuzov*, the Russian-American Company vessel
Suvorov had sailed to the North Pacific settlements from Kronstadt in
1816-17. The little squadron, commanded by Leontii A. Hagemeister on
his second voyage to the Pacific, brought supplies and stores to Sitka by
the shorter "clockwise" route around Cape Horn.[58] *Kutuzov* was commanded by an impecunious but bright naval lieutenant on secondment to

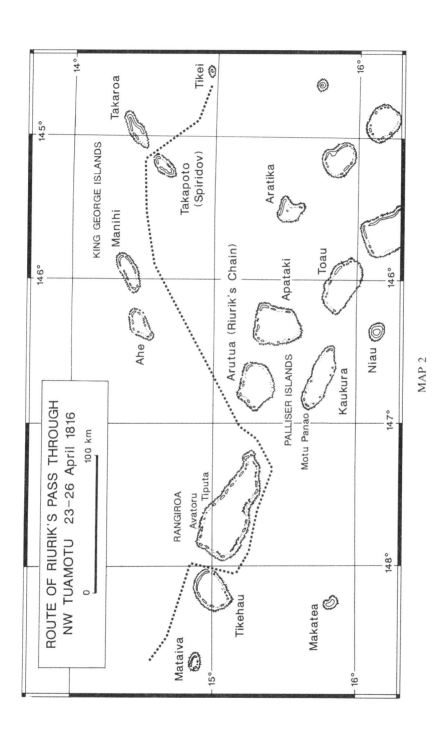

ROUTE OF RIURIK'S PASS THROUGH
NW TUAMOTU 23–26 April 1816

0   100 km

MAP 2

the Company, Zakhar Ivanovich Ponafidin, later Senior Inspector at the School of Navigators in St. Petersburg. Proceeding independently from Chile, Ponafidin reached Sitka on 19 July 1817. *Suvorov* was unladen, fumigated, beached, given a copper sheath, caulked, and reladen with peltry for St. Petersburg. She sailed for Cape Horn again on 12 January 1818. Port Chichagov (Hakaui Bay), Nukuhiva, was reached on March 13 after a slow and troubled voyage south between 140° and 145° of longitude. Fresh fruit and drinking water were obtained.

The shortest route from Nukuhiva to Cape Horn took any ship across the Tuamotu Archipelago's easterly outliers, Pukapuka and Napuka, then east of the Gambiers and past the solitary islands ESE of Papeete and the Tuamotuan chains. Ponafidin was not acquainted with *Riurik's* surveying: Chamisso's and Kotzebue's works had not yet been printed. He was familiar, however, with John Hawkesworth's *Voyages* (London, 1773) and their account of Captain Wallis's adventures in *Dolphin*. Besides, he had more recent charts showing the Tuamotuan islands seen by Wallis on his way to Tahiti in 1767. One of these was Queen Charlotte Island (Nukutavake), where the British had encountered thirty-foot double canoes and seen even longer craft under construction.[59] Sailing south, *Suvorov* passed in sight of bare Nukutavake Island on or about 1 April 1818.

Working from *Suvorov's* log in 1846-47, the historian Nikolai A. Ivashintsov asserted that she also passed in sight of the Tuamotuan outliers "Trinity" and "Karnefut."[60] "Trinity" is not readily identifiable, but "Karnefut" is plainly Carysfort, the cursive *n* and *i* of Russian being similar in form and therefore easily confused.

Carysfort's Island had been sighted from a European vessel for the first and only time in March 1791. The vessel was HMS *Pandora* under Captain Edward Edwards, who had entered the Pacific to recapture the *Bounty* mutineers. Coming from Ducie and Marutea, Edwards found his Carysfort in latitude 20°49′S, longitude 138°33′W.[61] It lay along *Suvorov's* shortest route to the Atlantic. Even so, the fact that Ponafidin sighted it and estimated its position suggests a consciousness of hydrographic opportunity. His subsequent career underlined this. Carysfort is now known as Tureia.[62]

BELLINGSHAUSEN'S TRAVERSE OF THE ARCHIPELAGO, JULY 1820

The next Russian captains to enter the archipelago, Bellingshausen in *Vostok* and Mikhail Petrovich Lazarev in *Mirnyi*, were not only conscious of *Riurik*'s surveying work but also thoroughly prepared to complement it. Time was not as short for Bellingshausen and his company as it had been for Kotzebue. No surveying could begin along the fringes of Antarctica until its summer came, in mid or late November. Other factors, too, favoured the slow and careful sweep up to Tahiti that *Vostok* and *Mirnyi* made. For one thing, Kotzebue's data on a dozen coral islands had been added to earlier works and charts, of which a veritable library was carried in *Vostok*. Also, Bellingshausen had the temperament of the professional surveyor.[63] Calm and circumspect, he took the trouble to examine the appropriate literature on the Tuamotu Archipelago as he approached it from the south. Even before arriving, he understood the need, bearing in mind the routes of Schouten and Le Maire, Roggeveen, Byron and Bougainville, Wallis and Cook, to move westward or northwestward through the islands on a higher latitude than his compatriots. In broad terms, Kotzebue had been following the 15th parallel; for a week or so *Vostok* and *Mirnyi* would make their ever westward zigzag, between the 16th and 18th parallels, finally moving north to intersect the routes of *Dolphin*, *Resolution*, and *Riurik*. By this procedure, which would take the Russians into waters once traversed by Quiros and complement Cook's second voyage, fresh discoveries might be made. Like Kotzebue, Bellingshausen *intended* to discover coral islands and bent all his expertise in that direction. At the same time, he was ready for ethnography, zoology, and botany. It seemed improbable, as Rapa in the Austral Islands slid from view behind *Vostok*, that he would have as little luck in meeting Tuamotuan Islanders as Kotzebue had, or that Pavel N. Mikhailov the artist and Ivan M. Simonov the scientist would not land before arriving in Tahiti.[64]

Sailing practically due north from Rapa, Bellingshausen sighted his first coral island on 5 July 1820. It was Manuhangi (19°12′21″S, 141°16′W), a low but verdant island less than four miles long. Wasting no time, *Vostok* and *Mirnyi* sent their boats to its reef-encircled shore. The party from *Vostok*, which included Lieutenant Torson, Simonov, and Midshipman Demidov, spent more than two hours ashore, surveying, drawing, and collecting sea urchins with six-inch spikes, as well as pandanus fruit, large "snapping cormorants," and frigate birds. Demidov and a sailor named Gaidukov were first-class shots, and so of use to ornithology as well as to the galley.[65]

The Russians were impressed by this new island. The multicoloured coral glistened. Sea birds plunged from an enormous height onto their prey. The cloudless sky offered no drinking water, but it made determination of the island's latitude quite simple. Simonov and Navigator Iakov Poriadin made a dozen observations, on the strength of which their captain placed Wallis's islands, Nengonengo (Prince William Henry), Paraoa (Gloucester), and Manuhangi (Cumberland) 24′ west of the longitudes that Wallis's officers had reckoned. Not surprisingly, since Wallis had placed "Cumberland Island" 5' to the south and almost 20' to the east of Bellingshausen position, in a portion of the ocean full of islands, Bellingshausen failed to equate his own discovery with it.[66] The only disappointment was the absence of islanders.

Bellingshausen's second coral island, Hao, came in sight at dawn the next day, 6 July. By 9:00 am *Vostok* was three-quarters of a mile off its palm fringed southern point and the disappointments of the preceding day were forgotten. Natives armed with spears could be seen, "coppercoloured and quite naked."[67] They ran along the shore with *Vostok*, making gestures of "urgent invitation," till they tired. Three canoes were also spotted. Pounding surf along the reef made an attempt to land seem foolish, so the Russians drew and measured as they coasted. A central lagoon had a diameter of one and a half miles. Fires burning at the northwest end showed that the island was inhabited. Bellingshausen felt at home as a surveyor. Ignorant though he was of Hao's native name, he could identify it firmly with Bougainville's La Harpe and Cook's Bow Island.[68] He could also state with confidence that *Vostok* was now retracing *San Pablo*'s route of 1606 or closely shadowing it. (Cook himself had made the connection between Bow and San Pablo.)[69] It is significant that Bellingshausen's next four islands included three—Amanu, Takume, and Raroia—observed by Pedro Fernandez de Quiros. (To Quiros and successive generations of cartographers, Amanu was "La Decena" and Raroia "La Sagitaria.")[70] Like Kruzenshtern, Bellingshausen was a scholarly officer of much persistence.

Amanu was sighted and surveyed on 6 July under light south easterlies that made it hard to reach the island. It consisted of low-lying reefs around a central lagoon, with intermittent undergrowth and trees that included tall coconut palms. Two little apertures from the ocean into the lagoon were also spotted. Fires burned by day and night, and natives were in evidence. Not until 3:00 pm on 8 July did Bellingshausen, Mikhailov, Demidov, and a party of armed seamen from *Vostok*, then Lazarev, Surgeon Galkin, Novosil'skii, and Annenkov from *Mirnyi*, accompanied by sailors of their own, effect a landing on the island's northern end. The Russians were received with great suspicion and hostility:

> Some sixty native men rushed down to the shore and their number was constantly increased by others . . . They were all armed with long spears and a few of them carried in the other hand a wooden club with which they, like the New Zealanders, hit their enemies on the head. . . . As we approached to get ashore, the islanders, with frightful shouts and brandishing their spears, prevented our landing. . . .[71]

Gifts thrown onto the reef were soon scooped up, but the resistance continued. A rifle-shot over the natives' heads produced a momentary panic, then, seeing that nobody was harmed, the natives laughed and taunted. Finally, a cannon ball from *Mirnyi* crashed into the woods. The natives fled, regrouped, returned. Small bells and other trinkets made no difference to their hostility. Frustrated, the Russians made a last attempt to land and were again charged by spear-shaking warriors. Bellingshausen saw no option but to retreat. It was apparent that the natives thought the flash of muskets might inflict a minor burn, and so continually splashed their arms with water, but were otherwise ignorant of European weaponry. Disgusted at the thought of murdering in order to collect a few shells, plants, or artefacts, Bellingshausen finally swallowed his pride. "The women rushed out of the wood to the shore and, lifting up their dresses, presented their posterior parts to us, slapped themselves and danced about, probably to show their contempt at our feebleness."[72]

Unaware that the Spanish store ship *Jupiter* had called at Amanu in November 1774,[73] Bellingshausen named the island "Moller Island" in honour of the admiral under whose flag he had served in the Baltic Fleet. Again steering due north, the Russians sighted Angatau on 10 July. It was a genuine discovery.

> From noon until 6:00 am of the following morning the wind continually varied, shifting backwards and forwards. . . . I concluded that we were navigating to the leeward of an undiscovered island. . . . At daybreak we heard with delight that land had been sighted to windward from the top. . . .
>
> Towards noon, when the vessels were 12 miles distant from the shore, the natives surprised us by their great daring. From the lookout we noted first one canoe then a second and a third, and finally as many as six on their way out to us. They approached fairly close to the ships and stopped abreast of them. . . . Finally, one canoe did . . . catch hold of a rope which we let down from the stern. . . .[74]

Well might Bellingshausen be impressed by these thin, swarthy natives' daring: what they had in mind, it seemed, was nothing less than the attack and capture of *Vostok*, whose size they had misjudged. Seizing the rope, they tugged and tried to cut it off; seeing a Russian at a porthole, they strove to wound him with a spear. Not a man would step aboard, yet all were armed with little clubs, spears, or "plaited grass lassoes." In general, the Tuamotu Islanders whom Bellingshausen met in 1820 were decidedly aggressive. Only on Nihiru was friendly contact made. The

Angatauans wore their hair in a topknot, had "a rope made of grass round their waists," and wore a loincloth with which they would not part for any trifle. Three or four men sat in each canoe. The craft were twenty feet long and made of "several planks skilfully put together." They had a single outrigger and were evidently seaworthy.[75] The Russians left them axes, printed linens, even bronze and silver medals. Speeding back to Angatau's western shore, the natives pulled their craft up on the reef and into the lagoon, then lit a series of enormous fires. Bellingshausen took these blazes as a sign of hostility or warning and remembered the Amanu Islanders' indifference to European strength. He was piqued but found a way to vent his feelings. As *Vostok* sailed westward and away from Angatau, rockets were fired and coloured stars broke in the sky over the island, which the Russians called "Count Arakcheev Island."

The next coral clusters, Takume (Prince Volkonskii Island) and Raroia (Prince Barclay de Tolly Island), both appeared on 11 July. The wind was steady from the NNE, the ocean swell quite gentle, and the temperature pleasant. Daily highs and nightly lows fell in the range of 75° to 80°F. Flying fish leapt from the waves, their flights curved by the wind, and whales spouted. Ever willing to make amicable contact with the islanders, Bellingshausen ordered twelve rockets to be fired into the night sky off Takume. "These blazing streams of lights must have inspired these people . . . with unusual fear. . . ."[76] In the Russian view, respect verging on fear was the guarantee of amicable dealings. Bellingshausen was correct to think that any islanders would have had no prior contact with Europeans: Quiros had left the place, which he had named La Fugitiva, 214 years before. Smoke rose from the islands, but the Russians did not land on either low Takume or Raroia. The former was reckoned to be twelve miles long and three miles wide; the latter, twenty-one miles long and seven miles wide. Both were surveyed very precisely before nightfall. Nihiru appeared on 13 July to WSW. Again a surf-embattled reef and wooded shore were seen; again a smooth lagoon was visible; again a native craft came out towards the Russians. This time, however, the two natives showed a very different and altogether trusting attitude. It was the harbinger of a delightful interlude.[77] This proved to be the Russians' first contact with the Tuamotuan pearl trade that was to gain major significance in the next half century.[78]

A boat party from *Mirnyi*, meanwhile, attempted to land on Nihiru, but the underwater reef and raging surf prevented it. To compensate, the Russians spent another hour with the Tuamotuan chief, his associate, and an attractive native woman. The woman was presented with a mirror, earrings, a ring, and red material that she immediately wrapped around her waist. In return she gave the Russians fine matting and some well-dried cuttlefish. She and the chief were curly-haired, swarthy, of medium height, and, the Russians thought, of modest disposition. The chief, who was tattooed on thighs and haunches, was delighted to dress up in the bright red uniform of a Russian Guardsman. Improvising skilfully, Mikhailov drew all three islanders and later placed them as a group against a composite background: beach, pandanus trees, and flat-bottomed canoe ("Natives of the Coral Island of Nigera").[79]

From Nihiru, Bellingshausen moved northwest toward Taenga. Unaware that the British trader *Margaret* had sighted it in 1803, he named it "General Lieutenant Ermolov's Island." It was reckoned to be thirty-four miles in circumference, some fifteen miles long. Lightly wooded, it was temporarily inhabited by natives who had come for food. Two native craft in the lagoon had triangular sails. This, the eighth of Bellingshausen's coral islands, was seen at noon on 14 July. The ninth, Makemo (Prince Golenishchev-Kutuzov Smolenskii Island), was examined the next day. Again the few natives in sight seemed to have visited the place in search of food or raw materials: there were no villages or groups of huts, no coconuts, and no fires burning on the strand. Although they watched the Russians' slow approach, the Tuamotu Islanders decided not to visit *Vostok*. It was but a small disappointment for the Russians, who by 3:00 pm that very day were well in sight of other land to the SW. This was one of the Raevskii Islands, Bellingshausen's third discovery in five days.[80] The Russians saw and sketched a single island, Tepoto, which was the southernmost of three. The name Raevskii has been kept on modern maps. Mentally retracing Cook's routes in relation to his own, Bellingshausen wondered briefly if his latest coral island might not possibly be Cook's Adventure Island (modern Motutunga). He decided that the island seen by Cook in 1773 could be Raevskii. Cook had neglected to describe his island's size.[81]

After the Raevskii cluster, in a seemingly interminable series of similar low coral islands, came Katiu. Sighted towards 5:00 pm on the 15th, it was seen to have, along its eastern side, two narrow openings to the predictable lagoon inside.[82] The Russians call it "Graf Osten-Saken Island," this time honouring a Russian general and not a naval leader. Shortly after dusk, *Mirnyi* caught up with *Vostok*; she was by far the slower of the two, even in gentle winds. Lazarev had unexpected gifts for Bellingshausen. While off Makemo earlier that day, *Mirnyi* had traded with the natives there. Apparently they had had previous contact with European vessels, for they had asked for razors and had eaten Russian food without concern. Lazarev had left them medals and material. Their thigh tattooing had resembled that of Chief Tatano on Nihiru.[83]

By now, Bellingshausen had encountered and was following the more southwesterly of two great island chains, the one running from Motutunga in the ESE to Matahiva in the WNW, the chain that Kotzebue had not followed. Now, as in the early nineteenth century, a yacht can sail eighty miles along that chain and not entirely lose sight of land in one direction or another. These are, however, tricky waters for a sailing vessel, large or small: the reefs are numerous and winds are treacherous. Small gas powered cutters are preferred by the French, who now control the archipelago, and by the islanders. For Bellingshausen and his people, as their diaries and published narratives reveal, these were taxing but exhilarating days. Taxing because danger was so obvious, exhilarating because of the knowledge that discoveries were being made. Trevenen's forecast was realized at last.[84]

Moving west again, Bellingshausen arrived at the twelfth and thirteenth of his sixteen Tuamotuan islands on 16 July, Tahanea and Faaite. Neither was a new discovery, but Bellingshausen named them "Admiral Chichagov's Island" and "Russian Island." Again, it was the Spaniards' secrecy, not Russian chauvinism, that resulted in the many lengthy proper names. Tahanea had been sighted by Domingo de Boenechea in *Aguila* in 1774, but Madrid had not informed the world of this. Faaite's existence had been mentioned in John Turnbull's *Voyage Round the World* of 1805; Turnbull's associate, John Buyers, had spotted it in 1803, but its coordinates had not been specified.[85] By now the officers of both *Vostok* and *Mirnyi* were making running-surveys automatically. The processes had grown familiar through repetition. Signals sent by Lazarev were understood at once, even anticipated. Synchronizing routes, approaching capes or rip-tide entrances from different but complementary positions, Lazarev and Bellingshausen had reduced the time and energy required to survey a coral island. Tahanea was surveycd in two hours, with the help of favourable winds. Bellingshausen's narrative of 1831 was backed up by two dozen plans of Tuamotuan Islands, most of which were reproduced by Frank D. Debenham in his translation (Cambridge, 1945). Taken together with the Simonov and Novosil'skii texts and with Mikhailov's illustrations, such as "Natives of the Palliser Islands," Bellingshausen's narrative and island plans make it easy to trace his route, hour by hour, day by day. Such is his legacy to practical and historical comparative hydrography.[87]

After Faaite, on the northwest tending chain, came Fakarava and Toau. Fakarava (Count Miloradovich's Island), sighted on the 17th at 8:00 am, was later presented to the European public by Robert Louis Stevenson. It was there that the writer spent four months or so in 1888, a visit used in his romantic book *In the South Seas*. Toau (Graf Vitgenshtein Island) had been visited by Cook in *Resolution* on 20 April 1774.[88] Thus the Russians departed from the Quiros path of 1606 to meet Cook's path from the other side. Cook had discovered Kaukura and Toau, which together with the larger Apataki cluster he had called the Pallisers, as he was sailing southward.[89] Bellingshausen's route tended northwest.

Like the other islands, Fakarava had been visited by collectors of food or raw material. These evinced no interest in *Vostok*, neither attempting seaborne trade nor hiding out. Toau, too, looked less than fertile through Russian telescopes. A little undergrowth and intermittent clumps of twisted trees were interspersed with places "where nothing was to be seen except the sterile coral which had turned into limestone."[90] There, forty natives were observed, standing together on a narrow neck of land. Some waved the cloaks or mats that they were wearing, even tying stuff to poles in an attempt to catch the visitors' attention. But the wind was high, the surf was strong, and dusk was near. With regret, the sloops hauled off. The night was passed from ten to fifteen miles off Toau, in heavy squalls. Next morning, *Vostok* returned to take another look at what the Russians now conceded was Cook's Palliser Island No. II. An entrance into the lagoon was found five miles from its northern tip; the tidal streams were rippling across it. There were fine coconut palms, but no sign of the natives. All had departed to Fakarava Island, so the Russians guessed.

Over the next twenty-four hours, Bellingshausen did his best to collate his own bearings with Cook's of April 1774. There were so many islands now in sight that it was difficult to state with any certainty if *Vostok* was SE of Apataki or of Kaukura. Most probably, the Russians sighted both. Palliser Island No. II, the Russians recognized as Arrowsmith's Elizabeth placed too easterly. At length, the sky grew overcast and night descended. Unconvinced that he had settled the confusion on the chart, Bellingshausen coasted south by west. At 2:00 am, breakers were sighted straight ahead. Niau was in sight again at dawn. Again consulting Arrowsmith and Forster, Bellingshausen readied for a landing on a stretch of coast where the surf was slight. Nature collaborated, the winds fell off, and the sea grew calmer. Torson, Mikhailov, Simonov, Leskov, and Berkh were briskly lowered in a boat and rowed for shore.[91]

Niau, which the Russians call "Vice-Admiral Greig Island," was their sixth discovery among the coral islands. It differed from the others, being 26 feet high and rich in bird life. "Niggerheads," great coral masses thrust up onto the reef, gave it a wild, rocky look; and here and there trees grew thickly. The lagoon was even hidden by their leaves. The very air of the island made the Russians think, correctly, that they were leaving or had left the coral maze. Accordingly, they turned back to the north and, crossing eighteen miles of placid water, reached Kaukura at 4:00 pm on

18 July. It, too, was impressive, with its coral masses sixteen feet or more above sea level, pounding surf, and great lagoon. With daylight failing, Bellingshausen prepared for another landing on 19 July, then lessened sail. The temperature in the crew's quarters was 81°F at 1:00 am but, acclimatized to heat after a month, the crew slept well.

Kaukura's position was fixed early the next day. Then, in another of his sweeps designed specifically to mirror Cook's of fifty years before, Bellingshausen coasted up the island's southern shore, from east to west. His people drew and measured as they went.[92]

So ended Bellingshausen's painstaking examination of the more southwesterly and densely packed of the Tuamotu Archipelago's two island chains. It was with full justification that he named the coral islands he had seen from Angatau (Arakcheev) westward *Ostrova Rossiian*, "The Russians' Islands." It was true that Cook had seen the Pallisers, which were included in his group. But it was Russians, led by Kotzebue or himself, who had described all Cook's and other early navigators' islands in the region and "determined their actual extent and configuration."[93] The name *Ostrova Rossiian*, which seemed so reasonable at the time, was never internationally recognized because the islands were in fact only a section of a larger archipelago. Large Soviet atlases still show the native names of Tuamotuan islands with the Russian names in brackets.[94] But only the name Raevskii Group preserves the memory of Bellingshausen's effort in contemporary Western atlases.

Bellingshausen had already chosen Venus Point, Tahiti, as the best place to revictual, water, and rest his crews while checking the chronometers and precisely reckoning the longitudes of all the Russians' Islands.[95] Wasting no time, he chose a route to Matavai Bay and Venus Point "in such a way as to make it of all possible service to geography." Kaukura vanished behind *Vostok* to eastward toward nightfall on 19 July, and Bellingshausen made directly for the spot where Arrowsmith's most recent chart showed Makatea Island, 15°53′S, 147°28′W. He proposed to verify its true position. Makatea rose on the horizon on the morning of the 20th, some 50′ to the west of the position marked by Arrowsmith. Shaped like a wedge, its northern side had steep unbroken cliffs. Four islanders were seen ashore among the palms, waving green branches or matting at the ships under full sail. Surf was moderate and winds were steady, so Bellingshausen and Lazarev decided to send their boats to Makatea. Twenty Russians spent an hour and a half ashore. They would have tarried longer, had their visit not acquired a dramatic element as two young Tuamotuans, who had watched the strangers landing, suddenly revealed themselves:

> At 3:00 pm the party returned on board with an unexpected acquisition in the shape of two boys. One of them was about seventeen and

the other about nine years of age; two others had been taken on board the *Mirnyi*. . . . The sole possessions of these lads consisted of a fish-hook made of a kind of slate and a few cups made from the coconut shells, which also served them as vessels. There is not the slightest doubt that these islanders, like the Scotsman Alexander Selkirk whose adventures provided the occasion for the writing of the celebrated novel *Robinson Crusoe*, had to invent ways of obtaining the necessaries of life, but fortunately succeeded and suffered no privations. Had Providence miraculously saved a few girls together with these four boys, the history of the settlement on Makatea Island would have begun from that time. It is indeed probable that the colonization of other islands in the Pacific Ocean has had similar beginnings.[96]

By their unexpected, welcome appearance, the boys made it both feasible and necessary for the Russians to reflect on Makatea and the archipelago's westerly outliers in the context of the *Voyages* of Cook, Forster, and Turnbull, not the Spanish or the Dutch. It is at this juncture that Bellingshausen in his narrative of 1831 quotes at length from Turnbull's *Voyage Round the World* of 1805. Makatea, Turnbull wrote, had long been governed from Tahiti: King Pomare's deputy was met and the canoe sent to collect the local tribute was observed.[97] Bellingshausen and his officers gave thought to King Pomare, whom it would be useful to impress by friendly overtures and by evidence of firepower. Were the boys Tahitian, able possibly to facilitate the Russians' dealings with Pomare or with the English missionaries also present on Tahiti? They were not. They came, apparently, from Cook's Chain Island (Anaa), fifty miles south-by-east.[98] Suddenly, Bellingshausen found himself in a position to enquire into Tuamotuan inter-island navigational techniques and practices. What knowledge had the boys of the geography of the entire archipelago? What signs were used to steer by on the passage from Anaa to Tahiti? Language problems soon emerged. Bellingshausen took the boys to Tahiti in the hope that an interpreter might raise the curtain. His persistence was rewarded.

Vostok and *Mirnyi* spent six busy days (22-27 July 1820) at Tahiti. Bellingshausen was hospitably received both by the English missionaries then at Matavai Bay and by King Pomare II and his family. Passing Makatea for the second time, he arrived at Tikahau on the 30th. He promptly recognized it as Kotzebue's Kruzenshtern Island and, accordingly, went west bearing in mind that Kotzebue had steered north-by-west en route from Kruzenshtern to Penrhyn Island four years earlier. An island was in sight within five hours. It was Matahiva, twenty-two miles WNW from Tikahau, five miles in length and three across, the seventh and last of Bellingshausen's Tuamotuan finds.[99] He named it "Lazarev Island" after his associate and second-in-command. No further land was sighted till 3 August, when "Vostok Island" was seen in 10°5'50"S, 152°16'50"W. The Russians thus entered the Line Islands and Northern Cooks.[100]

In the course of their two traverses through the Tuamotu Archipelago (5-21 and 28-30 July 1820), the Russians sighted, described, and fixed the geographical positions of these islands:

1	Manuhangi	19°12'21"S,	141°16'00"W
2	Hao (Bow)	18°01'30"S,	140°58'04"W
3	Amanu (Moller)	17°49'30"S,	140°40'00"W
4	Angatau (Arakcheev)	15°51'01"S,	140°49'19"W
5	Takume (Volkonskii)	15°47'20"S,	142°11'00"W
6	Raroia (Barclay de Tolly)	15°55'45"S,	142°15'19"W
7	Nihiru (Nigera)	16°42'40"S,	143°44'50"W
8	Taenga (Ermolov)	16°21'45"S,	143°05'36"W
9	Makemo (Kutuzov)	16°36'40"S	143°24'32"W
10	Raevskii (Tepoto)	16°43'00"S,	144°11'00"W
11	Katiu (Osten-Saken)	16°28'35"S,	144°17'33"W
12	Tahanea (Chichagov)	16°50'05"S,	144°52'43"W
13	Faaite (Miloradovich)	15°47'20"S,	145°12'43"W
14	Fakarava (Vitgenshtein)	16°04'50"S,	145°33'55"W
15	Toau (Elizaveta or Palliser II)	15°55'40"S,	145°56'00"W
16	Niau (Greig)	16°11'18"S,	146°15'50"W
17	Kaukura (Palliser III)	15°50'20"S,	146°25'55"W
18	Makatea	15°52'35"S,	148°13'04"W
19	Tikahau (Kruzenshtern)	15°00'05"S,	148°41'00"W
20	Matahiva (Lazarev)	14°56'20"S,	148°38'30"W

Pinpoints though they are, on any map of the Pacific, most of these coral islands are some miles in diameter: Hao is twenty-five miles long, seven wide; Takume is twelve miles long and three across. The central lagoons, or lakes, of such low coral islands may be several miles long. The above coordinates are for specific *points* on the islands visited. Bellingshausen carried excellent chronometers and sextants, had the benefit of recent astronomical developments, and was an excellent surveyor. Readings of 00"W do not necessarily mean that he lacked the opportunity or time to make a fix to that degree of accuracy. It should therefore be noted that the longitudes determined for Hao, Raroia, Makemo, and Fakarava were for those islands' northern points; that for Kaukura was for its eastern point; and those for the remainder were for their centres. What cape or other feature of an island served the Russians as a fixed point in their reckonings depended solely on convenience; and this, in turn, reflected

Bellingshausen's course or path as he approached a given island. Not surprisingly, the Russians found it necessary to correct all but a few of the coordinates for Tuamotu Islands that they found in existing charts, notably Arrowsmith's. The corrections varied from 5′ to 50′.

Seven of the islands seen from the *Vostok* were unknown to Europeans: Angatau, Nihiru, Raevskii-Tepoto, Katiu, Fakarava, Niau, and Matahiva. According to Andrew Sharp,[101] Angatau could conceivably have been observed from Magellan's *Trinidad* in 1521. A close examination of the Albo narrative, as reproduced in M.F. Navarrete's *Coleccion* (Madrid 1837), suggests that it was not, for reasons touched upon by Sharp.[102] Bellingshausen was mistaken in asserting that other islands were his discoveries too, but the error was excusable. Captain John Buyers' sightings of Makemo, Faaite, and Taenga from the *Margaret* in 1803, which Turnbull mentioned casually in his *Voyage*, had not been followed up by closer inspections, and their coordinates were not accurate. The visitors of 1820 pardonably failed to associate John Buyers' Holt and Phillip's Islands with their own Ermolov and Kutuzov Islands.[103] As for Tahanea (Chichagov), Spain had chosen not to publish news of its discovery by Capitan Domingo de Boenechea on his passage to Tahiti from Callao in 1774.[104] Of course the Russians made mistakes, wrongly identifying certain islands in the Tuamotuan maze with others seen by the Spanish and the Dutch in other times. The point is that Bellingshausen's claims, which were reasonable at the time and made with modesty, were grounded in a competence at sea that equalled Cook's.[105] It fell to Kruzenshtern, while working on his *Atlas of the South Sea* in the period immediately following *Vostok*'s and *Mirnyi*'s return to Kronstadt (1822-25), to make superb use of the 1820 Tuamotuan plans and of a first-rate library and set of charts, and so eliminate three-quarters of the Bellingshausen errors.[106] Thus, collaborating smoothly with his protégés and brightest pupils, Kotzebue and Bellingshausen, the admiral contributed more to the cartography of Eastern Polynesia in the early 1800s than either Britain's Admiralty Hydrographic Service or its counterpart in France.[107]

Bellingshausen and his people made a conscientious survey of the islands. Boat landings were made on five of them: Manuhangi, Amanu, Nihiru, Niau, and Makatea. The periods ashore ranged from approximately twenty minutes to at least four hours. Most of these landings had a scientific aim; the possibility of watering or bartering for foodstuffs was an incidental factor. Matavai Bay was only days, perhaps a week, ahead, and Bellingshausen reckoned to provision there easily and amply. In any case, most low coral islands offered nothing to eat but coconuts. In short, ethnology and other sciences were uppermost in Bellingshausen's thoughts as he arranged these landings. Few historians of Oceanic exploration or ethnography have adequately recognized this fact.[108]

For all its shortage of non-naval scientific expertise, the Bellingshausen expedition was in various respects better prepared than any late eighteenth-century Pacific probe had been to undertake ethnography. By 1820, ample time had passed for the Rousseauesque approach toward the South Sea as La Nouvelle Cythère to have faded in St. Petersburg and in Russian naval circles. Even in public, Bellingshausen did not hesitate to present the Russian Crown's attitude toward the South Sea Islanders as fundamentally pragmatic, though of course also benevolent: "On despatching this expedition, His Imperial Majesty had in view the augmenting of our knowledge of the terrestrial globe and the acquainting of savage peoples with Europeans, and vice versa."[109] Coming relatively late to the Pacific Islands, Russians had examples to reflect upon and follow or reject. This was particularly true where the assembling of curiosities and native products was concerned. Cook had been issued "toys, Beads, and Glass Buttons"[110] and many other things for barter in the islands where supplies would be required. Once supplies had been secured, extra "toys" might be exchanged for local artefacts, but not before. These orders were reflected in the Russians' early dealings with the Nukuhivans in 1804. But *Nadezhda*'s and *Neva*'s supplies of trinkets were inadequate compared with the stores aboard *Vostok* as she approached the Tuamotu Archipelago by way of Rapa. Never, one may think, had any European vessel brought such quantities of trading articles into the coral island chains, "to induce the natives to treat amicably and . . . provide, by barter, fresh provisions, and hand-made articles of many sorts."[111]

The Tuamotu Islanders responded differently to *Vostok* and *Mirnyi* in different localities across the archipelago. The natives of Amanu were aggressive on 7 July, women as well as men standing along the fringes of the woods with clubs and spears ready. "Frightful shouts and brandishings" of weapons stopped the Russians on the reef itself.[112] At Hao (Bougainville's La Harpe), the natives made no effort to make contact with their visitors beyond pursuing them awhile: no canoes were put to sea although the wind was light and Russian progress slow. At Angatau, six canoes ventured out, but the atmosphere was belligerent. Had *Vostok* been smaller and inadequately armed, perhaps the islanders would have attacked instead of contenting themselves with thrusting at an officer with spears and attempting thefts of rope and iron objects.[113] At Nihiru and further west, the Russians were hospitably, if warily, received, and bartering was quite extensive. Pondering these various responses to the Russian presence, Simonov and Bellingshausen came to the conclusion that an inter-island war was being waged in the Amanu-Hao area. Most likely they were right. As members of the London Missionary Society informed the Russians at Tahiti, there were patterns of traditional hostilities among the Tuamotu Islands, vengeance raids provoking other raids, year by year.[114] Bellingshausen heard evidence of inter-island conflict in another area when he met the young survivors of a raid on Makatea. The survivors were natives of Anaa, the attackers very probably Toauans.[115] In this case, the Russians caught a breath of local wars that had been fought for many years between native factions known to the Tahitians as Auura and Parata. According to the missionary historian John Davies of Tahiti, "the Auura, inhabiting the Palliser islands, Rairoa [Rangiroa] . . . and some other small islands had a dialect very near to the Tahitian, but the Parata party had a different dialect, bearing a greater affinity to the Marquesan. They were all cruel cannibals, and had frequent wars among themselves."[116] Auura, also known as Kaukura in the rival dialect, was virtually uninhabited in 1820. Here, too, the Russian evidence corroborates Tahitian mission records. In the first years of the century, Davies remarks, "the Parata nearly exterminated the Auura, except those who had fled to Tahiti. . . ." Russian records offer further glimpses of political realities across the Tuamotu Archipelago. It is noteworthy, for instance, that Tatano, whom the Russians met at Nihiru but who had voyaged from Anaa, was familiar and even comfortable with Europeans. The Anaans had perhaps had more and happier relations with the British mission at Tahiti than any other Tuamotu Islanders: they had been worshipping at Matavai or at Papetoai (Roby's Place) since at least 1814, and a number had settled temporarily and had been baptized at Paofai Station.[117] It is reasonable to suppose that Chief Tatano represented those Anaans who had voyaged east and west since 1812, or had had enough contact with Europeans to know that the latter could give them many useful articles.

Whenever possible, the Russians gathered ethnographic data. All the journals kept by officers contain descriptions of the Tuamotuan individuals encountered, such as Chief Tatano and the boys at Makatea. Artefacts were purchased with the intention of assembling a representative collection from the archipelago, as from Queen Charlotte Sound and Rapa. Simonov, especially, was conscious of the value of the artefact that showed technique. Mikhailov drew Tatano, another male, and a woman at Nihiru, then two more males at Kaukura. As in his Maori studies, he paid attention to the details of tattooing.[118] His Tuamotuan studies show circular and horizontal patterns on the upper arm and vertical incisions on the thighs. Such data complement Tilesius von Tilenau's and Langsdorf's studies of tattooing on the south of Nukuhiva (1804) and Mikhailov's and Simonov's own evidence of *moko* in New Zealand.[119]

BELLINGSHAUSEN'S VIEWS ON THE ORIGINS OF CORAL ISLANDS

In developing his views on the origins and growth of coral islands, Bellingshausen had the great advantage of familiarity with Kotzebue's findings of 1817-18.[120] His views and Kotzebue's were essentially the same and have been shown to be correct by modern science.[121] Where Bellingshausen's writings on the subject diverge from Kotzebue's, they do so less in theory than in emphasis. Bellingshausen's interest in reef-building leads him to oceanography. It is a triumph of his thinking to have looked on coral islands as exposed, visible points along the crests of great submarine ridges, not as tips of isolated hills.

> The coral islands and reefs have been slowly built up by tiny organisms throughout many centuries [and] . . . constitute the greatest constructions on the face of the globe. . . . Their completion is accelerated by the heaping up of different kinds of soil and slimy and other organisms which fill the interstices, lodge in the outer edge of the coral, and form the beginning of the wall. When these edges get near the surface, the surf breaking over them changes them partly into coral sand; and this process again helps to fill up the spaces between the corals. . . . [122]

In Bellingshausen's view, Niau (Grieg) Island was a typical exposed ridge-top, "rising a little above the surface of the sea, and consisting partly of schist and partly of coral." Its soil foundation, like that of the other coral islands observed, was an accretion of "seaweed, rubbish thrown up by the sea, bird droppings, dead birds. . . . "[125] Here, modern science has pulled away from Bellingshausen.

Why was the Pacific Ocean's floor bare of ridges in some areas? Bellingshausen thought that there were no scientific grounds for stating that it was. More probably, enormous depths of water had prevented seamen like himself from noting them. Better equipment was required. Kotzebue duly brought it to Oceania in *Predpriiatie* in 1823.[124] Of course, the presence on the sea bottom of "high mountainous ridges, steep ravines, cavities and plains" bore directly on the growth of coral masses. "Often belts of coral islands indicate the direction of chains of submerged mountains hidden from our sight by impenetrable depths."[125] But what if underwater mountain summits were so far below the surface as to hinder coral growth? Here, Bellingshausen's thinking followed George Forster's, of 1777:

> Mr. Forster, who accompanied Captain Cook, says: "It would be by no means useless to enquire why, to the windward of the Society Islands, low-lying islands should form an extensive and numerous Archipelago, whereas to leeward there are only a few islands." I believe the reason is that, to the east of the Society Islands, there is a corresponding lowering of the upper parts of the submerged mountains,

which makes it possible for the sea creatures which construct the coral formations to exist. . . . To the westward a very great depth is to be found, with the result that the tiny organisms either cannot exist, or the coral formations have not yet reached the surface of the sea. . . .[126]

Two problems thus arose: first, the gauging of enormous ocean depths, and second, the investigations of conditions that promote or prevent coral growth. Bellingshausen was content to point the way for oceanography in future years by making one major prediction: "I am convinced that, when in future all the coral islands have been correctly charted, it will be possible to count the number of submerged ridges from which they have grown up." Of the soundness of his views, suffice it to say that Charles Darwin acknowledged that the Russians were essentially correct in their account of coral growth;[127] that Chamisso and Eschscholtz both acknowledged Bellingshausen's coral work and oceanography;[128] and that the great depth leeward of Tahiti was examined, eventually measured, and named the Tonga Trench. It is 11,000 metres deep.

PREDPRIIATIE IN THE TUAMOTU ARCHIPELAGO, 1824

In scientific terms, five Russian expeditions to the North and South Pacific in the early nineteenth century stand out from others. They are Kruzenshtern's in 1803-6, Otto von Kotzebue's in *Riurik* and *Predpriiatie*, Bellingshausen's, and Ferdinand Petrovich Lütke's in the sloop *Seniavin* in 1826-29.[129] Lütke did little work in Polynesia, but compensated by his multifaceted and brilliant exploratory and scientific work among the Caroline and Marshall Island chains of Micronesia. Of the four commanders, only Kotzebue led two extended expeditions into Central Polynesia. His role in Russia's Polynesian venture of the early 1800s was essential.

When he returned to the South Pacific as commander of Count Rumiantsev's *Riurik* in March 1816, Kotzebue was twenty-eight years old, still young and elegant in his appearance. And the atmosphere aboard the little brig, we know from Chamisso's account, was also youthful, though occasionally stressful. Eschscholtz was twenty-three and Choris twenty-one years old; most ordinary seamen were a little older. When he arrived in the South Pacific for the third time, with the armed sloop *Predpriiatie* early in 1824, Kotzebue was a prematurely dignified and sober officer approaching forty years of age. The joy and energy of youth were present in *Predpriiatie*, however. Eschscholtz's assistant, Heinrich Seewald (in Russian, Zival'd; 1797-1830) brought the memory of Heidelberg, where he had studied medicine, to Oceania.[130] And the other scientific gentlemen represented even younger generations. Vil'gel'm Preis

(1793-1839), astronomer and humbly-born associate and protégé of V.Ia. Struve of the Dorpat (Tartu) and St. Petersburg Observatories, was thirty-one, but Ernst Karlovich Gofman (in German, Hoffmann; 1801-71), the geologist, and Emil Lenz (1804-65), the physicist, had yet to graduate from Dorpat University when news of Kotzebue's expedition broke. Among such young savants and even younger midshipmen, no less than eight of whom were listed for the voyage, Kotzebue was a veritable father figure.[131] It seems that he did not mind playing that role.[132]

To such a company, work was pleasure. There were questions to be answered in the fields of zoology and botany,[133] hydrography and oceanography, ethnology, and physics; and the problems were pursued with energy until the day of *Predpriiatie*'s return.[134] The *Predpriiatie* expedition was perhaps most similar to Lütke's in *Seniavin*, which began within six weeks of *Predpriiatie*'s return to Kronstadt roads.[135] Both were designed with scientific tasks in mind. In place of Lenz and Gofman, Lütke had Karl Heinrich Mertens, who had missed the boat at Copenhagen when *Vostok* had called to take him to Antarctica, and Baron Kittlitz.[136] Like *Seniavin*, *Predpriiatie* was built for special work in Oceania as well as Arctic waters, and produced first-rate results in physics, botany, zoology, ethnography, and hydrography. Like Lütke, Kotzebue conducted physical and maritime experiments in many parts of Oceania. It is important to remember that the work he conducted in the Tuamotus was but a small portion of a comprehensive scientific program. Certain disciplines, such as geology, were hardly represented in the passage to and through the coral islands. Only in Tahiti was Gofman able to investigate the rocks and minerals of Central Eastern Polynesia.[137] Sciences such as physics and hydrography were as effectively pursued among the coral reefs and islands as elsewhere in the Pacific, while others could be undertaken only in that portion of the voyage. That portion was an early one. Kotzebue left the Spanish-speaking settlements of Talcaguano and Concepcion in Chile on 3 February 1824, after tense encounters with the local antimonarchists and with the new President Freire and his rivals.[138] Within a month, the Russians were among the Tuamotus. Patterns and routines were more fluid than they would be after she sailed from Tahiti for Kamchatka and the Arctic.[139] It was just as well: the Tuamotu Archipelago demanded swift responses if the crew were not to lose their vessel on a reef lying "so low" as to be visible at only "trifling distance."[140]

PREDPRIIATIE AMONG THE CORAL ISLANDS: FANGAHINA, ANGATAU, TAKAROA

From Concepcion, Kotzebue shaped a course toward the Juan Fernandez Islands. Fresh southerly winds carried *Predpriiatie* 660 miles in a mere three days. The air grew hot, too suddenly for Russian seamen.[141] Then, around the Southern Tropic and a week from Talcaguano, winds fell off. A tragedy at sea occurred—a sailor fell and drowned just as his fellows' amateur theatricals were about to begin. "The orchestra had even made the signal for the company. . . ."[142] Oppressed, the Russians were increasingly impatient for a sight of coral islands in the west, but the elements deserted them. The southeast trade wind vanished. In its place sprang up a grim northwesterly, bringing a tempest. Only three days later, on 2 March, did the expected trade wind blow again. That evening, land was sighted.[143]

It was Fangahina, forty miles ESE of Angatau. It might have been sighted by Magellan in 1521, but the Russians gave the first firm record of it.[144] Having tacked and stood well out to sea during the night, Kotzebue moved in early the next morning. Smoke was visible, then native craft.[145]

A band of warriors stood on the shore, but no canoes came out to meet the ship. In Kotzebue's view, such craft were meant for long-range inter-island navigation. Had the "boisterous" and foaming surf not made a landing inadvisable, the Russians would have made a closer study of these craft and ventured barter. As it was, the *Predpriiatie* could only circumnavigate the island. It was reckoned to be four miles across from ENE to WSW, and to lie in 15°58′18″S, 140°11′30″W, with needle variations of 4°E. Kotzebue then steered west and reached Angatau. *Vostok* and *Mirnyi* had been approached by six canoes off Angatau on 10 July 1820, but in 1824 there were no traces of inhabitants on the island. Russian evidence of 1824 and 1820 thus indicates the mobility of people in the Tuamotus, perhaps because of inter-island tension or hostility.

From Angatau, Kotzebue went northwest past Takume (Volkonskii) on his way to Tikei (Rumiantsev), which he had visited in April 1816. At both Takume and Tikei, coordinates were checked with great precision and adjusted. Kotzebue reckoned the former to lie 5′ further west than Bellingshausen had in 1820; the latter he now moved 4′ westward from his own previous estimate. Like Bellingshausen, he used British chronometers of recent make, not Russian ones.[147]

As he proceeded west from Tikei, Kotzebue struggled to accommodate the logic of his route and situation to his sense of bruised, if not quite injured, pride. The point at issue was legitimacy of discovery: Kruzenshtern and Bellingshausen had wondered whether he had really discovered "Rumiantsev" and "Spiridov" (Takapoto). It was suggested by the admiral that Captain Roggeveen might well have seen Tikei in *Arend*. As for Takapoto it, too, lay in the path of Roggeveen, and might have been visited later by Commodore John Byron in *Dolphin*. As Kruzenshtern observed, "Spiridov Island" seemed to lie where Byron's own "King George's Islands" lay, at least according to the data found in Hawkesworth. In addition, Byron's and Kotzebue's (1816) narratives agreed on the island's size, approximate appearance, and shape.[148] (It was on Takapoto that *Dolphin*'s landing party had discovered the worm-eaten remains of a Dutch rudder, relics from the wreck of Roggeveen's *Africaansche Galey* in June 1765.)[149]

Kotzebue was a man of academic disposition. He accepted Kruzenshtern's contention that the Dutch or British had been active in the area much earlier than *Riurik*. Still, it was natural for him to entertain the deep, unspoken hope that Kruzenshtern might be mistaken. With his duty uppermost, he steered west again on 8 March 1824.[150]

Kotzebue's professional punctilio was unexpectedly rewarded. In the night, the *Predpriiatie* was carried so far south by a combined current and wind that Takapoto was invisible, and all attempts to struggle north were unsuccessful. Three years later, writing on the basis of his journal, Kotzebue could not resist a barbed remark at the expense of *Dolphin*'s officers: "So we remained uncertain whether this and the other . . . were the two King George's Islands, or not. I can only say that if they really *are* so, their discoverer has given their geographical position very inaccurately."[151] Kotzebue's censure was deserved. His need to vent his feelings further was softened, however, by the accident of drifting south at night:

> The sea being at the time remarkably calm, proved that we were surrounded by islands, and . . . we soon saw land directly before us. . . . This island stretches ten miles in length, from East to West, and is only four miles broad; it appeared to be a narrow strip of land, thickly overgrown with low bushes, surrounding a lake in the centre. Sea birds only, of which we saw a vast number, appeared to inhabit this waste. . . .[152]

Kotzebue's experience of controversy over claimed discoveries now made him cautious. Could the island be the Carlshof attributed to Roggeveen? That island, after all, was "given differently on almost every chart." It was, however, a true discovery for Europe: Aratika.

As Bellingshausen had in 1820, Kotzebue added laurels to his fame as a hydrographer by complementing Cook's surveying work. Where Cook or others had proceeded north, *Predpriiatie* would steer south; where others had examined coral islands from the north, he would survey them from the south. Thus, Kotzebue worked his way along the south side of the Pallisers: Apataki, Toau, Kaukura, Aratua. His hydrography was of the highest order. Finally, to clear the archipelago, he went southeast and past Niau (Greig), en route to Matavai Bay and the comforts of Tahiti.[153]

Kotzebue reckoned the positions of these islands on his way across the Tuamotu Archipelago in 1824:

1	Fangahina (Predpriiatie)	15°18′18″S,	140°11′30″W
2	Angatau (Arakcheev)	15°51′20″S,	140°50′50″W
3	Takume (Volkonskii)	15°47′00″S,	142°02′38″W
4	Tikei (Rumiantsev)	14°57′00″S,	144°28′00″W
5	Takapoto (Spiridov)	14°41′appr.	144°59′appr.
6	Aratika (Carlshof)	15°27′00″S,	145°31′12″W
7	Apataki (Palliser II)	15°34′25″S,	146°06′49″W
8	Kaukura (Palliser III)	15°44′52″S,	146°28′92″W

The coordinates are for the southernmost point of Apataki, the eastern edge of Kaukura, and the centres of the other six islands. Estimates allow for a 6′30″ westward adjustment made on the basis of errors in chronometers, as ascertained at Venus Point in March 1824. Kotzebue's enumeration of "the Pallisers" does not quite tally with Cook's because, as the Russian narrative explains, Cook had on 19 April 1774 supposed that he had seen four groups of clusters where there are but three.[154] Conversely, Kotzebue's enumeration harmonizes with Bellingshausen's of 1820. He took great pains with his estimates of longitude. The position of Takapoto could not be reckoned, and it seems that no attempt was made to fix a precise latitude for Takume. All eight islands were observed between 2 and 10 March. Though Fangahina and Aratika were discoveries,[155] no landings were considered feasible.

The Kotzebue expedition also made important contributions to zoology, meteorology, and physics while in the Tuamotu Archipelago. "On the second expedition, Eschscholtz observed and, according to his own words, collected 2,400 forms of animals . . . many of them were described and illustrated in his *Atlas* and in his monograph on the *Acalephae*."[156] The *Zoologischer Atlas, enthaltend Abbildungen und Beschreibungen neuer Thierarten . . .*(Berlin, 1829-31) was Eschscholtz's magnum opus, barely completed before his death from typhus. Also zoologically significant was his elegant appendix to the third volume of Kotzebue's account of *Predpriiatie*'s Pacific venture, "Uebersicht der Zoologischen Ausbeute" (*Neue Reise um die Welt . . .* , Weimar 1830).[157] In early March, Eschscholtz also examined the flying fish he saw.[158] His fish studies in mid-Pacific waters complemented the earlier work of George Heinrich Langsdorf and Tilesius von Tilenau and did credit to his teachers in Dorpat.[159]

The meteorological records from the *Predpriiatie* expedition are especially complete. In this respect, Kotzebue was the true pupil of Kruzenshtern.[160] In the Tuamotu Archipelago, he examined the influence of low islands on local weather:

> An opinion had been hitherto entertained that the coral islands, from lying so low and in small masses, could produce no change in the atmosphere, and that the trade winds, to which they offered no obstruction, would continue to blow uninterruptedly in their neighbourhood. Repeated expedience, however, convinced me that this is an error. . . .[161]

Evidence was offered that even tiny coral islands cause a turbulence from which arise black thunder clouds, and that the upward air movement is by no means localized. At certain times, low-lying islands cause significant and fairly widespread "variations from the ordinary tropical weather" of the archipelago.[162] Together, dozens of such islands could produce an interruption of the powerful southeasterly still called the mid-Pacific trade wind.

Lenz, meanwhile, was sampling water 2,000 metres down, an immense depth by contemporary standards. He arrived at three major conclusions. First, he noted a continuous but ever smaller drop in water temperature in the Pacific Ocean, from 5 to 1,950 metres, between the equator and 45°. Second, he theorized that water is warmed in the tropics and moves toward the poles at shallow depths, while cold water is moved towards the lower, warmer latitudes at greater depths, thereby producing oceanic circulation.[163] And third, he established the existence of salinity maxima both north and south of the equator, with a minimum between, rightly explaining the phenomenon in terms of more intense evaporation in the trade wind zones.[164]

Lenz was a painstaking and cautious physicist. Important though they were, his findings were not published until 1830, in his *Physikalische Beobachtungen*. This fine display of patience in a man of modest means, in his late twenties and with a young wife to support and a career to establish, was handsomely rewarded. Lenz secured the chair of physical geography and physics at St. Petersburg University in 1836 and lived to be its rektor. He was prominent in the Academy of Sciences for thirty years.[165] His Pacific temperature measurements at depth were still regarded as authoritative thirty years after his death.[166]

Taken together, all these accomplishments were proof of the enormous scientific benefits that could result from a venture such as *Predpriiatie*'s. The strictly naval benefits were apparent too: an entire company was given sea experience, the Russian flag was shown from San Francisco to Manila, and the Russian claim to Sitka was asserted again. But what of politics and strategy? It is a fact that Russian influence in the Pacific was reduced in 1824-26 as a result of Anglo-Russian and Russo-American agreements that delimited the Russian Northwest Coast as an extensive lisière.[167] It is also a fact that the accession of Tsar Nicholas I signalled a policy of withdrawal from involvement in the North Pacific basin. Only Company commitments or interests, such as at Fort Ross north of San Francisco Bay, were to be guarded. Nonetheless, it is remarkable that even Russian nationalists and arch-imperialists of the early nineteenth century at no time seriously argued that the Russian claim to South Pacific islands should be pressed. "Neither then, indeed, nor later, did Russia show the slightest intention of annexing to her possessions those numerous islands to which she might have laid claim, by right of first discovery."[168] As academician L.S. Berg remarks, the ten islands in question are today a part of French Polynesia.

Russia could have claimed the Tuamotu Islands, not with settlement or economic benefit in view but as a pawn in future international chess games. France annexed them in precisely such a spirit. Russian pragmatism vis-à-vis Pacific islands, demonstrated first by Karl R. Nesselrode in the wake of Dr. Georg Anton Scheffer's grandiose and doomed adventure in Hawaii (1815-17),[169] sprang not from a disinterest but rather from another set of problems nearer home. Nevertheless, the fact remains that the Russian Crown acted in concert with its agents in the Pacific to leave a spotless non-imperialist record. From Russian and Polynesian vantage points, this has residual significance today.[170]

MOLLER AT AHUNUI, 1827

> At the beginning of 1826, and on the pattern of earlier expeditions, two warships were to have sailed with cargoes for Petropavlovsk harbour and Okhotsk; they were also to have cruised off the Russian-American Company's colonies. Since, however, in consequence of a treaty concluded at about this time with the United States of America, the colonies no longer needed any warships, the commanders of the sloops in question were instructed that the year... should be employed in surveying and exploring....[171]

The sloops in question were the *Moller* (Captain-Lieutenant Mikhail Nikolaevich Staniukovich) and *Seniavin* (Captain-Lieutenant Ferdinand Petrovich Lütke). Both had recently been built on the Okhta River, were 90 feet in length, and had an internal depth of 12 feet 9 inches; both were sheathed in copper and prepared for lengthy cruising in the tropics; both were armed as barks at Kronstadt, given stores for three full years, and superbly manned. As the senior officer, Staniukovich was given overall command of the new squadron, which sailed from the Baltic Sea in August 1826.

Moller and *Seniavin* sailed independently from Copenhagen to Brazil, in company towards the Horn, then independently again to Valparaiso. From there, Lütke made for Sitka. Crossing the Tropic of Capricorn in 10°S, 116°W and the equator in 125°W, *Seniavin* passed more than a thousand miles northwest of any Tuamotu Island.[172] On the other hand, Staniukovich's route brought him directly to Tahiti, *Moller*'s arc from Valparaiso towards the Russian Northwest Coast being deliberately deeper, or more westerly, than her companion's.

Staniukovich knew about the work recently done by Kotzebue and Bellingshausen in the archipelago that lay between him and Tahiti. Reckoning the prospects of discovery to be more promising in somewhat higher latitudes than 15° to 18°, he steered past Tureia to the 20th parallel. Unwittingly, he was in Frederick William Beechey's track of January 1826. Like *Blossom*, *Moller* moved past Vanavana NNW toward the Tuamotu chains; like her, she came in sight of Ahunui, 27 April 1827. Staniukovich did not know of Beechey's sighting, as Beechey's *Narrative* was not available till 1831. He therefore paused to fix its longitude and latitude by astronomical procedures, placing its western point in 19°38′40″S, 140°25′35″W. No landing being possible, the Russians did not learn the island's native name. Kruzenshtern referred to it as "Lito," thus dismissing Beechey's "Byam Martin."[173]

Moller spent two weeks in Matavai Bay, Tahiti (29 April–15 May 1827), then pressed north to Matahiva. Staniukovich's navigators, Aleksei Rydalev and Filip Larionov, had but lately checked the ship's chronometers, so that it seemed a useful exercise to fix the island's longitude again. It was estimated at 148°37′5″W, 1′25″ east of Bellingshausen's fix of 1820.[174]

Unlucky in his search to the south of the Tuamotu chains and to the north of the Societies, Staniukovich at length made his discovery on the remote northwestern fringe of the Hawaiian archipelago, where twenty-three years earlier *Neva* had almost grounded on Lisianskii Island.[175] It was Curé (Kure) Island, low, small, dangerous, and uninhabited, but for Staniukovich, as Tikei had been for Kotzebue ten years earlier, a source of "pure and heartfelt joy."[176]

2

THE RUSSIAN TEXTS

LUDOVIK CHORIS, 1816

On 5 April, a small coral island was sighted and was taken, at first, for Lemaire's and Schouten's Island of Dogs;[1] but since the latitude which those navigators had given it differed from our own by twenty minutes, we entertained some doubts about the isles' identity.[2] The island was consequently named "Sumnitelny ostrov," or Doubtful Island. It is well wooded, but still appears to have no palms.[3] It is situated in latitude 14°50′S, longitude 138°44′W.

On the 8th another island very similar to Doubtful came into view. This one was of equal lowness and breadth, but was more thickly wooded, coconut palms especially being very numerous.[4] This evening, a boat was put off to search for a landing spot in the island's lee. We had not managed to find such a spot on Doubtful Island, because of the violence of the surf all along its shoreline. We did not fare much better here, in this regard: the surf was, indeed, fairly low in the island's lee, but our boat proved unable to draw close to that side, which was fringed with coral outcrops, some of which extended far out to sea.[5] A seaman reached the island by swimming, though, gathered a number of coconuts, and found paths that made it clear that men visited the isle. It was in vain, on his return on board ship, that this sailor spoke of the difficulty, if not impossibility, of making a landing. Our curiosity to see the place's interior was at a tremendous pitch, the more especially as we were certain that this island was truly a new discovery.[6] It was accordingly resolved to land and, with that in mind, a raft was constructed. Next morning, the ship's boats approached the island to within a hundred and fifty feet and there dropped anchor. Two strong sailors then plunged in and swam, carrying ropes, one end of which was attached to the boats, the other to the raft. Thus, it was simple to go, by raft, from the boats to the shore and from the island back to the boats. We disembarked in this manner, one after another. We were not in any danger, indeed, but we were so thoroughly drenched by the waves that broke on the shore that we could not use our firearms: our cartridges were soaked through.[7]

We crossed the island, which was about a mile and three-quarters long in all directions. Everywhere we discovered paths, coconut shells, and sites where fires had been lit; and finally, we came across two old huts that were collapsing in ruins[8] and a rather poor canoe dug out of a tree trunk. But despite all these indications of human presence, nothing showed that the island had been visited of late.

The shoreline is low and consists of pieces of coral madrepores.[9] The whole island is made up of it, in fact. A layer of fertile earth, one foot deep, covers the rock of the interior. We also found some reservoirs, in which the water had kept very well. The commonest trees were baquois[10] and coconuts. We took many coconuts aboard in the evening, on leaving this island, which we named very justifiably after the generous man who had undertaken to support our expedition at his own expense. May the name of Rumanzoff Island [Rumiantsev or Tikei], which that place will now bear, serve as a lasting indication of our gratitude.[11] It is situated in latitude 14°57′S, longitude 144°28′W.[12]

Another low isle, well wooded but lacking coconut palms, was sighted on 10 April and was named Spiridoff Island. It lay in latitude 14°40′S, longitude 144°58′W. Then, on the 11th we discovered a long chain of islets joined together by reefs. Again, no palms were observed. This chain was named Tzep Rurika [Tsep' Riurika, or Riurik's Chain]. Its centre lies in latitude 15°22′S, longitude 146°40′W.

LUDOVIK CHORIS, 1826[14]

The Great South Sea contains large numbers of islands of very remarkable form. These might be considered as the summits of high mountains, rising up from the ocean floor. Sounding the depths round their shores, one finds no bottom. The surface of the rock that serves as the base of the island is covered by water; and the island's circumference is fringed by a large dike of reefs, which the low tide uncovers and which in turn supports sandbanks formed by the waves on the windward side. These reefs and islets thus surround an internal basin or lagoon. When the mountain has only a modest circumference, this basin is full of water; and in that case, there is but one isle instead of a cluster.

It was at Romanzov Island (Tikei) that Mr. A. de Chamisso, the expedition's naturalist, was first able to study the singular fashion in which such isles are produced. He has given a most ingenious explanation of the process. . . . [15]

Romanzov Island is small. The skirt, made of madrepores or corals of bright red colour, is almost three feet hight. When the waves break on it, they entirely cover it. The sand to be found further inland rises from six to nine feet, is of dazzling whiteness, and supports a stratum of vegetable matter or mould which is between two inches and a foot in depth. The dike is broken in several places on the side of the island in the lee of the wind, and at very high tide the sea probably penetrates into the island's interior. The rain water, that filled several pits,[16] was sweet. We came across varieties of cistern, made by man, dilapidated huts, an old canoe, and, finally, traces of fires. All this showed that this empty island is sometimes visited by the inhabitants of other South Sea islands. The verdant aspect of Romanzov Island is extremely pleasant. The number of plants to be found there is, however, very limited. Such varieties as there are form a dense brush, above which rise coconut palms and in which the baquois stands out by its odd form. The isle was not yet shown on any map, and so we were within our rights to give it a name. We could not have chosen a more suitable one than that of the generous man who had conceived the idea of our expedition and had so liberally borne all its expenses. Count Romanzov [Rumiantsev] died in 1825, leaving behind cherished and venerated memories.[17]

ADELBERT VON CHAMISSO, 1821

The writer of these essays will leave it to learned hydrographers, who demand the most rigorous enquiry into the many and similarly formed isles of the Great South Sea, to compare, on the one hand, those low islands that we ourselves saw in about latitude 15°S and between longitudes 128° and 149°W from Greenwich and, on the other hand, the discoveries of earlier mariners, notably those of Le Maire and Schouten.[18] Those sighted by us in the year 1816 were, from east to west (which was the direction of our course), Doubtful Island (Sumnitelny ostrov), Romanzoff and Spiridoff Islands, the Riurik Chain, Dean's Chain, and Krusenstern Island. At the same time, the hydrographers may be left to seek these islands on the chart of Tupaya,[19] in the limits of which they must fall. The former enquiry has, in fact, already been made by Krusenstern himself in his *Beyträge zur Hydrographie*, p. 173. We are unable, however, to accept the desolate Spiridoff Island as Sondergrondt Island, which is said to be very populous, and to be rich in coconut palms.[20] And in view of this, we must throw some doubt on Krusenstern's findings on other points.

The islands that we all saw, at all events, seemed to be lacking inhabitants and indeed to be inhospitable. Of all the isles on which we made landings, only little Romanzoff Island [Tikei] was covered by coconut palms. . . . A glance at the atlas will be more instructive with respect to those isles' positions than anything we might say.[21] Of modest circumference, Romanzoff Island has an outer edge or raised dam of madrepore, enclosing a level area where, apparently, the vegetable mould is of greater depth. Here and there, coconut palms rise from this area, without forming an actual wood. . . . And shrubs, with entire, simple, and generally fleshy leaves and colourless flowers, comprise an easily penetrable thicket, above which the coconuts rise. Only the leafless *Cassyta* climbs, with its reddish fibres. Through this sparse vegetable covering, the soil is everywhere visible.[22]

We did not see the rat which, it is true, hides itself during the noon heat, (in which we visited the island).[23] But we did see a good number of forest birds (*Numenius*, *Scolopax*), which had no fear of mankind: like tame chickens in a farmyard, they merely moved to avoid being trodden on. Most numerous among the water fowl was the *Sterna stolida*, whose name has justly been acquired through a foolish over-confidence. In these waters, it literally flew into our hands. We set some free, having first tied labels around their necks, giving the name of our ship and the date. A small lizard appeared to be the only wingless creature on Romanzoff Island.[24] A little butterfly was particularly common, but proved to be the only insect that came into our possession.

The inhabitants of other isles, invisible from Romanzoff, certainly visit the latter island. The landing place is on the windward side; and from there, several shining footpaths, trodden in the sharp-edged coral, lead right across the island in various directions. In the island's interior, we discovered small craft, quite decayed, which had been hollowed from a coconut palm trunk and supplied with an outrigger. In two different places, there were light circular huts, consisting merely of a few poles, rough mats, and coconut leaves. In one of these huts, we found an instrument like a wooden comb, bound together with coconut fibre cords. Several pits had been dug, to collect rain water, and fires had been lit on various parts of the earth. Nowhere, however, did we find earth ovens for baking. In the lee of the island, on the shore, was a place designed to stretch lines; and not far off, we saw a young tree with branches lopped off, on which hung coconuts, leaves, and a coconut fibre string. There were no established dwellings and no *morais* on Romanzoff Island, nor did we find any sign that people had lately visited it.[25]

ADELBERT VON CHAMISSO, 1836

16-17 April. Doubtful Island was sighted in latitude 14°50′11″S, longitude 138°47′7″W. Then, on the 20th, we discovered Romanzoff Island, landing on it next day, 14°57′20″S, 144°28′30″W. It was the only island among those mentioned here upon which the coconut palm was growing. The others all had sparse vegetation. All, in fact, have the appearance of sand banks, with their broad white beaches; and so they were considered by the seafarers of old, who marvelled at their own failure to find any bottom with the plumb-line even in the close proximity to such isles, a fact that those seafarers never fail to note.[26]

On 22 April, Spiridov Island was seen, in latitude 14°51′00″S, longitude 144°59′20″W. Then, on the 23rd, we sighted the Riurik Chain in the vicinity of Captain Cook's Pallisers and moved southward from it. We sighted the chain in latitude 15°10′00″S to 15°30′00″S and between longitude 146°31′00″ and 146°46′00″W. Their further extent to the northward was not examined. Land was observed off to the SSE, too, but was not investigated.[27]

On the 15th of this month, we had seen many seabirds, notably frigate birds and pelicans, and we had suffered several wind squalls and had not sailed on during the night. The skies were heavily overcast, it had rained very hard, and there had been lightning flashes in all directions.

The shout of "Land!" excited us in a joyful manner at noon on the 16th of April. Anticipation is great when land emerges, as one might say, voluntarily and not at the behest of seamen who have made for it, that is, when unknown land emerges from a mirrored surface and gradually takes a shape. The eyes eagerly search for smoke, that waving flag that announces the presence of humans to other humans. If rising smoke is seen, the heart pounds remarkably. But these sad reefs soon lost all interest save that offered by a certain idle curiosity.

Nevertheless, it was a great occasion when it was decided on the 20th to attempt a landing on little Romanzoff Island, which was rich in palms. The captain ordered Lieutenant Zakharin to seek out some landing place, at the same time ordering me to accompany him. I got into the boat filled with joy and hope, and we pushed off. We rowed in quite close to the island, separated from the shoreline only by surging breakers. Then a daring seaman swam to shore with a rope. He walked along the shore, discovered human traces, coconut shells, trodden pathways. He listened in the bushes, picked up a few green branches, and returned to the rope. Zakharin now gestured to the island with his hand, saying to me, "Adelbert Logginovich, would you also care to go?" I do not think that such a feeling of embarrassment will ever again penetrate my whole being!

I record this for my own humiliation. What the sailor had done, I was incapable of doing, so he swam back to the boat and we rowed back to the ship. And there, after we had made our report, a pram was put together out of all the available wood on board. Next day, we went in to the island in two boats, which anchored in deep water beside the breakers. The same sailor then swam with a rope in his hand, and with the aid of our pram or raft we were able, one by one, to reach the shore, the foaming waves breaking right over us.

We wandered happily through the wood and explored the island. We collected all possible indications of human presence, followed the paths that others had beaten, and looked around the deserted huts that had served them as shelter. I would liken the feeling to the sensation that one might have in the house of a person who, although unknown, is dear to one. In the same spirit I might have entered Goethe's country house to take a look at his study. As I have said elsewhere, in my Observations,[28] this isle has no permanent inhabitants and appears to be visited from other islands unknown to us.

The day, which was in any case the Russian Easter, became a festive one for us, and we celebrated it on board the *Riurik* with cannon fire. The crew received double rations and we brought coconuts to those who had stayed aboard. In order to get those coconuts, an axe had been put to the trees, a procedure that cut into my soul. The axe itself was left there in atonement.

A few birds were observed in the vicinity of these low isles, the recording of which occupied us in the following days until the 25th. And there were numerous flying fish. Here, I also once saw a water snake swimming in the ocean.[29]

OTTO VON KOTZEBUE, 1821

On 16 April, we found ourselves in latitude 14°51'S, longitude 138°4'W. After daybreak, we pressed on westward.[30] A strong wind from ENE drove the *Riurik* on swiftly. At 3:00 pm that afternoon, a seaman at the masthead shouted, "Land!" a word that struck me like lightning. Hope alternated in my mind with fear of another disillusion. The state of anxiety did not last long, however, for I soon had the inexpressible delight of seeing, with my own eyes, the object of my most ardent wish. The land was seen to the NNW, on a WSW course, and we made directly for it. The island seemed so small and low to us that the grove, plainly discernible now, appeared to us to rise straight from the surface of the water.[31] The greatest distance from which the island can be spotted from the masthead is, in fact, ten miles; and, because we had been accustomed to seeing nothing but elevated lands,[32] the contrast made a very strong impression on us. We doubled the island's northern extremity at a distance of a mile and a half. We saw that the whole island was covered with dense brush, at the centre of which a small lake had quite a pleasant appearance.[33] The shoreline was surrounded by coral reefs, and so violent was the surf on it that any landing seemed impossible. And so, as soon as the sun had set, we departed from this lovely isle, which was seven miles long from NW to SE, and tacked throughout the night under light canvas in order to return at daybreak and take another look at it. The wind was varying from N to NE. It is hard to say why the trade wind should change its general direction hereabouts, since no high land is close by. All the sea birds went to the island at sunset, returning to us at the crack of dawn. I venture to state, on the basis of my repeated experience, that mariners may conclude that an unknown island is near when many sea birds, particularly pelicans, are spotted fluttering about. But this holds good only in the Tropics. It might also be observed here that at sunset the birds will all, save those that remain at sea during the night, go off in the same direction: so that they may be followed and their home may be found.[34]

At dawn, we again moved in closer to the island, doubling its northern and western points at a distance of a mile and a half. We busied ourselves by taking sketches of it. No landing place was seen except at the NW point, where a landing might conceivably have been effected had the waves, driven by a powerful wind from the north, not created so tremendous a surf.[35] The island's centre, where the lake lies, is very low. Its extremities, to north and south, are higher. We searched in vain for any palms, but the bushes at least relieved the eye with a luxuriant greenness.

In appearance, this island did correspond with the description of Schouten's Dog Island; but we could not be sure that it was in fact that isle, since our reckoning for latitude differed from Schouten's by 22'; a mistake which can hardly be regarded as possible, even in view of the period of the Dutch discovery. I pay no heed to the longitudinal variance, as it was necessarily several degrees out at that time.[36] Unquestionably, a number of islands must lie close to this area, as was indicated by the innumerable sea birds that we had been seeing for two days: they could scarcely all have found room on the island we had found. Being uncertain, I named the place Doubtful Island. We found its latitude, calculated from two noon observations, to be latitude 14°50'11"S, longitude 138°47'7"W. The inclination of the magnetic needle was 5°E. The day before he sighted his Dog Island, Schouten had no declination and he fixed its latitude at 15°12'3"S. Our own survey was complete by 11:00 am. Being by now quite convinced that no landing could be made without great risk, we also recognized that the place was only the retreat of sea birds. Schouten had stated that his Dog Island was further south than our present position, so I immediately set a course in that direction. An hour was vainly passed searching for his island, before we once again headed westward. We had had a constant wind from the ENE or NE since we had been sailing in the 15th parallel, but in the night, this wind had been accompanied by rains and heavy squalls from the NW.

On 19th and 20th April, we made excellent observations of sun and moon, and I had the great pleasure of finding that the longitude, as reckoned by our chronometers, agreed quite exactly with those observations of ours.[37] But my joy was augmented when the cry of "Land!" from the masthead struck my ear. The land had been sighted to SW, and by noon we could see a little island not far distant, some three miles in length. It differed from Doubtful Island in that no lake was visible at its centre, and this time a number of coconut palms rose majestically above all the other vegetation.[38] This time I was sure that I could, with full justice, claim to have made a fresh discovery. We all longed to land and unanimously agreed to satisfy our desire, regardless of the risks. So the ship was immediately brought under the lee of the isle and Lieutenant Zakharin was sent off to examine what needed to be done if we were to answer our wishes. For we could see, soon enough, that a boat could not pass through the surf.

Lieutenant Zakharin confirmed this on his return; but two of my seamen, determined not to leave this new discovery unexplored, now swam through the surf. I admired their courage the more for their lack of any such ability as the South Sea Islanders possess, practically to live in the ocean. The pair landed safely but did not venture far, there being many indications that the island was inhabited. To prove that they really had been ashore, though, they returned with several coconut shells and a woven cord, which was attached to a pole. And now I was seized with an even sharper desire to make a landing, resolving, as it was too late to act today, to satisfy it on the morrow at all events. A pram seemed to me the most appropriate means for the purpose, and in a trice all the boards and poles aboard *Riurik* had been gathered. We laboured right through the night, and at dawn on the 21st, to my great pleasure, our pram, which was constructed large enough to carry one person easily, was complete. During this night, we had been tacking against a north wind, in rain; but as soon as it began to dawn, we approached the shore to within half a mile. Two boats were at once put off and Lieutenant Shishmarev, I, and our scientific gentlemen left *Riurik*, with our newly made pram, by 7:00 am. We anchored the boats, some forty fathoms from the shoreline on a coral bottom, in ten fathoms of water; and my two seamen repeated their hazardous attempt, taking hold of one end of a rope, the other of which was fastened to the two boats, so establishing communication with the shore when they landed. One of them next placed himself on the pram and pulled himself along the rope as far as the surf. He left it to a rising wave to throw him ashore again.[39] The pram was drawn back just as soon as this man had a firm footing on the beach, and a second man started his unsteady passage. At length, we were all ashore except two seamen who stayed in the boats. We were all, moreover, more or less hurt, since we could not get ashore without being swept by the surf over a sharp coral bank. It was, of course, of no consequence here in the tropics that we were also drenched to the skin. And now we proceeded, well armed, into the island's interior.[40] At every step, we found traces of humanity. After a while, we came upon a well-worn footpath, which fully convinced us all that the island was inhabited. Looking about in all directions, for fear of surprise attack, we continued on our way, so coming to a grove, the aromatic smell of which refreshed us, and at length arriving at a level spot shaded by palms. Here, we found a small craft like those used generally in the South Sea, only with outriggers on both sides of the hull.[41] We were now in a truly delightful place, not far from the centre of the island. Considerably fatigued by the heat, we sat down under some coconut palms and, for the very first time on our voyage, refreshed ourselves with the milk of the nuts. I felt indescribably happy in this little place. For, though the discovery itself might be a minor one, I would not have exchanged the pure and genuine joy that it had afforded me for all the treasure of the world.

As soon as we had recuperated a little, we proceeded on our trip, finding some uninhabited huts in which were a number of articles of native workmanship. We exchanged these for European wares, which we left there.[42] Nowhere, however, did we find fresh traces of people. A few poles from which fishing nets were hanging confirmed me in the idea that the islanders came here at a particular season of the year for the fishery. In four hours, we had crossed the whole island from north to south. As we returned, we came across several well-made reservoirs, in which there was sweet tasting water. As is well known, coral isles lack springs and so their inhabitants must satisfy their needs with rain water, collected in large pits dug out for that purpose. When we returned to our landing place, I had a bottle of wine opened, and we all drank to the health of Count Rumiantsev with loud cheers, naming the island after him. Our boats were adorned with flags and fired off several guns; and the *Riurik*, expecting this signal, hoisted the imperial flag and fired her own guns.[43] During this time, we drank to the health of our beloved emperor. We reached our boats with the same difficulty as we had landed, but we returned safely to the *Riurik* at 2:00 pm. I handed our coconuts, just brought from Rumiantsev Island, to those men who had remained behind; and the whole crew had double rations. The seaman who had first spotted our island was given six piastres as his reward. We tacked the whole night under small sails, because more such islands might be expected in these waters and, being low-lying, they could occasion the wreck of our ship in the darkness. We continued westward at daybreak. The latitude of the centre of Rumiantsev Island, as reckoned by three sextants with good meridional observation, is 14°57′20″S. Longitude 144°28′30″W was arrived at both by observation and by readings of the chronometers. Magnetic needle variation was 5°36′E.[44]

Land was spotted from the masthead, off to the NNW, at 9:00 am on the morning of 22 April. We made straight for it. This island, with a central lake from the surface of which many large rocks rose, was of the same sort as the preceding islands. It was eleven miles long along a NNE-SSW axis but only three miles broad. We doubled its northern tip at a distance of half a mile, without seeing either signs of habitation or a single coconut palm. Its southern point lay to our east by midday. We had an excellent observation, which enabled us to fix its centre as lying in latitude 14°41′S. The chronometers informed us that its longitude was 144°59′20″W. I had no doubt that this was also a fresh discovery, and I named it after my own former commanding officer, Admiral Spiridov.[45] Since the island seemed to me uninhabited, and as a landing could not be made without the same problems as we already encountered at Rumiantsev Island, I decided to lose no time and so steered WSW, with the object of examining Cook's Palliser Islands and comparing my longitude with his.[46] We were borne swiftly towards our destination by a fresh easterly wind and, immediately after sunset, I hove to, in order to keep the ship in an area where the sea was very calm and even. In itself, this area proved that a number of islands must lie in the surrounding waters. So powerful did the ocean current prove to be here, however, that by noon the next day, we discovered the ship had been carried twenty-eight miles to 82°NW.

We sailed on at dawn on 23 April. According to calculations, we ought by 10:00 am to have been close to the meridian of Palliser's Islands and a little north of them. Hoping to find those islands, we now steered SSW. Land was duly announced, at about 10:30 am, both to port and to starboard. I shifted course from south to east at this juncture, so steering that we must go straight into the passage that separated the islands sighted. The land on our starboard side, which consisted of a number of small coral islands, well wooded and joined by coral reefs, I declared to be a new discovery. The cluster's position was more northerly than that of the Pallisers, which we clearly saw off to the left and whose meridian we had already passed. This was not feasible, according to our ships chronometers, and again I questioned their accuracy. But I was soon comforted by an excellent meridional observation, which clearly showed that the ocean current had played a trick on us, pushing us thirty miles westward. My reckoning of the longitude of the Palliser Islands agreed with Captain Cook's to within 3′, and our latitudinal fix and Cook's were identical, so I had no cause to complain about my time keepers. Being quite certain that the islands to the SE were indeed the Pallisers and did not need to be examined, we turned toward the newly discovered ones, which stretched in a chain to the SW as far as the eye could see. I will not enter into details with regard to their position, as a single glance at the chart, which was most carefully drawn, explains that far better than any words.[47] I am inclined to regard these islands as uninhabited. Certainly, we saw neither signs of people nor any coconut palms, though we sailed along the entire chain, from its SW part, only half a mile off shore.[48] Throughout this run, we enjoyed a most delightful view: even the trees, agitated by the wind, were plainly visible to us. The length of even the largest of these isles, which lie at intervals of one to two hundred fathoms from each other and are linked by little coral reefs, is not more than two miles; and the breadth ranges from a quarter to half a mile. Every one of them, even the smallest, which are not more than a hundred fathoms long, are densely covered by fine trees. These islands may be imagined to form a circle as, from our masthead whence the horizon was visible beyond the chain, the sea looked quite still whereas on this side of it the surf was fierce. . . . By dawn next day, we perceived that the current had borne us far from the land to our east, bringing us to new islands in the west.[49]

On the 24th, the islands of yesterday lay to windward of us; and, having tacked for several hours, we found that we were still barely able to see land off to the east from the masthead. Every moment now being valuable to us,[50] I was now obliged to abandon any longer examination of that land, which I called Riurik's Chain and regarded as a discovery.[51] It is assuredly a pity that we were not able to inspect another island, spotted the day before to SSE from the point of this chain, but it is certain that it exists; and another navigator, trying his fortune amongst these dangerous clusters of islands, may perhaps finish what circumstances prevented me from examining. . . . I directed my course westward, toward land that had been sighted at daybreak.

We soon saw that this land was similar to Riurik's Chain and that it appeared to lie from east to west. When we had coasted along its southern side at a distance offshore of half a mile, I was sure that it had to be Dean's Island, as shown on Arrowsmith's chart.[52] The eastern point of that island coincided with our findings here, both in latitude and in longitude. So we sailed swiftly on, with the help of a brisk easterly wind. . . . Once again, we saw neither coconut palms nor any signs of habitation. Yet one can hardly suppose that such a considerable extent of land should in fact be quite uninhabited. We tacked about during the night, resuming our survey the next morning at the point where we left off. But just as we were about to reach the southernmost point of Dean's Island, on 25 April, and just as we became able to see that that chain ran in a NE direction, yet more land was sighted off to our WNW. I gave up further inspection of

Dean's Island, which already lay to windward of us, and steered for the new land spotted in the west, which I believed to be a fresh discovery. The position of Dean's Island as marked on Arrowsmith's chart, I may note here, is incorrect; nor does it seem to have been remarked that that island is in fact composed of a number of small isles linked by coral reef. I have so frequently on my voyaging found groups of coral islands that form a circle that I am disposed to think that it is the same with those. The lay and dimensions of Dean's Island according to our own survey, which rested principally on points fixed astronomically, are expressed by NW 76° and SE 76°, over an interval of seventy-two and a half miles.[53] The latitude of its easternmost point is 15°16'30"S, and its longitude is 147°52'00"W. . . .[54]

We soon arrived at the land in the west, which likewise consisted of small coral islands connected by reefs, which extended thirteen miles from NNE to SSW; this also was the greatest length of the group, which formed a close circle, in the middle of which a large lake, with a thickly wooded island in it, renders this group very easy to be recognized. I call it Kruzenshtern's Group, after the man with whom I had made my first voyage around the world, since it was certainly a new discovery.[55] Our noon observation was again excellent. The NW point of Kruzenshtern's Group lay to our west and we still saw Dean's Island off to the east, where it tended NE and vanished on the horizon. We steered between the two groups, heading northward. We were very glad to have escaped all the dangers of the coral labyrinth, which have cost many a navigator his life. If the weather had not proved fair in every respect during our sojourn among them, *Riurik* would inevitably have been exposed to many hazards; and, besides, lack of sun would have removed credibility from our astronomical observations. A storm in gloomy weather in these parts would be the inevitable destruction of the ship; and even the possession of an accurate chart of all the islands of the group could not ensure its safety, because the current is strong, the land low, and the wind too violent to ply back.[56] This last factor would be significant if one were so unfortunate as to come too near a reef. Only two hundred fathoms or so offshore, the ocean is bottomless. Consequently, the lead can afford no timely warning of the danger. After all I have said here, anyone may imagine our delight when, once again, we saw the open sea ahead. Nonetheless, and in spite of all hazards, I would gladly have remained in these parts a few days longer to complete the surveys of the several isles we had seen, had not the need to arrive at Bering's Strait at a certain time made every moment valuable to me. According to my orders, therefore, I now headed NW towards where Bouman's Islands were supposed to lie.[57]

The latitude of the centre of Kruzenshtern's Group was fixed in

15°00'S, and its longitude at 148°41'W, the needle's declination being 5°37'E. During the night that followed, we experienced rain and powerful winds from the NE: we thought ourselves lucky to be out of the coral islands. Yet, despite the strong winds, the ocean remained extremely smooth hereabouts, which led us to surmise that more land might be close, to the NE. On that account, we could only sail under light canvas.[58]

F.F. BELLINGSHAUSEN[59]

5 July. At dawn, which was at 6:00 am, we again set a course N 16°35'E, and after perhaps an hour land was observed to the NE from our lookout. I steered directly toward it, on a course N 50°E, putting on more canvas. By 9:00 am, we found ourselves one and two-thirds miles distant from a small, low-lying island, with a lagoon in its centre and a small opening on its SE side. I then moved northward, along a line parallel with this coral isle, which had a breadth of about half a mile, less in some places. We came to its northern tip by 10:00 am, and I sent Lieutenant Torson ashore in a boat to a spot where there appeared patches of dense, low growth. Mr. Torson was escorted by Messrs. Simonov, Berkh, and Demidov, and Mr. Lazarev also sent off a boat with his own navigator in it. The day was a very fine one, and we were able to fix our position by observation as being latitude 19°11'34"S, longitude 141°16'W. . . . The island is a mile and three-quarters long and eight miles in circumference.[60] Although it strikes one externally as do Prince Henry or Cumberland islands, both of which were discovered by Captain Wallis on 13 June 1766, the latitude of Prince Henry Island is actually different by 11½' and the longitude by 13½' (to westward). And Cumberland Island lies 5' southward and 19½' eastward of this island we were visiting. For the purpose of these comparisons, I fixed the positions of the isles that Captain Wallis had discovered 24' further to the west than he himself had, since he had determined Matavai roadstead in Otahiti [Tahiti] 24' further west than the true longitude as fixed by Captain Cook on his first voyage. The disparity in the position reckoned for the aforementioned islands leads me to suppose that Captain Wallis passed this new island in stormy weather and consequently made an error in reckoning its latitude, mistaking it for Prince Henry Island.[61]

Once the geographical position of the island had been fixed, I signalled with a gunshot to the boats that they should return from the shore; and they arrived back at the ships by 12:30 pm. Messrs. Torson, Simonov, and Berkh informed me that the narrow strip of land in question consisted of differently coloured corals, and that the trees were low and poor. They had shot some sea birds and had returned aboard with a number of quite large sea urchins (*Echinus*) with spikes or prickles some six inches long, of a lilac hue like slate pencils. Of all the numerous known varieties of sea urchin of the Coral Islands, this was the only one we found here. Mr. Mikhailov brought back the fruit of the tree known to naturalists as Pandanus. The boat was hoisted and we proceeded on a course to the northward and slightly to the east. . . . While we were lying off this island, frigate birds and cormorants flew around us. Seaman Gaidukov, who was our top marksman, brought down a few of them, but he only wounded them: they lived on for some time. In the end, we poisoned them and prepared their skins for taxidermy. . . . The frigate birds were observed to dive vertically into the water from considerable heights, catching whatever might be thrown out from the galley at the wake of the ship. We examined the birds' insides and found that the breast bone and the "wish bone" fused into a single bone. It is probably this fact that enables the birds to withstand the impact on the breast when plunging down from such heights. We lost sight of the island at 5:00 pm, ten miles away.[62]

6 July. There was a gentle wind, and clouds, appearing intermittently, did not obscure the light of stars throughout the night. At 5:30 am, when dawn came, small clusters of coconut palms were visible. We went due east towards them. By 9:00 am, we were off the southern extremity of an island and perhaps one mile distant from the palm grove. Men armed with spears were clearly visible to the naked eye. They were all copper coloured and naked, and they were making signals to invite us ashore.[63] I coasted along this shoreline, and two natives ran along it, keeping parallel with our ship; but finally they wearied, stopped, and looked back at their compatriots, whom they then rejoined. A canoe had been drawn up beside a group of coconut palms and two other canoes could be seen, further off in the lagoon, hastening to the same spot.[64] A heavy surf, which broke with much roaring against the coral reef, prevented our sending any launch ashore; but we could already see the opposite shore of the island, a mile and a half away. A number of low sandy hillocks were visible on that part of the isle which was nearest to us . . . and the northern and eastern parts were clearly covered more densely with scrub, though some areas were bare there too. We observed a number of islanders near the northwestern end. Burning fires indicated that the place was quite well populated. The island, which extends N 40°W for twenty-five miles, has a maximum breadth of seven miles and a circumference of thirty-nine miles. Coral reefs were also to be seen within the lagoon. . . . This was the island discovered by Captain Cook and called by him Bow Island. . . .[65] By 2:30 pm, land was again sighted from the lookout. This time, it extended from NE to SW, so I kept close to the wind on a course S 55°E, moving as near to the SW extremity of the new land as the light southeasterly wind would permit. Until nightfall, we were able to move along its western part at a distance of three miles, inspecting the shoreline thoroughly and observing that, like Bow Island, this one consisted of low-lying coral reefs with a central lagoon. The part lying closest to us was covered with bush and undergrowth. Coconut palms were to be seen at several places, rising high above the other vegetation, and we also noted two small apertures or entrances into the lagoon, across one of which several islanders were seen wading. The western side, on which surf was breaking, was lower and consisted of a coral reef protruding above the water, with bushes visible on it. At 6:00 pm, the thick, overcast weather prevented our seeing anything save fires lit in two places on the central headland, where the large coconut grove is situated and near which, of course, the islanders live in some numbers.[66]

7 July. At night, we attempted to maintain our position, under very light canvas, but at daybreak next morning we found that the current had carried us away from the shore. Since it was my intention to come close in to the island to see something of its inhabitants, I beat up towards it again; but a continually shifting light wind prevented our reaching its northern end before 2:00 pm on the 8th. . . .[67]

8 July. Having come up to this end of the island, I went ashore in our launch, taking with me Messrs. Mikhailov and Demidov. Mr. Lazarev came over in his cutter accompanied by Messrs. Galkin, Annenkov, and Novosil'skii.[68] All officers and oarsmen were armed, in case of any hostile acts by the natives. When we had approached the coral shore, on which a heavy surf was breaking, we saw that it would be easy to get ashore without risking damage to the launch on submerged coral. But meanwhile as many as sixty native men had gathered on the shoreline where we were, and their numbers were constantly increasing. Some had beards and all had short and curly black hair. The islanders were of middling height, the face and torso being burned bronze by the sun's intense rays, as is the case with all the natives of the Pacific Ocean. The genitals were covered by a narrow girdle. They were all armed with long spears and some grasped, in the other hand, a wooden club with which, like the natives of New Zealand, they strike their enemies on the head.[69] Women stood a little way off by the brush, some twenty fathoms distant, but they were likewise armed with spears and clubs. These women were covered, from the navel to the knees, by a fine wraparound matting.

Just as soon as we approached the shore in order to land, all the islanders, with a frightful shriek and with threats, began to brandish their spears in order to prevent us from doing so. We tried, by friendly gestures and by throwing gifts ashore for them, to calm and appease them; but in that we failed. They gladly picked up the things that were thrown to them, but they would *not* consent to our landing. We then fired small shot over their heads from a musket, and they were all frightened. The women and some of the younger natives withdrew further into the scrub, and all the rest sat down. Seeing that we had inflicted no harm on them by this step, however, they took courage. Still, after each shot they sat down in the water or splashed water over themselves; and then they would taunt us, laughing at us because we were unable to cause them harm. This clearly shows that they were quite ignorant of the fatal effects of firearms. Seeing the flash from our muskets, they most likely concluded that we wished to burn them, and so they threw water over themselves, scooping it up in their hands from the ocean. When the sloop *Mirnyi* approached and, on a signalled order, fired a single cannon ball into the scrub above the islanders' heads, they were again terrified, crouched down, and soaked their bodies. The women and several young men now ran into the wood and set fire to the trees all along the shoreline, so forming a long unbroken belt of crackling fire with which to cover a retreat over a considerable extent of land.

Of all the gifts, the little bell that we had earlier rung appeared to delight them most; and so I threw a few more small bells to them, supposing that their pleasant sound would establish harmony between us. But as soon as our boats started to approach the shore again, the natives' mood switched, with wild cries, from one of great joy to one of great anger.

Such obstinacy compelled us to turn back. Their stubbornness was, of course, the result of ignorance of the effects of our firearms and ignorance of our superior strength. Had we resolved to fell a few islanders, I am sure that the others would have taken flight and we should have managed to land without hindrance of any sort. But having satisfied our curiosity at fairly close range, I had no particular desire to land on this isle, the more especially as, though it might indeed offer a small field for natural historical investigations, and particularly for collecting coral, shell, and plant specimens, I had concerned myself very little with natural history and we had no naturalist with us.[70] A landing would have brought very little benefit. And so, not wishing to use firearms at the natives' expense, I postponed the time of the latter's real acquaintance with Europeans. When we had moved some distance from this island, the women ran out from the wood, and lifting up their clothing on the shoreline, presented their posterior parts to us and slapped them with their hands, also dancing about. By all this, they probably wished to make us feel the feebleness of our forces. Several of my people sought permission to open fire with small-shot at these islanders, to punish their insolence, but I would not permit it. From observations, we had found that the position of this island was latitude 17°49′30″S, longitude 140°40′W. Its greatest length was sixteen miles in a NE direction, the width being seven miles. I named this island Moller, in honour of Rear-Admiral Moller 2nd,[71] under whose flag I had commanded the forty-four gun frigate *Tikhvinskaia Bogoroditsa*. I steered north from Moller Island,[72] inclining slightly eastward to make the 16th parallel. . . .

At dawn on the 10th, we heard with joy that land had been seen to windward from the cross-trees; we ourselves then saw it, lying to our ENE, and, with daybreak, we began to beat up towards it. In reply to a request from Mr. Lazarev, signalled by telegraph, I gave permission to bring the coast due east of him at noon to fix the precise latitude. But towards midday, when the two ships were still some twelve miles offshore, the natives amazed us by their audacity. From the cross-trees, we noted first one canoe coming out towards us, then a second, and a third, and finally as many as six of them. They came quite near, then stopped abreast of our ships. The islanders yelled to us but could not, though they yelled frequently, quite bring themselves to come up alongside. At last, one craft did approach *Mirnyi*'s stern and then moved over to *Vostok*, the islanders catching hold of a rope that had been let down from her stern.[73]

These natives were all of medium height, lean rather than stout; their face and body were swarthy and therein they differed from us Europeans. Their hair was bound in a topknot, they had small beards, and all wore a rope of woven grass around the belly and a strip to cover their genitals: these comprised the whole of their clothing. I wished to acquire one of these girdles, but no islander would barter his in exchange for anything.[74] This would seem to show that the exposing of the parts concealed by it is regarded as improper.

The craft in which these islanders received us at this distance from the shore were about twenty feet long and broad enough in the beam for two men to sit side by side. They were made of a number of planks, very skilfully bound together. In cross-section, these craft resembled a low milk pan. There was an outrigger on one side, to steady the hull, and the oars were like those used by all the South Sea Islanders, at least with little variation.[75] These craft go well enough and are certainly better suited to the open sea than any canoes that I have hitherto encountered. In each craft, there were three or four agile islanders; and each man had a lasso made of woven grasses, a spear, and a small club.[76] We inferred from these indications that they had come out to attack us from various sides and, if feasible, possess themselves of the sloops. Perhaps, having never seen European ships, they had mistaken them at a considerable distance for canoes going from one island to another to trade or on a warlike expedition and supposed they could overwhelm them. When they drew near, they were probably astonished by the huge dimensions of our vessels, which were obviously disproportionate with their own strength and martial skills. All the same, they seized hold of the rope at our stern and constantly tugged it towards themselves in hopes of cutting it off. And, in treacherous fashion, they attempted to wound with a spear an officer who, from his cabin, was giving them evidence of our amicable intentions. Both I and Mr. Lazarev gave them gifts of axes, pieces of printed linen, and silver and bronze medallions; but we were unable to induce these people to come nearer to the sloops, still less to come aboard. At 4:00 pm, the islanders started off back toward the shore. Shifting a little to the north, the wind enabled our sloops to reach that shore at the same time as the natives. Turning onto the starboard tack, we then proceeded along the western shoreline, at times within a mile of it.[77] The islanders landed within sight of us, dragged their craft up with the aid of some of their fellows who were already ashore, raised them onto their shoulders, and carried them to the interior lagoon. Then, without delay, they set fire to the trees and bushes in many places along the shore where we stood, producing a terrible blaze. I believe that the setting alight of these lines of trees signifies hostility and serves as a warning of the arrival and attack of an enemy, as had happened on the occasion of our encounter with the natives of Moller Island.[78]

The centre of this island lies in latitude 15°51'05"S, longitude 140°49'19"W. It has the shape of a spherical triangle, with the acute angle facing SSE.... Its circumference is some sixteen miles: I call it Count Arakcheev Island.[79] The thermometer stood at 78°F falling to 76° at midnight.... Both to awe and to engage the natives who were ignorant of the power of European fire, we sent a few rockets up from both sloops. Several scattered multicoloured stars in the air. Such a pyrotechnic display, engrossing enough even for contemporary Europeans, must have amazed people living on a little island in the middle of the ocean. They could only have seen falling meteors that might have resembled the demonstration, but even that would have been on a small scale because of the distance, and would have been lacking any accompaniment of flashing and noise.

11 July. At 1:30 am, under bright moonlight, we kept a headway of three to four knots. I signalled to proceed full and by, so as to remain in this place for the night. We had a gentle NNE wind, and the swell from the east was now so slight as to indicate the presence of land to the east of Count Arakcheev Island. At 6:00 am, at daybreak, we bore away from the wind, steered WSW, and put on more sail. At 11:00 am, land was sighted from the cross-trees, away to the NW. I altered course and sailed WNW, close-hauled, under a northerly wind. At noon, we reckoned our position to be latitude 15°53'25"S, longitude 141°40'22"W. But the wind was so very light throughout the day that it was really impossible to rely on the accuracy of our measurements of headway, which must serve as the basis for our determination of this new island's size. Under such a light wind, the way of a vessel is affected by the unknown speed and direction of the stream. Therefore, I hove to for the night. . . .[80] Since no European ships had ever called at or sighted this isle before, it was inevitable that all the natives' attention be already focused on *Vostok* and *Mirnyi* as upon enemies. So, when it had grown dark, I ordered twelve rockets to be sent up one after another. These fiery streams must assuredly have inspired great terror in the natives, who could never before have witnessed anything like them.[81]

12 July. At 1:00 am, we turned back towards the shore . . . coming along the island's southern littoral until we were lying off its south cape. This proved also to be a coral island with a central lagoon. The eastern coral shore was extremely narrow, only some 200 yards across, and was quite bare; only at rare intervals could isolated shrubs be seen. The northern, southern, and western shores, though, were all covered with woods, amongst which we spotted coconut palms. Smoke was being spread by the wind from several places in the woods, proving that the island was an inhabited one. . . . This discovery of ours I named "Prince Volkonskii Island."[82] And soon we had sighted yet another island ahead, bearing S 28°W from the southern tip of Prince Volonskii Island and separated from it by a strait some four miles across. Heading for it, we lay at midday off the NE side of this island and one mile offshore. From observations, we now fixed *Vostok*'s position as latitude 15°57′52″S, longitude 142°12′11″W. From noon till dusk, we coasted along the narrow coral shore on the eastern side at a distance of a mile and a half or two miles. . . . Smoke was to be seen rising up out of the trees at various points along the NW shore, and Mr. Lazarev reported that he could see both natives and canoes on the shore. The northern extremity of this island, which I named after Field-Marshal Prince Barclay de Tolly, lies in latitude 15°55′45″S, longitude 142°15′19″W. . . .[83]

13 July. Mirnyi caught up with us in the night and by daybreak we were able to proceed under all sail. When it was full daybreak, we sighted from the lookout a low-lying shore off to the WSW and altered course towards it. Very soon thereafter, yet another and similar shoreline was observed to the south. I preferred to inspect the latter first, since it lay on our present course, and so we moved a little further southward. Excellent weather favoured us at this time, but the wind was very light and indeed prevented our proceeding as fast as we would have wished. Still, at 11:00 am we passed within half a mile of the shore and along the NW cape of the low-lying reef of this new island, which was washed by a roaring surf. The whole island now lay before our eyes.[84] The entire northern shore was elevated and covered by low scrub, but on the other shores vegetation was growing only in places. We spotted only three coconut palm trunks. They were quite without foliage. They had perhaps been torn off by gales and uprooted, or had simply fallen from old age. The surf broke over the elevated coral reef with a terrible roar, flowing across it into the interior lagoon of the island, which lay on a NW-SW line and was seven miles in length, two in width, and seventeen in circumference.[85]

Soon, to my pleasure, I saw a craft paddling out towards the *Vostok*. To give it the possibility of reaching us the sooner, I hove to; whereupon, without any detours, the canoe containing two men came right alongside us, as invited. We were surprised at the unusual boldness of these islanders. One of them at once clambered up onto our gangway and offered to us, for barter, fish-hooks made of mussels or snail shells, used by those islanders.[86] Then, having taken from his girdle a little packet tied up with coconut fibres, he tore some of the latter off with his teeth and handed me a few little pearls. To my question, "Are there any more?" he answered, "*Niui, niui*," meaning "Many, many!" pointing to the shore. And when we asked, "Are there women?" he at once dispatched his companion, who was very evidently a servant, to the shore in his canoe, while he himself stayed on board our sloop.[87] From what he said, we gathered that he was a chief from the island of Aniui[88] and had come to this island, off which we were lying, in order to trade.

Dinner time was fast approaching and so I sat our guest at table beside me. He ate everything offered, only with great caution; and he attempted to imitate all our own actions. The proper use of the fork, however, he found a difficult matter, for he feared he would prick himself. Mr. Lazarev and a number of officers from both sloops, meanwhile, had gone off to the shore in two boats; but they had found, on approaching it, that there was no prospect of landing, thanks to both submerged coral reefs and a violent surf, so had returned to the ship. On this occasion, they had also lost a drag anchor, which had become so firmly caught up in the coral that they had proved unable to raise it.

After dinner on the quarterdeck, we dressed our guest in the red regimental uniform of the Lifeguard Hussars. His inward delight was plainly visible on his face. Then, while three cheers were given, I hung a silver medal round his neck and, in sign of friendship, we touched noses.[89] In order to give greater significance and value to the medal, each one of us then walked up to examine and admire it. We thought that, after this, the islander would take good care of his medal, at least until he next met Europeans; and then he would appreciate the value of our gift yet more fully, since the medal would secure him new friends and, by extension, further gifts.

The native messenger, meanwhile, had landed quite easily in his little craft, which was flat, light, and keel-less. And he returned quite soon, bringing with him a young woman, some dried cuttle fish,[90] and some shelled mussels, also dried and strung on a tree bark fibre cord. Very likely, these foodstuffs that he had brought out from the island were the article of these people's trade with the inhabitants of this island, and the reason for their journeying among uninhabited ones. We invited the woman into the wardroom, and I presented her with a little mirror, earrings, a ring, and a piece of red cloth, which she wrapped around her lower body above the knees. Her own grass mat, very skilfully woven, she left for us, and it is now kept among the rarities at the Museum of the Admiralty Department.[91] This native woman showed particular modesty while changing her clothing and attempted to conceal as well as possible those parts of the body which modesty forbids one to reveal.

Our guests were of medium height and had curly hair. The chief was tattooed on his thighs and haunches in a bluish-black hue, the marking resembling those to be seen on the faces of natives of the Marquis de Mendoza [Marquesas] Islands and of New Zealand. His nakedness was covered, as is usual on all the islands of the Great South Sea, only by a narrow belt. The woman was not tall but had a full and well developed figure and black, curly hair. Her pleasant, swarthy face was embellished by flaming black eyes. Mr. Mikhailov very accurately sketched our visitors, the chief standing, the woman and the other man seated. His sketch also depicts a coral shore and the scrub growing on it.[92] At noon we fixed the position of Nigira [Nihiru] Island (so our guests call it) at latitude 16°42′40″S, longitude 142°44′50″W.

These islanders had a large craft in the lagoon, which they used to visit other islands: this canoe lay behind bushes from our position, so we could not examine it well. Very likely, the natives who came aboard us had other companions who did not show themselves. I brought our guests a little further inshore at 4:00 pm. On taking their leave from us, they loaded up their little craft with the treasures they had received and returned to the shore. Once having completed my survey of Nigira Island, I turned NW towards the island that we had first spotted at daybreak, when it had been WSE from us. . . . At noon on the next day, our position was latitude 16°28′38″S, longitude 143°07′26″W. The nearest headland of coral reef off this other island lay at a distance of three miles from us, extending from N 68°E to N 29°40′W. We observed two canoes in its central lagoon, under sail; but except for the triangular sail with one point downward, we could make out nothing at that range. I believe that natives come here from other islands in search of food and that this island is uninhabited, for we nowhere saw any signs of habitation; besides, there were no coconut palms, which provide food and sustenance for these islanders.[93] The latitude of this island is 16°21′45″S, longitude 143° 05′ 36″W. . . . I named it, as it was our discovery, Lieutenant-General Ermolov Island,[94] then, under a light south easterly wind, proceeded parallel with its shore until 5:00 pm, when we rounded its wooded western section at a distance of three and a half miles. Mr. Lazarev now signalled that a well wooded island had been sighted by his lookout to the SW. . . .

15 July. At 3:30 am I again turned towards the shore of this isle, the wooded eastern headland of which lay, at daybreak, eight miles to windward of us.[95] I was anxious to get closer still, but variable winds made this impossible, and so I coasted along the coral shore. . . . We saw a narrow entrance into the central lagoon towards the east, and made our way towards it, under a freshening wind. Soon thereafter, a canoe containing two men was seen putting out from shore. I hove to and took in the main topsail, but the islanders could not bring themselves to approach our sloop and so, wasting no time, I filled the sails and went on my way along the narrow shore, which was overgrown with scrub and bushes. . . . This island is thirty-two miles long, seven miles wide, and seventy-one miles around. We proceeded along its largest and finest part; yet we spotted only those two men, nor did we see any signs of fire or any coconut palms, which might have supplied natives with food. So we concluded that this island, too, which I called Prince Golenishchev-Kutuzov-Smolenskii Island,[96] was uninhabited. I further concluded that the two natives seen were probably there merely in search of foodstuffs or raw materials. We had not yet got clear of this island before two others were reported from the lookout, the first SW by S, the other SW from us. . . .[97]

The wind favoured our surveying of the next island, which had been sighted to the westward. I ran parallel with this island's east side, then rounded its northern point. No inhabitants were observed. I named this island after General Count Osten-Saken, hastening to make an examination of it before nightfall.[98] As a result, we moved quite some distance ahead of *Mirnyi*. . . . So we reefed in the topsails and shortened sail for the night, and *Mirnyi* was in due course able to come up to us. Mr. Lazarev sent us, in one of his boats, some fresh fish that he had received from the two aforementioned men in the small canoe off Golenishchev-Kutuzov Island. Mr. Lazarev informed me that these two islanders had their thighs tattooed and dyed with a bluish-black colour like Eri Tatano,[99] who had visited us from Nigira Island, but that they seemed to have met Europeans before, as they begged for razors, pointing to their beards, and readily consumed everything that was placed before them without fear.[100] They were presented with medals and assorted European wares. . . .

By 1:30 pm next day, we were standing abreast of the western point of another island, very similar to those in its vicinity and also of coral formation. The northern side was covered with trees; the other sides formed a sort of mole, on which the surf broke with a great roar; and on the eastern side, there was seen a narrow opening into the large lagoon. There were a few coconut palms on the north shore, some two miles from the western cape; and here we saw two men who were very probably, like those on Nigira and on Kutuzov islands, collecting food. The latitude of this island, which I called Count Miloradovich Island,[101] is 16°47'20"S, longitude 145°12'43"W. It stretches fifteen miles along a WNW-ESE axis, is five miles broad and has a circumference of thirty-nine miles. Even while passing its western cape, we observed other land to the NW, towards which we proceeded without delay. . . .[102] Before dusk, by 5:30 pm, we were lying off a point near the centre of this island on its south side. And here we observed some forty people, standing on a bare and narrow isthmus. Some of them had pieces of material or mats thrown over their shoulders. They waved to us with mats or pieces of cloth which were attached to long poles, and with various other things. Near the islanders, on this narrow coral neck, two sizable craft had been drawn up: one of them had two masts.[103] I regretted very much that the lateness of the hour, the briskness of the wind, and the heavy rollers crashing against the coral shore prevented our sending a party ashore. Both our vessels were now about one mile offshore. There was a high wind with squalls from the SE, blowing straight onto the shore. . . . At daybreak the next morning, we again turned in towards this island against a fresh wind. The wind made it impossible for us to reach the spot where we had seen people ashore the previous evening. . . . The distance between this island's N and NW points was eleven miles; the shore was covered here and there with sparse bush, but the greater part was bare coral. . . . We named the island after Count Wittgenstein.[104] Its northern point lies in latitude 16°04'50"S, longitude 145°33'55"W. . . . Although, as was mentioned above, we did see people on this island, it seems to me that they had come only for food or fishing and had stationed themselves around the boats pulled up on the shore.

While *Vostok* was off the northern cape of Count Wittgenstein Island at a distance of one mile, a shore was sighted from the lookout to our WNW; it was separated from this present island by a strait some nine miles wide. Soon after 10:00 am, having completed my survey of Count Wittgenstein Island, I set a course for the southern point of that newly sighted land.[105] We . . . found its eastern extremity to lie in latitude 16°00'40"S, longitude 145°47'20"W. It extends ESE-WNW nineteen miles, is six miles across, and forty miles in circumference.

I recognized this island as the one discovered by Captain Cook when on his way from the Marquis de Mendoza [Marquesas] Islands to the Society Islands on 19 April 1773, and named, together with three other isles, the Palizer [Palliser] Islands. I will distinguish them by numbers, as they were discovered one after the other.[106] When Captain Cook lay off the first Palizer island's southern point (in latitude 15°31'S, longitude 146°23'W), having coasted along it, he observed from the masthead other land away to his SE.[107] Had it been possible for his line of vision to be extended twenty-four miles in that same direction, Captain Cook would inevitably have seen the island that we ourselves now saw. Being off the northern extremity of this island, we had sighted, away to the WNW of our own lookout, that shore where Captain Cook had been, namely Palizer I; and so the island off which we were lying was Palizer II. That island is called Elizabeth Island on Arrowsmith's chart, where it is indicated on the same latitude, but 12' to eastward.[108] There can be no doubt that the second Palizer island is the same island as the one called Elizabeth by Arrowsmith.[109] While lying a mile to the west of the western extremity of this second Palizer island, we sighted more land towards the west. But it was already growing dark and so, for safety during the night, I bore away close-hauled under the fresh trade wind to the SW.[110] The sky, covered by cloud, was only occasionally lit up by moonlight.

18 July. After midnight the clouds scattered, the moon shone, and the wind moderated. Just after 1:00 am, thanks to the vigilance of our officer on watch, Lieutenant Torson,[111] breakers were seen through our night glasses, directly ahead of the ship. We immediately went about and at daybreak again turned towards this shore. On this course we caught two sharks, from which we prepared fish soup for the crew's breakfast. To improve the taste, we added red, or cayenne, pepper. I was very pleased that our sailors had no prejudices and would always eat everything that was prepared for them, completely confident that they would be offered nothing harmful. When the light was stronger, we spotted ahead of us a little island, more elevated than any of the coral isles that we had hitherto sighted, not a few of which now lay astern of us.[112]

By 8:30 am we had moved to within half a mile of this island's eastern edge, and steered westward along its northern shore. At 9:30 am we were abreast of its steep NW cape, consisting of sandstone strata. Behind this cape, the sea was perfectly caim and there was very little surf along the shoreline, so that our rowing boats could easily land on the coral reef that formed the beach. I took advantage of these facts to approach the shoreline to within half a mile and to lower a launch, sending ashore Messrs Torson and Mikhailov, accompanied by Messrs. Simonov, Leskov, and Berkh. As on all such promising occasions, I remembered and regretted that the naturalists Kunze and Mertens, having earlier given their word to join us, had changed their minds when it was already too late to find replacements. . . .[113] Torson, Mikhailov, and the others stayed ashore only a short time, then returned to the sloop.[114] They had cut off branches from various trees, all of softwood, collected mussels and shells, and shot a small species of parrot, about the size of a sparrow, which had beautiful blue feathers, and claws and beak exactly like morocco leather. They had also shot a small turtle dove of a gray green colouring and had gathered a few sponges with coral encrusted on them.[115]

Mr. Torson announced, on his return, that he had noted signs of human habitation, even including places where fires had been lit, but that he had seen no natives. They had observed various small land birds, small lizards, and little turtles that had slipped away into the water and hidden among the corals. In the lagoon there was an old craft, drawn up onto the shore. Very probably this island, like many others, is merely visited by the inhabitants of larger islands who come for food or other articles.

All my companions were pleased to see an island higher than all the preceding coral islands. They imagined that we had already left the archipelago, navigation through which is indeed rather difficult, as stated by the earlier navigators Rogevein [Roggeveen], Shuten [Schouten] and Lemaire, Commander Byron, Wallis, Bougainville, and Cook. Although this island was more covered with high trees than the others had been, a central lagoon was spotted from our lookout through the vegetation. And we observed clayey boulders on the shore.[116] At noon, according to observations, *Vostok* lay in latitude 16°10′04″S, longitude 146°19′46″W, about a mile due north of this island's western headland. . . . Since it was a discovery, I named it after Vice-Admiral Greig, under whose command I had served in the Black Sea.[117] Soon after midday, having completed my survey of Vice-Admiral Greig Island, I steered NW towards the eastern point of the island we had sighted from the lookout to our west . . . the previous evening.

19 July. At 11:00 am, on approaching this island, we observed a wooded headland. The southern side consisted for the most part of a coral reef;[118] the northern shore we had not yet seen, on account of both distance and fading light. Captain Cook had proceeded along this same northern shore from the eastern point of the island.[119] He states that the island is exactly like the other low-lying islands, except that the shore is less continuous and consists, as it were, of several islets. While coasting along this island at a distance of half a mile, we observed natives armed with spears, those islanders' huts, craft, and structures on which they dry fish. We also spotted a number of huts on the island's western shore, near the woods, and islanders standing by them. Some dogs were running about. Two islanders now sat in a canoe and paddled out towards our sloop. We hove to in order to allow them to overtake us. They came on board at our first invitation; at first, they were a little timid, but when I had hung medals round their necks, given each of them a piece of printed linen, a knife, and other things, they soon took courage and were then as free and easy with us as if we had been old acquaintances. Like the previously mentioned Eri of Nigira Island,[120] one of the pair drew a small packet from his girdle containing a few small pearls, handed them to me and, pointing towards the shore, cried, "*Niui! Niui!* [Many! Many!]." I gave him a mirror. Both islanders were swarthy in face and body, no doubt because while out fishing they had been constantly exposed to the sun. Their facial features did not differ from those of Europeans, and they had curly hair. Mr. Mikhailov drew very good likenesses of them; and they themselves, remarking the resemblance, were as pleased as children with them.[121]

On the basis of our noon observations, we fixed the following positions: the eastern point of this island lies in latitude 15°50'20"S, longitude 146°25'55"W.... Captain Cook fixed the eastern point in latitude 15°47'S, longitude 146°80'W. With regard to length, *Vostok* reckoned that it stretched 23½ miles along a WNW-ESE axis. *Mirnyi* calculated that it extended in that direction 26¼ miles, and Captain Cook had reckoned the total length to be 21 miles. Such similarities in the observations fixing the island's position and extent leave no doubt that this was, in fact, Cook's second Palizer island.[122]

This whole chain of coral islands, beginning at Count Arakcheev Island and ending with Kruzenshtern Island, has been surveyed and made known by Russian navigators. Though indeed those islands include the four Palizers, which were discovered by Captain Cook, it seems fitting, since these too were subsequently described and had their true extent and configurations determined by Lieutenant Kotzebue and ourselves, that this entire chain should be called the Russians' Islands.[123]

In this part of the Pacific Ocean, the longitude of Venus Point had been determined with great precision by the astronomers Green and Baillie, who had accompanied Captain Cook on his first and second[124] voyages round the globe. So I selected Otaiti [Tahiti] as a port of call in preference to other Society Islands, to check our own chronometers by the longitude of Venus Point and to fix more accurately the longitudes calculated from our last observations, as well as those of the coral islands we had discovered, and their positions relative to the Society Islands. I decided to make a stay at the island of Otaiti for the additional reasons that we could there take on fresh water and the crew could rest and recuperate with the fresh air of the island and the fruits and other fresh supplies that abound. I set my course thither in such a way as to bring all possible advantage to geography. On 19 July, we proceeded westward from noon until evening, under a light trade wind from the SE quarter.... The last of the Palizer Islands vanished from view astern to the east, at a distance of eighteen miles....

At 6:30 the next morning, there were no signs of land on the horizon for the lookout; but we were now in the parallel of Matea [Makatea] Island, which was shown on Arrowsmith's chart as lying in latitude 15°11'53"S, longitude 147°28'W.[125] I steered west under full canvas in order to verify its position on our way. The following morning, Mr. Lazarev signalled to me that, in his opinion, the land we had sighted the previous evening and the day before it had been an island sighted by Lieutenant Kotzebue.[126] This inference struck me as well grounded and I concurred. Captain Cook had rounded that isle on its northern side.[127]

We were now making good headway, but still it was not till 9:30 am that we saw Matea Island, lying twenty miles westward of us. . . . It was wedge-like in form, cut away sharply on the northern side but sloping, on the southern edge, down to the water's level; there were slight elevations in the centre. . . . We saw four people ashore when we were abreast of the island's NE point. Three of them were waving to us with branches and one with a piece of matting tied to a pole.[128] The weather was favourable, and there was no heavy sea or surf near the island, so I made for the headland, raised the ship's ensign, and hove to while a boat was lowered. Lieutenant Ignat'ev, Mr. Mikhailov, Father Rezanov, and Midshipman Adams went ashore. Mr. Lazarev also sent a launch. . . . The party returned to the sloop at 3:00 pm with an unexpected addition, in the shape of two boys. One was about seventeen and the other about nine years of age; two others had been taken on board the *Mirnyi*. Mr. Ignat'ev told me that, except for these four boys, they had seen nobody, but that there was plenty of fresh water on the island. Breadfruit and coconuts that were with these boys would seem to prove that there is enough food on the island to sustain a few people. All the property the boys brought out to us consisted of a fish-hook made of stone resembling slate and a few coconut-shell cups, which served them as vessels. There can be no doubt that these islanders, like the Scot Alexander Selkirk, whose wanderings served as the basis for the celebrated novel *Robinson Crusoe*, had had to devise various ways of obtaining the necessities of life. Happily, they had found them and did not suffer great privations. Had Providence saved a few girls together with these four boys, who had so miraculously been spared, the history of the settlement of Matea Island would have begun from that time. Very likely, the settling of other islands in the Pacific Ocean, which are now well populated, had similar beginnings.[129]

The west side of Matea Island is also well wooded and is more suitable for landing purposes, as the shoreline is less steep. We fixed the latitude here at 15°52'35"S, longitude 148°13'04"W. It extends WNW and ESE, is four and a half miles long, two in width, and twelve miles in circumference. Our determination of its latitude agreed with that given for Matea on the Arrowsmith chart; but its longitude is actually, by our calculations, 51'40" more westerly than suggested by that chart. Mr. Turnbull was at Matea Island in the course of his voyage from 1800 to 1804. . . . [130]

21 July. In the morning, we managed to discover from the elder of the boys who had been brought out, not without considerable difficulty, that they were from the island of Anna [Anaa] but had been carried from there by a high wind and borne to Matea. Natives from yet another island had also been saved on this island. These natives were constantly at war with each other: those to whom the boys had belonged had been killed and eaten by their enemies. The boys had saved themselves by hiding among the bushes in the island's interior; then, when their enemies had departed, they had remained there. I ordered that they should be shorn and washed, dressed in shirts, and given jackets and trousers specially made from striped ticking material. This attire diverted them greatly and they willingly wore their clothes; but being unaccustomed to shoes, they would always cast them off and go barefoot. [131]

I several times questioned the elder boy about the direction in which the island of Anna lay, and, before answering, he invariably worked out where Taich', as they call Otaiti, was situated. When I pointed out to him the direction in which Otaiti lay, he would point with his hand to the SE quarter, against the trade wind. The younger boy did not agree with him. . . . At 9:00 am, the island of Otaiti showed green on the horizon from our lookout, away to the SW. . . . [132]

PAVEL M. NOVOSIL'SKII

On 5 July, we passed near the atoll marked as Prince Henry Island. Its centre lies in latitude 19°11'S, longitude 141°16'W. It is not settled, though its windward side is covered with low woods. [133] Navigator Il'in, sent ashore in the launch, brought back sea urchins (*Echinus*). They were six inches long in the spike, lilac-coloured like slate pencil. On the 6th, at dawn, groups of coconut palms on another atoll revealed themselves. We approached this new island to within a mile; and even with the naked eye, it was possible to discern a high coconut grove and, on the seashore, natives armed with long pikes. Two of them ran for some time alongside the sloop. A heavy surf that broke against the coral reefs prevented our sending the boat ashore. The centre of this atoll lies in latitude 18°12'S, longitude 140°53'W. It is twenty-five miles long and about seven miles across at the widest part. It had been discovered by Cook and called by him Bow Island. [134]

By 9:00 pm, another atoll had revealed itself. We remained by it during the night and at daybreak, under a gentle wind, tacked toward it. It was only on 8 July, however, that we succeeded in getting up to its northern point.[135] *Vostok*'s launch and *Mirnyi*'s cutter set off for the shore; in the former were Captain Bellingshausen, Midshipman Demidov, and Mr. Mikhailov the artist; in the latter Captain Lazarev, Lieutenant Annenkov, Dr. Galkin, and I. All officers and men at the oars were armed. Perhaps sixty men with spears and short clubs[136] had assembled at the spot where we proposed to land and where a heavy surf was running. They were naked save for the usual loincloth. The number of these islanders on the seashore was continually growing, and it was evident that they intended to give us a hostile reception. Women stood a little way off, also armed with pikes.

As we were coming up to the actual coral reef in order to make our landing, the islanders shook their hands at us, yelled, and were ready to do battle with us quite seriously. In order to appease them and dispose them to give us a kind reception, various little articles were thrown to them; and these were promptly picked up. But still the natives were not willing to allow us to land of their own free will. Next, small shot was fired from several muskets over their heads. They squatted down and splashed water over themselves, and the women took off into the woods. Seeing, however, that the shots had caused them no harm, the savages continued to brandish their spears, remaining firmly entrenched in their position right by the seashore. A genuine discharge would, of course, have forced them to take flight, but we really had no special need to go onto this island, whose inhabitants wished to have no dealings with us. And Captain Bellingshausen was mindful of his instructions from our Sovereign, the Emperor, given him verbally: he was "only in extreme need to make use of firearms."[137] He therefore merely instructed that *Mirnyi* should send a cannonball over these islanders' heads and into the bushes. When this was done, they once again all squatted down and poured water over themselves, but the women, in fright, set fire to the woods. The fire spread like a long ribbon along the shoreline as the woods burned with a crackle, and clouds of thick smoke were borne away by the wind. But when our boats returned and reached a good distance from the shore, the women ran out and to the water's edge, where they made expressive gestures, as if to say, "Well, we settled you!" And then they danced and pranced.

The length of this island is sixteen miles, its breadth is seven miles, and its middle lies in latitude 17°49'S, longitude 140°40'W. Since this atoll was not previously known, it was named, in honour of Rear-Admiral A.V. Moller, Moller Island. From here, we bore northward in order to attain the 16th parallel and then to proceed westward, examining that hitherto unexplored portion of the ocean lying between the Angry Sea and the Dangerous Archipelago.[138]

At dawn on 10 July, we sighted yet another coral atoll. We were lying some twelve miles off it when a few sizable canoes came out to meet us; in each craft sat four or five naked islanders. Having thus approached our sloops, they lacked the courage to come on board, merely seizing hold of a rope that was thrown from the stern. These natives were armed with spears and clubs, and some among them had lassos made of grassy rope. It seemed that they had had the intention of attacking us and taking possession of the two large craft that we had; but, on examining these craft from close quarters, they had convinced themselves that the struggle would be too much for them. We gave these natives a few axes, as well as silver and bronze medals, on one face of which was a representation of the Emperor and on the other, the names of our sloops.[139] Even while accepting our presents, the savages in cunning fashion very nearly wounded an officer aboard *Vostok* with a spear. We sailed to the very shore where the islanders had just disembarked from their craft. They hastened ashore and, with help from their fellows who had collected on the seashore, swung the canoes up on to their shoulders and carried them to the lagoon. At this juncture, fire broke out at various places in the woods. Turning onto the other tack, our sloops moved along the shoreline, now enveloped in flames. This line of fire served, of course, as a signal to warn of the coming of an enemy to the island. The centre of this newly discovered atoll lay in latitude 15°11'S, longitude 140°49'W. That night, a number of rockets were fired for the islanders: they burst in the air, with stars of many colours.

Our voyage along the 16th parallel westward proved a most fortunate one. Almost every day, we were finding and surveying new atolls, with the result that, between 140°49'W and 146°16'W, the whole archipelago of the Russians' Islands was discovered. . . . Several of them were inhabited, and all belonged to the class of true atolls with the exception of Greig Island, which was composed of, as it were, the emerging summit of a mountain ridge of layered rock.[140]

It should here be mentioned that, on 13 July and as we were lying by an atoll covered with woods and known to the Polynesian natives as Nigera [Nihiru], a canoe with two islanders deftly and boldly came up onto her gangway and offered little shell fish-hooks in trade. One of the islanders drew from out of his loincloth a small packet, wrapped around with coconut fibre, pulled the fibres away with his teeth, and took out a small pearl which he gave to Captain Bellingshausen. In reply to the question as to whether there were pearls on this island, he said, "*Niui! Niui!* [Many! Many!]." This islander gave us to understand that he was not a commoner but a chief from the island of Aniui, who had come to Nigera only for foodstuffs or other articles. When asked if there were women on this island, he said something to a native who was with him, and the latter at once went off to the shore in their canoe. Meanwhile, dinner time had come and Captain Bellingshausen seated his guest beside himself. The Aniui chief tried to copy those seated with him at table in everything. . . .

The messenger sent ashore brought back with him a young native woman. We invited her into the wardroom and Captain Bellingshausen presented her with a small mirror, earrings, a ring, and a length of red cloth, in which she decided then and there to wrap herself from waist to knees. Her own material, which was skilfully woven from grasses, she left on the sloop; and it is now with other rarities in the Admiralty Museum. . . .

On 20 July, on our passage to Otaiti, we sighted the island of Matea. As we coasted along its northern shore, its edge resembled the dark walls of a high fort, on the summit of which a grove of coconut palms waved in the wind. Coming level with the island's NE cape, we noticed four people standing on a finger of land right by the water; they were waving a piece of red material tied to a long pole to attract us. The sloops hove to and boats went ashore. Lieutenant Annenkov, Dr. Galkin, and I went from our ship. We made an easy landing and found on the shore four boys, two of whom were taken to *Vostok*, two to *Mirnyi*. On this island we observed, as well as coconut palms, the breadfruit tree; and we also saw several streams of good fresh water. The boys brought to our sloop were aged about fifteen and perhaps ten. With the aid of gestures, the elder boy related the following tale to us: They were from the island of Anna and had been carried by a storm, with their relatives, to the island of Matea. Later, other craft with enemies aboard had also arrived here; and these newcomers had slaughtered and eaten the earlier arrivals but for these four boys, who had managed to flee and hide in the bushes. They had remained concealed there until the enemy canoes had departed from the island. Seeing our sloops, and having heard that Europeans do not eat people and do not injure others, they had resolved to ask us, by signs, to take them off this island. The boys were intelligent and had facial proportions similar to Europeans'. They knew the island of Otaiti, which they called Taich', and they indicated that their own island lay to the SE of where we were. The boys were shorn, washed well, and dressed in trousers and jackets made of ticking material; and they no longer looked in the least like savages. . . . [141]

IVAN MIKHAILOVICH SIMONOV

The following day [6 July], at 9:00 am, yet another island revealed its beauty before us, replete with people and coconut palms. It seemed that this island was settled by a populous tribe. This was indicated by fires lit in numerous places and by crowds of natives, armed with spears, who were yelling something and making various signs to us. They were apparently inviting us to land, and with such eagerness that two men actually ran for awhile abreast of the sloops, which were at the time coasting along the shore at a distance of no more than two versts [2,330 yards]. On reckoning the geographical position of the island, Captain Bellingshausen recognized it as Bow Island, discovered and so named by Captain Cook.[142] In shape, the middle of the SW shore of the island does indeed resemble a weapon of that sort, used before the invention of firearms, whose name it bears.[143] Since the island was already known, Captain Bellingshausen had no wish to remain longer by its shores; nor did he even send officers ashore here to fetch coconuts, because the white hue of the water and the mighty roar of the surf gave us pause, obliging us to believe that by its shores it was just as shallow and difficult of access as at Cumberland Island.[144]

At 2:30 pm that same day, a seaman in the lookout, a little platform built over the second topmast section, spotted more land. Toward evening, we passed by it at a distance of five versts and could see that it lay as close to the ocean surface as Bow Island, and had a similar coral foundation and a lagoon at its centre. Its NW shore was covered with woods, over which majestically soared coconut palms, and it was inhabited by men. By 6:00 pm, the sky had grown dark and we could no longer see anything on the shore except the fires lit in a few spots. Throughout the night, *Vostok* remained in one position under light canvas; still, the current had carried her quite far from the shore. Meanwhile, the wind had died away, so our sloop was not able to draw near the shoreline in question before 2:00 pm on 8 July.

According to observations, the latitude was 17°49'S, and the longitude 143°W.[145] The maps aboard *Vostok* and *Mirnyi* showed no land whatever on this spot, and so Captain Bellingshausen considered this island a fresh discovery and named it after Moller. This was the first discovery made by the commander in a beautiful tropical clime and was the first populated island found by us on our Southern expedition. For this reason, Captain Bellingshausen examined it with great attention, made a hydrographic survey, and wished to make the acquaintance of the inhabitants. Since the latter were not coming out to us, the captain himself went to them in the launch, taking with him the expeditionary artist, Mikhailov, and Midshipman Demidov. After he had set out, Captain Lazarev, the surgeon Galkin, Lieutenant Annenkov, and Midshipman Novosil'skii put off for the island from *Mirnyi*. All the officers and men were armed, in case of hostile actions by natives. And here very soon what I remarked earlier about the hostile attitude of savage islanders towards Europeans was proved to be just.... [146]

Vain blood-letting is not in the tradition of the Russian people, and Captain Bellingshausen, ever mild and ever noble, was unwilling by such means as that to open a way for the satisfaction of a useless curiosity. And what, indeed, would we have found or learned there of any utility to science or humanity? A tropical climate, properties of coral isles, the appearance and character of natives, or products of nature? We trusted to see and learn all this, in the near future, from other coral islands, where the inhabitants would be more amicably disposed toward the reception of European wanderers.

When *Vostok*'s and *Mirnyi*'s launches had rowed a good distance from that shore, women were the first to run out of the woods and down to the sea, even up to their knees, where they mocked the unsuccessful visit of our captains with various grimaces and antics, some of them pretty indecent. Several sailors sought permission to teach these jeerers a lesson with small-shot from a musket; but the captain would not hear of it. I think that, nonetheless, the event will long remain in the memories of the natives of Moller Island. Let Dumont D'Urville give another name to Moller Island and ascribe its discovery to another mariner: Captain Bellingshausen's fame will not be diminished a whit for that, for nobody can dispute his discovery of a subsequent and numerous chain. [147]

Until 10 July, the sloop *Vostok* and her inseparable companion *Mirnyi* continued in an almost northerly direction and there, in latitude 15°51'S, longitude 143°09'W, they found another inhabited coral island, which Captain Bellingshausen named Count Arakcheev Island. From here, the leader of our expedition gave orders to proceed due west and sailed on between southern latitudes 15°40' and 17°, inclining now to one side, now to the other. Within that band of 1°20', or 140 versts, and over an expanse of 5½° of longitude, or 554 versts, Captain Bellingshausen discovered during an eight-day period twelve new isles. These formed a veritable archipelago, and the captain called it, with full justice, the group of the Russians' Islands. They were found in this order: [148]

10 July	Count Arakcheev Island	15°51'S,	143°09'W
11 July	Prince Volkonskii Island	15°47'S,	144°31'W
12 July	Prince Barclay de Tolly Island	16°06'S,	144°39'W
13 July	Nigiru	16°43'S,	145°05'W
14 July	General Ermolov Island	16°22'S,	145°26'W
14 July	Prince Golenishchev-Kutuzov Isle	16°32'S,	146°30'W
15 July	General Raevskii Island	16°43'S,	146°31'W
15 July	Count Osten-Saken Island	16°29'S,	146°38'W

16 July	Admiral Chichagov Island	16°50′S,	147°13′W
16 July	Count Milodarovich Island	16°47′S,	147°33′W
16 July	Count Wittgenstein Island	16°21′S,	147°53′W
17 July	Admiral Greig Island	16°11′S,	148°36′W

In addition, Captain Bellingshausen during this same period looked over and described two islands previously discovered. These were:

| 17 July | 2nd Palizer | 15°31′S, | 148°43′W |
| 18 July | 3rd Palizer | 15°46′S, | 148°54′W |

The name Palizer was given to four islands by Captain Cook in 1774; and Captain Bellingshausen marked them, on his own chart, by the numbers and in the order described by Cook. In fact, though, they had been discovered before Cook's time by Roggeveen and originally named by him the Disastrous Isles, because one ship in Roggeveen's squadron was lost by them and another two saved themselves only with great difficulty.[149] All these islands, as well as many others that remained far away from us, have an identical appearance: all were created on coral or madrepore foundations, all are low and narrow, and all have a central mediterranean sea, usually termed a lagoon.... Vegetation is meagre and poor. Before Europeans brought cattle, horses, goats, rabbits, and cats, the only quadrupeds known to the islanders were swine, dogs, and mice.[150] Fresh water is obtained from wells some two fathoms deep, where a calcareous layer of madrepore, hard and rough on the surface, becomes softer and more porous. It very likely strains sea water, so purifying it of saline and dirt particles. The natives of Arakcheev Island received us with as much hostility as had the natives of Moller. Our captains and officers did not go ashore to visit them, but they themselves came out to the sloops in six canoes, to the number of twenty-five men, armed with lassos, spears, and clubs. Despite our kindnesses and gifts, they refused to draw any nearer, let alone board our sloops. It seemed that, having rather miscalculated their own strength when far off, they had set out with the aim of attacking and taking possession of our vessels; but they no doubt soon recognized their powerlessness and were, for that reason, in a hurry to return to shore....[151]

By noon next day, 12 July, we were already close to Barclay de Tolly Island, on whose shores both people and craft were visible. And on 13 July, at 11:00 am, yet another island revealed itself to our sight: it was covered partly by woods, partly by low bushes; but we saw only three trunks of coconut palms, without leaves. Certainly, we observed no signs that would have led us to conclude that this island was inhabited. However, two islanders came out toward us from the shore, one of whom, it seemed, was the proprietor of the canoe, and the other his labourer. Without any preliminary explanations whatever, the pair came onto *Vostok*'s quarterdeck, where the senior native, Eri-Tatano by name, offered the captain a number of sea pearls in trade. He further assured us that many pearls could be had on the island. At lunch time, our captain sat our guest by his side and he gladly ate everything; but he was bothered by a fear that he might cut himself with his knife or prick himself with his fork, so he carefully watched how we ourselves ate. After luncheon, the captain delighted Eri-Tatano by giving him a magnificent gift, a red Lifeguard Hussar's jacket. The officers at once dressed him in that dazzling attire, hanging around his neck a silver medal of our expedition. . . . Our guest's servant had meanwhile returned to shore and, on his instructions, come back to the sloop *Vostok* with a young woman. Our guests, both the men and this woman, were of middling height, had bronze coloured skin, and black, curly hair. The chief was skilfully tattooed on the thighs and haunches, and his female companion was distinguished by a very pleasant expression on her swarthy face, by lively and gleaming black eyes, and by particularly white teeth. The captain called this newly found island Nigira, because the guest so named it. . . . [152]

On the wooded island named after Prince Golenishchev-Kutuzov, a fire was spotted through the tropical dusk. The next morning (15 July), *Mirnyi* was approached by a craft with two islanders aboard who brought out fresh fish, which M.P. Lazarev shared with us. When we met, Captain Lazarev told us that the natives who had paid him this visit had been tattooed just like Eri-Tatano. [153]

On 18 July, we discovered an almost circular and unusually high coral island, which Captain Bellingshausen named after Admiral Greig. [154] Behind its NW cape, which was quite steep and elevated, it was totally calm: no surf was crashing onto the shore. The leader of the expedition took advantage of this happy circumstance to send ashore a launch with several officers, including me. We saw on Greig Island shores that were far higher than those of other coral isles, indeed, but still we found the same sparse vegetation, the same low and spindly trees, the same thick, close bushes, their branches intertwined, the same ferns and couch grasses. Here there was no branchy shade from the sun of the kind we had found on other similar islands, nor any fruit to please the taste, nor any flowers to captivate the eye. But standing on the narrow ring of the coral island, amidst the silent majesty of the ocean, I reflected on the ring-shaped mountains of the moon, imagining the latter's similarity to Greig Island if the sea were drained dry. And our visit to the shore of Greig Island did enlarge *Vostok*'s collection, adding numerous objects from the three kingdoms of nature that were rare for us Europeans.[155] These included a beautiful blue parrot of Polynesia, with red beak and red claws, about the size of a sparrow,[156] which was shot by Lieutenant Leskov. In addition, we brought back a small but very interesting collection of corals, conches, and snails.

The third Palizer island disappeared, at a distance of thirty-one versts, on 19 July; and throughout the next night, we had no indications of new islands. But at this time we were already near Matea Island, called Mate-Giva [Matahiva] by the Tahitians. Turnbull was the first of the European navigators to see it, in 1803.[157] He found the island subject to the king of Tahiti and governed by an official sent out by the king. . . . We ourselves sighted it at 10:00 am on 20 July, at a distance of thirty-five versts. Here was no longer that nature that we had seen in the labyrinth of low coral isles, from which we had emerged with honour, so successfully and so happily. Here, instead of shores that barely reached above sea level, were crags and cliffs on which grew luxuriant verdure, with coconut palms and other shade-giving trees. . . . Passing this island at a range of under two versts, we spotted ashore four human figures who, it seemed, were making signals of invitation to us. The captain sent off the launch and. . . . a cutter was likewise dispatched from the *Mirnyi*. Our boats had not even arrived at the shoreline before two youths were swimming out to each and begging to be taken out to the sloops. The two islanders who fell to *Vostok*'s lot were called Alarik (the elder boy) and Tuloin: the former was perhaps seventeen years of age, the latter about twelve. The two boys taken into *Mirnyi* were of the same ages as ours.[158] Our young guests brought out, in the launch sent from *Vostok*, coconuts and breadfruit. They were thanked and given in return, as they requested, gimlets and other trifles. Alarik and Tuloin greatly entertained us. We gave them clothes, washed them, cut their hair short, and provided them with footwear. . . . And on Otaiti we learned all the details of the adventure experienced by these four boys, taken from Mateo Island in *Vostok* and *Mirnyi*. In our presence, they related the tale of their misfortune to the king, and an English missionary translated it for us.[159]

They belonged to the tribe of natives on Anna Island, (which Cook calls Chain Island).[160] Having put out to sea as a group of ten, they had been carried by a powerful wind to the deserted shore of Matea. Subsequently, and also by chance, there had arrived on the same shores a number of canoes carrying natives of another island, who had doubtless been conducting hostilities against the people of Anna Island; and these foes, being stronger than Alarik's and Tuloin's countrymen, had attacked and consumed six people. The four boys had escaped a similar fate by hiding from the cannibals in bushes and caves. The officers who visited the coastline of Matea Island saw there abundant springs of fresh water. In the place where they were, however, they observed no signs whatever of permanent settlement.

OTTO VON KOTZEBUE, 1824

Finally, on 2 March [1824], the tropical wind returned and regained its sway,[161] bringing us clear weather. Although it was indeed extremely hot (the Réaumur thermometer stood even by night at no less than 24°), the whole company felt well. This evening, we calculated that we were in latitude 15°15'S, longitude 139°40'W.[162] Just as the sun was about to set, our lookout cried from the masthead that he could see land immediately ahead as we lay. So swiftly did the fresh wind bear us forward now that, even before darkness fell, we could clearly see part of a very low-lying, wooded island. Since no mariner known to me had ever been in this spot before, which was marked as an empty space even on the most recent charts, we were within our rights to consider ourselves as the first discoverers of this island and I named it, in honour of our vessel, Predpriiatie [Fangahina] Island.[163]

When it was dark we stood off from the shore, tacking all night at some distance from it. At dawn next day, we again moved in closer and, impelled to do so by curiosity, stuck to our telescopes. Some believed they could see what others could not, and what was perhaps a product of their imagination; but columns of smoke, observed by all, convinced us that the island was assuredly an inhabited one. And not long afterward, it became possible from the mast-top to examine the entire island. The dazzling whiteness of the coral shore fringed a bright green ground, upon which rose a wood of palms.... From pretty huts of plaited reeds, under the shade of breadfruit trees, women were flying to conceal themselves in the woods. Some had children, whom they had caught by the neck. Such was the terror that we inspired in this little nation! Among the islanders there were, indeed, a few heroes who dared to come out right to the water and to threaten us with their long spears. But not one of the numerous craft lying on the coast ventured to put off and approach us. Judging from the size of those canoes that we saw, and by their good rigging, these islanders are quite capable of visiting other, even quite remotely situated, isles. We sailed right round our island but found no landing place, even so. The sea was not calm, and rollers were everywhere distinctly high and boisterous, so we were obliged to renounce our intention of making the closer acquaintance of the Predpriiatians. The clear sky allowed us, nonetheless, to fix by observation the exact latitude and longitude of this islet. The horizon, too, was perfectly clear. We reckoned the latitude of its cen-

tral point to be 15°58'18"S, longitude 140°11'30"W, needle variation being 4°E.

Once these calculations had been completed, I ordered that a course be
set to the west, in order to approach Arakcheev Island, found in 1819 by
Captain Bellingshausen of the Russian Navy. . . . From our reckonings
there, its centre lies in latitude 15°51'20"S, longitude 140°50'50"W. According to Captain Bellingshausen's chart, it lies in 15°51'S, longitude
140°52'W. Had his observations not made it known that the island is inhabited, we would have been bound to come to the opposite conclusion,
for we saw no signs of man. Towards night, we moved some way off
from that island and lay to, lest in the darkness we strike against some
other, yet unknown, island. At daybreak I gave the order to steer NW and
to proceed to Rumiantsev [Tikei] Island, which I had discovered during
my voyage in the brig *Riurik*; for I wished to be certain of the accuracy of
astronomical observations then made. At 8:00 am we sighted the northern
point of the Volkonskii Group, found by Captain Bellingshausen, away to
the SW. But the wind was so feeble that it was not until the morning of 8
March that we were finally able to see Rumiantsev Island. Taking advantage of a clear sky, we now took many measurements of lunar distance, so
arriving at a very precise determination of this island's longitude:
144°28'W. According to the observations made from *Riurik*, it had been
reckoned at 144°24'W, so the difference was merely 4'.[164]

Now we steered deliberately westward in order to establish if I had really discovered the island that I had named after Admiral Spiridov
[Takapoto], on my first voyage, or if it were in fact merely the more
southerly of King George's Islands.[165] A fresh breeze helped us on our
course, and even by 6:00 pm we had sighted that island, the honour of
whose discovery is not ascribed to me.[166] It lay directly ahead of us, six
miles to westward. . . . But throughout the night, we found ourselves
quite becalmed, and a current had borne us so far to the south that . . . the
attempt to regain Spiridov Island would have been attended by an exces-
sive loss of time. I was accordingly obliged to leave open the question of
whether the island in question and another, seen by us to the north, were
the two King George's Islands. I can only say that, if they really are so,
the navigator who first discovered them gave their geographical positions
very inaccurately.[167]

The SE trade wind was succeeded at this juncture by variable winds,
blowing now from the north, now from the south or west; and these
brought with them incessant storms and downpours. Such was their great
violence that our sails were torn. Nonetheless, the sea stayed wonderfully
calm, a sure sign that we were surrounded on all sides by islands. It was
thus essential to observe the greatest caution, the more so in view of the

significant currents running in these waters. Very soon, we saw land directly ahead of us; and since it is impossible to sound the bottom every fifty fathoms off these and all such coral islands, we decided to approach the land to within one mile. The isle stretched ten miles from east to west, its width not exceeding four miles. In the centre was a lagoon, girdled by a narrow strip of land that was densely overgrown with low bushes. Only sea birds, of which there are vast numbers here about, inhabit that desolate spot. By our calculations, the centre of the island[168] lay in latitude 15°27'S, longitude 145°31'12"W. Judging by the chart prepared by Admiral Kruzenshtern, one might suppose that this island was in fact Carlshof Island, discovered by Roggeveen in 1722.[169] The geographical location of that island is given variously on almost every chart, and its very existence, indeed, has been questioned. . . .[170]

By 6:00 pm this same day, lying near the eastern extremity of the third group of the Pallisers, we sighted Greig Island, discovered by Captain Bellingshausen. We resolved to steer between the two clusters,[171] wishing to leave the Dangerous Archipelago and enter the open sea. . . . The SE trade wind resumed, and with its aid we were able to take the direct route to Otaiti.

All longitudes within the Dangerous Archipelago adduced by me without reference to the method of reckoning were calculated by our chronometers. But on our arrival in Otaiti, it transpired that these were showing a longitudinal error of 6'5". Longitudes given here have all been rectified accordingly. . . .

Most of the islands of the archipelago are inhabited, but we have not yet managed to make the necessary acquaintance of these natives. The latter are, in truth, a very unsociable people. Unlike the other South Sea Islanders, they do not come out to vessels and they attempt to impede mariners' landings. Byron made a landing on one of these islands by force.[172] But many islanders were killed on that occasion, and others fled. The stores of coconuts found in their huts were plundered. It is possible that the tale of that attack spread across all the islands in the archipelago. Cook likewise sent some people ashore. Those seamen did not encounter opposition, indeed, but the gifts they brought were received extremely coolly. And when the English were putting off from shore, they had stones cast at them instead of thanks.[173] In general, these natives greatly resemble the Tahitians in appearance and language. One may therefore think that the Tahitians, as a related and neighbouring people, will exert a beneficial influence on them when true enlightenment spreads in Otaiti itself.[174]

3

RUSSIAN SCIENCE

INTRODUCTORY REMARKS

Surveys are offered here of the botany, zoology, ethnography, surveying, and geodesy that Russian expeditions undertook in the Tuamotu Archipelago from 1816 to 1824. Marine astronomy is discussed under hydrography, which, in the Oceanic context, has remained firmly connected with the name of Admiral Ivan F. Kruzenshtern (1770-1846), distinguished author of the *Atlas of the Great South Sea* (*Atlas Iuzhnago moria*, 1823-26).[1] And since the physics and pioneering oceanography of Emil Lenz (in Russian, Emilii Kh. Lents; 1804-65) have been discussed in many histories of science and Pacific exploration[2] and have only incidental bearing on the Tuamotus, they are touched on very briefly. Interested readers are directed to the works of Otto Krümmel, Admiral S.O. Makarov of the Russian ship *Vitiaz'*, and Joseph Prestwich, FRS.[3] Adequate overviews of Lenz's oceanography of 1824-25, while in *Predpriiatie* with Captain Kotzebue, and of his innovative use of the bathometer for sampling water at a predetermined depth with the assistance of a depth-gauge, may be found in works by L. Fersman and H.R. Friis.[4] The maritime astronomy undertaken in the Tuamotus by the scientists aboard *Riurik*, *Vostok*, and *Predpriiatie* (Vasilii S. Khromchenko, I.M. Simonov, and Vil'gelm Preis)[5] was altogether practical and functional. Of Preis (1793-1839) suffice to note that he had risen from an early life of poverty and labour in a weaving shop to the position of assistant to the eminent astronomer V.Ia. Struve; and that, in the view of his professional contemporaries, his astronomy was thrown into the shade by his results with the theodolite and pendulum.[6] His monograph of 1830, *Astronomische Beobachtungen auf des...Reise um die Welt in den Landungsplatzen angestellt*, reflects great competence. It led directly to appointment and promotions at the Dorpat (in Russian, Derpt) Observatory.[7]

Botanical and zoological specimens collected on atolls in the Tuamotus by Kotzebue's or Bellingshausen's people were, at the end of the voyages in question, submitted to several institutions. Some went, with Kotzebue's naturalists Adelbert von Chamisso and Johann Friedrich Eschscholtz, to the Royal Botanical Garden in Berlin and Dorpat University, respectively.[8] Others went to the private estate of Count Nikolai P. Rumiantsev, patron and financial backer of the *Riurik* expedition, and after Rumiantsev's death in 1826, to Moscow.[9] The great majority found their way, through naval channels, to the Imperial Academy of Sciences; and some remain to this day in the keeping of that academy's (Russian) descendant, the Komarov Institute of Botany and Zoological Institute (Division of Ornithology) of the Academy of Sciences in St. Petersburg. It seems appropriate, in the context of this survey, to comment on the fate and whereabouts of natural historical specimens such as dried plants in herbaria and preserved birds brought to St. Petersburg from the Tuamotus in 1821 or 1826.

As Bellingshausen conscientiously complemented the earlier survey work in the Tuamotus of Cook and Kotzebue, so the latter, returning to the scene in 1824, deliberately avoided sailing along Bellingshausen's track of 1820. The results were a wider hydrographic coverage of the entire archipelago and a more useful set of meetings with the islanders themselves. The fact that Kotzebue's two traverses of the atolls occurred in Southern autumn (March and April) while Bellingshausen passed through in mid-winter (July) has ethnological significance.[10] As in other parts of Polynesia, Russian officers and scientists took pains to complement their written narratives with assorted artefacts. Hostility on the part of many natives, however, made the assembling of a representative collection from the Tuamotus more or less impossible. This heightens the ethnographic value of the drawings, aquarelles, and other records left by Ludovik Choris and Pavel Nikolaevich Mikhailov. The ethnographic data in their works are summarized below. Because their records are so pertinent to study of the Russian enterprise in Oceania in general, they are also discussed from an artistic and historical perspective.

Western scholarship has been as generous in recognizing the magnitude of Russia's contribution to the accurate surveying of the Tuamotu Archipelago as it has been unwilling to examine it.[11] Here, therefore, attention is paid both to the scope and to the method of surveying undertaken by the Russians and to principal results of that surveying: Kruzenshtern's prompt use of it, in printed maps and essays, and a general acceptance of its usefulness by English speaking nations.

Chamisso's and Bellingshausen's theorizing on the origins of coral islands are considered, lastly, in the context of contemporaneous geodesy; and Eschscholtz's sound but neglected ideas on that subject, later favourably viewed by Charles Darwin,[12] are advanced in the hope of rescuing his memory from near oblivion.[13]

BOTANY

Kotzebue was a cultivated naval officer and an effective diplomat but he was not a major scholar compared to Kruzenshtern or Lütke.[14] His contribution to Pacific studies, besides his surveying of the Caroline and Tuamotu atolls, lay in bringing to Oceania scientists greater than himself. Four of his academically distinguished passengers aboard *Riurik* (1816-17) and *Predpriiatie* (1824-25) were famous in their lifetimes. These were Eschscholtz (1793-1831), the Dorpat doctor and zoologist who served as *Riurik*'s naturalist; Adelbert von Chamisso (1781-1838), the multitalented and cosmopolitan chief representative of natural and other sciences aboard the brig; Ernst Karlovich Gofman (in German Hoffman; 1801-71), the mineralogist and naturalist in *Predpriiatie*; and the distinguished geophysicist and oceanographer Emil Lenz (1804-65).

Among the other scientists or surgeons whom those vessels also brought to Polynesia, and who certainly had interests in botany, were *Predpriiatie*'s astronomer, Vil'gel'm Preis; the naturalist Heinrich Seewald (in Russian, Zival'd), also on *Predpriiatie*; and the most brilliant assistant navigator to arrive in Polynesia on a Russian ship during this period, Vasilii S. Khromchenko, marine surveyor.[15] These men were under orders to pursue the naval, natural, and human sciences, collaborating fully with the ships' official artists and savants. At the same time, they were to maintain a detailed journal of their doings on the far side of the globe. As Kruzenshtern observed three months after *Riurik*'s return to St. Petersburg in November 1818:

> It was supposed that crossing of the whole of the Great South Sea, twice and in entirely different directions, would assuredly do much to increase our knowledge of that ocean and of peoples inhabiting the many islands strewn across it. Furthermore, a rich harvest of objects of natural history was anticipated, since Count Rumiantsev had appointed not only a ship's surgeon but also a competent naturalist. . . .[16]

Chamisso and Eschscholtz were at liberty to arrange and organize their own natural sciences. It was an independence jealously protected from a captain never altogether comfortable with Chamisso's prerogative to take his orders only when they bore on naval matters and the working of the ship or the successful prosecution of the voyage as a whole.[17] There was little risk they would be idle where their scientific duties were concerned. In 1823-25, the presence of so large a group of scientists[18] under a captain resolved to gain more laurels for discoveries in the Pacific, augured well for certain sciences at least. Kotzebue's preface to the 1830 Weimar edition of his *Neue Reise um die Welt* shows which sciences were favoured: "We were amply supplied with astronomical and other scientific instruments, and had two pendulum apparatuses besides a theodolite made expressly for our expedition by the celebrated Reichenbach. . . . "[19]

The Baltic German element was even stronger than it had been aboard *Riurik*, as Dorpat University made its major contribution to Pacific studies: Eschscholtz, Gofman, and Lenz were all alumni of that venerable Swedish-Russo-German institution, and all returned to it, in one capacity or other, at the expedition's end.[20] Such men were worthy aides and comrades of the botanists, among whom Chamisso was the most diligent and the most erudite: it was with justice that he claimed, after long wanderings in the Napoleonic years, that "I have no fatherland but the Republic of the Sciences, nor could I ever have another."[21]

Chamisso's sole opportunity to botanize in the Tuamotus came on 21 April 1816, at Tikei. He describes the excitement with which, after so long a sojourn at sea, he "wandered happily" through that atoll's bush.[22] He says nothing, however, of his concentrated and highly productive botanizing while ashore. Though, as he observes, the flora of the low atolls of the Eastern Pacific is poor in comparison with the more western islands,[23] he managed to identify a number of *Rubiaceae* and *Hedyotideae*. All were carried aboard *Riurik* on a raft built for that purpose, and there carefully dried by Chamisso for later study and description. His botanical collection reached St. Petersburg on 3 August 1818.[24]

Chamisso left Russia for Berlin within three months of his return from the Pacific. Part of his herbarium remained behind, part went to Germany. Like Choris, he maintained a correspondence with Kruzenshtern but felt no real inclination to return to Russia. In Berlin, he was received with royal honours and appointed the curator of that city's well-financed Botanic Garden. His herbarium was large, but its Pacific Islands section did not capture his attention. His Pacific specimens were ultimately lost to bombing raids in the Second World War. On the other hand, the specimens that the St. Petersburg Academy of Sciences obtained from Rumiantsev and Chamisso survived. They are held today at the L. Komarov Institute of Botany of the Academy of Sciences in St. Petersburg, in storage cupboards, backed by stiff folio sheets, and individually labelled. The labels are, however, not in Chamisso's own hand.[25]

From the scientific standpoint, the timing of Chamisso's return to Prussia was particularly happy. After ten years, during which the state's stability was shaken by the Napoleonic Wars, Berlin was free again. The occupying forces had departed, and the recently established Friedrich Wilhelm University was complemented by a major new museum. The Botanic Garden, too, was undergoing a renaissance thanks to the energy and legacy of Karl Ludwig Willdenow (1765-1812), whose plant collections were renowned throughout the scientific world and whose herbarium grew to 20,000 specimens before he died. Chamisso brought his own Pacific plants to a herbarium enlarged by contributions from the greatest French and German botanists and travellers. He soon established contact with particularly qualified collaborators, men like Georg Friedrich Kaulfuss (1773-1830) and George Bentham (1800-84), who were among the most able systematists of their generations.[26]

It was Kaulfuss who undertook the listing and minute description of the Filices in Chamisso's collection, in a work entitled *Enumeratio filicum, quas in itinere. . . . legit Adalbertus de Chamisso* (Lipsiae 1824). As for the brilliant young Bentham, whose father, Samuel, had worked in Russia as a naval architect and whose more famous uncle, Jeremy, the eminent philosopher, employed him as a private secretary, he was available and willing to describe Chamisso's family of mints.[27] But the work of Kaulfuss, Chamisso, and Bentham all depended, by the early 1820s, on the competence and enterprise of Chamisso's publisher, the German botanist Diedrich Franz von Schlechtendal (1794-1866). It was Chamisso's good fortune that his publisher was scientifically and economically in a position to launch *Linnaea: ein Journal für die Botanik* in 1825, as it was Schlechtendal's to have the voyager's materials to offer in his first several issues. From the botanists' collaboration sprang a comprehensive, ten-part listing and description of the plants brought from the *Riurik* expedition to Berlin. That work, which treated plants by family and genus and was introduced by Chamisso, had the general title "De Plantis expeditione speculatoria Romanzoffiana observatis." Each family of plants was, in turn, provided with a geographically ordered preface. To find the specimens taken from Tikei, therefore, one refers first to Insulae aequinoctiales Oceani magni, and then to a generic index. Only five specimens were probably collected on Tikei and comprised the greater part of the Tuamotuan collection taken to Berlin by Chamisso. As Chamisso noted in *Bemerkungen und Ansichten* (1821), the flora was "extremely poor—we counted only nineteen species of perfect plants, one fern, three *Monocotyledones*, and fifteen *Dicotyledones*, and we do not think that many escaped our observation."[28]

Here are further extracts from the passage in *Bemerkungen und Ansichten* that bear on the flora of "Romanzoff Island":

Low *Acotyledones*, with which vegetation begins in the higher lati-tudes, appear to be missing here, and even lichens appear only on the trunks of old trees, like a covering of powder. A black mould, to be observed on stones, did not seem to be of a vegetable nature. One moss, and a few fungi which we later discovered at Radak, were not present on Romanzoff Island. The plants that we did observe there were a *Polypodium*; the coconut palm; pandanus; a grass; *Scaevola koenigii* [Malay rice-paper plant]; *Tournefortia argentea*; *Lythrum pemphis* [salicaria L. or loosestrife]; *Guettarda speciosa*; a *Cassyta*, i.e., *Cassytha* L. or scrub-vine; an *Euphorbia* [milwort]; and a *Boer-havia repens* or hogweed, a herbaceous nettle.

In addition to these, all of which are also to be seen on Radak, we encountered the following few plants which are wanting there: two shrub-like *Rubiaceae*, another shrub, *Heliotropium prostratum*, *Portulaca oleracea* [chickroot or pigweed], a *Leipidium* [pepper-grass or cress], and a *Buchnera* [Boerhavia?].

Shrubs with entire, simple, and on the whole fleshy leaves and colourless flowers comprise an easily penetrable undergrowth, above which the palm bearing the coconut rises and where the pandanus alone is distinguished by its remarkable form and where only the leaf-less *Cassytha* climbs with its reddish fibres. The soil is everywhere visible under a sparse vegetable covering.[29]

In his private diary, Chamisso left the following remarks on his method of botanizing on Pacific Islands: "I have always carried handkerchiefs and never carried botanists' tin boxes on my excursions. One spreads out the kerchief, places the collected plant specimen across it, presses it with one hand, and with the other hand and with the teeth then ties the opposite ends of the kerchief into a knot. The lower corner can then be tied to the others, and the fourth can be used for carrying. . . . "[30]

Eleven of the plant species named by Chamisso in *Bermerkungen und Ansichten* were at the Institute of Botany of the Academy of Sciences (BIAN) in 1989, in the keeping of senior research associate Dr. Andrei E. Bobrov. Like BIAN's important "1820 Sydney-Parramatta" plant collec-tion, brought to St. Petersburg from Australia in 1822 and largely made by Simonov and Bellingshausen of *Vostok*,[31] Chamisso's collection from Tikei is an accurate albeit miniature reflection of his interests and move-ments on the atoll. But of course those nettles, grasses, vines, and shrubs that met his eye were of little interest to him compared with the problem of the visitors whose feet had worn shiny paths across the coral reef, or with the question of the reef's silent genesis. The artist, Choris, who landed on Tikei with Chamisso, was aware of his main preoccupation at the time. "It was on Romanzoff Island that M. Chamisso was first able to study the singular fashion in which such isles are produced. He gave a most ingenious explanation of that process...."[32]

Chamisso in fact discussed the origins of coral islands twice in his writings from the *Riurik* expedition.[33] Together with complementary remarks by Bellingshausen on the same topic, his published reflections were a major contribution to the scientific study of the growth of coral reefs.[34] Ever stubborn in adhering to the truth, Bellingshausen frankly stated in *Repeated Explorations* (1831) why his own cruise through the Tuamotu atolls was so barren of botanical results. Beyond satisfying idle curiosity by forcing a landing on Amanu (Moller) atoll despite the hostility of islanders, he writes, he "had no particular desire to land.... I had concerned myself very little with natural history, and we had no naturalist with us."[35] The allusion is to the unfortunate way in which, in July 1819, the botanist-surgeons Karl-Heinrich Mertens (1796-1853) and Gustav Kunze (1793-1851) had literally missed the boat at Copenhagen.[36] Had the two young German naturalists sailed with *Vostok* as planned, both would have followed up Chamisso's work in Polynesia. Kunze was a student of bacteria and fungi and an advocate of microscopes afloat. Mertens gave ample proof of his abilities and zeal as a botanist in Micronesia, when in 1827 he arrived in the Pacific with the Russian sloop *Seniavin* (Captain F.P. Lütke.)[37]

ZOOLOGY

The ablest Russian zoologist to visit the Tuamotus in the early nineteenth century was Johann Friedrich Eschscholtz. In 1816 Chamisso lent him support in his work. In 1824, returning to the atolls as naturalist on *Predpriiatie*, Eschscholtz enjoyed the moral and practical help of Heinrich Seewald and Ernst Gofman. In both expeditions, he benefitted from his personal friendship with Kotzebue, who in scientific matters gave him all the scope and liberty he could.[38]

Circumstances, however, did not favour zoology among the Tuamotu atolls. As Eschscholtz himself drily observed:

> It may easily be conceived that the naturalist has fewer opportunities of enlarging his collection in the course of a voyage, than when he travels by land. And this is particularly true if the vessel is obliged to move swiftly from one spot to another, with a view to reaching her destination within a limited period.... It is true that interesting creatures are to be met with occasionally on the high seas, and that a day

may be pleasantly passed in examining them. It is equally true, however, that certain sectors of the great ocean appear to be almost completely untenanted near the surface.[39]

Riurik left the town of Talcaguano, in Chile, in the early days of March
1816. The Russians were at sea six weeks before Pukapuka was sighted.
At 180 tons, the brig was cramped below decks, so that no large creatures
could be stowed aboard for eventual examination.[40] Eschscholtz and
Chamisso had, in any case, a large number of creatures that had yet to be
studied properly or preserved when *Riurik* entered the Tuamotu Archipelago. In particular, Eschscholtz was busy with Chilean fauna.[41] Nonetheless, the few new creatures that presented themselves to the voyagers, as
they moved southwest-by-west, were welcomed gladly. Most, not surprisingly, were sea birds such as noddies, pelicans, and petrels.[42] Others were
fish. One even slithered into Kotzebue's hammock ("I found that it was a
flying fish that I had in my hands; and I am probably the first man that
caught such a fish while in bed").[43]
Eschscholtz and Chamisso shared the meagre zoology on Tikei. Here is
the latter's summing up of what they saw:

> We did not see the rat which, admittedly, does hide itself during the
> torrid midday hours (at which time we were visiting the islands). Var-
> ious species of forest bird were numerous, including *Numenius* and
> *Scolopax*, nor did they appear to fear mankind. Like tame poultry in a
> farmyard, indeed, they merely moved to avert being trodden on! The
> commonest of water birds, it seemed, was the *Sterna stolida*, which
> name it has justly earned by its foolish confidence. In these seas, it lit-
> erally flew into our hands, and we released a number of them after we
> had tied labels around the neck, recording the name of our ship and
> the date. A small lizard seemed to be the only wingless creature on
> the island; and a small butterfly was very common, and the only in-
> sect that fell into our hands.[44]

Such was the pressure of events that no one aboard *Riurik* had time for
taxidermy even though Eschscholtz, Chamisso, and perhaps others were
familiar with the Abbé Dennis Joseph Manesse's seminal *Traité sur la
Manière d'empailler et de conserver les animaux* (Paris 1787) and with
its Russian translation by the naturalists Timofei G. Bornovolokov and
Aleksandr F. Sevast'ianov.[45] Thus none of these birds found their way to
the Academy of Sciences to join today's survivors from the early Russian
ships in Polynesia, such as Bellingshausen's sloop *Vostok*.[46]

Coasting off Manuhangi on 5 July 1820, *Vostok* was encircled by curious frigate birds and cormorants. A number were winged by shot, and of these a few were later preserved for the Academy ("in the end, we poisoned them and prepared their skins for taxidermy").[47] For all their want of specialized training in the natural sciences, the naval officers with Bellingshausen were acute, thinking observers of the fish and birds that they saw in Polynesia. While crossing the Tuamotus, for instance, several wondered how frigate birds could survive the impact produced by their long, vertical dives into the sea. Practical steps were taken to investigate the birds' anatomy: "We examined the birds' insides and found that the breast bone and the 'Wish bone' were fused into a single bone. It is probably this fact that enables the frigate bird to withstand the impact on its breast when plunging vertically down from such heights... seizing whatever might be thrown out from the galley, in the wake of our ship...."[48]

Two weeks later, in the course of a brief landing on Niau, Lieutenant Konstantin Petrovich Torson, the artist Mikhailov, and a small landing party shot other birds for science, not the pot. Among them were a parakeet "about the size of a sparrow, which had beautiful blue feathers and a claw and beak exactly like morocco leather" and a small gray-green "turtle dove."[49] *Vostok*'s versatile astronomer, Simonov, was keen to examine such birds on the sloop's quarterdeck on the afternoon of 18 July. From him we learn that the parakeet ("beautiful blue parrot of Polynesia") had a red beak and red claws, and that Leskov also brought off from Niau an assortment of coral pieces, conches, and snails.[50] The bird in question was most likely the blue-crowned lory, *Vini australis*. The coral specimens were later presented to the St. Petersburg Academy of Sciences and are today in the collections of the Geological Museum, in St. Petersburg, together with "scoriaceous lava" picked up in 1816 near Mount Hualalai on Hawaii Island's Kona Coast by Eschscholtz.[51] Almost certainly, the conches were presented by Kotzebue to his patron, Count Rumiantsev, on his return to St. Petersburg in 1818. They found their way into Rumiantsev's personal museum, which was transferred to Moscow after his death in 1826 and formed the basis of the (Moscow) Rumiantsev Public Museum in the mid-nineteenth century.[52] The natural historical and ethnographical components of that institution, sadly for Polynesian studies, suffered enormous damage and losses during the Second World War. The items contributed by the *Riurik*'s officers, notably artefacts and conches from the Tuamotus and Tahiti, were last seen in the early 1940s.[53]

Eschscholtz's passage through the Tuamotus in February–March 1824 was in many respects like his first passage in 1816. Like *Riurik*, the larger and more comfortable *Predpriiatie* spent time in Chile, before moving west. Again the expedition worked its way across the atolls; and again the Tuamotus were an incidental call along that way, not the real destination of the voyage.[54] Finally, *Acalephen*, not *Mammalia* or fish or birds, comprised the core of Eschscholtz's Pacific work. His book, *System der Acalephen* (Berlin 1829) has no connection with the atolls. Nor do Polynesian fauna occupy a place of any note in his magnum opus, *Atlas Zoologischer* (Berlin, 1829-31). Such zoology as he pursued among the Tuamotu Islands forced itself on his attention, like the flying fish whose relatives were painted by Mikhailov in New South Wales for the Bellingshausen *Atlas*, which was published in St. Petersburg within a month or so of Eschscholtz's own volume. Here are Eschscholtz's remarks, taken from *Neue Reise um die Welt*: "In the immense space of water between Chile's shores and the Low Islands or Dangerous Archipelago, very few creatures seem to live near the surface. We, at least, observed none. However, great numbers of flying fish were in evidence, resembling *Exocoetus volitans*, only with the rays of the breast fins parted towards the extremities. . . ."[55]

The fate of the zoological collection brought to St. Petersburg aboard *Riurik* was unclear because, although she had flown the Russian Navy's flag, she had actually been Count Rumiantsev's property. Had she been sailing on a regular naval mission, as did *Predpriiatie,* all such collections would have been handed to the Naval Ministry.[56] In 1826, when *Predpriiatie* returned to Kronstadt with her stores of Polynesian artefacts, flora, and fauna, the right of the imperial authorities to take such objects, and to store and use them as they chose, was indisputable.[57] But what were the authorities to do with a dozen parakeets from Polynesia or a thousand mounted insects?

Deliberate acquisition of South Pacific fauna had begun at the Academy in 1776-80.[58] First-hand Russian collecting began in 1804 with the arrival of *Nadezhda* and *Neva* in Oceania. Aboard *Nadezhda* had been Georg Heinrich Langsdorf and Wilhelm Gottlieb Tilesius von Tilenau, both efficient natural historians.[59] The latter's diary of 1803-06, now held in the Academy of Sciences's archive,[60] is replete with first-rate drawings of Pacific fauna. Langsdorf returned with what was certainly the richest zoological collection to have reached the Russian capital from Oceania till then. More important from the standpoint of zoology at the Academy, however, was the energetic Langsdorf's recognition of the urgency of building up a program of exchanges. By 1806-8, Russian botanists had been developing such exchanges for half a century.[61] By exchange with foreign scientists and institutions, Langsdorf remitted, among other things, 6,000 insects. Specimens from Oceania were among them, though Pacific insects were almost lost among the thousands from Brazil, where from 1813 to 1829 he was Russian consul-general.[62]

The first large zoological collection to reach Russia from Polynesia in a Russian vessel came aboard *Vostok*. Among the items presented to the Naval Ministry in the final weeks of 1822 were preserved mammals and birds, corals, and shells. Space was already wanting in the Admiralty's museum, and these items were transferred to the Academy in 1828-29. But the latter, too, was filling up: great quantities of "curios" from Oceania had been submitted since 1826 by the commanders of *Predpriiatie*, *Moller*, and *Seniavin*. Many more might be expected. Zoological and other specimens had, for the last several years, been put in boxes squeezed between display cabinets or simply stored away. In 1830, the need for a new building was discussed at two official gatherings of the Academy. The crucial funds were voted, finally, in 1832. That year, on the recommendation of the celebrated German naturalist Alexander Humboldt, a young professor at Berlin University named Fedor (Friedrich) Brandt (1802-79) was named director of the future Zoological Museum.[63]

Brandt was a palaeontologist. He was interested in the Polynesian fauna in St. Petersburg in the context of palaeontology or zoogeography. While he examined skeletons of animals, two other German specialists, E.P. Menetrier and E.K. Schader, worked as "primary preservers" or taxidermists. In 1836 Schader was named first curator of the infant Zoological Museum and, with Brandt's encouragement, taught taxidermy to selected Russian-born apprentices. These, in turn, took their skills to Moscow and to Dorpat universities in 1841-44.

In 1829, however, when Eschscholtz returned with his collection, the St. Petersburg Academy had been unable to give it proper housing, treatment, and protection, let alone adequate study. Nor was any man at the Academy as well acquainted with the specimens or with the nature of the work needed as he was. So, under cloudy circumstances and without official orders from the naval or Academy authorities, the bulk of Eschscholtz's collection went to Dorpat University in 1829-1830.[64] Tragically, that great collection was largely lost to fire, damp, neglect, and, as the final blow, artillery bombardment during the Second World War.[65] It would be wrong to think, however, that the Central State Historical Archive of Estonia (TsGIAE) and the archive of Tartu University are bare of records that illuminate the original condition and holdings of Eschscholtz's collection. Lists survive.[66] Like extant lists of aquarelles made by *Otkrytie*'s efficient artist Emel'ian Korneev while in Oceania and New South Wales in 1820,[67] those materials provide for reliable, albeit tantalizing, outlines for collections and drawings that one cannot see. They are archival silhouettes of vanished prints, perhaps, but they should not be cast aside as lacking value for the history of science.[68]

Health, Food, and Diet

The Russians made swift passages across the Tuamotu Archipelago and were essentially concerned not with ethnography but with hydrography and naval science. Boat landings were made on six islands (Tikei on 21 April 1816, Amanu, Nihiru, Niau, and Makatea between 5 and 20 July 1820), but Tikei proved to be unpeopled, the landing on Amanu was aborted by the islanders' intense hostility, and periods ashore were never longer than a morning or afternoon, and sometimes less than twenty minutes. Nonetheless, the Russian records from the Tuamotu atolls are of major ethnographic interest, both in themselves and in conjunction with the evidence of other European mariners, such as Cook and Banks, Wallis and Byron, Lesson, Wilkes, and Duperrey.[69] For all their lack of trained ethnographers (and where, in the early 1800s, would a man have taken courses in ethnography?),[70] the early Russian expeditions in the South Pacific Ocean were better prepared than any late eighteenth century Pacific probe had been to collect artefacts in situ, to describe Pacific Islanders, to take the infant science forward. Kotzebue, Bellingshausen, and their officers and "gentlemen of science" went to Polynesia with thoroughly objective attitudes, with the aim of forming various collections when they could, with notebooks ready, and with ample stores of trading goods for barter.[71]

All Russian texts concur that the Tuamotuans were strong and healthy, despite scarce food supplies on many atolls. "The islanders were of middling height"; "the natives were all of medium height, lean rather than stout" (Bellingshausen). Although "swarthy" (Novosil'skii) and "with bronze coloured skin" that made them seem "copper coloured" (Bellingshausen), daily exposure to the sun while they fished in the lagoons or off the reefs did not harm the skin. Nor did the Russians see a scabby individual or any man with evidence of yaws or open sores. The women were "not as tall" as the men but were adequately nourished. One woman, at Nihiru, had "a full and well developed figure"; and others, on Amanu, were willing and able to bear weapons if need be. Men and women on the atolls had "curly black hair" and "flaming black eyes" (Bellingshausen); and the woman accompanying the chief encountered at Nihiru, whose function was apparently to gather *Tridacna* clams and other foodstuffs, "was distinguished by particularly white teeth." Many men had small beards "and their hair was bound in a topknot." To be so bound, the hair was obviously long, like that of the two Anaan boys found on Makatea, whom Bellingshausen found it very necessary for cultural reasons to "have shorn." Presumably, the men whose hair was bound "in a topknot" at Angatau on 10 July 1820 wore it loose to the neck at other times, as Commander Wilkes of the United States Navy saw, at Napuka in 1839.[72] Tuamotuans gave ample evidence of agility afloat. At Angatau they were threatening, and one native actually wounded a Russian with a spear thrust. They were obviously accustomed to travelling considerable distances from one atoll to another; and, as the Russians correctly deduced, voyages in search of food were unavoidable, given the limited natural resources on the Tuamotus. ("Europeans wrecked on one of the uninhabited atolls of the eastern Tuamotus, still in its pristine state, would probably be utterly dismayed over the prospect of maintaining themselves. No fresh water would appear available and, in the absence of the coconut, no vegetable food of any kind. . . . And the flesh of some fish was very poisonous.")[73] Ivan Mikhailovich Simonov, *Vostok*'s versatile astronomer, was one of several Russians to appreciate the islanders' skill in subsisting on such unpromising terrain: "We saw on Greig [Niau] Island shores that were far higher than those of other coral atolls, indeed, but still we found the same sparse vegetation, the same low and spindly trees, the same thick, close bushes, the same ferns and couch grasses. Here, there was no branchy shade from the sun . . . nor any fruit to please the taste, nor any flower to captivate the eye. . . . "[74]

Surviving on a diet of fish, *Tridacna* clams, coconuts, pandanus fruit, and turtles, these people had no choice but to be mobile. The Russians leave useful evidence of their wanderings from island to island, as also of their ability to provide themselves with an adequate diet in normal times, based first and foremost on fish and clams.[75]

On Tikei, the Russians found "a place designed to stretch line" and, nearby, "a young tree with branches lopped off" (Chamisso). This was a primitive drying rack (*toko*) and the tree was *Guettarda speciosa* or *Tournefortia argentea*. Both were observed by Chamisso and specimens of their foliage were taken aboard *Riurik*.[76] At Takaroa in 1765, Commodore Byron had seen "quantities of fish hanging on the limbs of trees to dry."[77] On Niau, however, the men of *Vostok* saw traditional West Tuamotuan drying frames consisting of sticks or coconut-leaf midribs laid across parallel poles, the whole being raised on forked stakes. These "structures, on which they dry fish" (Bellingshausen) were known as *takere* and kept fish out of reach of dogs and rats.[78] "A few poles from which fishing-nets were hanging" fully persuaded Kotzebue that Tuamotuans went to Tikei "at a particular season of the year, for the fish-

ery." Four years later, at Fakarava, Bellingshausen drew the same conclusion from the evidence he saw along its shore: "Although we did see
people, it seems to me that they had come only for food or fishing and had
stationed themselves around the craft pulled up on the beach." The deduction was almost certainly a just one, though there might have been additional factors in certain areas, such as around Amanu, where flight from
enemies was a necessity throughout this period. At Makemo (Golenishchev-Kutuzov Island), two natives fishing in a small canoe offered to barter part or all of their haul with the Russians in *Mirnyi*. The men had left
sufficient fish with M.P. Lazarev to allow him to send some to *Vostok*, so
it is clear that the islanders had fished very successfully in shallow water
off the reef edge.[79] Regrettably, the Russians leave no indications as to
species, merely mentioning in passing that flying fish and bonito were in
evidence off Angatau.[80] Naturally, the Tuamotuans were fishing for certain fish at the time of the Kotzebue (March–April) and Bellingshausen
(July) visits, and would have had other catches in view in Southern summer.

Bellingshausen fully recognized that shellfish were as important to the
Tuamotuan population as fish. On Fakarava, he noted, fishing and food
gathering were not synonymous. Fish apart, the native visitors might have
been hunting turtles, or octopus, or simply gathering *Tridacna* clams
(*Tridacna giges*), pearl-shell oysters, or other shellfish. It is significant
that Mikhailov's study of a Tuamotuan trio on the shore of Nihiru (see
Plate 7) illustrates many types of shellfish, including the great pearl oyster
(*Pinctada margaritifera*), but not a single fish. The complementary narratives of Bellingshausen and his subordinates amplify this point. The natives had with them "some dried cuttle fish and some shelled mussels,
also dried and strung on a tree-bark fibre cord." The "cuttle fish" was
octopus that had been hung to dry from a suitable stretching stick (*titoko*),
suspended from a tree or wooden rack.[81] The "shelled mussels" were
cured *Tridacna* clams. Such clams, strung on untwisted fibres of aerial
pandanus root, were frequently seen by the 1929-30 Bernice P. Bishop
Museum Expedition to the Tuamotus, on Napuka.[82] The clams were both
abundant in the atoll lagoons and easily procurable.

> The extent to which the *Tridacna* clam was important in the diet of
> the Tuamotuans is attested by the huge shell heaps that dot most of
> the lagoons. . . . A fisherman in the ordinary course of a morning's
> gathering of *Tridacna* clams would leave enough shells to make a pile
> 60 cm in diameter and 30 cm high. The shells taken by one individual
> in his lifetime, if put on a single pile, would cause one to gasp in as-
> tonishment.[83]

Tatano, the Tuamotuan regarded by the Russians as a local chief at Nihiru, had obviously come to collect pearls. He offered some to Bellingshausen and recognized their full value in trade. "He further assured us that many pearls could be had on the islands" (Simonov). Eri-Tatano had most likely voyaged to Nihiru from Niau,[84] with the specific object of gathering pearls for later barter, perhaps in Tahiti. Niau was westerly enough to form part of a Matavai based inter-island trading pattern in the early 1800s. Normally, men of Amanu and Hao would have been wholly unaffected by that trade, being a little too far east to feel its pull. Whether or not Eri-Tatano had brought dried octopus and clams to Nihiru for barter, as the Russian texts suggest, cannot be said. It seems unlikely that Nihiru Islanders could not, and did not, cure their own.

On Tikei, Kotzebue saw fishing lines and sticks on which to dry or stretch them. Russian evidence suggests that hook-and-line fishing was widely practised in the Central Tuamotus and Russian texts are strangely silent about net fishing, spearing, and poisoning. Occasional and brief encounters gave no opportunity for questioning the Tuamotuans on those other matters. In Tahiti, where the Russians stayed for days on end, with time and energy to spare from their shipboard duties, nothing stopped them from collecting such material. Eri-Tatano had available for barter "fish-hooks made of mussels or snail shells." He had almost certainly been using them and was responding to the strangers' curiosity and wealth, which they so grandly demonstrated, by presenting hooks for barter. On the shore of Makatea, the Anaan castaways had put another form of fish-hook to essential use: "All the property of the boys consisted of a fish-hook made of a stone resembling slate and a few coconut-shell cups" (Bellingshausen). Eri-Tatano's offerings were pearl-shell hooks of *tangoro* or *numi* form, then used throughout the Tuamotus. The slate-like substance seen in a hook at Makatea was, in all probability, black turtle shell. The Russian texts contain no references to the solid, large bone hook observed by Wilkes and the Americans in 1839.[85]

At Manuhangi, the artist Mikhailov landed and picked the fruit of the pandanus, whose drupe or seed cone he wished both to study and to draw. It seems that the Russians failed to recognize the considerable value of pandanus as a food source. On the other hand, they indicate the unreliability of coconuts: some atolls, such as Pukapuka, had no coconut or other fruit-producing palms whatever, and on Nihiru a hurricane had evidently caused terrible damage to the palms. "We spotted only three coconut palm trunks. They were quite without foliage, and had perhaps been torn off by gales and uprooted" (Bellingshausen). On Makatea, the Anaan castaways had found both coconuts and breadfruit. It is obvious that breadfruit had been introduced there in the early 1800s, if not earlier, despite remarks by Kenneth Emory suggesting a more recent introduction.[86]

The Russians periodically referred to other flesh foods. On Kaukura, "some dogs were running about" (Bellingshausen); "Before Europeans brought cattle...the only quadrupeds known to these islanders were swine, dogs, and mice" (Simonov). Kaukura was known for its dogs in the 1770s, when the Spaniards were compiling a list of the Tuamotuan atolls known to the Tahitians.[87] Kaukura dogs were said to have "good coats," valued by the Tahitians as fringing material for gorgets but of little interest to the Tuamotuans, who raised the dogs as food. Simonov was mistaken in thinking that swine were being bred in the Tuamotus in pre-contact days; as for his mice, they were rats. The Russians saw no sign of pork consumption in the Tuamotus. They saw no earth ovens on any island where a landing was made;[88] nor did they see the least indication of taro cultivation. "These natives [of Anaa] were constantly at war: those to whom the boys had belonged had been killed and eaten by their enemies...."[89]

Russian narrative evidence suggests that, while human flesh may have been eaten on occasion and regarded as the meat par excellence, it was a rare delicacy. Cannibalism was certainly practised by the people of Anaa and their neighbours, and doubtless on many other islands. Flesh from victims killed in battle, though, cannot be treated as a regular or significant constituent of native diet in the Tuamotu Islands. It was nothing but a tasty supplement.[90]

While crossing Tikei in April 1816, *Riurik*'s artist Ludovik Choris noted "many indications of human presence." Among other signs, there were "some reservoirs, in which the water had kept very well." "The rain water that filled several pits was sweet," Choris adds in his text of 1826, *Vues et paysages*. "We also came across varieties of cistern made by man."[91] Choris was very probably mistaken in thinking the water had been stored in both natural and man-made depressions or pits. His cavités were probably merely the shallow remains of older man-made "cisterns" of the classic Tuamotuan variety described by I.M. Simonov: "Fresh water is obtained from wells some two fathoms deep, where a calcareous layer of madrepore, hard and rough on the surface, becomes softer and more porous. It very likely strains sea water, so purifying it of saline and dirt particles...."[92]

The numerous coconut shells seen by Kotzebue's men around the cisterns of Tikei were evidence, perhaps, of the use of coconut-shell "buckets," that is, perforated shells in which the water could be drawn up to the surface. Such wells, containing slightly brackish water, had been seen at Takaroa by Commodore John Byron in 1765.[93]

Even in 1820-24, a quarter-century after the missionary ship *Duff* reached the area, the Russians of *Vostok*, *Mirnyi*, and *Predpriiatie* found Tuamotuan society essentially unchanged from classic patterns where subsistence foods and diet were concerned. Fish, giant *Tridacna* clams, pandanus fruit, and coconuts were the important items, supplemented by assorted other shellfish types, by turtle, and on rare occasions by dog. Pigs and poultry were unknown to the majority of islanders. The coconut was not the crucial staple for the atolls that it has become, thanks to the planting out of palms for copra export. Nor were the people of those islands that the Russians chanced to visit and describe engaged in cultivating yams, taro, or *kape* (*Alocasia macrorrhiza*). Fundamentally and even regularly transient, they moved from place to place in search of foodstuffs, trading articles, and medicinal and other herbs. As a whole, the Russian evidence suggests that they were physically robust, well nourished, and despite the early winter months most likely to remain so.

BODY ORNAMENT AND CLOTHING

Tuamotuans observed by the Russians were in general naked, clad only in the traditional girdle. "They were naked save for the usual loincloth" (Novosil'skii). Indeed, Tuamotuans were as scantily clad as any Polynesians. "Their genitals were covered by a narrow girdle" (Bellingshausen). Efforts were made by the Russians to acquire one such "strip to cover the genitals, but no islander would barter his for anything." The Russians concluded that modesty made it imperative for the Tuamotuans to conceal their private parts, and that this modesty was culturally a more potent force than greed. Even Eri-Tatano, a man of rank, had "only a narrow belt" to cover his nakedness (Bellingshausen). This was the loin-girdle (*maro*), commonly plaited from pandanus leaf or rootlet fibre.[94] In classical style, "all also wore a rope of woven grass around the belly" (Bellingshausen). These stomach bands or narrow belts of plaited fibres were worn until very recently on the remoter atolls. Some looked like fine hempen cordage. One notes the eagerness with which, off Angatau on 10 July 1820, armed warriors "seized hold of the rope at our stern and constantly tugged it towards themselves, in hopes of cutting it off." A belt braided from fine pandanus fibres and held at the Bernice P. Bishop Museum in Honolulu is said to have come from Angatau. It sheds light on this incident and explains why *Vostok*'s stern rope was of such interest.[95] The warriors would have perceived its regular weave and strength, and would have envisaged other uses for the rope.[96]

Women were traditionally dressed in pandanus-leaf skirts or plaited matting. On Amanu armed women "were covered, from the navel to the knees, by a fine wraparound matting'' (Bellingshausen). At Nihiru, the single woman encountered was similarly clad. Mikhailov depicts her skirt in his painting "Natives of the Coral Island of Nigiru," and Belling-shausen records that "her own grass mat, very skilfully woven, she left for us, and it is now [1824] among the rarities at the Museum of the Ad-miralty Department." "Her own material," Novosil'skii adds, "was skil-fully woven from grasses." When offered a piece of Russian red cloth aboard *Vostok*, this woman naturally and immediately wrapped it "around her lower body above the knees" (Bellingshausen). Accustomed to wearing the *kareu* or *reu*, she adapted the Russian cloth to her cultural norm, as the Russians watched and approved.[97] While at Angatau on 10 July, the Russians presented "pieces of printed linen" to the belligerent islanders. The Russian texts do not suggest that the material was joyously received: although Eri-Tatano at Nihiru delighted in a uniform of the Lifeguard Hussars, he did not request more Russian garments as the Maori had done a few weeks earlier, when the *Vostok* was in their midst,[98] and as Hawaiians had been doing for at least a quarter-century. The Tuamotuans, in short, seem to have felt no great desire to get European clothing from the Russians.

At Fakarava on 16 July, Bellingshausen saw some forty natives stand-ing on an isthmus. Unlike the Tuamotuans encountered on Amanu and at Angatau, they seemed friendly. "They waved with mats or pieces of cloth, attached to long poles" and "some of them had pieces of material or mats thrown over their shoulders." These were the "straw sacks" hung over natives' shoulders at Vahitahi, when Beechey arrived in HMS *Blossom* in 1826.[99] They were woven fibre capes of ancient type.[100]

In view of the natives' occupations and the Russians' lack of contact with Tuamotuan high chiefs or descent group heads,[101] it is not surprising that the texts contain no references to such marks of social rank as feather headdresses or to such ornaments as necklaces and ear-tufts. Conversely, Russian evidence for Tuamotuan tattooing (*nanako*) is particularly rich. Narrative descriptions are usefully complemented by Mikhailov's illus-trations of the native trio met on Nihiru and of two young men at Kaukura. Eri-Tatano, it seems, "was tattooed on his thighs and haunches in a bluish-black hue," in a manner that reminded Bellingshausen of what he had just seen among the Maori of Totaranui (Queen Charlotte Sound), New Zealand, and of depictions of the Nukuhivan people met by Kruzenshtern at Taio-hae Bay in 1804.[102] At Makemo, too, men seen by Lazarev had "thighs tattooed and dyed with a bluish-black colour." In the view of Simonov, who had been in close contact with the Maori six weeks or so before and so had standards for comparison, in point of ele-gance Eri-Tatano's *nanako* was "skilfully" executed.[103]

In the Tuamotus, as elsewhere in Polynesia, Mikhailov worked with a loose-sheet folder comfortably carried under his arm. Not knowing when he would be able to obtain more paper or what he might need to draw in coming weeks, he used his paper very economically. On some sheets measuring nine inches by twelve, he crammed rough outlines or sketches of several human heads or figures beside embryonic landscapes. Today these sheets are in the Drawings Division (Otdel Risunka) of the State Russian Museum (Gosudarstvennyi Russkii Muzei). Few have been published, but they are of major ethnographic value as immediate, authentic reportage and as the elements from which assorted published illustrations were derived in 1823-24 and later.

In its present form, the Mikhailov Portfolio consists of large light blue cardboard backing sheets to which original graphite or pen sketches, pencilled roughs, and aquarelles of various dimensions have been fixed. It is accompanied by a card catalogue and register, from which it emerges that the 1819-21 work has been supplemented by a range of other illustrations made by Mikhailov aboard the armed sloop *Moller*. The latter, dating from 1826-29, reflect the *Moller*'s route of 1827 from Chile to Tahiti, and include several portraits of individual Tahitians at Matavai Bay. Like *Vostok*'s third lieutenant, Arkadii Leskov, Mikhailov was to return to the Tuamotus (April 1827) and to meet Tahitian friends he had made at Matavai in 1820.[104]

The portfolio contains three sheets on which are roughs and cameos made at the Tuamotus, specifically at Angatau, Amanu, and Kaukura. These sheets also contain shorelines (of NW Rapa in the Austral Islands, for example,)[105] and aborted graphite sketches or commencements. In addition, there is rough work for the portraits of the group which met on Nihiru, and, on other sheets, unfinished sketches of pandanus fruit and other plants picked by the artist in the course of his hurried walk along the shore of Manuhangi on 5 July 1820.[106] Like Korneev of *Otkrytie*, Mikhailov was a master at extracting every possible advantage from the unexpected visit and the casual adventure.

Sheet R-29068 in the Russian enumeration of Mikhailov's original portfolio is described in the card catalogue as *Aracheev Isle: Natives' Heads, Craft, and Other Roughs*. It is in graphite, with some watercolour added, and measures 12.78 cm by 25 cm. Among the heads are commencements of two waist-up portraits of Tuamotuan men which, after his return to St. Petersburg, Mikhailov worked up for the use of the lithographer who was employed to illustrate the pending Bellingshausen narrative.[107] (That work occupied him for one year, and the album that he handed to the Naval Ministry, with its tincture of white lead, is today at the State Historical Museum on Red Square in Moscow.) The lithographer was Ivan Pavlovich Fridrits, an undistinguished craftsman still completing courses at St. Petersburg's Academy of Arts in 1824.[108] The native portraits, two young males with their hair "bound in a topknot,"[109] lacking ornaments, bare, seen from the left, duly appeared in the Bellingshausen *Atlas* (1831), with the inscription *Natives of the Coral Island of Count Arakcheev*. The portraits comprised Sheet No. 47 in the 47-sheet completed album and are shown here as Plate 5. The two men were among those encircling *Vostok*'s stern on 10 July 1820 and attempting to seize a hanging rope. In the lithograph neither has tattoos of any sort.

Sheet R-29069 in the portfolio is also a pencil-watercolour sketch. It measures 12.7 cm by 24 cm and bears an inscription by the artist: *The Coral Island of Moller*. Begun on 8 July at Amanu, it struck Mikhailov as a significant subject in view of the islanders' belligerent reception of the Russians. That same day or shortly afterwards, he developed elements in this original attempt to fix the nature of the Russians' thwarted landing in another, larger sketch. Again he preferred to work in graphite, not in colours. This second effort, R-29285 in St. Petersburg, measures 26.6 cm by 38.2 cm and brings together a number of the tentative roughs of the first attempt. Two boats, each rowed by eight Russian sailors, are shown bringing five officers into the coral skirt of Amanu Island, where two dozen or so unfriendly islanders with long spears are awaiting their next move. Women clad in "wraparound matting" stand off to the left, while in the middle ground the bush is burning fiercely in three separate spots (see Plate 6). This piece, too, was polished by Mikhailov in 1823-24 and included in the Bellingshausen *Atlas*. The finished original is No. 29 in the album held in Moscow and has the inscription *A View of the Coral Island of Moller*.

The third of Mikhailov's Tuamotuan sheets of July 1820 is R-29070 in the Soviet enumeration and is described at the State Russian Museum merely as *Island, Natives, and Roughs*. It is more significant ethnographically than the Nihiru group portrait. Its relevant part is given here as Plate 4. Shown in the lower left corner are the heads of two men encountered off the south shores of Kaukura on 19 July. Mikhailov has pencilled, at the left of the left-hand head, the date (19 July) and the name Balisair.[110] Together with roughly drawn elements at the right of this same sheet, showing *nanako* designs on arms and buttocks, these two heads were later worked up as *Natives of the Palizer Island*. It is No. 33 in the album in Red Square and appeared in the Bellingshausen *Atlas* under the same heading.[111]

As presented in the *Atlas* accompanying Bellingshausen's long delayed monograph, *Dvukratnye izyskaniia . . . (Repeated Explorations in the Southern Icy Ocean)*, the right-hand figure of the plate entitled "Natives of the Palizer Island" has four almost horizontal pairs of interrupted parallel lines on his upper right arm (see Plate 8). The rough torso on the lower right side of R-29070, however, has the left arm so tattooed, suggesting that the other natives seen off Kaukura were similarly pricked and dyed above the elbow. One certainly had slightly curving, almost vertical pairs of lines tattooed on his back and running up his right shoulder. In my view, the right-hand figure also has a pair of lines tattooed along the collar-bone, and other marks are visible on the man's left shoulder. As for the buttocks depicted at the right of sheet R-29070 (Plate 4), they show two forms of traditional tattoo: the patch of close parallel lines by the lower right hip and the rosette (*poteke*).[112]

The Mikhailov album held at the State Historical Museum in Moscow lacks the finished original used as the basis for the plate entitled *Natives of the Coral Island of Nigira* in the 1831 *Atlas*. It is therefore impossible to compare the detail of tattooing on that published plate with the original of 1820-23. It is certain that a good deal of detail was lost during the process of lithography and printing, over which the artist had no control. As presented in the Bellingshausen *Atlas*, the chief met at Nihiru has *nanako* as shown in Plate 8. In the words of Kenneth Emory, "A design of two or three concentric circles, edged with triangles pointing outward, is a motif applied twice on one hip and once on the other. A patch of vertical, parallel lines covers the inside of one thigh. Large, concentric semicircles come in from each side of the body and reach the belt of the malo [*sic*]."[113]

Mikhailov's sheet R-29070 shows tentative sketches of two double circle tattoo designs, of a sort that he had seen at Kaukura or at other places in the Tuamotus, though the literature indicates that men of Angatau and Amanu did not practise the art.[114] This double circle design, which the Wilkes Expedition was to see on Raraka men in 1839 ("large rosettes on their legs")[115] was apparently traditional on Western Tuamotu atolls like the Pallisers (Kaukura, Arutua, Apataki) and Niau. "The *poteke* was a circle containing a tiny circle at the centre, both circles being edged with a continuous border of small triangles."[116]

The number and placement on the body of such rosettes indicated warrior status and sent a message that the Tuamotu Islanders could read. It may be noted, in connection with Mikhailov's illustrations, that certain traditional tattoo patterns were placed exclusively on the loins and buttocks. In John Davies's Tahitian and English Dictionary of 1851, such skin-marks or "species of tatau" are termed *aie*.[117] As for the pairs of almost vertical but slightly curving lines across the backs of the Kaukura fisherman, they have the look of preliminary *ngangie* (Pemphis) lines.[118]

In general, the Russian narrative and illustrative record of tattooing in the Tuamotus confirms that *nanako* was widely practised in the west but hardly practised in the east. For all the curiosity of local styles, such as the checkerboard and the rosette, tattooing in the atolls was considerably cruder than in either the Washington-Marquessas Group or New Zealand.

WEAPONS AND CONFLICT

At Amanu, Angatau, and other atolls, the Russians saw spears, clubs, and slings ready for use, but no fish-jaw knives, daggers, or paddle-clubs. The Russians had limited opportunity to handle Tuamotuan weaponry and the textual record is generally poor. Mikhailov's drawings are of some interest, but again detail is lacking.

At Amanu, Bellingshausen notes: "All the islanders were armed with long spears and some grasped, in the other hand, a wooden club with which, like the natives of New Zealand, they strike their enemies on the head." So, too, at Angatau, the natives came out to *Vostok* well armed: "Each man had a lasso made of woven grasses, a spear, and a small club." According to Novosil'skii, the Amanu men had "spears and short clubs." Women also, as both officers remark, bore clubs as well as spears in case their participation in a battle proved necessary or unavoidable. Simonov tells us that the aggressive Amanu party "came out to the sloop in six canoes, to the number of twenty-five men." In short, Tuamotuans tended to use spear, club, and sling and to approach possible conflict with all three weapon types at hand. Naturally, the three types were used at different phases of collision; slings first, clubs last.[119]

Mikhailov's *View of the Coral Island of Moller* shows twenty-two islanders, and all but one or two of whom are carrying spears approximately twice their height in length. In 1769 Joseph Banks had seen a number of Tuamotuan spears "as long again" as their owners.[120] At Takaroa in 1774, Forster had seen spears "fourteen feet long," but noted that many men carried shorter "pikes," perhaps nine feet long.[121] The spears seen by the Russians in 1820 were evidently slender, one-piece spears of ancient type, almost certainly tipped with bone or stingray points. It may be noted that the strangeness of the circumstance of Europeans approaching the shoreline in boats of unknown use, from giant craft, affected the warriors' preparations. The almost chaotic situation on the shore, at least as described by the Russians, in no way reflects any known and traditional challenge procedure, for instance, chanting while spear points were banged on the earth or drilling in organized rows.[122] But then, the Tuamotuans might be forgiven for hesitating in their usual preparations for battle. In the first place, the visitors were apparently unarmed, no spears or clubs of any sort were visible. And in the second, their hostile intentions could only be assumed: hard proof was lacking.

The "short wooden clubs" observed, which reminded the Russians of Maori *patu* or *mere* in form and function, were not oar-shaped paddle clubs or sword clubs of the type seen at Vahitahi by Beechey.[123] They were simply bludgeons (*tongere*). The wood used was almost certainly *tou*, or *Cordia subcordata*, which was and still is readily available on Amanu, and the club would have had an oval striking blade.[124] As for the "lassos" seen, they were traditional *maka*, made of *ronga* or pandanus root fibres. Such slings had been used against the Dutch at Takapoto in 1616 and against the Spanish at Anaa in 1774. They had been seen by numerous late eighteenth-century mariners.[125] The Angatau warriors who approached *Vostok* on 10 July, evidently with aggressive intent, had stones or shells or even wooden missiles in their craft, which they declined to use. Spears were better suited to their needs, and they were put to good effect.[126]

The Tuamotu Islanders responded differently to the appearances of *Vostok* and *Mirnyi* in different parts of the archipelago. At Hao they made no effort to make contact with the Russians beyond pursuing them for a little while: no canoes put out to sea beyond the reefs, although the wind was very gentle and the Russians' progress very slow. At Angatau six canoes put out. There, as at Amanu, where women as well as men stood ready to repel an attack and where "frightful shouts and brandishing" of weapons stopped the Russians at the reef edge, the air was distinctly menacing. At Nihiru and further west, by contrast, the Russians were hospitably, albeit warily, received and Russian-Polynesian barter was extensive.

Pondering these varied responses to their arrival, Simonov, Novosil'-skii, and other Russians deduced that inter-island war was being waged in the Amanu-Hao sector. They were probably right; certainly there were patterns of traditional hostilities among the atolls, vengeance raids provoking other raids, year by year.[127] There is no record of wounds or scars observed, but at Makatea the visitors heard first-hand evidence of ferocious inter-island conflict when they met youthful survivors of an attack on Anaa men.[128] In this case, the Russians caught a breath of local wars that had been fought for many years between native factions known to the Tahitians as Auura and Parata. Bellingshausen learned from the missionary John Davies of Tahiti that "the Parata nearly exterminated the Auura, except those who had fled to Tahiti."[129]

Ignorant of the use of guns, the warriors of Angatau and of Amanu had initially supposed that they could overpower their unexpected visitors. At Fangahina, on 2 March 1824, the alarming appearance of the sloop *Predpriiatie* led to a prompt kindling of "piles of wood," evidently in a precautionary spirit and in hopes of warding off "the unknown sea-monster."[130] Significantly, Kotzebue found no traces of humans on Angatau when on 3 March he swept its shorelines with his telescope. In the Central Tuamotus, as in the Western groups, populations were very mobile in the early 1800s. Voyages by ocean-going craft were a response to constant danger.[131]

Russian narratives offer assorted hints and glimpses of political realities across the Tuamotu Archipelago. It is significant, for instance, that Tatano was familiar, and even comfortable, with Europeans. The Anaans had perhaps had happier relations with the British mission at Tahiti than had other Tuamotuans. They had been worshipping at Matavai or Papetoai since 1814, and many had settled temporarily and been baptized at Paofai Station.[132] We may reasonably think that Chief Tatano represented those Anaans who had voyaged east and west since 1812 or had had sufficient intercourse with Europeans to appreciate that they were carriers of many useful articles.

Bellingshausen was at pains not to inflict wounds on islanders and, despite his men's occasional indignant remonstrations, he left the Tuamotus with his hands unstained by blood. Kotzebue, too, was careful not to emulate the Dutch and other earlier explorers. Nonetheless, the Tuamotuans could not have failed to connect them with extraordinary authority and power. The Russians, for their part, wished to impress the Tuamotuans in just that way, for example, sending up numerous rockets in the night.

Russian evidence for weaponry and conflict in the Tuamotu Islands is essentially the evidence of educated passers-by. It is valuable both because of the visitors' sharp-sightedness and because of their ignorance of the importance of their own comments and data.

CANOES

Thanks partly to the dangers of navigating among the low atolls of the Tuamotu Archipelago and partly to the meagre trading opportunities offered, these coral atolls were among the Pacific Islands least frequently visited by Europeans in the nineteenth century. There are few reliable sources of information on the types and structures of canoes used by the Tuamotuans in earlier times. Slender though it is, therefore, the Russian evidence is a most welcome addition to the records left by such European mariners as James Cook, the Forsters, Byron, Wallis, Wilkes, and Admiral Francois Edmond Paris.[133] Again, the usefulness of Russian narrative material is immensely enhanced by the pictorial records left by Choris of *Riurik* and Mikhailov of *Vostok*, both of whom made a point of drawing Tuamotuan canoes. For example, sheet R-29070 in the Mikhailov portfolio shows a two-man craft and a simple paddle that may logically be associated with the Tuamotus.

Wherever the Russians saw men in the archipelago, they also saw canoes. Sometimes, these were drawn up or being paddled by the outer reef; sometimes, as at Hao, they were in the lagoon. Most craft were small, carrying one or two men, and were designed for local fishing. Larger craft were observed at a distance in Nihiru's lagoon, at Fakarava, and at Fangahina on 2 March 1824 ("judging from the size of those canoes that we noted and their good rigging, these islanders are quite capable of visiting . . . remotely situated islands" [Kotzebue]). It was at Angatau, however, that Bellingshausen had his best opportunity to examine an outrigger canoe. Six craft had come twelve miles offshore, to the Russians' surprise, and all were handled with the greatest skill and boldness:

> The craft . . . were about twenty feet long and were broad enough in the beam for two men to sit side by side. They were made of a number of planks, very skilfully bound together. In cross-section, these craft resembled a low milk-pan. There was an outrigger on one side, to steady the hull. . . . These craft go well enough, and are certainly better suited to the open sea than any canoes that I have hitherto encountered.[134]

Ever ready for duty, Mikhailov made a quick sketch of one of these six Angatauan canoes and its four native paddlers. He later worked it up for lithographing as *The Coral Island of Count Arakcheev*. It is sheet No. 34 in the Mikhailov album in Moscow. As shown in that illustration, the Angatauan canoe is a three-boom outrigger craft, with booms attached directly to the float. The bow piece slants upward at a gentle angle, not sharply, and lacks ornamentation. The stern piece slopes up at approximately the same angle but ends in a downward curve or volute turned in exactly the manner to be seen on a model Tuamotuan canoe collected by J.L. Young and now held at the Bernice P. Bishop Museum in Honolulu as specimen B-3477.[135] Such craft were better suited to the open sea than many other canoes of Oceania, and a major contributing factor was the presence of a keel. Together with the internal strength provided in larger canoes by cross-ribs, the "good rigging" admired by Kotzebue in 1824 made it possible for the Central Tuamotuans to venture many miles from land. "Outstanding characteristics of the old island craft . . . were the sharpness of the bottom, due to the presence of a primitive keel formed of a narrow longitudinal timber, usually channelled above, and the use in the building up of the sides of many short lengths of plank of irregular shape. . . . "[136]

Bellingshausen's approval of the neat sewing of planks together echoed that of his predecessors.[137] Solid though the canoes were, however, they could easily be carried on several men's shoulders across of a spit of land to the lagoon.

Mikhailov recorded other Tuamotuan canoes, as *Vostok* moved west-ward toward Tahiti in July 1820. The left foreground of his *Natives of the Coral Island of Nigira*, for example, shows the very end of a solid, composite-beam craft seen at Nihiru (Plate 7). And on sheet R-29070 of the Mikhailov Portfolio is a pencil rough of a two-man canoe, almost un-doubtedly the canoe met off the south shore of Kaukura. The connections between it and the central band of the aquarelle *The Coral Island of Count Arakcheev* are self-evident.[138]

Choris's sketch of the abandoned canoe found on Tikei in 1816, which appeared together with a canoe from the Penrhyn Islands as Plate XII of *Voyage pittoresque autour du monde* (1822), was subjected to very criti-cal scrutiny by James Hornell in 1935. Hornell claimed that many of Choris's figures had been "carelessly drawn" and that many details should, therefore, "be disregarded."[139] In my view, the blame for certain weaknesses in Choris's evidence lies as much with the lithographers em-ployed in Paris in 1821-22, notably Langlumé and Auguste-André Bovet (1799-1864),[140] as with the original sketches, most of which have long been lost.[141] It cannot justly be stated that Choris was a casual or careless observer of the Polynesian scene. Here, in any case, are extracts from Hornell's commentary on Choris's sketch of a Tikei canoe:

> Choris figures one canoe hollowed out of a tree trunk with three booms lashed to the gunwale of the dugout hull and attached directly to the float, which, as usual in Tuamotuan canoes, is nearly as long as the hull. Another common feature of Tuamotuan canoes is a tendency to employ multiple booms: this is a practice highly characteristic of Melanesian types and may be due to ancient influence from that quarter. The booms are shown straight in Choris's figure, but this is undoubtedly an error. . . . The ends of the hull show sheer, each ter-minating in a blunt point.[142]

In shape, Choris's craft bears a striking similarity to the Kaukura canoe sketched four years later by Mikhailov (Plate 4). Equally clear is the simi-larity between Choris's and Mikhailov's illustrations of the common working paddles seen in the Central and Western Tuamotus. Both draw-ings, it is suggested, are of *tipoka* paddles of ancient type, such as J.L. Young collected from Napuka and Beechey saw at Vahitahi or Vairaatea in 1826.[143] While neither paddle has a visible terminal knob, both have rel-atively long, narrow blades and handles extending as ridges down the blade-backs, thus producing well-defined, sloping shoulders.

Russian evidence for the use of double canoes in the Tuamotus in 1816-24 is conspicuous by its absence. It is true that Bellingshausen re-cords having seen, drawn up by "a narrow coral neck" on Fakarava, "two sizeable craft . . . one with two masts."[144] And it is true that Kotzebue, at Fangahina in 1824, observed canoes of a good size, "quite capable of visiting other, even remotely situated islands."[145] But single-hulled outrigger canoes often carried two masts (*tira*), with "triangular sails with one point downward" of the sort seen by the Russians at Taenga atoll on 14 July 1820.[146] Russian evidence lends no support whatever to Haddon's and Hornell's supposition that ancient Tuamotuan sails were hung like Oceanic lateen sails,[147] and similarly fails to support the contention that rectangular lug sails were used among the atolls in early contact times.[148] Nor did the visitors of 1816-24 see large steering oars of the type described by Paris and Duperrey, though such oars are known to have been used on islands visited by *Vostok*, *Mirnyi*, and *Predpriiatie* in the 1820s.[149] This would seem to indicate that the Russians chanced not to encounter the large double canoes, whose bulk would have necessitated the use of massive, broad-bladed steering oars even under gentle winds.[150] Taken together with the contemporaneous French and American evidence, Russian narrative and illustrative records indicate that the great Tuamotuan double canoes seen by eighteenth-century visitors, called *pahi* by the Tahitians and which Tuamotuans had built for Tahitian high chiefs,[151] were becoming rare in the Central Tuamotus by the 1820s. On the other hand, Tuamotuan canoe builders still enjoyed a high reputation in the Society Islands and were still employed in Tahiti, on Raiatea, and elsewhere to take full advantage there of the fine lengths of timber that were unfortunately lacking on Central and Eastern Tuamotuan atolls.[152] They were also accustomed, as the Russians recognized at Nihiru, Niau, and Makatea, to voyaging out of sight of all land and over considerable distances. All Russian texts insist on the Tuamotuans' maritime competence and daring. Such accidents as the one that had swept an Anaan party west to Makatea in 1819 were exceptions to the rule of planned, successful transits from one low coral island to another.

HYDROGRAPHY

How seriously Bellingshausen took the hydrographic portion of his *Vostok* mission is very plain from his actions in London from 1 to 11 August 1819.

> Mr. Troughton, the celebrated instrument maker, obliged us by providing us with the best sextants, with a transit instrument, and artificial horizons. Our chronometers were by two masters, Arnold and Barraud; and from Mr. Dollond we received circles as well as several

sextants and achromatic telescopes, two feet or four feet in length. And for the voyage itself, we obtained maps from Mr. Arrowsmith and books from a number of booksellers.[153]

Of Kotzebue's readiness in 1824 to undertake hydrography in the Tuamotus, suffice it to say that his scientific staff was the largest that had ever entered Polynesia in a Russian ship; that he carried assorted instruments for measurement of air and water movement, temperature and depth, and geographical position, that *Vostok* had lacked in 1820; and that hydrography was uppermost in his mind. "It was my intention to ascertain more precisely the geographical positions of islands which I myself had discovered in these waters during my previous voyage, and then to proceed to Tahiti specifically in order to check the correctness of estimated longitudes, and to get the necessary rest. . . ."[154]

Knowing the tracks of Le Maire and Roggeveen, Byron, Wallis, Bougainville, and Cook across the archipelago, Kotzebue, Bellingshausen, and Lazarev deliberately kept to the north or south of them as they coasted westward toward the Society Islands.[155] When intersections with the routes of predecessors occurred, they were deliberate and calculated. When they came up on atolls hastily inspected by an earlier explorer, all three Russians did their best, given the limits set by wind, current, and light, to make a survey of the shores not seen before. Moving rapidly through "Drown'd Isles" that he named after Sir Hugh Palliser, Cook had in April 1774 sailed due west from a location slightly south of Apataki. He had seen no island west of Kaukura (Palliser III).[156] Yet the Tuamotu chains clearly extended on a roughly SE-NW axis. Atolls stretched a hundred miles to the ESE or SE of Kaukura, so that land might not unreasonably be supposed to lie NW of it. Kotzebue steered deliberately west from Aratua in the Pallisers, knowing that only the Dutch had probed that way and had discovered Vlieghen Eylandt (Rangiroa). He was searching for, and found, another island, Tikahau, on the basis of available data.[157]

Bellingshausen, for his part, proceeded to the southeastern extremity of the Tuamotu Archipelago, moving north, on 14 July 1820, in longitude 142°31'W and entering the "thick" part of that archipelago. His ships then moved westward toward the island of Tahiti. But on traversing the Tuamotus, Bellingshausen held a course in approximately latitude 16°S. This proved extremely fruitful as a track for discoveries, for it lay to the north of the routes taken by Quiros, Wallis, Carteret, Bougainville, and Cook. . . .[158]

In 1824, Kotzebue steered first south and then north of his earlier track in *Riurik*.[159] In sum, the Russians complemented their own and others' work among the Tuamotu atolls. Not only did their reckonings of position in the Tuamotus compare favourably with those of Louis Isidore Duperrey of 1822-25 and Frederick William Beechey of 1826-28, but they also equalled the degree of accuracy reached by navigators of a younger generation, notably E.W. Lacott and Charles Wilkes, and improved with each successive expedition sent from Kronstadt. Russian hydrographic data were summarized, with an excusable degree of national pride, by many Soviet historians of exploration and discovery, including L.S. Berg (1962), D.M. Lebedev (1971), and Ia.M. Svet (1966).[160]

On his return to St. Petersburg in August 1818, Kotzebue handed all his charts and logs to Count Rumiantsev who soon dispatched the bulk of them to Kruzenshtern for full analysis. Kruzenshtern took the results of Kotzebue's expedition to his property, Schloss Ass, in southern Estonia, and there worked on them at intervals for eighteen months. He had a first-rate private library as well as access to the Admiralty's hydrographic store; corresponded with a range of foreign officers and scientists, who sent him copies of the latest charts and maps of Oceania, as well as news and lively controversy,[161] and was able to collate *Riurik*'s reckonings of geographical positions with the reckonings of many other navigators. By July 1820, he had sent off to the Admiralty a completed manuscript headed "Analysis of Isles Discovered in the South Sea by *Riurik*." It was published in Volume 2 of Kotzebue's narrative, *Puteshestvie v Iuzhnyi Okean* (St. Petersburg 1821), immediately after the description of the voyage, before Eschscholtz's and Chamisso's contributions, and as an honorary appendix. In Hannibal E. Lloyd's translation, *A Voyage of Discovery into the South Sea*, it appears in Volume 2, pp. 291-313. Pages 295-300 are devoted to discussion of *Riurik*'s movements from Pukapuka to Tikei, then west to the Pallisers and Tikahau. It is superfluous to repeat here a text that is readily available in English and lucidly written besides. Suffice it to say that Kruzenshtern's chief interest in the discussion of *Riurik*'s movements of 21-23 April 1816 centred on the possible identification of Spiridov (Takapoto) with Commodore Byron's King George Islands.[162] Kruzenshtern erred, uncharacteristically, in identifying Kotzebue's Riurik Chain, that is, Aratua in the Palliser Group, as a new discovery.[163] Tikahau was Kotzebue's only genuine discovery in the Tuamotus in 1816.[164] "The voyage of Lieutenant Kotzebue has cast significant light on the discoveries made by Le Maire, Schouten, and Roggeveen. One must only hope that the islands that he has found, between the 138th and 149th degree of western longitude, will soon be subjected to a second close examination. . . ."[165] Even as Kruzenshtern wrote these words, Bellingshausen was at work among the Tuamotus. His results, together with the *Riurik* expedition's, found their way into Kruzenshtern's own hydrographic studies of 1823-36.[166]

Six of the coral atolls seen and described by Bellingshausen were hitherto unknown to Europeans: Nihiru, Raevskii-Tepoto, Katiu, Fakarava, Niau, and Matahiva. Angatau may have been seen from Magellan's *Trinidad* in 1521, but the eminent New Zealand student of Pacific exploration, Andrew Sharp, indicates otherwise.[167] Bellingshausen, however, was mistaken in supposing that Amanu and Takume were discoveries. Nor was he familiar with the activities of Captain John Buyers and others who in 1803 had sighted Makemo, Faaite, and Taenga from *Margaret*.[168] It would be foolish to reproach the Russian mariners for ignorance of what they could not know because of Spanish silence in the cases of Raroia, Tahanea, and Amanu,[169] or clumsy and indifferent cartography in other times. What should be noted is that Bellingshausen's claims, which were both reasonable and advanced with modesty, rested on competence at sea that rivalled Cook's. It fell to others in this century to stress that point.[170]

The Russians' survey work among the atolls had practical significance for other seamen. Fifteen months before the end of Kotzebue's expedition in *Riurik*, accounts of his discoveries were being published in Europe and in the United States. The earliest European notices were German (Hamburg and Berlin) and the longest were English. In New England, news of Kotzebue's finds were first published in Salem, Massachusetts, on the basis of reports sent from St. Petersburg on 15 March 1817, five months or so after the Russian Naval Ministry received despatches from Kamchatka on the subject of *Riurik*'s routes and doings in the South Pacific Ocean.[171] On 16 May 1817, the *Salem Gazette* reported: "Lieutenant Kotzebue, commander of the ship Riurik, has discovered on his long voyage round the world several new islands, which he has named Romanzow's, Sperisow's, Krusenstern's, Kielurow's, and Suwarrow's Islands." The notice was reprinted, almost verbatim, by the *Boston Patriot* and in *Niles' Weekly Register* (Baltimore, Maryland) within twenty-four hours.[172] "Kielurow's Island" was presumably a typographic mangling of "Kutuzov's," that is, Utirik atoll, sighted from *Riurik* on 21 May 1816.[173] "Suwarrow" is clearly Taka atoll in longitude 11°05′N, latitude 169°42′E.[174] By early August 1817, the significance of Kotzebue's voyage was more obvious to sea captains and shipowners in New England ports, and more detailed accounts of *Riurik*'s sightings appeared both in Boston and in Salem. On 1 August the *New England Palladium and Commercial Advertiser* offered its readers this item on the basis of a London newspaper report that had, in turn, come from "a Prussian gazette":

> Letters of an earlier date which, after having doubled Cape Horn, Otto von Kotzebue sent from the coast of Chili, have been lost. Mr.

V. Kotzebue discovered three new islands in the South Sea, 14° of lat. and 144° of long. To these islands he gave the names of Romanzow (the author and equipper of the whole expedition), Spiridour (an admiral under whom Kotzebue formerly served several years), and Krusenstern. . . . Besides, he discovered a long chain of islands in the same quarter, and two clusters of islands in the 11th degree of lat. and 190th deg. of long. . . . These he called after the ship, Riurik Chain. . . . All these islands are very woody, partly uninhabited, and dangerous for navigators. The discoverer has sent to Count Romanzow a great many maps and drawings.[175]

In North America and Europe, Kotzebue's and Bellingshausen's nomenclature of Tuamotu atolls examined in the period 1816-24 was accepted throughout the nineteenth century. To such English-speaking commanders of expeditionary ships in Oceania as Edward Belcher and Charles Wilkes, it seemed both natural and proper to adopt the Russian names or, in the case of particularly long ones, to adapt and shorten them.[176] But over time, the use of Russian names for atolls has completely vanished in the West, save for Tepoto and the nearby outcrops, the Raevskii or Raevsky Cluster.[177] Large Soviet atlases provided Russian names, together with the native names, in brackets. Russian memories are very long where the achievements of Russians in discovery and science are concerned. Thus, in Antarctica the physical research facilities Vostok and Mirnyi remind the world, and especially young Russians, of Bellingshausen's ships. For decades, the Soviet space program showed particular awareness of the planet Venus, whose elliptic rings were first observed by Mikhail Vasil'evich Lomonosov in the eighteenth century, and which, a generation later, brought James Cook and Joseph Banks south to Tahiti.

Part Two

TAHITI

4

AN OVERVIEW

INTRODUCTORY REMARKS

Though not an earthly paradise, Tahiti had seemed almost paradisiacal to Cook and Bougainville in the late 1760s. Polynesian socio-political and economic structures generally worked very much to the visitors' advantage; initially at least, the Europeans were treated by Tahitians as superhuman. Fresh, sweet water, meat, and fruit had been available in inexhaustible supply, and native girls had offered sex to common seamen for a trifling price, or gratis. This was Bougainville's Nouvelle Cythère, an Elysium protected from the Eurocentric world of profit, industry, and gunfire by 14,000 miles of essentially unknown and empty sea.

British missionaries were first in the field in Tahiti, striking hard and striking earlier than representatives of science, trade, or even empire. The London Missionary Society was established on 21 September 1795 by evangelicals, and with the Great South Sea in view. Thanks to the overwhelming energy and widespread contacts of the Reverend Dr. Thomas Haweis, personal chaplain to the Countess of Huntingdon and one of the Society's prime movers,[1] funds poured in from Presbyterians, Calvinists, and Methodists alike. For none could turn away "in ease of soul" from the extraordinary challenge that Haweis painted of "innumerable Islands . . . where savage Nature feasts upon the Flesh of prisoners, appeases gods with human sacrifices," where the first-born child was regularly slaughtered and societies of thousands "lived and died" in the abyss of promiscuity.[2] The London Missionary Society, contended Haweis convincingly, was duty bound to do what the authorities had not: send out its people and, with "Otaheite" as their headquarters, save countless souls from the eternal flames of hell.[3]

Within four days of the creation of the Society, its board had decided to accept the services of Captain James Wilson, ex-East India Company, to command a transport ship yet to be purchased.[4] Within twelve months, *Duff* had been bought for five thousand pounds and fitted out for a similar sum.[5] As for missionaries to be sent to Polynesia, the directors had precise ideas on the qualities required: "Godly men who understand Mechanic Arts" were needed, not a set of dreamy scholars.[6]

> The Society had nothing to do with the fashionable or scientific world of Walpole and Joseph Banks. It was essentially a lower-middle class organization made up of dissenting clergymen, of lay preachers, and of respectable artisans and tradesmen who were Protestant to the core and who believed utterly in the Bible. Their faith and their proselytizing zeal were admirable but they were not perhaps absolutely suited to undertake the conversion of the South Sea Islanders. . . . They were practical workers in the Cause of the Lord. It was a strange boat load that drew up to the black sand beaches of Matavai Bay in March 1797, after sailing nearly 14,000 miles without sighting land.[7]

In fact, there were only four ordained clergymen, James Cover, Thomas Lewis, John Eyre, and John Jefferson, in the pioneering group of thirty-nine who reached Tahiti. One of these ministers, aged twenty-eight, had a wife aged sixty-four; and another had two children at his side.[8] Among the other men who gazed at the luxuriance around them, at the islanders who capered on the foredeck of *Duff* "like frantic persons," yelling "*Tayo! Tayo!*" and at the backdrop of the blue-green, soaring mountains, were four carpenters, a wheelwright, a bricklayer, a draper, a brazier, a tailor, a harness-maker, an under-gardener, and three or four domestic servants. All were certain that the Lord had made Tahiti their vineyard and that they, the Lord's good labourers, were destined for Tahiti and salvation.[9]

In its quality and scope, the Russian evidence for life and culture in Tahiti at the height of missionary success is entirely different from Russian evidence of native culture in the Tuamotu atolls, life on Nukuhiva in the Washington-Marquesas Group, or for the Rangitane element in Maoritanga. For in 1804 the Russian visitors to Taio-hae Bay on Nukuhiva had made skilful use of European beachcombers they found there, Edward Robarts and the Frenchman Jean Le Cabri, and had so handled relations with a Polynesian group whose ancient customs and beliefs remained intact despite the European presence.[11] Likewise, they took advantage of the presence of assorted other English-speaking castaways or settlers on Hawaii Island and Kauai.[12] In New Zealand, only weeks before his visit to

Tahiti, Bellingshausen had found ample evidence of ways in which potato cultivation, an important legacy of Cook's three sojourns in Queen Charlotte Sound, had changed the local way of life, migration, diet, even attitudes toward the future. The Maori had also shown their knowledge of the usefulness of ironware and European cannon. In their dress, decoration, beliefs, customs, and skills, conversely, the New Zealanders encountered in the sounds still lived the labour-filled, traditional life of their people and tribe.[13] Had Easter Islanders been influenced by European visits in the early 1800s or by memories of Roggeveen's arrival and aggression in another age? Of course: Lisianskii in *Neva* (1804) and Kotzebue in *Riurik* (1816) received tense and angry messages reflecting other Europeans' acts and attitudes.[14] Still, in their socio-political and economic life and their beliefs, the Easter Islanders had yet to fall under the Europeans' sway. In the Tuamotus, too, the Russian visitors dealt with people essentially untouched by the influences of Europe or the United States.

It was a very different matter in Tahiti. When *Vostok* and *Mirnyi* called at Matavai Bay in July 1820, English missionaries had been toiling there for twenty years with conspicuous success. Bellingshausen and his people were obliged to gain the missionaries' favour, or at least their understanding, before dealing with the islanders around the bay. The Russians liked neither this fact nor the rule imposed on the Tahitians in the name of God the Father by the Reverend Henry Nott and his companions.

Russian visitors made a persistent effort to record those features of native life and culture that they saw. At Matavai Bay and in surrounding areas, they noted what remained of local mores and traditional Tahitian crafts. They collected artefacts and kept journals that made it possible for us to determine the provenance and value of those objects. All this description and collection, however, was secondary to the main thrust of the Russian undertaking in Tahiti, which was the recording of the missionaries' effort to "supplant Venus with Mary Magdalen," in the emotive phrase of Alan Moorehead. The nature of the missionary task placed a burden on the Russians' objectivity. It would be pointless to deny that Russian evidence of life and culture in a totally transformed and calm Tahiti is not impeccably objective. Kotzebue, among others, viewed with a profound distaste the joylessness and discipline that had accompanied the missionaries' destruction of traditional Tahitian song and dance. His opinion, expressed in print in 1830, offended London Missionary Society apologists, who publicly rebutted all his charges and attacked both his judgement and his character.[15] No comparable situation had arisen, or was ever to arise, as a result of Russian visits to localities where Polynesian life was less affected by the missionary thrust. Thus the Russians' concerns about, or distaste for, the activities of Nott and his companions affected both the ethnographic record and ethnohistory. Happily, heavy biases such as Kotzebue's are those that are most readily discerned.

Russian illustrative records for Tahiti, like the artefacts held in St. Petersburg, have a value that does not require explanation. But what of Russian narrative accounts? Bias apart, why are they worthy of attention? Here is C.J. Newbury:

> The theme of the mission histories is the rise of a single Tahitian dynasty to power accompanied by a religious conversion to Christianity, though the extent of this conversion and the abandonment of older beliefs remained a debated point. . . . The mission historians, Ellis and Lovett in particular, emphasized, rightly, the hardships of early settlement for the missionaries and, less accurately, the magnitude of the benefits of religious conversion compared with the "barbarity" of pre-mission times. It was an easy comparison to make, but . . . is an endless topic, full of hidden and overt value judgements. . . . [16]

Simply put, the significance of the Russian narrative evidence lies in its being not only non-missionary and non-Anglo-Saxon but also self-consciously foreign. The Russians were thoroughly aware of their ignorance of local life and culture, and of their dependence on a questionable source of information: a fraternity whose truth had changed that culture and continued to attack its psychololgical foundations. [17]

CAPTAIN BELLINGSHAUSEN AND THE EUROPEAN COLONY AT MATAVAI BAY

The sloops *Vostok* and *Mirnyi* anchored in Matavai Bay precisely where HMS *Dolphin* had stood fifty-three years before, in June 1767. [18] Within the hour, the Russians were visited by hundreds of Tahitians and by two castaways, one British, the other a New Englander named Williams. The Englishman entered Captain Lazarev's service as interpreter aboard *Mirnyi*. Williams remained aboard *Vostok* and told his tale of adventure and migration from New England to the Russian Northwest Coast, and from Taio-hae Bay on Nukuhiva, where Bellingshausen too had spent some time, to Matavai Bay. Shortly afterwards, at 1:00 pm, the Reverend Henry Nott also came out in a Tahitian craft. The Russians found it significant that he preceded, yet was spokesman for, the king. [19]

A bricklayer by trade, Nott had been twenty-two years old when he had left England aboard *Duff* on 24 September 1796. [20] He was among the original party that had landed on the beach at Matavai Bay in March 1797.

After one year on Tahiti, he was in that small group who resolved to remain there despite the difficulties, the lack of success thus far, and the want of victualling. It was Nott who proved to have the greatest linguistic aptitude and who, on 10 August 1801, preached a sermon in Tahitian. . . . Nott had, in fact, very great influence on the king, in his councils and policies. In 1812, Nott went to Sydney where he wed a Miss A. Turner, one of the four "godly young women" sent out from London in 1809 by the prescient directors of the society. . . . In 1815, back in Tahiti, Nott played his part in the conversion of Patii, the high priest of the marae of Papetoai, who burned his idols.[21]

Nott played a crucial role in Tahiti, from 1815 onward. He preached to large, attentive audiences, who connected his message with Pomare II's military triumphs. In 1818-19, he devised the so-called Pomare Code, promulgated in May 1819, for the godly and equitable government of the land. From his station at Huahine, he moved in June of that year to the site of the missionaries' earlier setbacks and disgrace, Matavai Bay.[22] By moving there, he intended to remain in constant contact with Pomare II. So he did. Whether the king derived more benefit from the mission than Nott did from his access to the royal ear has been debated for a century and more. The two men certainly drew huge and lasting benefits from the connection; and, as Bellingshausen noted, Pomare II appreciated fully how the missionaries' influence depended upon him. At times, indeed, he found Nott's watchful presence irksome. Bellingshausen witnessed the king's furtive attempts to drink forbidden liquor and records how once Pomare II simply closed a door on Nott to gain a moment of seclusion with the Russian.[23]

Physically, Pomare II was a big man with a commanding presence, but he was self indulgent. A pitched battle had taken place in 1815, and in the auto-da-fé that followed the *marae* and ancient idols were torn down, unbelievers were put to death, and congregations were hunted to church by warriors armed with bamboo sticks. In place of the *marae*, Pomare built himself a vast cathedral, 700 feet long, with a mountain stream running through it. . . .[24]

Nott was interpreter and intermediary at meetings between the king and Bellingshausen, Lazarev, and their senior lieutenants. He took part in, and to some extent directed, conversations. From the first, the Russian visitors were conscious of his power as Pomare's right-hand man, advisor, minister, and priest. And it was clear that his influence was not declining.

When the Russians first landed at Matavai Bay on the morning of 23 July, they headed straight for Nott's residence, at Nott's own earlier suggestion. And it was Nott who "kindly led" his fellow Christians, first to Venus Point, where Simonov, Mikhailov, and others from *Vostok* started work on astronomical and other observations and on sketches, then to King Pomare's house. It, too, was painted by Mikhailov, replete with palms and board enclosure, a traditional and most effective anti-pig device.[25] Nott breakfasted with the two visiting captains and the king and royal party as though by right. Later that day, he took the Russians through the settlement and into native huts, whether or not their owners were at hand. He had the power to inspect whatever place he might select, and he used that power widely. On the other hand, the Russians saw no evidence of irritation or hostility on the Tahitians' part, and they were certainly alert for any sign.

For Bellingshausen and his people, Matavai Bay was a delightful and extraordinary spot. It was delightful because the climate was superb, the population friendly and obliging, the supply of food unlimited, and drinking water readily accessible and excellent. At the same time, however, it was not even an echo of the place described by early British mariners: it was another place entirely, another populace, another outlook. Nott was justly proud of the transformation that had taken place since 1800. Bellingshausen and his officers were conscious of the many benefits to the Tahitians and applauded them, but at the same time they viewed those victories askance. It would be foolish to paint either Bellingshausen or his second-in-command as sentimentalists, or to suppose that they had secret sympathy with Rousseauesque approaches to the Polynesian-European meetings of their day. They were hard, practical seamen, and could recognize the value of the mission's work in making Matavai Bay completely safe for visitors and in ending brutal practices such as human sacrifice and institutional infanticide. And yet, Tahiti had paid a price for these gains, and the Russians could not forget it as they wandered through the village and the area around it for the next five days (23-27 July 1820).

> He found that the natives, though gay and ebullient, were changed beyond belief. All those who could wore European clothes. . . . Tattooing had been discouraged, liquor was banned, and no one danced any more or played Tahitian music. Even the weaving of garlands of flowers was now forbidden. Of prostitution there was not a sign: only men came to barter on the Russian ships. . . . Morality police roamed the countryside by night, pouncing on illicit lovers. On Sunday all activity ceased, and the people attended church, the women with hats on their shaven heads. Perhaps the most remarkable thing of all was that the natives had been induced to work.[26]

The Russian visitors of July 1820 made as thorough an inspection of the Matavai settlement, and of Tahitian mores, crafts, and attitudes, as time and language barriers allowed. And as in other parts of Oceania, *Vostok*'s and *Mirnyi*'s officers wrote accounts of their experiences, and their data were made available to Bellingshausen. "Observations on the Island of Tahiti," which appeared in the Bellingshausen narrative of 1831, is an accurate reflection of the range of their enquiries at that time. To their credit, Bellingshausen, Novosil'skii, Simonov, and others manfully struggled against the impulse to condemn what they regarded as the missionary society's excesses in Tahiti. Later visitors in 1823-24 were less constrained, and so their evidence is easier to process.

The profound transformation of Tahitian life and mores that Bellingshausen saw continued for a time after his visit and is well reflected in the records left by Russians of at least six later expeditions: those of the frigate *Kreiser* (Captain M.P. Lazarev again) and the armed sloop *Ladoga* (Captain Andrei Lazarev, his brother) in 1823; the large sloop *Predpriiatie* (Kotzebue, on his third Pacific voyage) in 1824; *Moller* (Captain Mikhail N. Staniukovich) in April 1827; *Krotkii* (Captain L.A. Hagemeister, also visiting the South Pacific Islands for the third time), in February 1830; the transport *Amerika* (Captain von Schants) in 1835; and the Russian-American Company vessel *Nikolai* (Captain Evgenii Berens) in the early weeks of 1839. Taken together, these accounts comprise a useful but neglected commentary on the missionary enterprise in its triumphant or climactic phase under Pomare II and his infant son (1820-26), and on the wild "time of troubles" (1827-31) still connected in Tahitian memory with Queen Pomare Vahine IV or Aimata and the atavistically disposed Mamaia Sect.[27] In short, they reflect the rise and fall of missionary power and the Europeanizing of Tahitian monarchy.

The Russians' attitudes toward Pomare II and his family and entourage thus form the frame and tinge the substance of their record as a whole. They were sympathetic toward Pomare but reserved and cool toward Nott. The Russians themselves were profoundly monarchist, not evangelical, in outlook, and, as Bellingshausen recognized, it was Pomare II, not the missionaries, who gave instructions that *Vostok*'s and *Mirnyi*'s holds be filled with pork, fresh fruit, and other welcome foodstuffs.[28]

BELLINGSHAUSEN AND POMARE II

Like the missionaries, Russian visitors to Matavai Bay commonly misinterpreted the signs and workings of indigenous authority. They tended, naturally, to consider social rank and local hierarchy in Northern European terms. As Robert Williamson observed so well in 1924, any early nineteenth-century European record of the changing situation in Tahiti must be examined for irrelevant presumptions and for overtones reflecting European feudalism as a socio-political and psychological inheritance.[29] The Russian visitors of 1820 had, in any case, too little time for any serious assessment of the functioning of Polynesian chieftainship. What they report about the tribal and political divisions of Tahiti is entirely derivative and so of no intrinsic worth.

Pomare II was a king by European as by Polynesian standards. Bellingshausen and his people rightly recognized his power as a function of inheritance and military success, and rightly recognized that *mana* and authority had been deliberately intertwined with London Missionary Society success. From the outset, the Russians were favourably predisposed towards a native ruler who, in several respects, answered their deeply European expectations: he was physically commanding, fully conscious of his dignity, familiar with European visitors' own expectations and conventions and prepared to accommodate them, and generous, even magnanimous. To such qualities, he added others that reminded the Russians of their own Peter the Great: intelligence, boundless curiosity, and willingness to learn from other nations. Like Kamehameha I of Hawaii, he was "laudable."[30]

Bellingshausen spent some hours in Pomare's company ashore and aboard *Vostok*. Nott was often present, and was evidently glad to be at hand whenever possible during the Russians' formal meeting with the king. There were occasions, however, when Pomare was alone with Bellingshausen, such as on the morning of 23 July 1820.

> I noticed that the presence of Mr. Nott had not pleased the king, and that he now hastened to shut the door. Then he showed me his watch, map, exercise-book for the rudiments of geometry, and took out . . . a pen and a scrap of paper. This he handed to me with the request that I write in Russian that the bearer of the note should be given a bottle of rum. I wrote that the bearer should receive three bottles of rum and six bottles of Teneriffe wine. At this moment, Mr. Nott and Mr. Lazarev came in. The king became confused, quickly hid the note, ink, paper, and changed the conversation. . . .[31]

Minor incidents are sometimes eloquent. Pomare II died of drink within eighteen months of Bellingshausen's visit; and by then his queen and court had fallen hopelessly under the spell of alcohol, which Yankee whalers were about to bring in quantity to Matavai.[32] Bellingshausen's narrative does not insist upon Pomare's weaknesses. Unlike Herman Melville, who would look on King Pomare II as "a sad debauchee and drunkard even charged with unnatural crimes,"[33] he chose to emphasize those features of his host that were commendable by Russian cultural and social norms. Again, one is reminded of the Russian attitude towards that other major Polynesian monarch of the age, Kamehameha I of the Hawaiian Islands.[34] Like Kamehameha, but unlike his weak and self-indulgent son, Pomare II conformed to the Russians' notion of the reforming native king. Were the Tahitians being overworked, exploited by the mission-driven chiefs, forced to pay taxes to the Missionary Society in arrowroot, coconut oil, and other products? It was possible, and visitors in 1820 caught a glimpse of those religious "impositions" from the corner of their eye.[35] But they elected not to scrutinize the missionaries' tax-collection processes. Decorum, lack of time, and a sense of gratitude to Nott all tipped the balance against open indignation. Kotzebue took a harder look in 1824 and indulged himself in just such public criticism of the missionary venture as Bellingshausen's people had avoided. Did the officers aboard *Vostok* and *Mirnyi* regret Tahitian willingness to dress in European cast-off clothes, to beg incessantly for European trifles? Did they recognize that Christian worship was enforced and that the populace were, physically or otherwise, compelled to fill the recently built churches? Indisputably they did; but in 1820 it sufficed to appreciate the safety and sobriety and order that prevailed at Matavai Bay thanks to the union of monarchy and mission. King Pomare II had the Russians' gratitude and their respect. It was for later Russian visitors to note the limits of accord between the missionary band and the Pomare dynasty, and to record the consequences of a parting of the ways under Pomare Vahine IV.[36]

There are no warmer or more delicate portrayals of Pomare II of Tahiti than those left by *Vostok*'s artist Mikhailov (see Plate 10) and by Bellingshausen. As the pen is complemented by the brush, so the Mikhailov portrait gains both context and perspective from the narrative.[37]

KREISER AND *LADOGA* AT MATAVAI BAY, 14-20 JULY 1823

Sailing by the Straits of Dover, Rio de Janeiro, Cape Horn, and either the Society or Sandwich islands, any voyage from the Baltic Sea to Sitka (Novo-Arkhangel'sk) was more than 18,000 miles. Nowadays, Russian submarines complete that voyage in a week or less, passing of course beneath the (former Soviet or the Canadian) High Arctic ice cap.[38] In the early 1800s, Russian vessels were at sea eleven, even thirteen, months depending on the winds, the time of year, and chosen route between St. Petersburg and Russian settlements along the coasts of northwestern America and the Aleutian chain. The voyage was most wasteful of material, ships, and men. Fir hulls deteriorated in warm waters; illness struck at Russian crews in South America;[39] morale was often low even before

Cape Horn was sighted. Yet by 1840 at least thirty ships had been despatched from Kronstadt to the cold, fur-rich littorals of North America.
Only the British Admiralty sent more ships of war. But then, only the
British government had military and economic interests of comparable
breadth in that remote part of the globe and, hence, a comparable need to
guard those interests.[40]

Confronted by the need to halt Bostonian and other foreign "pilfering"
of furs within the territories that it governed and exploited as an agency of
the State, the Russian-American Company Board, under massive Navy
pressure, banned all sales or deliveries of peltry to non-Russians on the
Russian Northwest Coast in 1818 and 1820.[41] New England shipmasters
and other foreigners ignored the bans, so the Company sought imperial
assistance. No doubt, the Company had undertaken more than it had
power or resources to accomplish, but its own disgrace would shame the
nation. Both politically and economically, therefore, it was essential to
enlarge the Navy's role in regions that were theoretically under the Company's control.[42] The stage was set for the imperial ukases of 4 and 13
September 1821, by the first of which Russia claimed sovereignty over
territory in America down to 51°N, extending to 115 miles offshore on
both the North American and Asian sides of the Pacific Ocean. By the
second, the Company was granted a monopoly of fur hunting, trading,
and fishing in those areas and on islands of the Kurile and Aleutian chains
for a further twenty years.[43]

The tsar was ill-advised in this attempt to claim exclusive rights "to all
commerce, whaling, and fishery, and all other industry on all islands, and
posts, and gulfs, including the whole northwestern shoreline of America . . . to latitude 51°N."[44] It was predictable that the United States and
Britain would protest in heated terms. "The American Government,"
wrote Count Nesselrode, the minister of foreign affairs, to D.A. Gur'ev of
the ministry of finance, on 3 June 1822, "protests against what *it* calls the
expansion of imperial possessions."[45] Though a Eurocentric diplomat par
excellence and ill at ease with North American and North Pacific issues,
Nesselrode perceived the awkwardness of the entire situation. It was not
in Russia's interests to clash with Britain over such an issue. Alexander I
wished to bring order to the Balkans as a whole. British neutrality was
wanted. On the other hand, the Company for whose specific benefit the
edicts had been promulgated was in deep financial straits.[46] And edicts
were not to be ignored by the Americans or British if imperial authority
was to remain unquestioned in the Company possessions. In short, measures were needed to support the tsar's ukase.

In September 1822, the 28-gun sloop *Apollon* (Captain Irinarkh
Tulub'ev) "cruised" to the Northwest Coast of North America, "there to

move as close as possible to land, though not beyond the latitude to which the Company at present enjoys all its prerogatives and rights."[47] Another ship or two, the Navy argued, would help to counter British influence and, equally important, to control the flood of daring and importunate New England shipmasters. Accordingly, it was resolved to send two other Navy vessels round the world. The frigate *Kreiser*, mounting thirty-six guns, and *Ladoga* (formerly *Mirnyi*), a sloop-rigged transport armed with twenty guns of varied calibre, were promptly chosen. M.P. Lazarev was offered the command of the small squadron and accepted it, naming his younger brother Andrei to the ship that he himself had brought to Polynesia two years earlier. For M.P. Lazarev, this voyage, his third to Oceania, was to seal professional success. Since 1812-13, when he had seen close action both off Riga and at Danzig, he had been marked by his superiors as an officer of evident potential. Now, in 1822-24, he made a move toward flag rank. His seamen, midshipmen, and officers formed a particularly able company. Among the officers were future admirals P.S. Nakhimov and E.V. Putiatin, four future captains, and a future chief staff surgeon of the Black Sea fleet, P. Aleman. Two of the *Kreiser*'s five lieutenants, Kupreianov and Annenkov, had already served with Lazarev in *Mirnyi*, and so had worked among the Tuamotu atolls.[48] As for *Ladoga*, her navigator, M.P. Kharlov, was to overcome the disadvantages of humble birth and lack of patronage to reach the rank of lieutenant-colonel purely by merit; and her surgeon, Petr Ogievskii, was a natural historian of some distinction. Of the total company of two hundred and thirty men, however, only D.I. Zavalishin, the incipient Decembrist, would, in later years, equal or surpass the elder Lazarev in fame.[49]

Kreiser and *Ladoga* reached Rio de Janeiro in January 1823 after a slow and troubled South Atlantic crossing. Reprovisioning, repairs to the transport, and weather all conspired to delay their further progress. (When at length they did reach Sitka, political and trading conditions were quite different from when they had left St. Petersburg.) In May 1823, after a stormy twelve-week passage from Brazil, they approached Van Diemen's Land, modern Tasmania. The ships dropped anchor in the Derwent, hard by Hobart Town, at 4:00 pm on 17 May and were generously welcomed by the colony's lieutenant-governor, William Sorell.[50] Their presence provided Sorell with a respite from mounting pressures and preoccupations: bush rangers at large, new convict parties in from Sydney, building schedules. *Kreiser* and *Ladoga* left Hobart on 9 June minus one leading seaman, Stanislav Stankevich, who had taken to the bush and was never to be seen again by Europeans.[51] To the last, Colonel Sorell was ignorant of Lazarev's true mission on the Northwest Coast of North America.[52]

M.P. Lazarev was received in Matavai Bay, on 9 July 1823, by the

Reverend Henry Nott, his wife, and three other servants of the London Missionary Society: the Reverend Charles Wilson (1770-1857), a member of the second group of missionaries to depart aboard *Duff* in 1798, and two "Deputies" sent on an inspection tour of "various stations in those uttermost parts of the sea," the Reverend Daniel Tyerman and the Reverend George Bennet.[53] Tyerman and Bennet were accompanied by servants. Lazarev reciprocated their hospitality almost at once, inviting Tyerman, Wilson, and others to dine aboard his ship. The meeting was civil, but later Tyerman and his party became apprehensive of the Russians' real motives for a call at Tahiti and suspected grand imperialist schemes. Tyerman, indeed, was alarmed even by Captain Lazaroff's "procuring" a Tahitian flag. How could it benefit Tahiti or the mission if his Russian visitors received or gave such "potent" objects? As for Nott and Wilson, they were both already coping with the pressure brought to bear by New England whaling captains who, by 1823, had made Tahitians too acquainted with the Stars and Stripes and cheap New England liquor.[54]

Like Bellingshausen, Lazarev approved certain results of the missionaries' energy but found it little to his taste. It was commendable, of course, that the Tahitians were so peaceable, pious, and sober; but the missionaries were a sombre presence in their midst. Within five days, *Kreiser* was ready to depart. Only the hope of seeing *Ladoga* restrained her captain, and the transport's masts were duly sighted on the morning of 14 July.[55]

With the help of eighteen young Tahitian men, *Ladoga*'s rigging was restretched and raised within two days. Fresh fruits and viands were acquired in considerable quantity and Tahitian barterers were given what they obviously wanted: Russian clothing.[56] Waistcoats, uniforms, kerchiefs, and linen shirts were in demand among a people whose tastes had been considerably influenced by Captain Duperrey of *La Coquille*. "The women stood in need of straw bonnets! We had none, not having known that the French had introduced their fashions here."[57] *Ladoga* was formally visited by Pomare II's widow; her son, the two-year-old Pomare III; and assorted retainers and advisers on 16 July. The meeting was pleasant.

The Matavai Bay scene had changed since 1820, though. Then, Pomare II and his court had surreptitiously asked Russian visitors for liquor while publicly standing by the missionaries' rule of abstinence. In 1823, neither the queen or any chief challenged the rule by asking either of the Lazarevs for spirits; yet the appetite for alcohol had grown apace and, thanks to visiting New Englanders and others, the demand had its supply. *Vostok* and *Mirnyi* had re-provisioned at a modest cost in "little mirrors, needles, fish-hooks, knives, scissors, and so forth."[58] Three years later, no Tahitian would accept even an axe or polished knife without demur, but interest in European fashion, which in Bellingshausen's day had been restricted to the island's chiefly stratum, was becoming universal and intense. Such were the symptoms of intensifying European influence and of increasing drunkenness.[59]

Kreiser and *Ladoga* set sail on 20 July, fully provisioned with bananas, coconuts, yams, breadfruit, pork, and sweet drinking water. Officers and men were relaxed and fit. They made for Sitka Sound, arriving on 3 September after an easy six-week cruise.[60] Regrettably, no artist accompanied the Lazarevs to leave an illustrative record of the visit to Tahiti. Nor had scientists of international reputation been appointed to the basically non-scientific venture.

Andrei Petrovich Lazarev, however, did in due course publish an account of the *Ladoga*'s voyage entitled *Plavanie vokrug sveta . . . (A Voyage Round the World in the Sloop Ladoga, in the Years 1822-25*; St. Petersburg 1832). Its fourth chapter offers a wide-ranging description of Tahiti, its resources, people, missions, and prospects at the time of the second Russian visit. Almost half of that chapter comes from Surgeon Petr Ogievskii's pen. A talented and energetic botanist, Ogievski had had instructions to examine and report on all he could within the three days and nights at his disposal. Flora and fauna, local husbandry and crops, the geological configuration of Tahiti, mission buildings, roads and groves, Pomare II's mausoleum, huts and furniture, diseases, cures, local diets, attitudes, and mores: all were noted with economy and balance. Ogievskii's contributions to the history and ethnohistory of Polynesia and Australia, while minor compared with those of Bellingshausen, Simonov, or Kotzebue, merit notice. Hitherto, they have been totally neglected in the West.[61] Taken together, Lazarev's and Ogievskii's accounts of the situation at Matavai Bay in 1823 complement the 1820 records and the mission histories or annals. Their account is supplemented by material from Mikhail P. Lazarev, first published in the *Zapiski Admiralteiskago Departamenta (Transactions of the Admiralty Department)*, Volume 6 (1834).[62] There are fine cameos of Henry Nott ("His face shows liveliness yet perfect calm; his words breathe a religious feeling"); of Pomare II's heavy widow, clad in silks; and of the infant king whom Russian whistles, bells, and other baubles bored.[63]

KOTZEBUE IN TAHITI: "ETERNAL REPETITION OF PRESCRIBED PRAYERS"

Well pleased with his hydrographic work among the Tuamotus, Kotzebue brought *Predpriiatie* to Matavai Bay on 14 March 1824. Like Bellingshausen, he was both surprised and glad to find a Russian-speaking pilot, Williams, and resigned himself to the considerable crowds of native traders who immediately swarmed around and over his ship. The deck was speedily "transformed into a busy market, where...the bargains were concluded with laughter."[64] To the visitors' amusement, name exchanges were proposed within the hour. Shortly afterwards, Tahitians and Russians could be seen "walking in couples, arm in arm." Were these procedures a device to make it easier for the Tahitians to extract what they most wanted from their new brothers and allies—Russian clothing? Kotzebue thought it likely, but allowed his men to give away old clothes. The native visitors, all male, were provisioning the ship as he had hoped, and they were friendly and honest in their dealings. All was calm. A message was despatched to the authorities ashore, who were agents of the monarchy but also members of the Missionary Society. Kotzebue's first shore encounter was with Charles Wilson, not Henry Nott.[65]

Kotzebue was an officer of dry and sober temperament. By training and by nature, he was predisposed to scrutiny of concrete evidence, a man unlikely to be favourably struck by the enforced preoccupation with the rituals of mission life that marked Tahiti in the early 1820s. What he saw deeply offended him, and he expressed his feelings crisply:

> The religion taught by the missionaries is not true Christianity, though it may possibly comprehend some of its doctrines, but half understood even by the teachers themselves. That it was established by force, is of itself evidence against its Christian principle. A religion which consists in the eternal repetition of prescribed prayers, which forbids every innocent pleasure, and cramps or annihilates every mental power, is a libel on the Divine Founder of Christianity....It has put an end to avowed human sacrifices, but many more human beings have been actually sacrificed to it than ever were to their heathen gods.[66]

It is difficult to read the long Tahitian section of the 1830 Kotzebue narrative and not be conscious of the author's deep antipathy toward the London Missionary Society. We read, for instance, that on Sunday, 15 March, the natives stayed indoors "where they lay on their bellies reading the Bible and howling aloud." It being the Sabbath day, "the very birds seemed to celebrate by silence."[67] As for the missionaries themselves, they were lacking that "careful education and diligent study at schools and universities" without which, in Russia, no man can become a teacher or religious educator. "The London Missionary Society is more easily satisfied: a half-savage, confused by the dogmas of an uneducated sailor, is, according to them, perfectly fitted for the sacred office."[68] In the church itself, "surrounded by its black wooden crosses" and filled by "the most profound stillness," Tahitians dressed in their extraordinary, motley, comic clothes and listened gloomily to Wilson's sombre homily. A psalm or two, when ventured, were sung to "incongruous tunes" and "in defiance of harmony." When children chattered for a moment, they were silenced by the threatening and chilly eyes of "Messrs. Tyerman and Bennet."[69] As for what was termed the "Code," or constitution, it was nothing but a product of the missionaries' grandiose ambition; and their power and control "over the minds of the Tahitians" was "unbounded." Mission policy had led to the selection, as guardian of the infant king, of "the tributary king" of Borabora. He was a seven-foot giant of "enormous corpulence, which almost prevents his moving."[70] This "mountain of flesh," in whose name the British missionaries acted as they chose, and who was indolent enough to be their "mouthpiece," was Tapoa II of Borabora and Taha'a. Since December 1822, he had been married to the late Pomare's daughter, Aimata, the future Queen Pomare Vahine IV. Fully conscious of their temporal as well as spiritual control, Kotzebue wrote, the aggressive missionaries had not yet produced a text of their Tahitian constitution. They were "still employed upon it, well convinced that whatever they should insert would be received without opposition."[71] Wishing to consolidate their own, as well as the infant Pomare III's authority "they had resolved to confirm the title...by a solemn coronation."

Many more examples might be given of Kotzebue's disapproval of mission efforts in Tahiti, but the point is clear. First, Kotzebue saw the spiritual consequence of London Missionary Society activity in Oceania as negative, and it was this that most enraged the Society's apologists. What Wilson, Nott, and their associates had been purveying to the natives with the military and psychological assistance of the monarchy, so Kotzebue claimed, was a travesty of Christianity. Second, he objected to the missionaries' involvement in political affairs while claiming to be acting in the spiritual sphere alone. From his perspective, Nott's and Wilson's patent meddling in Tahitian political affairs was hardly more objectionable than their blunt yet disingenuous denial of their interest in all temporal matters. If the missionaries were simply acting as religious servants, why were they drafting constitutions, legal codes, and other documents of non-religious content? They were planning to present the infant king with an imported English crown and with a Bible, not a copy of their Act of Constitution! "Was not a sly mental reservation perhaps intended by this? If the Constitution should not have exactly the effect intended...might not the pupil of Nott come forward to the Tahitians boldly and force them back under the yoke of the missionaries?"[72]

Third, Kotzebue took exception to the burden of taxation placed on all

Tahitians by mission orders and to benefit the Missionary Society. Was it equitable that these natives should be forced to send large quantities of arrowroot, coconut oil, or any other product of Tahiti to Great Britain to defray the costs of printing tracts and Bibles and of sending missionaries to Oceania? Together with the narrow and sectarian approach toward the Gospel that the missionaries had taken in Tahiti, and their mixing of religious and political concerns and edicts, this taxation, which converted chiefs exacted with a horrible enthusiasm from the commoners, had "driven joy away" and cast a pall of apprehensive pseudo-piety over the land. And yet, had Christ not saved mankind? And was the Gospel not a cause for endless joy and celebration?

Kotzebue's whole view of Tahiti was coloured by his deep dislike of certain aspects of the missionaries' enterprise. Thus, we find him noting sadly that "the making of mats and canoes" was in decline; that imported, purchased boats were now used for long sea voyages and ancient navigational skills were fast being forgotten; that traditional agriculture and husbandry were disappearing; that Tahitians possessed almost no horses and no cattle; that "no kind of mechanical trade" was carried on, and no industry was prospering; that "dancing, mock-fights, and dramatic representations" were all banned; that music was absent from everyday life; that obese and idle chiefs, "solely employed in praying, eating, and sleeping," were grossly fat even in youth; that hair was cropped so close to the scalp as to produce an ugly, "ape-like appearance."[73] Like a fine mist, disapproval settles lightly on the Kotzebue narrative and penetrates it. One regrets the fact, for it renders Kotzebue's evidence less valuable and more difficult to use.

In the course of his stay at Matavai Bay, Kotzebue had at least three audiences with the queen and so had a number of occasions to examine her relations with her court and with the mission and, moreover, to observe the infant king. Among the brightest vignettes in the 1830 Kotzebue text are those depicting the Tahitian royal visits to *Predpriiatie*. The royal fashions (wide straw hats with black crepe streamers, swaddling silks), the royal conversation (Did the captain pray to God each day, and was the world really round?), major gift exchanges (pigs for calico, glasses, and silks), all make an interesting cameo, of value in conjunction with the Duperrey account and with the mission histories of Davies, Ellis, Lovett, and Horne.[74]

While *Predpriiatie*'s navigators Grigor'ev and Ekimov surveyed Matavai Bay and the adjacent coast from Mount Tahara (One Tree Hill) in the southwest to Port Papeete and Motu Uta islet in the northwest, for a chart printed in 1830 and reprinted in the first English and subsequent translations,[75] Eschscholtz botanized and took the butterflies, insects, and birds that "willing islanders" had brought him from Tahiti's "furthest corners." His collection was of interest to *Predpriiatie*'s Tahitian visitors.[76] While Kotzebue dealt with matters of diplomacy, his youthful naturalist, Gofman, took a hike through the interior to Lake Wahiria with a trio of Tahitians.[77] Gofman's principal concern was with geology. Rock samples that he brought from Oceania are still in St. Petersburg today.[78]

Kotzebue left Tahiti on 24 March, after a ten-day stay, and set a course for the Samoan Group, the Marshalls (Eastern Carolines), and Petropavlovsk-in-Kamchatka. He departed with the bitter taste of bigotry still in his mouth, and he had not lost it when he wrote his narrative in 1828-29.

"SLANDERS, SARCASMS, AND INSINUATIONS": JAMES MONTGOMERY

Kotzebue's *Novoe puteshestvie vokrug sveta* . . . appeared in English as *A New Voyage Round the World in the Years 1823, 1824, 25 and 26* (London 1830). It at once caught the attention of the London Missionary Society, for whom the Scottish journalist and poet James Montgomery (1771-1854) was then preparing Bennet's and Tyerman's reports, letters, and journals for the printers.[79] From the outset, the Society and James Montgomery regarded Kotzebue's published comments on the mission in Tahiti as offensive slander.

Montgomery, whose missionary parents had died in the West Indies, had been raised by the Moravians in Yorkshire. A precocious, needy youth, he had had numerous adventures, published many wretched poems, written hymns, and dabbled in politics, typesetting, and love before becoming the proprietor and editor of an anti-Tory newspaper, the *Sheffield Iris*. Both his time with the Morvaians and an essential wanderlust were reflected in such poems as *The World Before the Flood* (1812), *Greenland* (1819), and *Pelican Island* (1826). Mid-life brought him a measure of security, and his innumerable local benefactions and probity were recognized by Robert Peel with a small government pension.[80] As editor of Tyerman's and Bennet's papers and a long-term friend of the Society, Montgomery considered it his duty to rebut Kotzebue's charges. He did so with heated indignation in a massive introduction to *The Journal of Voyages and Travels of the Reverend Daniel Tyerman and George Bennet, Esq.* (London 1831). Coincidentally, he brought the Kotzebue narrative to the attention of a large, middle-class readership in Britain. One year later, an American edition brought the Kotzebue *Voyage*, and especially its South Pacific portion, to the notice of another growing audience. Montgomery's unintentional but major contribution to the sales and publicity of Kotzebue's book deserves attention. For it largely compensated for the fact that Kotzebue himself had directed his account first to a Russian, then to a German, readership. The *Neue Reise um die Welt in dem Jahren 1823-1826* had appeared in its Weimar edition within weeks of the St. Petersburg edition[81] and ensured that the English-speaking world would be more aware of the influence of Russian ships and men in Oceania. It was a small step from awareness to apprehension and, among the English living in the South Pacific, to alarm.[82]

Here are extracts from the introduction to Montgomery's edition of *The Journal of Voyages and Travels*:

> In chapter xxxii, vol. ii, p. 217 of this work will be found some mention of a visit paid by the Russian Captain Kotzebue to Tahiti, at a time when the deputation were there. There has lately been published in England what is called 'A new Voyage Round the world,' etc. by this gentleman. In a section of more than a hundred pages, entitled 'O Tahaiti,' the writer has thought proper to assert as facts things which never happened under the sun, and to express sentiments concerning the mission which no man could entertain who was not under strong prejudice, if not actual delusion . . .
>
> The captain says: "After many fruitless efforts, some English missionaries succeeded at length, in the year 1797, in introducing *what they called Christianity* into Tahaiti, and even in gaining over to their doctrine King Tajo, who then governed the whole island. This conversion was a spark thrown into a powder magazine, and was followed by a fearful explosion. The marais were suddenly destroyed by order of the king, every memorial of the former worship defaced, the new religion forcibly established, and whoever would not adopt it put to death. . . ." How much truth is there in this straightforward statement? Let the reader judge. There never existed such a personage as King Tajo. Pomare the First was king of Tahiti during the early residence of the missionaries in that island. He died in 1803, having never so much as pretended to embrace Christianity. . . . Christianity was not received, "after many fruitless efforts," in 1797; nor till 1814 were a "praying people" found among the inhabitants. . . . There are indeed on record shocking instances of the murder of natives for embracing the "new religion" by the bigoted adherents of the old, but Captain Kotzebue may be safely challenged to produce one example of an individual being put to the alternative of preferring "death to the renunciation of his ancient faith." What he means at page 169, by "the bloody persecution instigated by the missionaries, which performed the work of a desolating infection," he would find hard to explain before the bar of God or man. At each he is answerable for it.
>
> "The religion taught by the missionaries *is not true Christianity*"

(vol. i, p. 168). If that which Captain Kotzebue practices be "True Christianity," assuredly that which missionaries teach is not. Try him by his own test. In an interview with the queen, he says, "She asked me whether I was a Christian, and how often I prayed *daily*." "I merely replied, that we should be judged according to our actions, rather than the number of our prayers" (vol. i, p. 183). Every page of his fables and lucubrations respecting the missionaries and their people proves that he is not of that religion which says, "Thou shalt not bear false witness against thy neighbour. . . ."

The rest of his slanders, sarcasms, insinuations (especially at pp.196-7, which are fitter for a court of justice than of criticism), may be left for the present, to the exposure which awaits them. . . . One cannot help wishing that he had left one solitary specimen of his "prayers." If he had, it is not uncharitable to suppose that it might have begun thus: "God, I thank thee that I am not like," etc.[83]

Kotzebue's summary of the events following the arrival of the English missionaries in 1797 is unworthy of his narrative and is indeed replete with factual errors. Some, no doubt, reflect his difficulty in fully understanding his informants at Matavai Bay; others, however, show a failure to verify assertions in a sound, scholarly way. There was no reason why a Russian should, in 1830, have imagined that Tahitians had accepted Christianity the year that *Duff* first reached their island. Nor was Kotzebue acting professionally or scientifically when he accepted, untested, the contention that Tahitians who would not embrace the missionaries' faith had soon been "put to death" and that the missionaries personally instigated "bloody persecutions" and vendettas.[84]

On the other hand, Montgomery himself, posing as champion of real Christianity, a risky avocation, shows precisely that uncharitable animus of which he pointedly accuses Kotzebue! Disingenuously stressing Kotzebue's small but irritating error in misnaming Tu (Tajo, Teiu), whom, as Montgomery certainly knew, the early missionaries *had* always called Teu,[85] he takes all Kotzebue's "slanders" out of context. Here, for example, is the London text to which Montgomery takes violent exception after editing it first: "But the religion taught by the missionaries is not true Christianity, though it may possibly comprehend some of its doctrines. . . ." As for the Russian text, it gives one *less* room for offense: "Though the missionaries' teaching is not genuine Christianity, it does contain the latter's dogmas, albeit wrongly understood. . . ."[86] Again, here is that passage supposedly demonstrating Kotzebue's irreligious and ignoble attitude towards the Church's teaching: "The queen . . . inquired how often I prayed daily. This last question afforded me an opportunity, had I thought fit, to give her Majesty some new ideas on the subject of the missionary religion; but I did not feel myself quite capable of entering into a theological dispute, and therefore merely replied that Christianity taught us that we would be judged according to our actions rather than by the number of our prayers."[87] In this case, too, the Russian text is milder and somewhat more circumspect than is the English one, laying stress on the author's feeling that he was "inadequately prepared for any theological disputation."[88] Would Montgomery have been mollified, had he been able to examine the original remarks in Russian? One thinks not. He was a man who liked the feel of indignation and could use it, like a wind, to fill his sails.

MOLLER IN TAHITI, 1827

Three years elapsed between Kotzebue's departure from Tahiti on 24 March 1824 and the arrival of the next Russian company, aboard the armed sloop *Moller* under Captain-Lieutenant Mikhail N. Staniukovich. In the interim, missionary power on Tahiti and especially at Matavai Bay had reached its zenith, King Pomare II's eldest daughter, known as Queen Pomare Vahine, having begun her troubled reign.[89]

> The high tide of the missionaries' success was around 1827, when Queen Pomare Vahine was set up on the sad little mockery of a throne. After this, the decline begins and accelerates fairly rapidly. The population figures are appalling. In Cook's time, there were probably around 40,000 people on the island.... By the end of the eighteen-thirties, the figure was down to 9,000 and was eventually to drop to 6,000.[90]

Since *Predpriiatie*'s sailing, other forces than the Church had spread their influence: tuberculosis, smallpox, dysentery, venereal disease, and prostitution were increasing, month by month, as whaling ships, most from Nantucket, brought in dozens of aggressive, hungry sailors. Sealers, too, brought new brutal elements as well as guns and liquor to their island. Among their crews were escaped convicts from Sydney and assorted armed "banditti," who, in the words of Joseph Banks, were happy to introduce "diseases, murther, barbarism...."[91] The collapse of the Tahitian way of life, morality, and local culture that was so to shock the Quaker Daniel Wheeler when he visited the missionaries in 1834 ("There is scarcely *anything* so striking or pitiable as the natives' aimless, nerveless mode of spending life")[92] was in its early phase when *Moller* called, in 1827.

Captain Staniukovich was conservative by temperament and, though an excellent sea officer, was certainly no academic in the mould of

Kruzenshtern or Bellingshausen. Not surprisingly, the Staniukovich reports on *Moller*'s sojourn in Tahiti from 29 April to 15 May 1827 have a dry and very "service-centred" character.[93] Disparaging remarks about the mission and the missionaries are missing from his letters and despatches; and so are all remarks and references to the men whose joyless piety had so frustrated Kotzebue. Like the equally conservative and bluff commander of *Otkrytie* in 1821, Captain Mikhail N. Vasil'ev, Staniukovich found it natural to treat his missionary hosts in Polynesia with politeness, to respect the Church, and to maintain a tactful silence, on the printed page at least, on the whole matter of European missionaries.[94]

Several men aboard *Moller* in 1827 had had previous experience in Polynesia. From the standpoint of Tahitian and Pacific studies, Pavel Nikolaevich Mikhailov, the artist, was by far the most important. Mikhailov had enjoyed good relations with Bellingshausen in the early 1820s. The period immediately following *Vostok*'s return to Russia had been bright with promise, as he worked up aquarelles for publication in the narrative that Bellingshausen was preparing for the service and imperial authorities.[95] That promise had deceived him. The appearance of the Bellingshausen text was postponed, then placed in doubt by the Decembrist insurrection on 14 December 1825, and Mikhailov's solvency began to vanish. Debts increased, frustration mounted. His dilemma has been summarized by the historian of art, Boris N. Suris:

> Using as his starting point the numerous drawings that he had brought back from the voyage, Mikhailov had, by the end of 1824, actually finished more than fifty large aquarelles, all intended as illustrations of the text that Bellingshausen still planned to produce. It was not until 1831, however, a full decade after the *Vostok* and *Mirnyi* expedition, that a comprehensive account of that venture appeared in print. . . . And in that interval, the artist managed to undertake a second voyage round the world, this time aboard the sloop *Moller*. He was "chosen and accepted for the campaign" in 1826, by Captain-Lt. Staniukovich. The *Moller* expedition . . . was not a success. The officers' harshness and maltreatment of sailors even drove the crew to open insubordination. As a result, the "disobedient elements" were subjected to severe reprisals on their return. The official cover-up of the expedition, which had been compromised by such a very undesirable conclusion, was caused, in part, by this outbreak of insubordination. In consequence, Mikhailov's new work went unpublished.[96]

Extant records of the insubordination shown aboard *Moller*, which evidently began with resentment of orders to "take to bed" and which remain in the Central State Naval Archive (TsGAVMF),[97] indicate that Mikhailov was in no way implicated.

While in Tahiti, in 1820 and again in 1827, Mikhailov worked with a loose-sheet folder that fitted comfortably under his arm. Those sheets are today in the Drawings Division of the State Russian Museum in St. Petersburg. In total, the Mikhailov Portfolio contains a dozen sheets with studies clearly deriving from the artist's two visits to Matavai Bay. Most originate from the first. Among the Tahitian chiefs sketched by Mikhailov were Hitoti or Vaiturai of Tiarei, who was later to flourish under the French administration of Tahiti, and Paofai, also known as Paihahi, a chief of the Arioi society. There are also a view of the Hapape River and at least two coastal panoramas. One of these was worked up by Mikhailov and lithographed in 1824 by Ivan Pavlovich Fridrits under the title *A View of the Island of Otaiti and of Cape Venus.* Together with the celebrated breakfast scene, showing two heavy Russian officers in full dress uniform awkwardly seated on stools six inches high, taking refreshment with Pomare II, his wife, Nott, and assorted native grandees, that view of a tranquil Cape Venus joined Mikhailov's major study from Tahiti, the portrait of *Pomari, King of O-Taiti* in the *Atlas* accompanying Bellingshausen's narrative of 1831, *Dvukratnye izyskaniia.*[98]

Mikhailov's work, together with Staniukovich's three long reports on *Moller*'s outward voyage to Kamchatka, makes it possible to reconstruct the outline of the visit to Tahiti. As for details, they have yet to be presented; as of 1990, they are under lock and key in the Central Naval Archive in St. Petersburg.[99]

KROTKII'S VISIT: 5-11 FEBRUARY 1830

> Captain-Lieutenant Hagemeister, known already for two voyages out
> to the colonies of the Russian-American Company, was early in 1828
> appointed commander of the transport *Krotkii*, lately returned from a
> voyage round the world. She was now sent to Kamchatka and the col-
> onies with a mixed cargo of rigging, ironware, carpenter's and
> joiner's tools, etc. . . . He left on 10 September 1828. . . .[100]

As recorded by Rear-Admiral Nikolai A. Ivashintsev in his seminal account of Russian circumnavigation (1848-49), Hagemeister took the *Krotkii* to Australia by way of Portsmouth, Porto Praia (Santiago), and Simon's Bay (Cape Town), then pressed north across the Fijis and the Marshalls to Kamchatka. Ever prudent, he proceeded in a measured, sober way: repairing spars and damaged rigging, landing goods at Petropavlovsk (11-16 July 1829) and at Sitka 27 October–2 November 1829), checking fixes, and surveying. From the colonies, where *Krotkii*'s presence was superfluous and placed a needless burden on supplies, Hagemeister set his course for San Francisco. He intended to revictual and water there in comfort, but conditions were unusually bad: a drought had ruined grain crops in the area, and little wheat or rye was to be had. Still, he remained in port about three weeks, until 13 December.[101]

Aboard the *Krotkii* on her homeward run was the distinguished Prussian physicist and student of magnetic force, Professor Georg Adolph Erman (1806-77). Like Emil Lenz aboard the *Predpriiatie* in 1823-26, Erman made major contributions to geodesy and physics, especially in the field of magnetic inclination/deviation. Inasmuch as he made use of Freycinet's and Bellingshausen's then unpublished data, Erman was developing the 1820 work of the *Vostok*'s Ivan M. Simonov.[102]

Coasting past Aratua on 28 January 1830, Tikahau on 31 January, and so intersecting the western Tuamotus, *Krotkii* entered Matavai Bay on 5 February. The objective was to water and provision quickly, but, as in California six weeks earlier, the elements proved hostile. This time, not drought but squally winds frustrated Hagemeister's efforts to revictual and rest his fifty-seven men. Day by day, the north wind blew into the bay, making relaxation an impossibility.

> Hagemeister made haste to take on fresh provisions; but for three whole days and nights, he could not even establish contact with the shore, the north wind was whipping up such waves that when she pitched, the *Krotkii* took in water through her stern windows, and when she rolled, through her gunports. Surrounded by breakers not a cable off, she could easily have been cast ashore. . . .[103]

Krotkii carried an unusual, even disproportionate, number of promising midshipmen. One of them, Evgenii Andreevich Berens (1811-78), left a narrative describing his experiences in the transport, which, unlike other narratives produced by *Krotkii*'s officers, was ultimately published in a journal. "Notes by Midshipman Evgenii Andreevich Berens, Taken During a Round-the-World Voyage in the Sloop 'Krotkii' in 1828-1830" appeared in 1903 in *Morskoi sbornik*.[104] Like other pieces that reflect Russian dealings in the North or South Pacific in the early nineteenth century, the "Notes" were printed first and foremost as a public recognition of political success. Midshipman Berens was an admiral by 1864 and a member of the Admiralty Council shortly afterwards—an elder naval statesman in the age of coal and ironclads. As such, he was remembered and, a quarter-century after his death, allowed to reminisce about Tahiti.

Hagemeister and his people found the Tahitians more than ready to trade but "not too importunate." The word taboo remained a mighty force and sufficed to clear a busy deck. Missionary influence was still extensive: Sunday was a day of public idleness or prayer depending on how the Lord's Day was regarded by the visitor.[105] In general, *Krotkii*'s was the least successful Russian visit of the period. The wind remained unhelpful. Native barterers were shrewder, and the native chiefs less docile, than European seamen might have wished. Even the oranges "were not quite ripe and . . . did not taste too good," while local coconuts, so Berens thought, had a "thin layer of meat."[106]

Hagemeister and his officers were all promoted and rewarded when they returned to St. Petersburg in September 1830, but no account of *Krotkii*'s voyage was presented to the public. As for Berens, he was marked out as an officer with special aptitude for expeditionary work and by 1834 was first lieutenant of *Amerika*, bound for the North Pacific settlements once more.[107] Second Lieutenant in that transport was Vasilii Stepanovich Zavoiko. Like Berens, he was destined for flag rank and was to leave a published record of his two fleeting visits to Mo'orea in December 1835 and January 1839. That text, entitled *Vpechatleniia moriaka. . . . (Impressions of a Seaman During Two Voyages Around the World . . .*; St. Petersburg 1840), lacks academic value. It is popular in tone, replete with tired purple passages, and clearly meant to entertain rather than educate the public. Still, it does provide a glimpse of the *Amerika*'s pedestrian but economically successful voyage, and, despite its shallowness, it makes a useful supplement to Georg Erman's *Reise um die Erde . . .* (Berlin 1833-48).

AMERIKA AND NIKOLAI AT MO'OREA, 1835 AND 1839

Both *Amerika* (Captain Ivan Ivanovich von Schants) and *Nikolai* (Captain E.A. Berens) carried mixed cargoes from Kronstadt to Novo-Arkhangel'sk (Sitka) on the Russian Northwest Coast. Both sailed in mid-August and called at Copenhagen and Portsmouth before making for the South Pacific Ocean by entirely different routes. *Nikolai* reached Sitka on 14 April 1838, and *Amerika* arrived in June, after a stop at Petropavlovsk-in-Kamchtka. Both carried heavy naval stores and ironware and both were laden with the Company's peltry for the homeward cruise. Both left the colonies as winter was approaching (October-November), making straight for Honolulu and its warm promise of fresh supplies, water, and rest. *Amerika* arrived there on 7 November 1835, *Nikolai* in mid-December. Both ships' companies were well received by the Hawaiian king and court; enjoyed the sights; took on supplies in smaller volume than expected; and proceeded to the Societies, Cape Horn, the South Atlantic, and the Baltic. As the overlapping patterns of their voyages suggest, Company efforts at provisionment along the Russian Northwest Coast of North America had grown routine and, by the thirties, were pursued with a deliberate, unhurried rhythm. Gone were almost annual attempts to send supplies around the world at huge expense.[108] Gone too, by 1835, were all but echoes of the Navy's golden age in Oceania, the age of exploration and of innovative science. Nikolai K. Kadnikov, Dionisii P. Zarembo, Andrei Iunker: such commanders of modest ships (*Abo, Naslednik Aleksandr, Nikolai*) on modest resupplying expeditions in the early 1840s were pale reflections of the great figures of Russia's naval venture in the North Pacific basin: Kruzenshtern, Lazarev, Kotzebue, Bellingshausen, and Lütke. They were well aware of this and understood that, scientifically, their contribution was exiguous. In 1835, the publication of the Lütke *Voyage* and associated *Atlas* brought the final curtain down upon the grand and generous, albeit nationalistic, enterprise that Kruzenshtern, Lisianskii, and their patron Count Rumiantsev had begun in 1802.[109]

And yet, for all the pattern and predictability of Russian shipping in the North and South Pacific by the later 1830s, there were elements of chance and private preference at work. Inadequately reprovisioned on Oahu for the passage round to Rio de Janeiro, von Schants elected to call in at Mo'orea (Eimeo) in the Societies, where foodstuffs were believed to be abundant. "On December 6, 1835, the island of Tahiti came in sight; but the transport was becalmed within sight of it for another four days. They finally entered Talu Bay, on the island of Eimeo, on the 10th. The King of Tahiti was there at the time."[110]

Was Captain von Schants really obliged to spend three weeks at Mo'orea? (In his despatch, he claimed that rigging problems and the lading of provisions had delayed him.) One is sceptical. Did Berens need to make a visit there, having spent twelve days and nights at Honolulu? Almost certainly, he *chose* to bring the *Nikolai* to Tahiti, or at least "to stop for a few days at one of the islands of that archipelago." *Nikolai* dropped anchor in Opunohu harbour on Mo'orea on 29 January 1839 and stayed four days. Neither she nor *Amerika* had any physicist, natural historian, or linguist aboard. No rock samples, animals, or flowers were collected, and no running surveys were made on the approaches to that island. In 1835 the Russian officers on Mo'orea were impressed by the persistence of the single British missionary there, William Henry of the Papetoai and Afareaitu stations.[111] Both *Amerika* and *Nikolai* took on fresh provisions in Opunohu harbour, at the head of which, half lost from sight beneath a thick carpet of green, stood the ruins of the Bicknell sugar-mill. In the words of the missionary historian John Davies: "It was first proposed to set up the machinery at Tahiti, but obstacles being found in the way, by the consent of the king the whole machinery, mill, boilers, etc. were removed to Eimeo . . . and a large piece of ground was inclosed, cleared, and planted with Cane. . . ."[112]

The enterprise collapsed within one year of its start (1819). When the Russians came, they found no trace of sugar, only breadfruit, bananas, lemons, oranges, pineapples, goats, chickens, and innumerable pigs. The pigs had free and easy access to the churches, where the islanders had thronged in other times but where the forest now pressed in on every side.[113]

5

THE RUSSIAN TEXTS

F.F. BELLINGSHAUSEN, 1820

At 9:00 am, we sighted from the lookout, far off to the SW, the island of Otaiti [Tahiti]. It was blue and took the form of two separate heights on the horizon. The larger ridge, that of Tahiti Nore (Great Tahiti), lay 13°30′SW from us; the smaller, belonging to Tahiti Tiarabu,[1] lay 2°20′SW as we steered. We continued on our southwesterly course under a gentle trade wind from ESE. The weather was beautiful. We were all impatient to reach the island as quickly as possible, and the wind gladdened us, blowing fresher at noon so that towards 7:00 pm we were only four miles from the island's northeastern point.[2] Although it had grown dark by then, fires burning along the shore showed the sites of the houses of those islanders so praised by Captain Cook and his fellow voyagers, Banks and Forster.

The night was dark; thick black clouds hung over the high mountains; and on the barely visible shoreline, fires twinkled. Often little waves stood out in phosphorescent belts against the dark waters. Stretching into the distance in various directions at different moments the weak glowing streaks of flying-fish would gradually fade away. In the presence of so wonderful a spectacle, we passed the whole night under small canvas, tacking in such a way as not to move away from the shore.

22 July. In the morning, we proceeded along the coast near Cape Venus [Venus Point].[3] We were all on deck and admiring the most beautiful view of the shores. The great mountains covered with forests; the deep vales; the steep cliffs; the broad, green, and level plain at the foot of the mountains covered with coconut palms, banana, and breadfruit trees, providing shade for the neat little dwellings of the natives; the yellow strip of the shoreline; the rivulets rushing down from the hills; the islanders bustling about here and there, paddling their craft or moving under sail in outrigger canoes, all these filled the heart of each one of us with the most delightful sensation. Such varied indications of well-being, in a perfect climate, inspire a peculiar feeling of confidence in the people inhabiting this beautiful country.

A European jolly boat, which had come out from the island, broke our contemplations. The men paddling were natives. The man seated in the place of honour we supposed, though we afterwards discovered our error, to be one of the missionaries who have been on this island of Tahiti since Captain Wilson arrived in the year 1797.[4] I hove to, so that the jolly boat could make fast alongside us. An individual of considerable height, thickset, with a swarthy complexion, hair cut short in front and hanging in one curl at the back like a woman's, came on board. This islander was wearing a calico shift, the lower part of which was wrapped round with another piece of calico right down to his heels. I invited him into my cabin, and he immediately went in and sat down. When I asked him, in English, what he wished to announce to me, he pulled a letter out from beneath his belt, handed it to me, and said a few words in a mangled English that I could not understand. The letter read as follows:

Tuesday Morning

Sir,
I have sent off a Pilot to conduct you in to Matavai Bay, and shall be glad to see you safe at anchor.

I am, Sir,
Yours, etc,
Pomare

Finding it hard to make out the poor English of this Tahitian, I invited Mr. Lazarev to come over; but he too understood the man's words very poorly, gathering, however, that our guest was a pilot and that there was another pilot in the jolly boat. I proposed to Mr. Lazarev that he take this pilot on board with him, announcing that we should drop anchor in Matavai Harbour behind the cape.

Having braced up, I set a course for Point Venus and we soon passed the coral reef that protects that cape on the outside from the fury of the sea, forming a sort of wall within which the natives are able to navigate without much danger of any kind. Moving on close hauled, I brought the sloop by a narrow channel into the road, between the aforementioned coral reef and a shoal situated to its west. The depth of water over this shoal is a mere two fathoms. At 10:00 am, we arrived in Matavai Bay and dropped anchor in eight fathoms, sand and mud bottom, in that very spot where Captain Wallis had had a clash with the natives on 14 June 1767, and where, on 13 April 1769, Captain Cook and the celebrated patron of science, Sir Joseph Banks, had been received with such friendliness by the very same people.[5] Soon after this, the sloop *Mirnyi*, which had rounded the shoal, was standing at anchor right beside the *Vostok*.[6]

Everywhere, the islanders were assembling along the shore and getting into their craft, a few of which were already on their way towards us. Given the brilliant sunshine and the calm sea, every object was reflected in the water as in a mirror. My pen, however, is too feeble to express the pleasure felt by the seaman who, after a protracted voyage, finds himself at anchor in a place which, even at first glance, fires the imagination. We were almost surrounded by land which presented an enchanting spectacle: the level, green plain of Matavai, with coconut palm groves and orange and lemon trees extending to the very shore; the enormous breadfruit trees towering above the coconut palms; and, to the right, the high mountains and the deep valleys of Tahiti, covered with woods and with little houses along the seashore.

We had not even taken in the sails before the Tahitians in their single and double canoes, laden with fruit, were surrounding our ships from all sides. Each one more keen than the other, they attempted to barter their oranges, lemons, coconuts, bananas, pineapples, hens, and eggs. The gentle behaviour of these natives, and their facial features so expressive of kindness of heart, had soon won our confidence. In order to preserve and not disturb these mutually amicable relations, to maintain order in the bartering for supplies and other things, and to keep the prices moderate, I entrusted Lieutenant Torson with direction of the purchasing through barter and appointed as his assistant Mr. Rezanov, who was on board *Vostok* as secretary and purser and who, in addition, had time enough to occupy himself with another matter.[7]

With the Tahitians there came out two sailors who had settled on this island and lived in their own houses. One of these men, an American named Villiam [Williams], had deserted from an American vessel, served for some time in the Russian-American Company, and knew all the officials in our colony,[8] even learning to speak Russian in the dialect of that region. He had set out in an English vessel for the island of Nukagiva [Nukuhiva], where he had married a beautiful young islander in Anna-Mariea Bay [Taio-hae].[9] Remaining there only a short while, he moved on with his wife at the first opportunity, again on an American vessel, to the tranquil island of Tahiti, whose present ruler, Pomare, received them in a friendly manner and granted him a decent plot on which to build a house. Williams now lives happily in that house, seventy-five fathoms from the shoreline, by Matavai Harbour. I took him on as interpreter aboard *Vostok*. The other sailor was an Englishman, and Mr. Lazarev took him on as interpreter aboard *Mirnyi*. They told us that the natives of the Society Islands were peaceable, well-behaved, and had all received the Christian faith.

We had prepared ourselves for the eventuality of an unfriendly reception: our cannon and firearms had been loaded, the fuses had been primed, and the sentries doubled. None of the natives had the right to board either sloop without permission, and this was granted, initially, only to chiefs. Subsequently, though, seeing the mildness and the calmness of the Tahitians, I allowed everyone without exception to come on board. In a very short time, the sloops then resembled ant-heaps: natives were crowding the decks, every man wandering fore and aft with his burden. Some would be offering fruit in hopes of selling it quickly, while others were examining articles obtained from us. I ordered that all the fruit should be purchased, not rejecting even the rather useless kava roots,[10] so that every islander could return home well pleased with his trading. We had the pleasure of seeing women, too, among the native traders and visitors. All their foodstuffs, including oranges, pineapples, lemons, Tahitian apples,[11] bananas both cultivated and wild, coconuts, breadfruit, taro roots, yams, a variety of ginger, arrowroot, kava, hens, and eggs, the islanders exchanged for glass beads, other beads, coral ornaments, little mirrors, needles, fish-hooks, knives, scissors, and so forth. We piled everything we had acquired in one corner and our people were allowed to eat as much as they cared to have.

At 1:00 pm, we were visited by Mr. Not [Nott], an English missionary who had arrived in the Society Islands together with Captain Wilson and his men in 1797. Since that time, Mr. Nott had continuously preached Christianity to the natives on these islands.[12] He told us that the king was coming on board the sloops. We were, all of us, most anxious to see him, and so everyone rushed to the gangway, repeating the phrase, "Here he comes!" The double canoe on which the king was seated approached slowly. On the horizontal, projecting fore part of the canoe, which resembled a drake's bill, a scaffold and seat had been erected. The king was seated upon it. Over a short calico shirt, Pomare wore a piece of white material with an opening in it, through which his head passed. The points of this cloth hung down, before and behind. The lower part of his body was wrapped with another piece of white calico, from the belt right down to the feet. His hair was cut very short in front, but at the back of the head it fell, twisted in a single hanging tress, from crown to nape. His face was swarthy, with deep-set black eyes under thick black eyebrows and a knit brow. He had thick lips and a black moustache, and his colossal stature gave him a truly regal appearance.

In the stern of the canoe, under an awning rather like the hood of our *ki-bitka*,[13] sat the queen, her ten-year-old daughter, her sister, and a number of comely women. The queen was covered from breast to feet by thin white material, over which another piece of the same stuff was thrown like a shawl. Her hair was cut short and her face was protected by a shade fashioned from fresh coconut leaves, plaited as we might make an eye-shade, to protect her eyes against very bright light. Her pleasant dark face was embellished by lively little eyes and a small mouth. She was of middling height, slender waisted and with well-shaped limbs, perhaps twenty-five years of age. Her name was Tire-Vagine [Tiara Vahine].[14] The daughter wore a European printed calico dress; her sister, a dress like hers except that, unlike the queen's, it was striped in a motley way. Their retinue consisted of a few attractive girls. All the other women were also in white or yellow dresses with red patterns on them, resembling leaves, and like all the other islanders they wore on their head green shades plaited from fresh leaves.[15] The paddlers were seated at their places and had small paddles.[16] The distance from the shore was not great and the canoes soon reached the *Vostok*. The king came on board first, extending his hand to me but waiting on the gangway until his entire family was also aboard. I invited them to my cabin and they sat on the divans. The king repeated several times the word, "Russian!" then pronounced the name Alexander, and finally, having added "Napoleon," he began to laugh. He wished to show by this, of course, that he was familiar with European affairs. The queen, her sister, and the other girls were meanwhile examining everything, and their fingers were also occupied: they felt the material covering the divans and chairs, and even felt our pocket handkerchiefs.

Mr. Nott, who knew the Tahitian language perfectly, did us the kindness of acting as interpreter during our conversation with the king. I invited the latter to dine with us, apologizing for a lack of fresh food and observing that all was salted. The king willingly acceded to my request and, smiling, said, "I know that fish are always caught inshore and not in the depths of the ocean." We sat at table in order of precedence. The king occupied the place of honour, with his queen to his right, then Messrs. Nott and Lazarev, while on his left side sat his daughter and I. The queen's sister did not see fit to eat at table with us, but selected a convenient spot for herself on the deck and there nursed the little heir to the throne of the Society Islands. The king and his whole family ate everything with zest and punctually drank off their wine, too. Since our water had been brought from Port Jackson and was consequently not very fresh, the king ordered one islander to serve coconut milk. And that native, having brought some coconuts to us, very expertly broke their tops with a small hammer. Meanwhile, the king, who had been drinking wine mixed with water, was continually wiping the sweat from his good-natured face.

When he drank wine neat, he would every time propose someone's health, in the English manner, nodding his head and clinking glasses. Having dined, he asked for a cigar, smoked, and drank coffee. Meanwhile, he had observed that Mr. Mikhailov had been stealthily drawing him (see Plate 10). In order to keep him calm, I handed him my own portrait, done by Mr. Mikhailov. He then expressed a wish to be sketched holding that other portrait in his hand. I said in reply that if he wished to be drawn holding anybody's portrait in hand, I would give him an incomparably more suitable one. Then I presented him with a silver medallion on which was engraved a likeness of His Majesty the Emperor, Alexander I, with which he was duly pleased. Portraits of the king and his wife are to be found in the *Atlas*.[17]

While Mr. Mikhailov was sketching Pomare, the queen took her infant son from her sister and fed him at the breast in front of everyone there, without the least embarrassment. From this it is evident that on Tahiti mothers are still not ashamed of breastfeeding their babies before other people and openly fulfil their most tender duty. I then led the king onto the deck, there showed him the cannon, cables, and other objects of interest, and there and then ordered that a fifteen-gun salute should be fired, in his honour. He was highly delighted by this mark of attention, but as each shot was fired, he held my arm and hid behind me.

After dinner, we were visited by the king's chief secretary, Paofai; his brother Khitota [Hitoti], (whom they regard as an excellent military leader);[18] and one of the local officials, the keeper of the general store of coconut oil, collected for the benefit of the Bible Society. Each of these guests of mine, as soon as he found himself alone with me, would assure me that he was my true friend and would then ask for a pocket handkerchief, or a shirt, or an axe, or a knife. First of all, I gave them each a silver medal. Then I obliged them in other ways, for I had on board many objects of various sorts that were meant specifically to be used as gifts or in barter for foodstuffs, so that no refusals were necessary. But these grandees preferred grog to ordinary Teneriffe wine, no doubt because the strength of the grog depended upon their own discretion.

At 5:00 pm, another royal craft came out to us, bringing gifts from Pomare consisting of four large pigs, a great quantity of coconuts, ground coconut kernels wrapped in leaves, some breadfruit, both cooked and raw, baked yams and taro roots, ordinary and mountain bananas,[19] some Tahitian apples, and a few sugar canes. From practically not having anything fresh apart from the few rather unattractive looking fowls that had remained from the voyages and that had been plucking out each other's feathers and tails, we now suddenly found ourselves extraordinarily well off: for the king's gifts were added to the quantity of edible supplies that we had already acquired through barter, so that we were even hard pressed to find space for them and time to stow them all away. Such abundance of everything and such friendly behaviour on the part of the Tahitians delighted our sailors. They were continually shaking hands with the natives and repeating the word, "*Yurana*! [Welcome!]."

At 6:00 pm, the king sent the queen and all those in her party ashore in the double canoe but remained on board himself. All the other islanders also dispersed. When it was quite dark and Pomare had expressed the wish to return to shore, I ordered that my cutter should be prepared, with Midshipman Demidov at the helm. I also ordered that two blue lights[20] should be lit at the bow of the cutter to illuminate it. On parting with me, the king asked that a bottle of rum be placed in the cutter and told me that rum was manufactured on his island and that much in fact could be produced. Since the Tahitians who drank strong spirits became unruly, however, he had altogether prohibited the drinking of rum, despite the fact that he himself was among its greatest devotees.[21] As the cutter pulled away from the sloop, one of the two blue lights was lit immediately, for the entertainment of the king, and twenty-two rockets were fired, some of them star rockets.

On his return, Mr. Demidov told me that the cutter had landed behind Point Venus right opposite the royal residence, and that the king had been very pleased by this, asked Demidov to wait a little, and had returned with gifts. He himself gave Mr. Demidov eight fathoms of Tahitian material and each of the oarsmen received four fathom lengths of the same stuff, which is made from the bark of the breadfruit tree.[22]

23 July. Scarcely had the sun's rays touched the masts before the islanders were again striving to be the first to reach us in their fruit-laden craft. Since we now needed some space in order to stretch the standing rigging, however, the islanders embarrassed us a good deal on board and were even likely to hinder us in that work. It was in order to avert that eventuality that I ordered Mr. Rezanov to take an assortment of things into a boat, pull away a little behind our stern, and there conduct barter. And I ordered that only the ranking chiefs, or *eri* [*ari'i*], should now be permitted on board the sloop. By this means, we prevented a great concourse of people on the deck and deflected them to a spot behind our stern, where various craft crammed with natives of both sexes soon encircled our boat. All did their best to barter their wares. What we principally acquired through this bartering were hens and lemons. I intended to preserve the latter for later use as an anti-scorbutic among my crew when we were in high Southern latitudes.[23]

At 8:00 am, I went ashore with Mr. Lazarev to visit the king, his secretary Paofai, and Mr. Nott. We went first to Mr. Nott's house on the shore.

It stood facing the bay. We found the master of the house in, and he introduced us to his wife. The young Englishwoman had grown accustomed
to her solitary life. Although not a beauty, she had the gift of relieving the
tedium of her husband's existence.[24] Having left England, neither of them
has any desire to return to their native land: both consider themselves happier in Tahiti.

Mr. Nott placed us under an obligation by undertaking to escort us to
the king. We proceeded along the sandy shore to Venus Point, where we
found Messrs. Mikhailov and Simonov surrounded by a great number of
islanders of both sexes and all ages. Mr. Mikhailov was busy sketching a
view of Matavai Harbour, while Mr. Simonov was busy checking the
chronometers on the very spot where Captain Cook and Messrs. Banks
and Green had, fifty-one years before, observed the transit of Venus and
so been able to determine the longitude of this cape with such precision. I
invited Mr. Mikhailov to walk with us, in hopes that he would see objects
worthy of his brush.[25] From here we had to cross a stream that flows down
from the mountains and, winding onto the Matavai Plain, debouches into
the sea. An old woman standing on the other side of the stream[26] waded
into the water right up to her knees, at Mr. Nott's request, and pushed toward us a boat, in which she dragged us to the far bank. As a recompense
for her labour, she received two strings of beads, with which she was well
pleased.

We stepped ashore on the other side and straight into a coconut grove.
Despite the fact that the sun stood very high in the sky, the thickness of
the palms' foliage was such that its rays penetrated only rarely here and
there, forming parallel, oblique shafts of light in the air. In the shade of
these tall palms, we walked up to the king's house. It was surrounded by
an enclosure of boards two and a half feet high.

We climbed over this by means of thick posts, which had been well
driven into the ground on either side and reached half-way up the enclosure, which was needed to protect the house from swine. These wander
here as they will, feeding on fruit fallen from trees and on coconuts. Having walked a few steps further, we passed through the house itself, which
was some seven fathoms long and five fathoms wide. The roof rests on
three rows of wooden columns. The central row is raised perpendicular to
the ground, but the two outer ones, which are not more than six feet in
height, incline inwards and are covered with mats. The roof consists of
two smooth sloping surfaces, covered with leaves from the tree called
faro.[27] In the chambers along either side stood broad bedsteads of the European type, which were covered with yellow blankets.

From this house, we again stepped over the enclosure onto the other
side, where, near a small hut, the king and his family were seated cross-

PLATE 1

Débarquement à travers les Récifs de l'Isle de Romanzoff (Landing over the reefs at Romanzoff [Tikei] Island). This piece by *Riurik*'s artist, Ludovik Choris, shows the events of 21 April 1816 as the Russians make their awkward landing on Tikei atoll in the Central Tuamotus. Lithographed in Paris by de Bovet, it appeared as Plate X in Choris's *Vues et paysages des régions équinoxiales* (Paris 1826). The flag is the cross of St. Andrew, flown by ships of the Russian Imperial Navy and, by special concession, in *Riurik* also, even though she was the private property of Count Nikolai Petrovich Rumiantsev, for whom Kotzebue named Tikei.

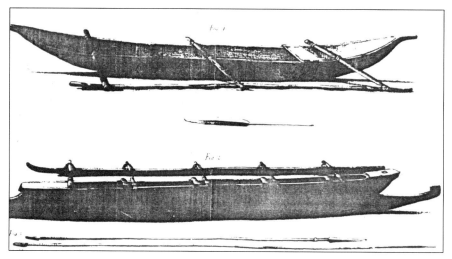

PLATE 2

Bateau à Rames de L'Isle de Romanzoff (Rowed boat of Romanzoff Island), with paddle at centre. Plate XII in Choris's first published record of his voyage in *Voyage pittoresque autour du monde* (Paris 1822).

PLATE 3

Ludovik Choris, or Khoris (1795-1828), artist aboard *Riurik* on her Pacific expedition (1815-18), friend of Chamisso, and expatriate after 1819. Lithograph by Langlumé of Paris (1821).

PLATE 4

Sheet R-29070 in the Mikhailov Portfolio held at the State Russian Museum in St. Petersburg. It shows, among others, the heads of two Tuamotuans encountered by *Vostok* on the southern shores of Kaukura atoll on 19 July 1820 and details of tattooing (*nanako*) designs. The upper part of the sheet shows the northern coastline of Rapa Island, in the Austral Group.

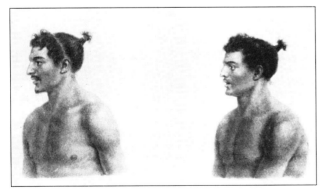

PLATE 5

Natives of the Coral Island of Count Arakcheev: Plate 47 in the Album held at the State Historical Museum (SHM), published in the *Atlas* (1831) accompanying Bellingshausen's narrative *Dvukratnye izyskaniia*. The pictures of the men were drawn off Angatau atoll on 10 July 1820.

PLATE 6

View of the Coral Island of Moller [Amanu] in the Alexander the First Archipelago: Plate 29 in the 1831 *Atlas*, based on Sheet R-29285 in the Mikhailov Portfolio. The latter, measuring 26.6 by 38 cm, contains sharper ethnographical data than the Fridrits lithograph, and offers a very lively picture of the Russians' hostile reception by the people of Amanu atoll on 8 July 1820 (see *Dvukratnye izyskaniia*, p. 253).

PLATE 7

Natives of the Coral Island of Nigera [Nihiru], published in the 1831 *Atlas* but missing from the SHM Album in Moscow. The chief and his two attendants were met by *Vostok* on 13 July 1820, and Bellingshausen himself comments on Mikhailov's drawing (*Dvukratnye izyskaniia*, p. 260).

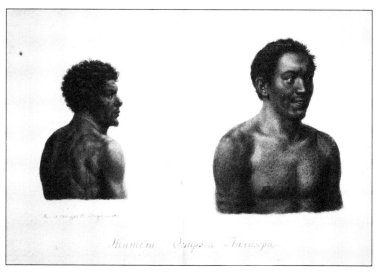

PLATE 8

Natives of the Palizer [Palliser] Island: Plate 33 in the 1831 *Atlas*. These portraits were worked up by Mikhailov in 1822-24, on the basis of his sketches on R-29070 (see Plate 4 here). The man on the right was named Balisair, to judge from the artist's pencilled annotation.

PLATE 9

Pavel Nikolaevich Mikhailov (1786-1840). This portrait was painted by Anton M. Legashev, ca. 1830 (Tret'iakov Gallery, Moscow, No. 206).

PLATE 10

Pomari, King of O-Taiti. Mikhailov's celebrated portrait of Pomare II, begun on 22 July 1820 in *Vostok*'s wardroom and published in Bellingshausen's 1831 *Atlas* as Plate 35. The king wears a European calico shirt beneath his *tiputa*.

PLATE 11

The Breakfast of the King of O-Taiti: Plate 36 in the 1831 *Atlas*. The Reverend Henry Nott sits with visiting Russian officers, in their heavy full-dress uniforms, facing King Pomare II, his wife Teremo'emo'e, and probably her sister, Pomare Vahine. The air temperature was 82°F. The menu included baked suckling pig dipped in sea water, fresh breadfruit, and crushed breadfruit with coconut. The royal sleeping hut, at right, was part of a compound or complex of structures very near the site of Cook's Fort Venus, near Te-auroa at the northeast end of Matavai Bay.

PLATE 12

A View of the Island of O-Taiti [Otaheite] from Point Venus: Plate 37 in the 1831 *Atlas*. Mikhailov faced south-southwest, so that Cook's "One Tree Hill" (Mount Taharaa) would lie at the centre of his composition. A large canoe shed at the far left balances the activity of several types of canoes to the right. Tahitians wear *ahu* and eyeshades.

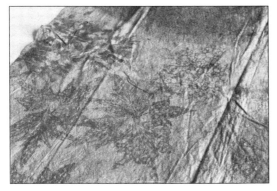

PLATE 13

upper Detail of fern-leaf patterns on *tiputa* No. 737-1.
lower Detail of "dull red spots" covering the surface of MAE's tapa specimen No. 737-21. Both pieces are of late eighteenth-century origin. The former was brought from Tahiti by the English shipmaster and adventurer Captain Henry Barber.

PLATE 14

upper Detail of patterning imprinted by a leaf on tapa No. 737-2.
lower Detail of Tahitian appliqué in multi-layered bark cloth.

PLATE 15

upper Detail of a soft, flexible Tahitian mat (No. 736-248) presented to Bellingshausen as a gift for Tsar Alexander I, by King Pomare II of Tahiti (1820).

lower An eyeshade, No. 736-230 at MAE, worn by Tahitians on a daily basis and made almost as frequently.

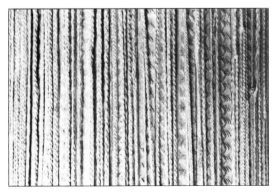

PLATE 16

upper Detail of the grooving on two working faces of a Tahitian tapa beater (No. 3117-271) of the variety seen in use by the men of *Vostok* and *Mirny* at Matavai Bay.

lower Detail of the sennit lashing on the outer walls of a large Tahitian drum (*pahu nui*), with traces of pink ochre (No. 736-231 at MAE).

PLATE 17

upper Detail of sennit lashing and carving at the base of *pahu nui* No. 736-231. The drum has a shark skin top and was collected at Matavai Bay in 1820.
lower Example of Tahitian stone-tool carving on the base of the drum.

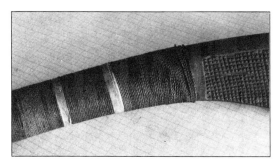

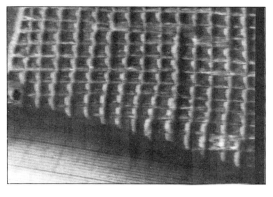

PLATE 18

upper Section of the haft and part of the striking portion of a Tahitian breadfruit or coconut splitter (No. 736-164 at MAE).
lower Magnified view of portion of this splitter's working end, with transverse, sharp-edged grooves.

legged on mats spread on the ground. They were breakfasting on suckling-pig, dipping the meat into sea-water that had been poured into smoothly fashioned coconut shells. All those breakfasting passed food from hand to hand, ate with great appetite, and licked their fingers. (Among the princes of Abkhazia's people, who live on the eastern shore of the Black Sea, dinner is eaten similarly. Those dining sit in a large circle on the ground and attentively watch every movement of the prince, who is dividing up a sheep, so as not to fail to catch the piece that is thrown to each man in turn.)[28] The bones that remained were being thrown to a dog. Instead of water they drank coconut milk from a nut, having skilfully broken off the top with a little axe. To the left of this spot, a native was preparing other food from breadfruit and coconuts, while to the right of the house itself stood assorted domestic implements.

Having first shaken hands with us, the king said "*Yurana.*" And on his orders, we were brought low stools, whose legs were no more than six inches long, and each of us was served a glass goblet full of fresh coconut milk. This cooling drink is also a most delicious one. Our conversation was most conventional: were we well, how did we like Tahiti, and so forth. Meanwhile, Mr. Mikhailov had moved some six paces off to one side and was drawing the whole party at breakfast. Other islanders surrounded him, laughing heartily and describing each new figure, as it was depicted, to the king. When breakfast was over, the king washed his hands and left us with the queen. Returning, he took me by the arm and led me into a small hut, about fourteen feet wide and twenty-eight long. This hut was divided halfway along its length by a partition. The part that we entered served as a study. A double bed stood against one wall, and by the other, on several shelves, lay English books and a rolled up map of the world. Beneath these shelves stood a trunk fitted with a lock and a redwood box, presented by the English Bible Society.[29]

I noticed that the presence of Mr. Nott did not please the king and that the latter now hastened to shut the door. Then he showed me his watch, map, exercise book for the rudiments of geometry—he was studying this from an English book and clearly understood it, copying it into his exercise book in the Tahitian tongue—and took out from a box an inkstand, a pen, and a scrap of paper. This he handed to me, with the request that I write in Russian that the bearer of the note should be given a bottle of rum. I wrote that the bearer should receive three bottles of rum and six bottles of Teneriffe wine. At this moment Mr. Nott and Mr. Lazarev came in. The king became confused, quickly hid the note, ink, paper, and geometry book, and changed the conversation. Having spent a little while longer with the king, we followed Mr. Nott along a winding path in the shade of a grove of orange and lemon trees. These fruit-bearing trees grow in a favourable climate here, under the open sky, just as do other trees, without the least attention on the natives' part.

We saw a number of neat little houses and went into one of them, which stood open. There was no one in the house. In the middle stood a double bed covered with a yellow bedspread—very tidy. A copy of the Gospel had been placed above the bed-head. A small, low footstool, a stone with which they scrape coconut shells, and a few cleaned shells comprised all the domestic utensils of these happy islanders. As for their food stores, they are ready on trees almost constantly, year round; when they need some, they pick them. There is no need whatever to lay in stores or to save for some future time. The owners of this particular house were evidently convinced of the security of their property and of everybody else's, and had left their dwelling with perfect confidence in their neighbours' honesty. Where, other than on the isle of Tahiti, could one do this and not afterwards regret it?

Having gone a little further down this same path, among bushes and small trees, we reached the church. It was built in the same way as the king's residence: in the middle, a passage ran its whole length between wooden benches placed on either side; and to one side a pulpit stood on four posts, some five feet in height, surrounded by a hand rail, whence the missionary preached the word of God. All in all, the church resembled a Reformed church in its internal arrangement.[30]

From the church, we went out to the shoreline, where, proceeding a half a mile to the east, we reached the house of Secretary Paofai. Posts driven into the earth enabled us, as before, to get over a low board enclosure. One side of the house faced the shoreline, and inside we caught sight of a beautiful young Tahitian woman, Paofai's wife, sitting with her friends on mats spread on the ground. She was breastfeeding her baby. All these women were dressed very cleanly in white Tahitian clothing, with flowers behind their ears. Paofai was not at home. Mr. Nott showed us a very clean sleeping chamber, in which stood a double bedstead with a yellow bedspread with red patterns on it and a small table on which lay a box. At his request, the good-natured mistress of the house opened this box and showed us the book that was kept in it. In that book, all noteworthy matters are recorded, in the Tahitian language, in an excellent hand. Mr. Nott praised the abilities of this islander very highly; and posterity will certainly be obliged to him for such a good beginning of a history of the Society Islands. His name will not be forgotten in the annals of Tahiti.[31] On taking my leave, I presented Paofai's wife with several pairs of earrings and gave one pair each to her friends. They seemed pleased with our visit and our gifts and, having examined the earrings, put them on.

It was already past noon, and we set off back by the same path, the route being somewhat shortened by the islanders' carrying us across the stream on their shoulders. At Mr. Nott's house, we rested and refreshed ourselves with coconut milk. This liquid, when fresh, seems to be the very best of all known beverages for dealing with fatigue on a sultry day. On Cape Venus we met Messrs. Zavadovskii and Simonov, the former having come ashore for a stroll after a serious illness that had begun as a chill and had lasted forty days. He had wanted to enjoy the balmy air of the shoreline in the shade of palms and the flowering trees. At Venus Point, we embarked in the cutter and so returned to the sloop *Vostok*.

After dinner, the king came out to us with his whole family and retainers. Although I had in fact ordered that only chiefs were to be permitted on board, it proved impossible to execute the order, for the chiefs themselves brought out other natives whom they named as their friends and whom they asked us to admit also. Many such guests assembled in the course of the day; and we regaled them in the usual way. There was not one Tahitian, man or woman, who did not drink grog with great pleasure. The decanters, indeed, were rather often drained, and on each such occasion I would instruct my servant Mishka to refill them. Not infrequently, though, we would leave the decanters empty for quite some time, so as not to find ourselves conversing with drunk islanders. The desire to drink exceeded their patience. The king and several chiefs began to shout out, "Missa! Missa!" and when he came to their summons, they would point out that the decanters were empty. He would carry them off quickly but would return with them slowly, and even then with very diluted grog. The chiefs disliked him for such craftiness, considering him extremely mean. When, in response to a request, I gave them some gift, or rather told someone else to do it, they would be delighted; but when I instructed my servant to present them with something or other, dissatisfaction would spread across their faces and they would repeat, "Missa! Missa!" In this way, he drew down upon himself the unfavourable opinion of the nobility of the island of Tahiti.[32]

On this day, I presented to the king the two boys who had joined me at the island of Matea [Makatea]. He questioned them and laughed and teased them when they recalled with horror how they had been chased by cannibals and made all those grimaces which islanders usually do at their feasts when a captive is being eaten. With the aid of Williams, the interpreter, we better ascertained the true causes of the adventure and mishap of the four boys. They had been carried by a high wind from Anna [Anaa] Island to Matea, and there had been ten in the party. But shortly afterwards, canoes had arrived there from the island of Tai, whose natives are called Vageitu.[33] These newcomers killed all those who had arrived before them and, in view of the perpetual enmity between the natives, devoured them, with the exception of the four boys who had saved themselves by hiding among the bushes of the island's interior. The natives of Tai, seeing no more enemies, then departed. Spotting the approach of European vessels, the boys had been overjoyed, for they had heard from their relations that Europeans treat people kindly and do not eat them. So they hurried to the cape and made signals, in order to be seen from the vessels. I gave them the choice of staying aboard the sloop or remaining in Tahiti. As soon as they expressed a wish to remain on the island, I entrusted the elder boy to Paofai's protection and the younger to the care of Paofai's brother, the general. Mr. Lazarev left the two boys that he had brought to the care of two other chiefs. The boys had found some of their countrymen from Anna on Tahiti, and they were delighted to see them. The eldest boy brought one of these natives to me, telling me that the man also came from Anna Island. When I expressed some doubt, the boy pointed out tattooing on the man's body that was exactly like the tattoo on his own and like that which I had seen myself on the thighs of the man who had come out to us from the island of Nigiru [Nihiru]. From this, I conclude that the craft of the latter island had come, for trade of some kind, from Anna Island.

Towards 8:00 pm, the number of our guests increased considerably. In order to keep them amused, I ordered that twenty rockets of various sorts should be sent up from the stern. During this spectacle, the king was continually hiding behind me. At the close of the entertainment, everyone dispersed well pleased. Taking their leave of us, they called out many times, "*Yurana! Yurana!*"

Mr. Zavadovskii and the other officers who had been ashore this day could not speak too highly of the islanders' honesty and friendly behaviour. Each of them had tried to be of service to our shipmates and to act as their guide. Mr. Demidov remained ashore all day to fill the casks with fresh water, having landed with the cutter right on the sandy seashore a half mile to the south of Cape Venus. The stream runs parallel with the shore there, at a distance inland of sixty fathoms, so that the casks could be filled very easily. Tahitian boys would most willingly wade into the little river, fill the casks, and bring them to the shore.[34] Our seamen had then no more to do than carry the barrels to the boats and had hardly time to go to the sloop and back before more barrels were waiting. The islanders showed our people the greatest good will and hospitality, inviting them into nearby houses and regaling them with coconuts and oranges.

Messrs. Nott and Lazarev came out to breakfast with me aboard the sloop *Vostok* next morning at 8:00 am, soon after which they and I set out for the shore in order to inspect the site of a former *morai*. (*Morai* is the name given by natives of the South Pacific Ocean to places and structures where they bury their dead and offer sacrifices.)[35] The site lay some two and a half miles to the west of Venus Point. The sea being calm, we soon covered that distance and landed our boat in the harbour of Toarkho [Taunoa], where Captain Bligh had stood at anchor in 1788.[36] Not having reached the *morai*, we halted at the so-called royal church. It was surrounded by an enclosure some two and a half feet high and the ground around it was paved with stones. Mr. Nott ordered that the doors should be opened and the shutters, too; and we went into quite a large building, seventy feet in length and fifty feet across with a roof supported by three rows of pillars made from trunks of breadfruit trees. The central row was perpendicular, the outer two inclined inward and were only half the height of it. The upper ends of the posts at the extremities had been carved, to a depth of six inches, to resemble forks. A stout beam had been laid in these clefts and ran the entire length of the building. The middle row of posts supported joists, and rafters, set on edge, extended from the middle row and from the joists that were likewise set on edge, to the outer rows. Poles of a lighter wood had been laid across these and skilfully bound together with ropes made of coconut palm and breadfruit fibres. This roof was also covered with leaves from the *faro* tree. The building is semicircular at both its ends. Everything is held together by ropes of various colours instead of nails or iron clamps, and everything has been done very skilfully and attractively. The sides of the building are faced with boards and there are elongated windows, fitted with shutters, through which light is admitted. At the northern end, there were three raised platforms, each resting on four pillars, for the priests. Benches had been arranged across the church in rows, double, leaving a central passage just as in the church already described here. The interior had been decorated in the Tahitian manner with particoloured materials that somehow, attached to the rafters and joists, comprised an unusual but pleasing embellishment.

This large building had been so constructed as to be light yet strong; it contained nothing superfluous or heavy, and it had no lacks or shortcomings. In itself, this serves as proof of the islanders' native ingenuity and taste. Mr. Nott led us to the spot where earlier a *morai* had stood, a huge structure erected with great labour, which Captain Cook had described.[37] We were much surprised to find only a pile of stones. On converting to Christianity, the islanders had destroyed the *morai*.[38]

After this, we proceeded westward along the shore in the shade of coconut palms and fragrant breadfruit trees. We had gone a mile or so when we spotted an old man of great height in a little open hut by the seashore. He was seated on clean mats spread on the ground and was dressed in white cloth. The pallor of his face and his sunken eyes and cheeks all indicated that he had long been suffering from some disease. His children surrounded him. An older daughter was about thirteen years old, a son was perhaps five. On his instruction, they offered us low benches and we sat down. Mr. Nott explained to him that we were captains of armed sloops belonging to the Russian Emperor Alexander and that we were on a voyage across the South Seas to find unknown lands. The old man asked if we wished to refresh ourselves with a drink and to eat, being weary, but we gratefully declined. Still, he ordered that fresh coconuts should be brought. A servant, having broken off the top of each shell with a small axe specially made for the purpose, then handed each of us a coconut. The cool milk quenched our thirst and restored our strength. On leaving, I gave the daughter a mirror and several strings of multicoloured beads and gave the son a little mirror and a small knife. The old man, whose name was Menono, loved his children and an expression of gratitude appeared on his pallid face for our kindness toward them. Menono governs the island and is the highest ranking grandee after the king. He sits in his little hut by the seashore solely in order to enjoy the cooling breeze that blows from the sea during the day. We saw a number of small cannon and one twenty-four pounder carronade in his shed.[39]

On our way back to the cutter, we followed a path to a large shed where a double canoe was being built. The lower part was made of a single tree, of the species called *apope*, which is felled on the mountains. The upper part of a canoe here is fashioned from breadfruit timber, which the natives make into boards that are then bound tightly together with ropes and caulked with pitch. Instead of planes, they use pieces of coral to finish the wood. In this same shed, there were a good many sections of bamboo, two and a half feet long and two or two and a half inches in diameter, in which the natives store the coconut oil offered to help the spread of Christianity by contributing to the costs of printing Bibles and so forth. Mr. Nott was just then expecting a vessel from Port Jackson with barrels into which the oil could be poured and so shipped on to London. Besides the oil, the islanders also provide the gift of a good deal of arrowroot.[40]

Reaching the cutter again, we set off to the sloop *Vostok*. The wind and current were both coming thence and, going against the stream here, we were amazed by the quantity of orange peel that had been cast overboard from our two sloops and was floating about. It was consoling to know that our crews had enjoyed such an abundance of fruit.

Whilst we had been looking over the royal church, Mr. Zavadovskii had gone to call on Paofai and had found all the latter's household busy with various forms of handicraft. Some had been colouring materials, others had been repairing stuffs by patching them with pieces of the same material from the underside, and others again had been preparing the red paint that they obtain from little berries containing yellow juice. This juice is squeezed from the berries onto green leaves, which are then wrapped around it and worked with the fingers until, in a very short space of time, the juice becomes a red colouring substance. These berries are the size of our cherries and are yellowish-red in colour.[41] One good-natured mistress of the house also demonstrated how they glue their materials together. The glue, a sort of starch, is extracted from arrowroot, which closely resembles the potato externally but is rather more yellow in hue. The natives first soak arrowroot then prepare the sticky paste, which looks like starch. The young and beautiful housewife regaled Messrs. Zavadovskii and Mikhailov, in the Tahitian way, with fresh coconut milk. Each man made her presents, on parting, in return for her kind hospitality.

Towards dinner time, the king and all his retainers again came out to *Vostok*. After the meal, he expressed a desire to visit Mr. Lazarev aboard *Mirnyi*, so the royal double canoe was brought alongside us. The women settled in the stern portion, while Pomare, several chiefs, two officers and I took places on the fore platform of the craft. Although the sea was as smooth as a mirror, the canoe was barely able to remain afloat because of the great number of corpulent people aboard. Mr. Lazarev received his guests and took them into his cabin, where he regaled them with their favourite beverage—grog. The king had soon grown hungry again, however, and ordered some baked taro roots and yams to be served from the stern of his canoe. Seeing this, Mr. Lazarev ordered that a few roasted hens should also be served, and all his guests ate them most heartily despite the fact that they had dined only recently aboard *Vostok*.

The queen, finding an opportunity to be alone with Mr. Lazarev, asked him to give her a bottle of rum; and when he replied that he had already ordered that the rum be sent to the king, she said: "He drinks it all himself and doesn't offer me a drop." After this, orders were given that two bottles of rum should be given to her. When our guests had examined the cannon on the sloop *Mirnyi*, it was the recoil after the shots that most entertained them.

Because of the great number of guests coming out from the shore, I soon returned to *Vostok*. We treated all these officials and their wives to tea, chocolate, and jam: but again they preferred grog to anything else. When any one of them succeeded in getting a word with me alone, he would assure me that he was my true friend and then ask for a present, despite the fact that he had already received gifts from me.

This custom derives from the time of Captain Cook and, more particularly, from the fact that Cook and Messrs. Banks, Forster, Green, Wallis, and many other officers had each, of necessity, his particular friends, who took care of him and would not allow any of the other islanders to injure or insult him.[42] Since that period and still today, Tahitians see the great advantage of being a European's friend, specifically in order to get presents; and on meeting you, the first thing they will say in English is: "You are my friend," and then "Give me a handkerchief!"

Barter was continuing in its usual way, meanwhile, only the natives were now bringing out fewer fowls and demanding a higher price for them. As for pigs, of which there were a great many on the island, we could not purchase a single one, for the following reason: the king had placed a prohibition or taboo on them. On the island of Eimeo, the missionaries had built a small brig.[43] The king had considered that he had a share in this vessel, because the timber and other necessary aid had been provided by him. But when the brig was finished, it had been suggested to him that he buy it outright for seventy tons of pork. Pomare had agreed to this proposition and had then forbidden his subjects to eat or to sell pigs.

25 July. On Sunday, the sun was already high in the sky but not a single islander had come out to us, to our great surprise. Our interpreter Williams then explained to us that they were all in church. As soon as all work on both sloops was done, we let half of the crews of each one go ashore to wash their linen and then to take a walk if they wished. Messrs. Zavadovskii, Lazarev, I, and almost all the officers of both sloops went to the church. On disembarking, we saw only children around the houses, all the adult islanders having gone off to the service. When we arrived there, the church was already full. The queen moved up a little and made room for me to sit down. All the natives were very neatly dressed in their best white and yellow attire, used on festive days; almost all of them had the umbrella-like headgear, and the women wore in addition red or white flowers over the ear. All were attentively listening to the Christian teaching of Mr. Nott, who spoke with particular feeling. Coming out of the church, the natives greeted us and then dispersed to their own dwellings, while we went off to the cutter. After dinner, the officers of both sloops again went ashore and were received kindly and treated to coconut milk. Some of the natives were even not accepting any gifts because it was Sunday. Such strict observance of the religious law regarding the Sabbath, in a people whose former savage and unbridled ways cannot entirely have faded from memory, must surely be regarded as exemplary.

26 July. During our barter on this day, the natives especially asked for earrings, which at first they had declined to accept at all, considering them useless. But since earrings can be carried easily in the pockets, I had, each time I had gone ashore, brought a few pairs with me and made gifts of them to the womenfolk of the nobility; and they had worn them from the ears. The other islanders, seeing the ornaments and wishing to emulate the nobles in their attire and customs, came now themselves or sent their relatives to exchange goods, above all for our earrings. As a result, our bartering was most profitable on this day and we finally ran out of earrings altogether despite the fact that we had brought many.[44]

The king and all those with him again dined with us. After dinner he presented me with three pearls a little larger than peas, asking me to point out to him those gifts that I intended to send to him. He had actually seen those articles several times already. Still, he asked that they not be sent ashore until his agent arrived on board, and not sent before darkness fell, so that none of his subjects would be able to see them. Pomare most likely feared that his officials, seeing our gifts, might want to have some of them or would envy his exceptional wealth in newly acquired European articles. The presents in question consisted of red cloth, woollen blankets, Flemish linen, striped ticking, motley kerchiefs, cotton prints of various patterns, mirrors, folding-knives, adzes, drills, and glassware. All these objects were among the stores provided for us by the Admiralty for distribution as gifts among the peoples of the Pacific Ocean. Pomare mostly felt the need for white calico, both fine and coarse,[45] because his clothing consisted entirely of such material. For want of calico, I was obliged to make him a present of some of our bed sheets, with which he was in fact more delighted than with the other things. All these gifts went ashore to him when it was dark.

27 July. The king and all the other islanders knew that we had already taken on water and were quite ready to sail, and so from morning onward they all hastened out to exchange something, bringing various artefacts along that we duly took from them in barter and which we later presented to the museum of the State Admiralty Department.[46] In the course of our stay at Tahiti, we had acquired a sufficient quantity of oranges and lemons to pickle ten barrels of them for each sloop. There can be no doubt that such fruit serves as an anti-scorbutic. We still had quite a large quantity of other foodstuffs left over, too, although every man had had the liberty to eat as much as he wished. We also had a fair number of hens left. On this day, the king and his whole retinue came out. He handed me a present for His Majesty the Emperor, with these words: "Although there are many finer things in Russia, this large mat is the work of my subjects, and for this reason I am sending it." Then Pomare made presents to all our officers. He put two pearls in Mr. Zavodovskii's pocket and gave him, in addition, a large piece of white material. He likewise gave native stuffs to Messrs. Torson, Leskov, and the other officers who, for their part, did their best to reciprocate the show of gratitude by giving the king various things.

At my request, Pomare kept a promise he had made, and sent six pigs out to *Vostok* and four to *Mirnyi*, together with quantities of fruit and roots suitable for use on the voyage. And the interpreter Williams too, notwithstanding the ban, sent four pigs out to *Vostok*, for which, and for his services as our interpreter, I paid him generously with European articles and clothing, as well as with powder and lead since he had a gun. During my final encounter with the king, I made him happy by dressing his faithful servant in a red Lifeguard Hussar's uniform and hanging my old naval sword across the man's shoulder. This gift was extremely pleasant for the servant, of course, who at once occupied himself with his new apparel.

On this day, all the chiefs came to call on us, each one bringing me a present of a piece of material. I gave them in return cotton prints, glassware, iron pots, knives, drills, etc. In addition, I gave silver medals to all the native functionaries and bronze medals to the commoners, explaining through Mr. Nott that they were given as souvenirs and that on one side was engraved the face of the Emperor Alexander, by whom we had been sent, and on the obverse face of the medals the names of our sloops, *Vostok* and *Mirnyi*. Although the islanders promised to keep their medals, they actually began to barter them for our seamen's handkerchiefs in our very presence.

A number of young girls who had come out with the queen sang hymns and psalms, which are now their only songs. For since their conversion to Christianity, the islanders regard it as a sin to sing their former songs, because they recall the old idolatrous rites. Of their own free will, indeed, the natives have abandoned not only their old songs but also their dances.[47]

Kaleidoscopes had been a source of amusement in Europe for some time, and so, imagining that they would also amuse and amaze the South Sea Islanders, I had bought a few kaleidoscopes in London. However, the natives here paid no attention to the toys.[48]

I informed the king that I should weigh that very evening with the land breeze. He begged me insistently to remain a few days longer, but when he saw that I had come to a firm decision to depart, he seized my hand and asked me not to forget him. He parted from us with the utmost reluctance, descending into his canoe with head bowed, muttering something to himself for a long time. He was probably saying a prayer, for he is said to be very devout. Thus, in a short space of time, had we come to know and like these islanders and now we were parting from them, most likely forever. A few natives wanted to set sail with me but I accepted no one, in deference to the wish of the king, who had begged me to take none of his subjects with us.[49]

OBSERVATIONS ON THE ISLAND OF TAHITI

The island of Tahiti was discovered in the year 1606 by the Spaniard Quiros, en route from Callao, and was named La Sagittaria.[50] Subsequently, it was visited at various times by other mariners, who renamed it thus: the English Captain Wallis called it King George III Island; the French Commander Bougainville called it Nouvelle Cythère because of the number of attractive women; and finally, since the time of Captain Cook's visit, the island has retained its true and present name; Otahiti. The island is actually composed of two round islands joined by a narrow and low-lying isthmus. In the middle of both islands there are mountains, whose summits are often lost in clouds. There are gentle slopes near the shoreline that are covered with beautiful palm trees, breadfruit trees, other fruiting trees, and bushes.

The breadfruit trees attain a very considerable height and great thickness and the timber is used in the manufacture of the upper parts of canoes, for posts in large houses, and for benches, which are usually fashioned, complete with little legs, from a single piece of wood. From the bark of breadfruit, the natives obtain a resin used to caulk the seams of canoes, and from the soaked bark they make cloth. The felled tree begins to grow again from the roots and after four years is again producing fruit six to seven inches in circumference and a little elongated in shape. The islanders cook these and eat them most of the year.[51]

The coconut palm is also large, the coconuts containing a liquid or milk that makes a refreshing drink. The natives eat the kernel raw or pounded. They also extract a great deal of oil from it and feed their pigs and poultry on the crushed remains. Polished shells are used in lieu of crockery, and ropes are woven from the fibres of the bark and used in the construction of houses and canoes. Out of young coconut leaves they fashion green sun shades, which are generally worn by islanders of both sexes and all ages.

The Tahitian apple tree bears fruit that resembles our ripe apple in appearance and has an excellent taste apart from the very centre, which is too hard to eat. Its flowers are red and white, and women embellish their hair with them. From the bark of the mulberry, the natives make their finest cloths. The banana tree bears fruit that is an excellent food. It is difficult to distinguish the new sprouts of this tree from coarse asparagus in colour, and they taste even better than asparagus when cooked.

The stout tree that the Tahitians call *apope* grows in the hills and is used in the lower part of canoes. As for the tree called *faro*, it is really a variety of palm. Its leaves are used to cover the roofs of houses, on account of their thickness and suitability. The natives of coral islands suck the fruit of this tree, and the Tahitians also, most likely, make use of it in famine years.

The *Aito* is a hardwood tree from whose timber the natives make spears and other weapons, little adzes for cleaning coconuts, and rectangular mallets with which they beat the fibres of soaked bark from breadfruit and other trees for the preparation of cloths. By contrast, the *purau* tree gives a light wood used for the rafters of buildings. The bamboo, a variety of cane, grows very high. Lengths of its stem, two and a half feet long and two or three inches in diameter, are used for storing coconut oil.[52]

The vine grows well, but it grows here in small quantity and is cultivated only by missionaries. On Tahiti, there are many trees suitable for the gathering of cotton; and there are others that bear a fruit rather like a small pumpkin. From the leaves of the *tao* tree, mixed with the yellow juice obtained from *mazhe* berries, they get a red colouring substance. Leaves or stems of different grasses are dipped into this substance, according to fancy, and then applied to various native cloths, on which they form perfectly printed red designs.

Fig, chestnut, orange, and lemon trees are cultivated by Europeans in large numbers and also provide a part of the diet of the islanders themselves. The missionaries have a fine garden, full of many other excellent trees and shrubs. Among the vegetables, we noted, such was the want of time, only yams, taro, potato, ginger, galingale,[53] pineapples, watermelons, pumpkins, cabbages, cucumbers, capsicums, and tobacco.

On the offshore shoals of the island, marine creatures[54] have here and there formed the foundations of coral walls, between which and the beach there are good sheltered harbours. The elevated mountains catch the moist clouds, which, falling as rain, form numerous creeks and rivers. Winding to the sea, these water the gentle slopes and plains of Tahiti. The high mountainous areas of the island are quite bare; on the other hand, the level places and plains are populated right to the shore.

Tahitians are in stature like Europeans, the men having swarthy faces and bodies, and black eyes, eyebrows, and hair. The women mostly have round and pleasant faces. Both sexes, of all ages, wear their hair close-cropped. Although many travellers have detected the presence of various races among the natives inhabiting Tahiti, I observed nothing of the kind. The apparent difference between the chiefs and the commonalty results from their quite different ways of life. High-ranking Tahitians are somewhat larger and stouter in build, and olive-toned, whereas the commoners are redder. But Tahitian grandees lead a quiet, sedentary life, and the common people are ceaselessly active, always practically naked and not infrequently out in the open all day long, fishing on the coral walls.[55]

The Tahitians received us with the greatest hospitality. Every one of them would entertain and welcome us when we came to their houses. They came out to the sloops every day and were always cheerful, and we never noticed any quarrelling or differences among them. The total number of the inhabitants of Tahiti has been estimated variously by different travellers. Indeed, the differences in estimates are so great that there never was a historical example of either an epidemic or a political upheaval producing such a population decrease as the following would indicate to the reader.

Captain Cook, on his first voyage round the world, says: "The whole island, according to Tupia's account, who certainly knew, could show 6,780 fighting men, from which the number of inhabitants may easily be computed."[56] If we suppose that the number of persons capable of bearing arms comprises five-twelfths of the population, then according to the above figures there were as many as 16,272 male inhabitants of the island. On his second voyage, Captain Cook reckons the total population of Tahiti to be 240,000, but Mr. Forster believes it to be only 120,000. The Spaniard Buenevo, who was on the island in 1772 and in 1774,[57] supposed the population to be from 15,000 to 16,000. Mr. Wilson, when here in 1797, also estimated it at 16,000 persons.[58]

The suppositions of these last two navigators agree pretty well, but they differ very greatly from the estimates of Captain Cook and Mr. Forster on the second voyage. Most likely, the considerable over-estimate of the total number of inhabitants arose either from ignorance of the language or from the desire of the chief of the island to exaggerate his military strength by telling Captain Cook that the fleet consisting of 210 large Tahitian canoes and 20 small ones belonged to four districts only, and not to the whole island. Captain Cook accepted this false statement as true, perhaps, and based his estimate of the total population on the premise that the other districts were like those four.[59] Mr. Nott was now telling us, in any case, that in the early days of May 1819 all the islanders had assembled at the royal church, and that they had numbered about 8,000 persons. If to this figure we add 2,000 old, very young, and sickly persons, who could not be present, the total population reaches about 10,000. The decrease of the number of natives from those given by Wilson, Buenevo, and Captain Cook on his first voyage was, according to Mr. Nott, the consequence of frequent civil wars, diseases that had raged there in former years, and the ruthless ancient custom of mothers murdering their own newborn children, so that of seven infants only four, or of five only three, were allowed to survive. The custom was to permit the better care of those who did survive.

The island of Tahiti and the Society Islands in general are under the rule of King Pomare, son of that King Otu who had flourished in Captain Cook's day. Pomare is very tall and has an august appearance. He began to learn to read and write in 1807. In 1809, a civil war that had flared up forced the missionaries to withdraw from Tahiti to the islands of Eimeo [Mo'orea] and Guageine [Huahine]. King Pomare also moved over to Eimeo; and for two years Tahiti was independent of him. When he became a Christian in 1811, however, he received support from the natives of Guageine and Raitea [Raiatea], who had likewise converted to Christianity. (The present queen, Tire-Vagine, was born on the former island.) With these fresh forces, he fell on the enemy in an attempt to recover the island of Tahiti, but he was repulsed and forced to withdraw with losses to Eimeo once more. Finally, in the year 1815, when the number of Christians on the Society Islands had increased, they all assembled afresh under the leadership of Pomare, who again returned to Tahiti, with many canoes. Fifteen hundred armed men were put ashore five miles west of Matavai Bay. From there, Pomare moved some twenty miles to the southwest to meet his enemy. His fleet also moved along the coast, parallel with his army. Saturday having arrived, the king halted, so that a Christian service might be celebrated on the morrow. The missionaries with him warned him that the enemy would surely take full advantage of the opportunity offered by his whole army's attending a divine service to attack him, and so everyone prayed with weapons in hand. Some men had guns, others had spears and clubs as well as slings and bows and arrows. The king often looked in the direction whence he expected the enemy to advance, and having finally sighted them, he instructed the missionaries to hurry the service along. Moving forward toward the advancing warriors, the islanders took a few steps and then, falling to their knees, beseeched the Almighty for a victory. The prayer was continued until they were quite close to the enemy. The king commanded from a canoe surrounded by a multitude of others. After an initial false move, the royal forces were thrown back; but they quickly took heart again and the enemy were routed. Then, contrary to the old Tahitian custom, Pomare ordered that the defeated should be spared, which utterly amazed the fugitives and was, as Mr. Nott relates it,[60] no small inducement to them to accept the Christian faith, so that now all the natives of the Society Islands and adjacent isles are Christians. Mr. Nott reckons that there are some 15,000 persons on Tahiti.

In 1819, during the early days of May, when all the natives had been summoned by royal command and had assembled at the royal church, Pomare walked to the central pulpit at the close of a prayer and thence delivered a short address to his people, explaining the benefits of laws for the safety of everyone's life and property, and then announcing the following statutes. A council consisting of twelve nobles of the island would be formed, with the king himself acting as president. They would draw up a short code of laws, in the first instance. The punishment for murder should be death; as punishment for theft, the guilty should be forced to pave the area around the church with stones or should work at shore defences, to prevent flooding from the sea; those convicted of adultery should be condemned to work as servants for nobles; and so forth. These punishments were to be strictly enforced. By raising their hands, the assembled people signified their assent. And since that time, these islanders have prospered under the benign control of those few laws.

Pomare later added to his possessions the island of Raivovai [Raivavae] or High Island, shown on Arosmit's [Arrowsmith's] chart as lying in latitude 23°41′S, longitude 171°57′W.[61] The occasion for this addition was a rumour that had reached him to the effect that the inhabitants of the island, recognizing his power, wished to become his subjects. In November 1818, Pomare himself set off on board an American vessel for Raivovai.[62] The rumour proved to be correct. The islanders there did, indeed, desire to accept his rule.

While he was thus extending the limits of his possessions, however, a fresh uprising broke out on Tahiti itself. A certain native from the Aropai district had decided to take advantage of Pomare's absence to usurp him. Panagia, as this rebel was called, began by declaring war against the king's adherents in the districts of Pare, or Matavai, and Faa. According to the Society Islands custom, he set fire to his own house on the side nearest to his enemies, so demonstrating his readiness to prosecute war to the utmost limit. Even before the king's return, though, he had been taken prisoner. Pomare, immediately upon his return, was not satisfied with having the instigator of the uprising in his hands already and wanted to wage war against the whole district of Aropai. In deference, however, to the suggestions of the missionaries, who were for peace and tranquillity, it was resolved that only two of the principal ringleaders should be hanged, and this was promptly done.

For the purposes of internal administration, the island of Tahiti is divided into five parts, each containing several districts and an equal number of chiefs. . . . There are nineteen principal chiefs in all. Each district has its own judge and tribunal, in accordance with the aforementioned laws that were put before the people. It is much to the credit of the missionaries that they have managed to bring the islanders to such a point of education in so short a time.[63]

A very great number of the islanders now read and write well. The Latin alphabet is used. Rum was earlier made, in Tahiti, from the roots of *ti*. Most probably at the urging of the missionaries, though, the king has forbidden the production of that liquor, despite his own great fondness for it. This ban has been of the greatest use in attaining the well-intentioned objectives of the good teachers here. It is a pity, however, that the enlightening of these islanders has been accompanied by the suppression of all their former innocent national amusements, dances, and other games. The missionaries say that all the festivities and dances of the natives were closely associated with their idolatry, and that therefore the Tahitians themselves, being now sincere converts to Christianity, have abandoned those dances and songs as pastimes reminding them of their former errors. Mere curiosity led me to ask the king to order his islanders to dance for us, but he replied that it was sinful and declined. The morality of these people has changed, for the better, to an incredible degree, since the change of religion.

Even though our sloops were visited each day by quantities of native visitors, filled indeed, we never had the least reason to doubt their good intentions or to expect any sort of trickery. They would always return home toward evening, parting with us amicably.

The king and members of his family each had a narrow tattoo mark of little stars on the legs, a quarter of the way up above the ankles, and by each arm joint. A few of the other natives also had tattooing on the body, but now they are no longer ornamenting themselves in this way.[64]

Mr. Nott gave us the chance to see some Tahitians who had been on coral islands lying to the east of Tahiti. During our stay, some natives from one such island, called Anna, came out to see us daily in a double canoe. While gathering information on the names of those coral islands from natives of Anna, as from the Tahitians in question, we had heard a variety of appellations, although all alike had indicated that the island of Anna lay northeast of Tahiti and that Matea lay midway between it and Tahiti. This would indicate that Anna is the very island that Captain Cook had found and named Chain Island.[65] The inhabitants of that island had exactly the same tattoo marks on the thighs as those I had observed on natives we had met at the coral island of Nigiru, who had sailed there to trade or collect food. They are invariably daring seamen and undertake long and difficult ocean voyages. They differ from the Tahitians only by the tattooing of the thighs and by their long, flowing hair. Although I attempted to persuade them that Anna lay northward from Tahiti, as indicated on Arosmit's (Arrowsmith's) chart, they just laughed at this and would certainly not accept it, urging as proof that, in order to return home, they needed to sail to Maitea and not to Matea.

During our sojourn on the island of Tahiti, the thermometer had reached 24.5°C [87°F] in the shade and from 17.5° to 18°C [71° to 73°F] at night. The latitude of Venus Point had been fixed by us at 17°29′19″S (Mr. Lazarev) and at 17°29′20″S (*Vostok*); its longitude we reckoned to be 149°27′20″W. This reckoning may be accepted as most reliable. We corrected our chronometers on the basis of it. Their error, accumulated during the fifty-three day passage from Queen Charlotte Sound to Venus Point, we now distributed on arithmetical progression, assuming that the rate of alteration had been gradual and not sudden. And on that basis, we also adjusted all the longitudes previously mentioned in this account of our voyage and entered them, corrected, on our charts.[66]

During our stay at Tahiti, moderate winds had blown from ENE in the daytime and a very gentle land breeze had blown at night. On the 27th, at

6:00 pm, we weighed anchor with just such a breeze. Having passed the coral reef, we held a course northward in order to get clear of the island as quickly as possible. Some of the islanders followed our sloops and asked us to take them with us, but since I had given my word to Pomare to take none of his subjects away, I refused their request. . . .

28 July. In the morning, perfect stillness reigned around us apart from the hissing sound made by the waves as the sloop cut through them. We experienced a strange emptiness, now, for we had grown used to the racket, shouts, and bustle of the islanders . . . but I was very glad on the other hand that it was again possible to have the sloop thoroughly cleaned down. We now stowed away all our lately acquired fresh provisions, including watermelons, pumpkins, bananas, breadfruit, and taro. The oranges, which were for the crew's daily use, we hung out over the stern and the chains. The remainder were suspended in large nets aloft. . . . The different sorts of Tahitian cloth were very carefully dried. Spears and other weapons, shells and hooks made of shell and coral, and all the other curiosities collected were well packed and stowed below.[67] Finally, when the sloop had been washed down, she was thoroughly aired. Fires were then lit in the stoves, and soon we had the pleasure of seeing our sloop in her former state of cleanliness.

P.M. NOVOSIL'SKII

The sloops laid a course directly for Venus Point, rounding the coral reef and passing through a narrow passage between it and the Dolphin Shoal to drop anchor in Matavai Bay, not far from the shore and in that very spot where Captain Wallis had had a fight with the islanders in 1767 and where Cook had also stood at anchor. We ourselves had scarcely dropped anchor before a quantity of craft were surrounding us. Islanders brought us lemons, oranges, bananas, pineapples, and coconuts, which they were ready to barter for trifles. The Tahitians had open, cheerful faces, and most of them wore trousers only, while others wore jackets minus the trousers, or merely camisoles. Among these guests coming out to us were two sailors, one an American, the other an Englishman. The former had served for awhile in the North American [Russian-American] Company, learning a little Russian. While on the island of Nukagiva [Nukuhiva], in the Marquesas Group, he had married a young island girl; then he had gone on to Tahiti, acquiring a house and enjoying the protection of the king, Pomare. Captain Bellingshausen took him on as interpreter, and the Englishman came into our own sloop in the same capacity. From him, we learned that the Tahitians now practised the Christian faith.

After midday, an English missionary, Nott, went out to *Vostok*. He had been here for more than twenty years. King Pomare, he announced, was coming to visit the sloops; and indeed we saw a large double canoe moving toward *Vostok*. On its platform sat a tall man of impressive appearance, in a white calico shirt, over which was thrown a piece of white material with an opening for the head. He was, in fact, wrapped in white stuffs from waist to feet. He was wearing blue spectacles. His hair was smooth and cropped short in front, but at the back it hung in a single lock, curling down. This was Pomare. Behind the platform, and under an awning that resembled a *kibitka*'s top, sat the royal family and the court ladies. This craft soon reached *Vostok*. Pomare went up first, extending his hand to Captain Bellingshausen and then waiting until he had been joined aboard by his whole family, consisting of the queen, his daughter, and a sister-in-law who was carrying in her arms an infant—the King's son. The queen, whose name was Tire-Vagine [Tiara Vahine], was about twenty-five years of age, quite short, a very slender woman with lively little eyes. She was clad in white material from the bosom down, over which another piece of the same stuff had been thrown, like a shawl. She wore a little shade on her forehead, fashioned from fresh coconut leaves. The daughter, Aimata, was perhaps ten years old and was wearing a coloured cotton print dress. Her aunt was dressed in the same manner as was the queen, and the courtiers, all good looking women, had gracefully draped themselves with white and yellow material of the sort made here from the bark of the breadfruit tree. They, like the queen, wore shades of fresh coconut leaves or else garlands of aromatic flowers.

The king, together with his family and suite, was invited into the cabin. The king and queen sat on divans. Pomare several times repeated the words, "Russian, Russian!"; then he uttered the names of Alexander and Napoleon, and finally he burst out laughing. It was evident that the recent gigantic struggle in Europe had even touched Tahiti. Captain Bellingshausen invited his guests to dine with him. The king sat in the place of honour with the queen at his right hand, and then Nott and our captain to her right, while Princess Aimata and Captain Bellingshausen sat on his left. The queen's sister sat a little way off and nursed the future sovereign of the Society Islands. The king ate with appetite, often pouring himself a goblet of wine and making witticisms of the following type: "I thought of making a road from my palace to the quay, but now this is unnecessary. I hope the Russians will beat a path there!" When Captain Bellingshausen apologized for the lack of fresh foodstuffs at table, Pomare retorted: "I know that fish are caught by the shore and not in the depths of the sea!" Having noticed that the water being served was not altogether fresh, the king then ordered one islander to serve coconut milk. The command was instantly obeyed; the man brought some coconuts, neatly broke their tops with a little hammer, and poured some milk into a glass. Pomare mixed it with wine. Then he again poured himself some neat wine, every time proposing somebody's health, moreover, and touching glasses. After dinner, he requested a cigar and drank coffee. During this time, the artist Mikhailov had been drawing his portrait. Pomare noticed this and gave his consent to it. He was then sketched holding a medal in his hand, while the queen, not embarrassed in the slightest, breastfed her son in our presence. Pomare was then shown the lower deck and the cannon, and a few shots were fired off in his honour. He was very pleased by this, but with each shot he hid behind Captain Bellingshausen.

Meanwhile, they were bringing out gifts for us from the king, quantities of various sorts of fruit, some sugar cane, and some taro and yam roots. The queen set off for shore again, with her family and retainers, at 6 o'clock, but the king stayed longer on board the sloop, until at length it was quite dark. Just before then, he expressed the desire to go ashore. A cutter was provided and Midshipman Demidov took him behind Venus Point and straight to a point facing his palace. While the cutter was on its way to the shoreline, false fires were lit from its bow, and several rockets of the star variety were sent up from the sloop and burst overhead. Pomare made Demidov a present of eight fathoms of white material and gave four-fathom lengths to each of the sailors too.

On 23 July, the sun's first rays having tinged the beautiful tropical sky with gold, islanders were already bustling about along the shoreline, loading their craft with produce and hastening to push them out to sea. A whole flotilla, paddling or under sail, set out towards our sloops. And once again the Tahitians brought us quantities of fruit, poultry, and beautiful shellfish, which we bartered for various trifles, even sheets of paper for writing on. Meanwhile, those officers who were free from their duties, including me, set out for the shore. We landed behind Venus Point and walked to the coconut grove beside which stood Pomare's Palace. At this same time, both captains, escorted by Nott, had also walked up to the royal residence, which was protected by a low enclosure of boards. Stepping over this enclosure at the place where little steps had deliberately been made, we walked through a spacious hut, along both inner sides of which there stood bedsteads with yellow coverings. This dwelling, most likely, was that of high court officials. Next, we crossed a small courtyard into Pomare's own little house. The king and his family were dining at the time. He greeted us and ordered that little low stools be fetched for the captains.[68] They gave us glass goblets and, filling them with fresh coconut milk, invited us to refresh ourselves. Taking Captain Bellingshausen by the arm, Pomare then led him off into another hut and there asked him to write instructions to the effect that one bottle of rum be sent from the sloop. His wish was satisfied: orders were written that three bottles of rum and six of Teneriffe wine should be allowed him. As we were leaving the royal residence, the king's little daughter, Aimata, handed me a bouquet of flowers and I made her a present of some earrings and a hand mirror. On the way, we met with some island girls, swarthy but of very pleasant appearance, though indeed they were not the beauties described by some of the navigators who had preceded us here. They offered us aromatic wreaths and received our various gifts in return. What they most liked were earrings.

On 25 July, Sunday, the sun was already shining and still nobody had come out to us. We found out ashore that the entire native populace had gone off to the house of prayer. We ourselves went to the church in question. It was full of people in their finest dress: one saw a strange collection of all kinds of European clothing there, indeed. Nott was delivering a sermon with much feeling, and the islanders, sitting or standing sedately, were listening with real attention. When the service[69] was over, we called on our friends among the islanders. They received us joyfully but, honouring the Sabbath day, would not accept any gifts from us whatever in return for their own small services.

The king visited our sloops several times, showing us great kindness. He had a natural intelligence and many good qualities. He always kept his word, for instance. Unfortunately, he was his own worst enemy. An unbridled fondness for strong spirits will probably send him to an early grave.[70]

The island of Tahiti actually consists of two peninsulas joined by a narrow isthmus. The larger is called Tahiti, the smaller, Taia-Rabu. Tahiti was discovered in the year 1606 by the Spaniard Quiros, whom the natives received peaceably. One hundred and sixty years later, it was visited by both Wallis and Bougainville. Wallis stood in Matavai Bay and was very nearly shipwrecked on Dolphin Bank. One morning he was surrounded by 300 canoes. The islanders began to cast stones at his ship, then stones positively hailed down. When the native canoes were closer, Wallis fired grape-shot into them and the savages fled. This lesson was a useful one: peace was established and the Tahitians became gentle and obliging. At that time, Tahiti was under the rule of Oberea, also known as Puria, a woman of about forty-five, of august appearance. She made Wallis's acquaintance and was friendly to him.

The Tahitians had a certain custom: if the ruler had a son, the latter was considered the true *otu* or tsar, the ruler himself being considered merely a regent until the son reached his majority. During the time that Wallis was at Tahiti, Oammo and his wife Oberera were the regents on behalf of the minor Temare.[71]

Bougainville called here in 1768 and represented the island in such a luxurious and enticing picture that all Europe began to talk about the discovery of a new and fascinating Cythera in Polynesia. But soon after his visit, there was a revolution in Tahiti. . . .[72] The subsequent arrival of missionaries on the island produced a great impression on the natives. Their chief priest, Manimani, pronounced himself in favour of the newcomers, to whom several parcels of land were at once allocated with full rights of ownership. The missionaries then set to their religious task with fervour, attempting above all else to master the Tahitian language. In 1802, missionary Nott went right round the island, preaching the Christian faith. He met with a friendly reception everywhere and even sympathy, to greater or lesser extent, with his message. On his way back, as he was passing through Ata-Guru [Atehure], he found the *otu*, his father, and many chiefs in the temple or *morai* there. They were making a sacrifice in honour of their principal idol, Oro. Nott was horrified to see men hanging from trees before the *morai*, as sacrifices for the idol. Vainly he attempted to persuade the idolaters of the errors of their ways.[73] No one would listen to him. Next day there was a stormy assembly in that *morai*. Both Pomares announced to the crowd that the mighty Oro wished to be taken from Ata-Guru in Tautara onto the peninsula of Taiarapu. Arguments broke out, and then an awful racket, and at a sign from Pomare I armed warriors threw themselves out of canoes, seized the idol Oro, and bore it off to the Taiarapu peninsula. A result of this was a bloody civil war known to the Tahitians as Rua's War, after the name of the chief of the insurgent Ata-Guru men. After some time, both sides were exhausted by the hostilities and there followed a temporary truce.

In 1803, Pomare I suddenly died, at the age of fifty-five. For thirty years he had been the principal figure on Tahiti. Intelligent, brave, a man of strong passions, which he was able to control, however, Pomare I had succeeded in keeping power despite the customs of the land and even after his son had grown up. And right until the end of his life, he had constantly protected the missionaries. On his death, power passed by right to Pomare II. Meanwhile, the missionaries were zealously pursuing their good work. Having perfectly mastered the Tahitian tongue, they translated the catechism into Tahitian in 1805, drawing up a Tahitian alphabet to serve as the basis for translations into that language of all the books of the Holy Scriptures.

Shortly after this, civil war broke out anew between the men of Ata-Guru and the Tahitians. The chief of the former party was Tuanta, formerly a general of Pomare's but now his darkest foe. He defeated Pomare II, forcing him to flee to the island of Vagine [Huahine], where there were a few missionaries. It was at this time that the whole crew of the schooner

Venus, which was visiting Tahiti, were very nearly sacrificed to the god Oro. They were happily released from captivity by the vessel *Urania*, which had hastened to their aid.[74]

In 1809, there were continual disturbances and uprisings on Tahiti and on other islands, so that almost all the missionaries were obliged to withdraw to Port Jackson. Only Heywood remained behind on the island of Vagine and Nott on Eimeo, whither the exiled Pomare II also betook himself. The latter's misfortunes, though, proved to be advantageous to him, for he became Nott's diligent pupil. Religious teaching opened up his heart and Pomare accepted Christianity from inward conviction. Several other islanders followed his example, and the former commanders, his comrades, began to join him from all directions. Pomare decided to make a ceremonial announcement of his conversion to Christianity, and it happened in this fashion. Once, a turtle was brought to him. He gave orders simply that it be cooked and served for dinner. But it is to be remarked that a taboo had been placed on turtles, which were to be used as food only if prepared with specific rites in the *morai* and if a certain portion were offered to the gods. Pomare just ate it, and left nothing for the gods. Horror seized all those present. Everyone thought the earth would open up and swallow the one who had dishonoured the idols. Nothing happened, of course, and Pomare knew how to take full advantage of the fact. Rising from the table, he said to the chiefs surrounding him: "Now you yourselves see that the gods are false and useless! They are soulless idols and can neither harm nor help you!" This simple speech, together with Pomare's example, had a powerful influence on the chiefs, many of whom converted to Christianity then and there.

Meanwhile, Tahiti had been given over to all the horrors of anarchy and debauchery. The islanders occupied themselves only with the preparation of the *ti* plant, in order to extract an intoxicating beverage from it. Stills were everywhere in evidence, with coconut shells under the liquid that flowed out from them. The natives would drink themselves insensible on the spot, rolling about while others made furious yells, fought and knifed each other. The most sensible of the islanders appeared before Pomare and urged him to return to the lost island of Tahiti. Pomare decided to do so, but he forbade the missionaries to follow him there until complete order had been restored. At first, only the district of Matavai declared itself under Pomare's authority.

The church was flourishing on Eimeo, though, and in 1813 a principal chapel was dedicated there. The island's high priest, Paii, who had been converted by Nott, cast all the idols into a great fire and declared himself a Christian. On the islands of Vagine, Ranatea, and Tagao there were likewise numerous conversions. It was now that idolatry, fading on the Tahitian archipelago, made its final struggle against Christianity. It was a desperate struggle to the death. The wild heathens resolved that they would cruelly pursue and, if possible, exterminate all Christians. To this end, they formed a conspiracy in the manner of the Sicilian Vespers, fixing on the night between the 7th and 8th of July 1814 as the time to knife all the Christians. Almost at the very hour when this was to occur, the latter discovered what fate was awaiting them and managed to get off in canoes and flee to Eimeo. The plotters moved on in the darkness of night, en masse, to do murder. One can hardly describe their surprise and fury on discovering that not a single victim remained in the houses marked for destruction! There were mutual accusations of treachery, and from arguments there grew fights and knifings; and fair Tahiti, lit up by the flames of fires, was that night an awful picture of murder and destruction. In cunning fashion, the idolaters then summoned Pomare again to Tahiti, together with his chiefs who had gone off to Eimeo. Pomare was not deceived, however, and returned only with 300 well-armed warriors. On 12 November 1815, a Sunday, as Pomare and his chiefs and fighting men were at prayer in the hamlet of Narii, in Ata-Guru district, the heathens fell on him with a savage cry, bearing the banner of Oro before them. "Do not fear," Pomare exclaimed to his own warriors, "for Jehovah will protect us!"[75]

There followed a bloody engagement in which Pomare was completely victorious. He ordered, however, that the fleeing enemy should be spared and even that the dead chief of the enemy faction, Upufara, should be buried with honour. Such magnanimity on the part of a victor toward the defeated was unheard of on Tahiti and demonstrated to the most stubborn idolaters how great was the superiority of the true religion! In the meantime, Pomare's warriors had on his instructions destroyed the temple of Oro down to its foundations, toppled to the ground the wooden idol with its crude human features, cut off its head, and burned the whole in a fire. So ended idolatry on Tahiti.

The missionaries then began, with renewed zeal, to distribute among the islanders those books of Holy Scripture that had earlier been printed in Port Jackson. Soon, the missionary Ellis brought thence to the island of Eimeo a printing press with letters. It was Pomare himself who set the first page and pulled the first sheet from the press. It is impossible to describe the general delight of the islanders, as the first printed sheets appeared! Initially, the books were distributed free of charge, but later the missionaries fixed a price for them, payable in coconut-oil. Not infrequently, new Christians would come to Eimeo, even from other islands, for spiritual food and would spend a night beside the printing press in order to get the sacred book before other people the next morning! Having obtained the books, they would hasten back to their craft, visiting nobody, in order to return home the faster with the new treasure.

Still, it is a pity that the missionaries subsequently, with Pomare's consent, placed on the new Christians various taxes to cover the printing of books, taxes that, during our stay in Tahiti, took the form of coconut oil, arrowroot, cotton, and such like, and which had already become too burdensome for the islanders. And lately, as was already mentioned, Pomare had given himself over to strong spirits to such an extent that they not infrequently clouded his reason and had lately undermined his health. One was sorry to gaze upon the ruler, thus lost, who had done so much for the Tahitian archipelago. And within the year, Pomare was no more. He died on 7 September 1821. Pomare II's young son was acclaimed sovereign as Pomare III, but he too died, in 1828. Then his younger sister, Aimata, became Tahitian tsaritsa, as Pomare Vahine I, and continues to reign over Tahiti to the present day under the protection of the French.[76]

On 27 July, having said our farewells to Pomare, the missionary Nott, and all our acquaintances, we regretfully left Tahiti, so happy an island and so blessed with all Nature's gifts.

I.M. SIMONOV

It was only the occasional native who had dared to board our sloop and offer his things in exchange for ours. Some who had already encountered Europeans, though, or had at least had some dealings with them, boarded us with confidence and returned to their island laden with various articles that were necessary for them. We, for our part, took from them cloths, spears, clubs, and so forth. From the Alexander the First Archipelago,[77] we made for the Society Islands, steering toward Tahiti; for we needed to check our chronometers in that place, so long known already and so accurately fixed. It was of course by the chronometers that we had been determining the geographical positions of those islands that we had lately discovered. . . .

At 9:00 am on 21 July, the two mountains of Tahiti were sighted from the cross-trees. By noon or shortly thereafter, the island was quite visible even from the quarterdeck, and by 7:00 pm we were looking at fires that were burning ashore. "Tahiti, Tahiti!" we exclaimed joyfully, gazing at the distant shore of that island. The joy was natural enough: it was a long time since we had been ashore or had fresh provisions, and even longer since we had a friendly reception from a people visited by us, among whom it was not necessary to have a gun at the ready, as in New Zealand, where we had been unable to land except in armed convoy.[78] To read the accounts of travellers who had preceded us here, one had to suppose that

Tahiti was an earthly paradise. Quiros, Wallis, Cook and his comrades, and Bougainville had all described the island as the Athens of Oceania. Bougainville had named it La Nouvelle Cythère, while Cook had exclaimed: "What a difference between the kind and gay nature of the Tahitians and the savagery of the peoples of other archipelagoes!" Tahiti had thus to be, for the mariner, a place of peace and true happiness.[79]

EGOR' KISELEV

22 July. We came to Tahiti Island, and a very wealthy island was spread out before us. There were up to three thousand savages. We stood at anchor here for nine days. And the king of the island and his suite came on board four times and brought us presents too: material and fruit. We made him a present of a sabre with shoulder band and eight medals and some rum, and four bags of white sugar, and mirrors of various sorts. The people were as peaceable and healthy as you can imagine. There are lots and lots of wild pigs and hens and goats, and as for fruit, we never saw such quantities on any other islands. There are breadfruit trees, on which bread grows, and there are coconuts. We made sail from Tahiti on the 24th.[80]

A.P. LAZAREV

On 8 July, the shores of the island of Tahiti opened up before us—Tahiti, with its two high peninsulas joined by a low isthmus and its transparent streams descending from tree-clad hills under a bright sunny light. We were impatient to reach a country whose mores were those of patriarchal times, and to greet our comrades from the frigate *Kreiser*, and to rejoice in pleasant strolls through delightful coconut groves, and to savour the cooling nectar of their fruit. But just then, contrary to everyone's expectation, the wind shifted to the ENE and became brisk, forcing us to make another tack and wait for another change in the wind.

On the 13th, we had reached latitude 18°40′29″S, longitude 147°50′29″W and a southeasterly wind was blowing, so we moved to the NNW. On the morning following, the 14th, the picturesque shores of the island of Tahiti once again showed themselves to us. Around noon, with the aid of tow boats because of a dead calm, we finally and slowly approached the landing place. Nor were we any less relieved by being able to rejoin *Kreiser*, which had been standing in Matavai Bay for a week already. Our commander had been intending to set sail the very next day, without waiting for us longer.[81]

The frigate *Kreiser*'s bare masts, standing up behind a grove of coconut palms, were for us a more pleasant sight than any palms or flowering shrubs along the shore. Nor did the great number of island craft that soon surrounded our vessel, bringing quantities of fresh fruit, have any significance for us in comparison with the single boat in which our comrades on the voyage greeted us, even while we were still under canvas. As for our friends' joy, it was not limited to mere verbal expression: the tongue answered the heart and our souls seemed to live in our mouths! Passing the remainder of the evening in pleasant conversation, we agreed that, as before, we would share our off-duty time.

At dawn on 15 July, we took in a warp to the NE and levelled the cables to fifty fathoms: light but variable winds and the current of a stream against which vessels are usually anchored call for such precautions, if anchors are to be kept clean. This was a Sunday, so we could have no dealings with the islanders, since on Sundays they were not permitted to leave the shore or even to occupy themselves with anything. They all had to be in church, listening to the preaching and divine services led by the missionaries, of whom there were two in Matavai Bay and nine in the Society Islands. These Englishmen know the Tahitian language perfectly, the senior man among them, Mr. Nott, having spent twenty-seven years there already. They have translated the Bible into Tahitian and many of the Tahitians know how to write, using Latin letters, and almost everyone except old men can read.

The day after our arrival, right at sunrise, we found ourselves surrounded by large numbers of craft laden with assorted produce, such as bananas, coconuts, breadfruit, yams, and so forth. Each canoe carried one or two people, and sincerity and good nature were evident in their very faces, attested to their friendliness, and demanded our complete confidence in them. The noise made by these islanders had woken us up, and now the welcoming word "*Yurona!*" was to be heard everywhere. We had no need to be cautious in allowing them on board the sloop, as we would have at other South Pacific islands. All these natives came up, trustingly and willingly, without any weaponry, and made our acquaintance. Barter commenced, and fruit was exchanged for nails, gimlets, axes, knives, and other small articles. Such things had already lost their earlier value, however, and the native traders now desired clothing and shirts. For this reason, I ordered that nothing should be accepted in exchange for clothing, so that we might take in those things that we truly needed for provisionment the quicker and more surely. This trading was carried on at the nearest point ashore, whither the natives betook themselves for the purpose. We ourselves had the greater liberty to busy ourselves with various tasks, putting the vessel to rights. Young Tahitians diligently helped our people in their work, willingly pulling on ropes with them, for instance, and these lads sought my permission to remain aboard the sloop to work. I selected eighteen of them, and those young men shared our food and spent the night with our own people for as long as the work aboard continued. I admit that they were not taken on in vain; by the third day, all the rigging had been restretched, adjusted correctly, and watered down. A three-day acquaintance resulted in genuine friendships, and at the end of the three days, I ordered that each individual who had collaborated aboard and had seen all the work to a conclusion should be given a shirt, a piece of soap, and a few iron objects necessary in the house. Having thus regaled our keen assistants, I wanted to send them all back to the shore. But what surprise struck us when they refused these rewards! Instead of the joy we had expected and grown used to seeing on their faces, we saw tears of grief flowing down from their eyes! They would accept nothing from us, and I supposed that they were highly displeased with me. Therefore, I ordered that the gifts destined for them should be rather generously augmented. But then I saw the truth: their weeping was not caused by bitterness but by regret that they were parting from their comrades, whom they had begged to take them to Russia. Forgive me innocent Tahitians, I did not know you and judged you by the European standard.

The island of Tahiti is the largest of the Society Islands and lies in latitude 18°S, longitude 149°W. Many ascribe its discovery to the Spaniard Quiros, who was on a voyage from Lima and who named it La Sagittaria. Sighting the island in 1767, Captain Wallis named it after George III; and in 1768 Bougainville, landing on its eastern side, found out its real name. Subsequently, Captain Cook was at Tahiti on all three of his voyages, observing the transit of Venus there during his first and accurately determining the latitude and longitude of Venus Point, at the northern end of the island and the easternmost extremity of Matavai Bay. The actual island consists, as was mentioned above, of two peninsulas connected by an isthmus that is level with the sea. It rises gradually for three miles inland from the shores and boasts high mountains covered with woods, from which there descend small streams.

Natural scientists who have visited the island's interior suppose that there once existed there a volcano, and that its activity ceased long ago. The best harbour is reckoned to be Matavai Bay, which, although open to sectors from the SW to the NNW, is still excellent, that circumstance being of little importance since the winds here always prevail from the east. And although winds from the SW and NW are indeed accompanied by very heavy seas, they are very rare, short-lived, and in any case occur only in October, November, and December. Calm weather under a cloudy sky serves as a reliable indicator of a change in the direction of the wind. While the trade winds blow, the weather is always clear.

The aforementioned bay may be distinguished by a high mountain[82] in the centre of the island, which lies directly south from Venus Point. On entering the bay, one must remain, for a half-mile or so, on the western side of a reef off that same point, in order to avoid a small coral bank over which the water is a mere two and a half fathoms deep.[83] While we were approaching Venus Point, the wind began to veer and soon prevented us from entering that passage. We were therefore obliged, leaving the bank to our east, to keep hard against the SW coast, where the passage in is completely safe. Going under tow eastward along the south shore, we dropped anchor in fourteen fathoms, black sand bottom, at a distance of one mile from both shores. The latitude of the aforementioned point is 149°35′45″W. The shore is entirely sandy and the little stream that waters it supplies the mariner with fresh sweet water although, as we afterwards discovered, it soon turns unpleasant in smell and taste. Work was carried out aboard the sloop with all possible despatch, and after three days we were ready to make sail. Each morning at 8:00 am, our people went ashore with trunks full of various articles and, settling in the shade of trees for barter with the islanders who gathered around in crowds with products of the land, they collected what was needed. The natives would point out the things in our trunks that they liked and, an agreement being reached, the word *matai* closed the deal.[84]

At the time of our visit to Tahiti, the queen had moved from Papaua to Matavai, most likely in order to show her respects to us.[85] Like all the other nobles of the island, she did her best to gain our friendship: each time we met, she brought us gifts of swine and fruit. But these really cost us far more than the articles acquired by regular barter, for we had to pay for favours with favours, and for gifts with gifts, and besides that it was necessary to entertain her with dinners and rum, of which all the islanders, even including the queen herself, are very fond. She was a woman of middling height, with large eyes and black, arching eyebrows. Her facial features were regular and it was evident that in her younger years she had been a beauty. And notwithstanding her want of education, she was much taken up by the importance of her position and even received all our gifts coolly. Large mirrors, crystal decanters, and glasses were accepted without particular remark; but the little bells, beads, rings, and other such trifles did not interest her in the least. Other islanders, too, would take them only reluctantly as payment for coconuts and bananas. In consequence of this, we had to obtain our pigs and poultry by offering shirts, axes, and other items; and the islanders were not less discriminating or capricious than our own people. Many of them would ask us if we had waistcoats, uniforms, and the like, and the women stood in need of straw bonnets! We had none with us, not having known that the French had introduced their fashions here. The novel little hats in which the queen's family visited us and the enticing little pictures in the hands of the populace served as clear indications of the recent visit of the French Capitaine Duperrey who, four months before our own arrival here, had taken on provisions.[86]

The natives of both sexes, including the royal family, wore their hair cropped short and covered themselves with cloths of various kinds. Some of the nobility now wore shirts and assorted other clothing acquired by barter from visiting vessels. It is noteworthy that all the officials here are tall, stout, and solidly built.

On Monday, at about noon, the still very youthful king and his numerous suite came out to visit us in two double canoes. The craft in which the king sat was guarded by warriors or bodyguards dressed in assorted worn European garments; and their armament was in keeping with their attire, consisting as it did of both spears and guns, which the Tahitians fire unwillingly. Our visitors were very pleased to be invited aboard the sloop, and, having first handed up the king, whom I took in my arms, his mother and aunt came on board, followed by numerous retainers who soon made our quarterdeck extremely congested. After spending some little time on deck, I invited the principal personages into my cabin; but as soon as I made to go below with the king, all his bodyguards wanted to follow us down, saying that they could not possibly leave him alone. We said, in response to this, that such mistrust was out of place and that their king was now with a high chief who received only those deserving of particular respect. They stayed behind, calm and content with their treatment on the deck. In the name of her son, the widowed queen thanked us with a pig and with much fruit of different kinds, in return for which I tried to give the king some little bells and whistles, placing a motley silk kerchief round the necks of both the queen and her sister. They admired these, and it seemed that with the silk kerchiefs alone they were well pleased.

The time for our dinner was approaching and the table was ready, so we all sat down together and I entertained my visitors as best I could. They ate and drank everything set before them with great appetite. Our ordinary table manners were, of course, not novelties for them, and they were quite familiar with the use of knife and fork. The queen showed a special fondness for rum, though, and amazed us by her resilience to it. Just before sunset, wishing to part company with these guests of mine, who were certainly disposed to remain a fair while longer, I told them that they would have to leave in accordance with procedures always followed in our warships. My visitors soon set off then, after inviting us to call on them ashore.

In view of the king's minority, Tahiti with its 9,000 inhabitants is presently governed by a man of advanced years chosen by the late king; acting in the young king's name, this man rules absolutely.[87] On his orders one islander, convicted of theft, had been hanged from a tree only a few days before our arrival. Another individual, for the theft of a sheet from our servants, was tied to a tree for two days and then sent off for two months of hard labour on the roads. Pomare, the late king of the Society Islands and of other isles in their vicinity, had died in November 1821 at the age of fifty. He had been buried in Papaua, the district contiguous with Matavai but having its own chief. This district lay some five miles to the west of our landing place, and the present king was spending the greater part of his time there. The late king, Pomare II, had accepted the Christian faith in the year 1809. On dying, he had left a wife aged thirty-five, a son of four and a daughter of twelve who, at the urging of the late king, had recently married the son of the ruler of certain islands to the west. By the general desire of the Tahitians, and despite the representations of the missionaries, the new king was entrusted for upbringing to his aunt, who is apparently a good natured and reliable woman.

The rudimentary education of these islanders, the eradication of idolatry, and the introduction of Christianity may all be attributed to certain unusual occurrences in this present century. In 1796 the English Missionary Society, founded for the propagation of the Christian faith, sent hither one of its most zealous members, a Mr. Nott, who remains on Tahiti to this day. The following account of the success of his enterprise is worthy of attention and is highly edifying.

On arrival in the Society Islands, Nott took up residence on Tahiti, as the principal island. Receiving no support whatever from his government, he was obliged to overcome every difficulty to earn the trust of the natives and especially that of their king, Pomare, who, from a deep attachment to idolatry, would pay no attention to the educated Christian. All Pomare's subjects followed his example. Mr. Nott drew solace from the future and considered himself fortunate simply because the islanders had proved indifferent to his presence. The broad-leafed trees served as his dwelling place and church, and there he prayed for the successes that were destined to him. Above all, he needed to know the Tahitian language and, establishing its rules, to translate the Holy Scriptures.

What abilities, what effort and care were necessary for this task! How many difficulties and obstacles were to be overcome! What strength had to be found! But nobody could stand in the way of Nott's zeal and great enterprise. He calmly bore not only poverty but even the islanders' contempt. For seventeen years he trampled the alien soil with bare feet, suffering, for want of clothing, from the heat of the sun. Despite the confluence of such hostile circumstances, Mr. Nott not only mastered the Tahitian tongue but also established the principles of its grammar and translated the Scriptures. It remained only to print the translation and other works and to teach the grammar to at least a few of the unenlightened islanders. The former task was handed to the solicitous Missionary Society, which fully justified Mr. Nott's expectations of it by printing and quickly sending him many copies. And in the interim, he was joined by another member of the Society, Mr. Wilson. While they were busy in England with the printing of the work in question, though, Mr. Nott was teaching the king and those closest to him how to read and write. To that end, he employed various means as inducements. The teacher's indefatigable efforts were rewarded by his pupils' swift progress. . . . [88]

It is remarkable that, despite all the difficulties that he has borne in the course of a twenty-seven-year sojourn in these half-savage islands, Mr. Nott has preserved all the fire of his imagination and all the energy of a great spirit. In his face, one sees liveliness and yet perfect calm. His words breathe a religious feeling; he is untiring in his labours and does not complain of want, though living in poverty. The islanders love and respect him, and the late king considered him a friend. Nor does Mr. Wilson deserve anything but praise and honour.

The missionaries' authority is limited to spiritual matters, which include, of course, the teaching of the Holy Scriptures and instruction in grammar. Under Mr. Nott's own supervision, exercise-books are being printed, and paper and ink are provided by the aforementioned Society free of charge. Only recently, the islanders agreed to sacrifice up to one hundred *pood* [3,600 lbs] of coconut oil each year, which is now sent off to England. As for the missionaries living on these islands, they are entirely free from avarice. Generous Nature feeds them with her products and clothes are supplied by the voluntary donations of those Europeans who call at Tahiti. The very houses in which the missionaries live differ from those of the common people only in having little windows. Still, their domestic arrangements are in an excellent state. Besides pigs and poultry, in which all the islanders are rich, each of the missionaries has a certain number of goats, sheep, and cattle, whereas the islanders make no effort whatever to raise them. Only a few that I happened to see had ducks and goats, but even they had them in small numbers.

The young Tahitian king has a pleasant and intelligent face. He has around him thirty guards, armed men, who never leave him and who keep sentry at night by his hut. I never saw a single islander who had weapons, though, and the very use of weapons would seem to be almost forgotten now. Those 300 or more armed and well ordered canoes and numbers of warriors ashore to embark in them, all seen by Captain Cook in Opara, no longer existed in Tahiti. The happy Tahitians content themselves with a small brig. Warfare and disorder seem quite unknown to them now, if not alien.

Upon the completion of our daily tasks, we would stroll through the localities of Matavai Bay, where majestic coconut palms and the delightful-
ness of the evening air itself would entice us imperceptibly into cooling
palm groves beyond. Birdsong would entrance our ear as the sun sank,
while slender and friendly Tahitian girls, walking in light dress, drew the
eyes of abstinent voyagers. Feeling weary, we would commonly move off
to the good Tahitians' huts, picturesquely scattered along streams of pel-
lucid water in which, having bathed, we were more than once regaled
with sweet coconut milk, breadfruit, and even piglet baked on stones. The
agility with which the islanders could procure a coconut amazed and
shamed us at the same time, for all our own attempts to reach the tops of
those tall, smooth tree trunks proved futile. On the other hand, the islanders would simply bind their feet with bast and leap up the tree with all the
lightness of a monkey. After just a few bounds up, they would reach the
very summit and tear off the wanted number of nuts; and they would descend in the same way. The taste changes in a coconut that has been
picked some considerable time before it is to be eaten; and it must be admitted that, without the islanders' assistance, no European would know
the full pleasantness of that nectar, coconut milk.

P. OGIEVSKII

The high mountains that comprise the interior of the island of Tahiti, being surrounded on all sides by gradually rising hills, lose their gigantic appearance as one approaches them but, at the same time, acquire the aspect
of a limitless labyrinth of inimitable nature. For the most part, the shores
incline toward the sea as sloping hills and valleys, covered with coconut
groves and intersected by clear streams. The natives' dwellings are scattered, in pleasant disorder, along these valleys, and the valleys themselves
present an enchanting view. Only on the southeastern side of the island,
for a couple of miles, is the shore steep and even sheer, rising to an elevated crest. From this hill or crest begins the extensive Matavai plain,
making a very convenient anchorage for shipping.[89]

Our first steps on disembarking were toward the place where stood the
splendid and yet simple church serving as the gathering place for all the
inhabitants of this district on festive days. Though splendid, it really differed hardly at all from other structures around. We had to cross a little
stream flowing near the church; but it did nothing to slow our swift progress. Zealous adherents to the Word of God, seeing our approach, came
out of the church to meet us and carried us across on their shoulders. They
would take no payment whatever for their trouble. The missionary, too,
who had just then finished his instruction, met us by its steps and congrat-

ulated us on our happy arrival, which, he said, the natives considered a sign of divine mercy. Neither great art nor deep knowledge are required to describe the architecture of this house of prayer, for it was built extremely simply. It was a hexagonal structure with wooden columns and roof beams, covered by a particular sort of matting woven from palm leaves. The roof stood ten feet from the ground, and the walls had been skilfully filled in with bamboo, plastered on the outside with lime. Bamboo had thus created regular walls. Large windows, closed over by shutters made of boards, gave the building a regular and at the same time attractive appearance. As for internal decoration, it consisted of three little lamps of simple workmanship hanging before the pulpit, which rose above benches placed there for the congregation, who generally sit during a sermon. The floor was strewn with leaves and clean sand, and there was no decoration whatever on the walls. These islanders put on clean material on Sundays or else shirts obtained in exchange for their artefacts from visiting Europeans. And they observe proper decorum on entering the church, listening with respect to the missionaries' exhortations. In the absence of missionaries, they themselves read from the sacred writings.

The positioning of Matavai district is truly delightful and, one might say, fortunate. In order to gain some idea of it, one must imagine an extensive field beginning on the slopes of high-peaked hills that shelter it from southeastern winds and ending on low shores beside the sea. The shores themselves are protected from the destructive effects of the angry waves by a reef that extends far out and by coral banks.

The surfaces of the Matavai valleys are covered by various species of trees, including the breadfruit tree, which grows in great abundance and quite without order right across them, coconut palms, and banana trees. These last are planted by human hands and here and there form the regular alleys of romantic groves. And among these main tree varieties, so to speak, grow many lemon trees and orange trees, indigenous and otherwise. Bushes or undergrowth are in such abundance that it is only with difficulty that the islanders manage to clear a sufficient area of land for their plantations or houses, which for that very reason are often located separately from each other and in the shade of trees. Streams flowing down from the mountain, and the cascades that tumble down along them, create three little rivers that provide the natives with a way of washing themselves frequently and of irrigating their plantations. These little rivers combine to form a single river, which debouches into the bay and supplies the navigators, too, with water.

Papaua district, like Matavai, is level; but it is less sheltered from the winds than Matavai. It is more extensive but poorer in streams, more populous but also less fertile than Matavai. The two districts are separated from one another by a hill that is large rather than high, over which a path has been laid that bears witness to the natives' art. From the foot of this hill, which of course increases in steepness right to its summit, they have cut a winding path that resembles the letter M in outline. It has been done with a precision that might only have been expected of Europeans. Equally worthy of attention is a raised road that runs straight across both Matavai and Papaua districts, passing through shady groves of trees. Traversing the aforementioned hill, one may, without any perceptible fatigue, reach the spot seven miles or so away where Christianity laid the first foundations of its extensive church on Tahiti. By its very great size, this building far exceeds all local structures: it is 700 feet in length and proportionately broad. Inside, there rise the pulpits from which the missionaries no longer preach. Nor does the populace gather there any more, such is the dilapidated state of the building, which, indeed, now threatens to collapse. After only thirteen years, the pillars that are its main supports and strength have become unsteady, and nothing can replace them. At present, another church is being raised nearby, on the same plan only with a single pulpit.

Broadly speaking, these churches have no majesty or internal embellishment, despite the fact that the latter is the surest means of inspiring uplifting reflections. The mere spectacle of the Cross of Our Saviour may produce Christian humility and grief in the heart. But here there is not even that sign of our faith. I had with me an image of the four Apostles, but I was wary of giving it to the islanders, for I foresaw the missionaries' readiness to interpret such an action in a manner uncomplimentary to Russia. I also had with me the design of a Greek Orthodox church, but again I decided not to offer it, knowing the cast of mind of these teachers. They would at once have begun to assert that God may be worshipped even under a tree in the same fashion as in the church of St. Peter and St. Paul. For all the Tahitians' good will and trust in these missionaries, they invariably expressed enraptured wonder on chancing to see the priest aboard our sloop cloaked in his vestments and conducting a prayer. And they listened to our own religious songs and gazed at our icons with the deepest benevolence.

I would have liked to offer here an obituary of the King Pomare, who had effected such celebrated changes on the island of Tahiti, but my superficial knowledge of his feats is inadequate for the purpose. I know only that the late Pomare descended from a royal line of that name and that he had assumed autocratic power even as a young man. He is said to have been unusually strong and very tall, with a swarthy face, protruding eyes, important manner, a store of courage in war, and decisiveness and a sense of justice in civil affairs. His subjects are said to have loved him, and certainly they recall him now with tears. Europeans visiting Tahiti found in him a man without avarice, friendly and serviceable. In the last years of his life, he had sought some way of conducting trade with New Holland and, for that purpose, had purchased a handsome trading brig with his profits from barter in swine and other things. His premature death robbed him of the possibility of enjoying that acquisition.[90] He was buried on a hill near the house that is now considered the principal residence of the royal family. (There is another house in Matavai district for temporary use.) The wooden coffin was placed on the earth, and an arched vault was constructed above it of brick and stone. Over this is a little house, replete with windows, in which a lamp always burns. A green grove of lemon trees adjacent to this mausoleum serves as a symbol of the late king's eternal memory; and waves breaking and foaming against the stony shore on the other side serve to remind us of the insignificant span of our lives in the context of eternity.

No better notion can be given of the royal residences, I think, than by comparing them with sheds or brickyards. The roof beams are covered with coconut leaves, the open spaces at the ends being filled in by sticks and more such leaves. The common natives' homes are just the same, only smaller. Internal decoration is unknown to the Tahitians. In one of the royal residences, I saw a table and five chairs acquired from some European mariner or other, but the Tahitians are not very anxious to use these things. The ground itself, strewn with leaves and covered with mats, substitutes for all ornamentation and serves in place of table and soft mattress alike.

Frequent visits by navigators are doubtless very useful for the natives of Tahiti, who have need of European articles, and for which, indeed, they have such a passionate fondness that they cannot do without them. Moreover, even the roughest manners of an unenlightened people are softened by intercourse with Europeans, and the islanders acquire new tastes and whims as well as the new requirements and the cares that are inseparable from a changed lifestyle. Furthermore, illnesses unknown here before the coming of Europeans, and which are made the more fatal by licentiousness and which spread easily, are the more dangerous because the Tahitians know no cure for them. Besides the sores that they consider to be a European disease, however, these natives do have their own sicknesses, such as dropsy, malevolent scabs, and a peculiar variety of tumours that they call *fefai*. This last is their worst endemic affliction and, again, they have no cure for it, which serves as a refutation of the view that Tahitians have remedies not yet known to European science. It does sometimes happen that they manage to cure themselves by rubbing or massaging the affected part. In my own opinion, however, such instances do not show that there was necessarily a real disease in the first case. The *casuarina* juice that they employ can certainly not be regarded as a sure remedy, for it acts only if assisted by superstition and blind prejudice.[91]

It seems to me that the origins of these diseases are largely connected with the torrid climate, which powerfully incites and yet debilitates sensitivity to illness. The principal cause, however, can scarcely be anything but the constant idleness with which the Tahitians are so well acquainted, for the reason that a generous nature can, even without the least assistance, supply them all year round with her products. Two or three breadfruit trees, which grow of their own accord, adequately supply a man with tasty and nutritious food for nine months of the year; and as for the remaining three months, they are provisioned with excellent foodstuffs also, in the form of assorted roots, such as *nateri*, which somewhat resemble earth apples; *iniak*, which is like our beetroot; potatoes; and taro, together with two varieties of *egue* quite like it, which for the most part grow wild, though the islanders also set them out in plantations for better cultivation and larger quantity. They are encouraged to do this not so much by necessity as by the profit to be had from sales of taro, from which the English produce a good paint.[92]

Despite the abundance of naturally nutritious plants, however, the islanders' caprice or discernment led to the development of a method of conserving vegetables through fermentation, which they in fact employ regularly at a given season of the year. This has induced them to plant out many coconut palms, banana plants, and many other fruiting trees, whose care, however, is far less demanding than is the care of all *our* garden plants. This is the result of the climate and of the fertile soil of the plains, which is black and abundant.

Leaving aside the bananas and other less important fruits, coconuts comprise practically the chief wealth of these islanders after breadfruit; for in the coconut that has reached full maturity, one finds a refreshing beverage that is unique in the tropics, and in addition to that, the kernel of the nut is highly nutritious when ripe, having an almond-like quality. The islanders extract from it a sweet-smelling oil, which they use to smear on their hair, for lighting, for trade with foreigners, and as an offering to the Missionary Society. From the shell that contains the kernel they make domestic utensils, and from the thick, hairy exterior of the shell they twist strong fibrous threads for fishing nets and cordage of different kinds. And they cover the roofs of their houses with the long leaves of the coconut palm, which they also plait and so make little baskets in which to carry fruit. From the bark of the trunk itself, women manufacture more or less fine cloths of many tones, which serve in place of our shirts, kerchiefs, and Persian shawls. The dried timber goes to make houses and canoes.

The seeds of European kitchen vegetables, brought to Tahiti by a number of navigators, are now disdained. Nor do the local natives trouble themselves with the care of horned cattle, sheep, or goats, very likely because those animals demand good supervision and far better feed than do pigs, which can be fed on various fruits that grow here in such abundance without cultivation.

Not all the islanders have cats, most likely because there are not rats in every house. Wild beasts and reptiles are not to be seen on the island of Tahiti, but there are great numbers of birds of various species. Besides yard hens and ducks, there are, in the bush, innumerable swarms of beautiful woodpeckers and swallows, and along the seashores there are blue herons, white gulls, and wild duck. In the waters surrounding the island, there are, besides whales, sharks and dolphins, flying and other multicoloured fish, oysters, crabs, sea snails, and many other creatures. We were casting seine nets in Matavai Bay and invariably bringing up sufficient fish to last the entire crew for one whole day. Among them were particoloured fish similar to bream, which proved harmful to us when eaten.

The mineral kingdom is, by contrast, very poor in Tahiti. Apart from black basalt, from which the islanders had earlier fashioned axes and other things, there is no rock matrix. The mountains here consist of firm, clay-like earth and porous limestone, their surfaces being covered by a thin layer of gray soil suitable only for the support of brush and insignificant trees.

It was not mere curiosity that led me to take daily walks. The friendly behaviour of the islanders themselves, their cheerful way of life and constant readiness to be of help, all attracted me to such an extent that I would pass a whole day with them and return to the sloop only reluctantly when nightfall approached. The pleasant evening weather in itself intensified the beauty of the Matavai meadows, which may, in all justice, be likened to those of the enchanted isle of Calypso.

THE REVEREND DANIEL TYERMAN AND OTHERS

21 July 1823. Captain Lazaroff, of His Imperial Russian Majesty's frigate *Cruiser*, of thirty-six guns, having just arrived in the harbour Matavai, paid us a friendly visit and invited us to dine with him on board his vessel. He and several of his officers speak tolerable English; and we found them polite and intelligent. The captain had been here about three years ago, with another ship in company, on a voyage of discovery northward of the Dangerous Archipelago. He had also circumnavigated New Shetland and particularly examined the coast to the south; but instead of one, he found the land so named to be a group of islands. Besides these, he had touched at upward of twenty small scattered islands, not laid down in any of the charts, most of which were low and of coral structure, and only a few were inhabited.

24 July. When the queen, with young Pomare, the other day went on board the Russian frigate at anchor here, they were received with distinguished honours. The captain got the people who accompanied his royal guests to procure the Tahitian flag from shore, which having obtained, he hauled up on some part of the rigging. He was very liberal with his presents and took great pains to impress upon the minds of his visitors that they and his countrymen were friends and neighbours, who ought to live on terms of the most pleasant intercourse. He pressed them also to accept a Russian flag and hoist it on shore. This equivocal gift, however, they resolutely declined, but were otherwise much pleased with his civilities. It is shrewdly suspected that he has some more politic purpose in view than putting in here for wood and water. Be that what it may, these islands are not worth stealing, either by Russia, America, or England.[93]

OTTO VON KOTZEBUE, 1824

It was not till the 14th of March that we reached the Cape, called by Cook Cape Venus because he there observed the transit of this planet over the sun; and from its beauty, it deserves to be named after this charming goddess herself. It is a low, narrow tongue of land, running out northward from the island, thickly shadowed by cocoa trees and forming by its curve the harbour of Matavai, not a very secure one, but generally preferred by sailors on account of the celebrity bestowed on it by Cook.

When we were still a few miles distant from Cape Venus, we fired a gun to draw attention to the flag hoisted at the foremast as a signal for a pilot. We soon saw a European boat steering towards us; it brought us a pilot who, to our great surprise, addressed us in the Russian language, having recognized our flag as belonging to that nation: he was an Englishman by the name of Williams, who had first been a sailor on board a merchant ship, afterwards entered the service of the Russian American Company on the northwest coast of America, and was at length settled for life in Tahiti. His wife was a native of the island; he was the father of a family and carried on the occupation of pilot in the Bay of Matavai. Wanderers of this kind often settle in the islands of the South Sea; but while they bring with them many vices peculiar to the lower classes in civilized life, they are generally too ignorant and rough to produce any favourable impression on the natives. They are not all liable to this censure; and of about twenty Englishmen and Americans whom I found so naturalized in Tahiti, some assuredly do not deserve it.

Having a pilot on board, we steered directly for the extreme point of Cape Venus, where floated the national standard of Tahiti. This flag displays a white star in a field of red, and, like many of the present arrangements, owes its origin to the missionaries, who do not indeed bear the title of kings of the island, but who exercise an unlimited influence over the minds of the natives. . . .[94]

As it entered the bay, our frigate attracted to the beach a crowd of curious gazers, who greeted our arrival with shouts of joy. Numerous boats laden with all kinds of fruits, provisions, and other articles of merchandise immediately put off from the shore, and we were soon surrounded by gay and noisy Tahitians. With their wares on their backs, they climbed merrily up the sides of the ship, and the deck was soon transformed into a busy market where all was frolic and fun; the goods were offered with a jest, and the bargains were concluded in laughter. In a short time each Tahitian had selected a Russian associate to whom, with a fraternal embrace, he tendered his wish to exchange names. . . . It is probable that these sudden attachments were *not* quite disinterested. . . .[95]

Our clothing appeared to be prized above everything we offered them, and the possession of any article of this kind set them leaping for joy as if out of their wits. On this day we saw no females; and when we were occasionally visited by the women, they always behaved with the greatest propriety.[96] When the sun set, our new acquaintances left us to return to their homes, satisfied with their bargains, delighted with the presents they had received, and without having stolen anything, although above a hundred of them had been on board at once.

I had sent a message to the missionary Wilson by an officer who now returned, bringing for answer an assurance that the missionary would with pleasure do all in his power to assist in procuring our supplies; a promise he faithfully kept.[97]

On the following morning we were greeted by the sun from a cloudless sky . . . and among the thickets of fruit trees were seen the dwellings of the happy inhabitants of this great pleasure-ground, built of bamboos and covered with large leaves, standing each in its little garden; but to our great astonishment, the stillness of death reigned among them, and even when the sun stood high in the heavens, no one was to be seen. . . . The inhabitants were celebrating Sunday, on which account they did not leave their houses, where they lay on their bellies reading the Bible and howling aloud. Laying aside every species of occupation, they devoted, as they said, the whole day to prayer. According to our reckoning, the day was Saturday. This difference proceeded from the first missionaries' having reached Tahiti from the west by way of New Holland, while we had come eastward by Cape Horn.[98]

I resolved to go ashore and pay a visit to Mr. Wilson, that through him I might procure a convenient place for our astronomical observations. We landed at the point of the cape because the shade of a thick palm grove there offered us immediate protection. No one received us on the strand; no human being, not even a dog, was visible. The very birds seemed here to celebrate Sunday by silence, unless, indeed, it was too hot for singing.[99] The loud prayer of the Tahitian Christians reached my ears as I approached their habitations. All the doors were closed, and not even the children were allowed to enjoy the beauty of the morning.

The small but pleasant house of the missionary, built after the European fashion, stands in the midst of a kitchen garden richly provided with all kinds of European vegetables. Mr. Wilson gave me a cordial welcome to his neat and simple dwelling, and presented me to his wife, an Englishwoman, and two children, besides two Englishmen whom he named as Messrs. Bennet and Tyerman.[100] They belonged to the London Missionary Society and had left England three years before to visit the missionary settlements in the South Sea.

The chief missionary, to whom the others are subordinate, is named Nott, and lives in the capital, where the king resides.[101] He is now far advanced in life. He has made himself master of the Tahitian language and was the first who ever wrote it. He has translated the Bible, a prayer-book, and some hymns; and has printed a grammar of the language under the title of ''A Grammar of the Tahitian Dialect of the Polynesian Language. Tahiti: printed at the Mission Press, Burder's Point.''[102]

He also first instructed the Tahitians in reading and writing, which acquirements are now tolerably common among them. I am sorry not to have known Mr. Nott better, and therefore not to have it in my power to judge the man as well as the missionary. His character stands very high.[103] Wilson, also an old man, has now lived twenty years in Tahiti; he was originally a common sailor but was zealously devoted to theology and is honest and good natured.[104] Including Nott and Wilson, there are six missionaries in Tahiti alone and only four among all the other Society Islands. Each missionary possesses a piece of land cultivated by the natives, which produces for him a superfluity of all that he requires, and he also receives an annual allowance of fifty pounds from the London Missionary Society. This Society has also sent missionaries to Tongatabu, one of the Friendly Islands, and to Nukashiva [Nukuhiva], lately made known to us by Krusenstern.[105]

Besides these English missionaries, some native Tahitians, after receiving a suitable education, are sent to spread Christianity among the islands of the Dangerous Archipelago.[106] In Russia, a careful education and diligent study at schools and universities is necessary to qualify anyone to be a teacher of religion. The London Missionary Society is more easily satisfied; a half savage, confused by the dogmas of an uneducated sailor, is, according to them, perfectly fitted for the sacred office.[107]

It was now church time, and Wilson requested me to be present at the service, an invitation which I accepted with pleasure. A broad straight path, planted with the cocoa and lofty breadfruit tree, leads from his house, about a ten minutes' walk, to the place of worship.[108] The church-yard, with its black wooden crosses, impresses the mind with a feeling of solemnity: the church itself is a handsome building, about twenty fathoms long and ten broad, constructed of light wood-work adapted to the climate and whitened on the outside, which gives it a pretty effect among the green shades that surround it. The numerous windows are large but remain unglazed because a free admission of air is here desirable in all seasons; the roof, made of ingeniously plaited reeds and covered with immense leaves, is a sufficient defence against the heaviest rain. There is neither steeple nor clock. The interior of the church is one large hall, the walls of which are neatly kept. It is filled with a number of benches placed in long rows so that the occupants can have a convenient view of the pulpit in the centre. When we entered, the church was full even to crowding, the men seated on one side, the women on the other; they almost all had psalm books lying before them; the most profound stillness reigned in the assembly. Near the pulpit, which Wilson mounted, was placed a bench for Messrs. Bennet and Tyerman, on which I also took my seat.

Notwithstanding the seriousness and devotion apparent among the Tahitians, it is almost impossible for a European seeing them for the first time in their Sunday attire to refrain from laughter. . . . As they know nothing of our fashions, they pay no sort of attention to the cut, and even age and wear do not much diminish their estimation of their attire. A ripped-out seam or a hole is no drawback in the elegance of the article. These clothes, which are brought to Tahiti by merchant ships, are purchased at a rag market and sold here at an enormous profit. The Tahitian, therefore, finding a complete suit of clothes very expensive, contents himself with a single garment; whoever can obtain an English military coat, or even a plain one, goes about with the rest of his body naked, except for the universally worn girdle; the happy owner of a waistcoat or a pair of trousers thinks his wardrobe amply furnished. Some have nothing more than a shirt. . . . The attire of the females, though not quite as absurd, was by no means picturesque. Some wore white or striped men's shirts, which did not conceal their knees, and others were wrapped in sheets.[109] Their hair was cropped quite close to the roots, according to a fashion introduced by the missionaries, and their heads covered by little European chip hats,[110] a most tasteless form, decorated with ribbons and flowers and made in Tahiti. But the most valuable article of dress was a coloured gown, an indubitable sign of the possessor's opulence and the object of her unbounded vanity.[111]

When Wilson first mounted the pulpit, he bent his head forward and, concealing his face with an open Bible, prayed in silence; the whole congregation immediately imitated him, using their psalm books instead of Bibles. After this, the appointed psalm was sung to a most incongruous tune, every voice being exerted to its utmost pitch in absolute defiance of harmony. Wilson then read some chapters from the Bible, the congregation kneeling twice during the intervals. The greater part of them appeared very attentive, and the most decorous silence reigned, which was, however, occasionally interrupted by the chattering and tittering of some young girls seated behind me. I observed that threatening looks directed towards them by Messrs. Bennet and Tyerman seemed to silence them for a moment. . . . [112]

I had assisted at a great religious assembly of the new, devoted, so-called Christian Tahitians; and the comparison naturally arising in my mind, between what I had seen and the descriptions of the early travellers, now introduced reflections which became less and less agreeable in proportion as I acquired a greater insight into the recent history of the island. . . . [113] The Tahitians, accustomed to a blind reverence for missionaries, consult them in all their undertakings, and, by means of the new Constitution, have so confirmed their power, both as priests and as rulers, that it would be difficult for governor, judge, or member of parliament to retain their office after having incurred their displeasure.[114] They have shown their artful policy in the choice of a guardian for the young king. It has fallen on the tributary king of the island of Balabola, distinguished by his giant height of seven feet and by his enormous corpulence, which almost prevents his moving, but by no mental qualification.[115] This mountain of flesh . . . is merely the mouthpiece of the missionaries, and, that their dominion may also be secured for the future, Mr. Nott has the sole charge of the young monarch's education and will not fail to bring him up in the habit of implicit obedience.[116]

The actual document securing the Constitution has not yet appeared; the missionaries were still employed on it, well convinced that whatever they should insert would be received without opposition. When complete, it will probably issue in due form from their printing office, and it will be interesting if some future traveller should bring us the translation.[117]

Firm as the foundation of the missionaries' power appeared, one little cloud was visible on the horizon of the political firmament. A son of the vanquished King Tajo yet existed and was not entirely without adherents.[118] If by any chance he should succeed in gaining possession of the throne, he might remember that these men had assisted in excluding him from it. For this reason, they resolved to confirm the title of the young Pomare by a solemn coronation; and to strengthen his party, all the tributary princes of the whole archipelago were invited to be present at the ceremony. The preparations for this solemnity had long been carrying on, and as it was now soon to take place, nearly all the kings, with numerous suites, had arrived in Tahiti. Among them was the powerful ruler of Ulietea, the grandfather of the infant sovereign.[119] He had brought with him several hundred men, many of them armed with muskets. We much wished to have been present at this first coronation of a king of the Society Islands; but as our time would not permit it, I obtained from Mr. Tyerman an account of the order and plan of the ceremony. . . .[120]

It is remarkable that the Bible, and not the Act of Constitution, was to be given the king as the rule of his government. Was not a sly mental reservation perhaps intended by this? If the Constitution should not have exactly the effect intended and the Tahitians, emboldened by it, should seek to withdraw themselves from their leading strings, then might the pupil of Nott, bound to them by no oath, not come forward to them boldly and force them back under the yoke of the missionaries . . . ? Religion and political institutions may raise a nation in a short period to a high point of civilization, and they may also serve, as in the case of the Turks, to retain them in a state of perpetual barbarism. . . . True, genuine Christianity and a liberal government might have soon given these people, endowed by nature with the seeds of every social virtue, a rank among civilized nations. Under such a blessed influence, the arts and sciences would soon have taken root, the intellect of the people would have expanded . . . Europe would soon have admired, perhaps have envied, Tahiti; but the religion taught by the missionaries is not true Christianity, though it may possibly comprehend some of its doctrines, but half understood even by the teachers themselves. That it was established by force is of itself evidence against its Christian principle. A religion which consists in the eternal repetition of prescribed prayers, which forbids every innocent pleasure, and cramps or annihilates every mental power is a libel on the Divine Founder of Christianity, the benign Friend of human kind. It is true that the religion of the missionaries has, with a great deal of evil, effected some good. It has abolished heathen superstitions and an irrational worship, but it has introduced new errors in their stead. It has restrained the vices of theft and incontinence, but it has given birth to bigotry, hypocrisy, and a hatred and contempt of all other modes of faith, which were once foreign to the open and benevolent character of the Tahitians. It has put an end to avowed human sacrifices, but many more human beings have been actually sacrificed to it than ever were to their heathen gods. . . .[121]

The Tahitians of the present day hardly know how to plait mats, make their paper stuffs, or cultivate a few roots. They content themselves with the breadfruit, which the soil yields spontaneously in quantities more than sufficient for their reduced population. Their navy, which excited the astonishment of Europeans, has entirely disappeared. They build no vessels but a few little paltry canoes, with which they fish off the neighbouring islands, and make their longest voyages in American or European boats which they have purchased. With the method of producing those commodities of civilized nations, which they prize so highly, they are still as much as ever unacquainted. They possess sheep and excellent cotton; but no spinning wheel, no loom, has yet been set in motion among them; they choose rather to buy their cloth and cotton of foreigners for real gold and pearls. One of our sailors sold an old shirt for five piasters. Horses and cattle have been brought to them, but the few that remain have fallen into the possession of strangers and have become so scarce that one hundred piasters was asked for an ox that we wanted in provisioning the ship. The Queen alone possesses a pair of horses, but she never uses them.

The island contains but one smith. . . . It is extraordinary that even the foreigners established here carry on no kind of mechanic trade. Can it be that the missionaries object to it? It is certain that they possess great influence over even the settlers. An American, however, was planning the introduction of a sugar manufactory and promised himself great profit from it.[122]

By order of the missionaries, the flute, which once awakened innocent pleasure, is heard no more. No music but that of the psalms is suffered in Tahiti: dancing, mock fights, and dramatic presentations are no longer permitted. . . . It is remarkable that the degenerate Tahitians are no longer even in person such as they are described by the early travellers. The large-grown *Yeris*, solely employed in praying, eating, and sleeping, are all, men and women, excessively fat even in early youth. The small common people, constrained to some degree of industry, look plump and well fed, but not so swollen as their superiors, and more fine forms are therefore to be seen among them than among the *Yeris*. The latter also suffer from a most disfiguring disease caused by want of exercise and excess nourishment: the legs swell to such a degree that from the knees downward the form of the calf and foot is entirely lost, and the thick cylinders that usurp the place of legs resemble nothing but the legs of elephants. . . .

All vanity is sin, and all care of the person is vanity. Hence the fat *Yeris* beauties no longer shelter their skins from the sun's burning rays and are become as brown as the rest . . . and the rancid cocoa oil with which they smear themselves may be smelt at a distance of many paces. I saw but one handsome girl at Tahiti; she was the sister of the little king, only fourteen years old but already the bride of her uncle, the prince of Ulietea.[123] The men far surpass the women both in form and in features.

The missionaries have abolished the custom of tattooing, and so far at least spared the Tahitians some useless torment. These marks are now only to be seen on people of the middle age and upward, never on the young. The first voyagers who visited this island describe the tattooing as representing half moons, birds, and irregular or zigzag lines; but on a better acquaintance with Europeans, the fashion changed and drawings of our tools, animals, and even compasses and mathematical instruments were executed with the greatest exactness on their bodies.

By the influence of Wilson, a small house situated on Cape Venus was cleared for our astronomical observations: we were told it stood precisely on the same spot where Cook's observatory had formerly been erected.[124] As a particular favour from the government, I was also accommodated with a royal pleasure house in its neighbourhood for my private residence. This very large building, resembling an ancient temple in appearance, had been a favourite abode of the deceased monarch Pomareh [Pomare], and since his death it had remained uninhabited out of respect for his memory. A number of utensils that had belonged to him, and a canoe on which he had obtained many splendid victories, were still preserved here as memorials of the beloved king. The house was wholly without walls ... the air was filled with the perfume of a neighbouring orange grove, which scattered its fruit upon the earth. Since I could only afford to remain a very short time at Tahiti, Dr. Eschscholtz and I immediately took possession of my new abode and erected our little observatory....[125]

In the morning, as we were drinking our coffee and smoking pipes, a messenger arrived from the queen requesting to speak with me. The queen had sent him to inform me that she was curious to see the commander of a Russian frigate.... I had scarcely time to prepare for the reception of my illustrious guests, when the concourse of people hastening to the shore announced their approach. A man soon appeared as avant courier, in the short, red uniform-jacket of an English drummer; an uncommonly showy, many coloured girdle; and the rest of his body, according to custom, quite naked. His legs were adorned by a tattooed representation of pantaloons; and when he turned his back and stooped very little, he showed also a drawing of a large compass, with all the two-and-thirty points executed with striking exactness. In his hand he held a rusty broadsword....[126]

At length, the queen herself appeared, followed by a numerous train of attendants. She walked first, carrying the little king in her arms, and ... after her came her three sisters, all, like herself, large, fat women; and then the whole crowd of the Court.[127] Little Pomareh, a pretty, lively boy, was dressed quite in the European fashion, in a jacket and trousers of bombasin; he wore a round hat, but his feet, like those of all Tahitians, were bare. They object that any kind of shoe hinders their walking. The young bride, a handsome girl, as I have before said, was very lightly clad in a short striped shirt, without any covering on her head. The giant *Yeris*, who formed the Court, mostly wore white shirts and round straw hats with black ribbons.

It was the first time since the death of her consort that the queen had entered these precincts, and a shower of tears fell from her eyes. . . . In the meantime, the master of ceremonies had vanished to prepare the repast.[128] When the queen, after surveying me from head to foot, had communicated her remarks and opinions to the company, I requested the interpreter to thank her in my name for my friendly reception on the island, for the presents she had made me, and for the high honour conferred on me by this visit. She received my thanks graciously and ordered some questions to be put to me, which I answered with all due respect. She inquired how old I was? Whether my voyage had been long? Whether I was a Christian? And how often I prayed daily? This last question afforded me an opportunity, had I thought fit, to give Her Majesty some new ideas on the subject of the missionary religion; but I did not feel myself quite capable of entering into a theological dispute and, therefore, merely replied that Christianity taught us that we should be judged according to our actions rather than the number of our prayers. I do not know how the interpreter rendered my answer,[129] or whether the queen considered me a heretic, but this I conjectured from her speaking no more on religious subjects and asking me, in order to change the conversation, whether the earth were really round? I assured Her Majesty that I could answer from my own experience, as I was now sailing round it for the third time.[130] This appeared to excite some astonishment, but my assertion concerning its spherical form still gained but small credit.

I then produced some presents for the queen, her family, and their immediate attendants, which, though in themselves extremely trifling, were received with great pleasure and produced a degree of hilarity little consistent with the symbols of mourning worn by the royal party. To the queen I presented a piece of calico four or five yards long, a coloured silk handkerchief, a small looking-glass, a pair of scissors, and some glass beads; to the young princess, a silk handkerchief, beads, and a looking-glass; to the sisters of the queen, cotton handkerchiefs, glasses, and scissors; to their attendants, among whom were four ladies, knives. During this time, the master of ceremonies had killed a pig and baked it in the earth in the Tahitian manner.[131] As soon as the royal family had resumed their seats, he brought it in and placed it before the queen on a great banana leaf, other servants spreading yams, potatoes, and breadfruit upon the ground. My chair was brought and placed opposite to the queen, who invited me, with much friendliness, to partake of the meal. I preferred, however, being an idle spectator, for it was still early in the day and I had no appetite.... When the repast was over, and a prayer said as before, the royal personages washed their hands with water and their mouths with cocoa milk, and then lay down altogether to sleep, the attendants retiring. I offered Her Majesty the use of my bed, which she condescendingly accepted, and during the siesta, I returned to my plans for our astronomical observations. On awaking, the queen expressed a wish to see my frigate. My time was not at my own disposal, but I entrusted to one of my officers the charge of doing the honours of the ship.... [132]

The officers exerted themselves to maintain the good humour of their guests by trifling presents and, among other things, gave them a piece of sham-lace, several yards in length, which was received with extraordinary eagerness. The royal sisters divided it between them and added it to the black crepe trimming of their hats; and so great was the admiration excited by this novel article of finery, that the rage for gold lace became an absolute fever among the more distinguished Tahitian ladies. The severe lessons of the missionaries forbidding all adornment of the person now proved vain. There was no end to petitions for lace and... tormented husbands came every day to the ship, willingly offering a fine fat pig and eight fowl for half an ell [22 inches] of the false lace.... While the royal family remained below in the cabin, their attendants were engaged on deck in purchasing from our sailors all sorts of old clothes for a hundred times their value, in Spanish piasters. The Tahitians have as yet no notion of the value of money, which they get from the ships that touch at the island and by their trade in cocoa oil with New Holland. [133] The missionaries have done their utmost to draw money into the country, and for this purpose they have fixed prices on every article of provision, under which no one dares to sell them to foreign ships. These prices are, however, so high that nothing but necessity would induce anyone to pay them, so that the ships in general rather provide themselves with old clothes, utensils of various kinds, and toys.... During this visit to my vessel, the young princess had found an opportunity to bargain with a sailor for a sheet.... After dinner, a general conversation took place, in which a man seventy years of age distinguished himself by his animation and intelligence. He was the only individual present who had personally known Captain Cook. He... boasted not a little of having accompanied Cook on his coasting voyages about the islands and of having often slept in the same tent with him. He knew the names of all Cook's company, and he could recollect the particular pursuits of each officer.... [134]

This visit being over, I hoped to be at liberty to pursue my occupations in peace, but in this I was disappointed. Though my habitation was surrounded by sentinels, I was continually disturbed by swarms of curious islanders who, troublesome as they were, were so gentle and good tempered that it was impossible to be angry with them. They were particularly pleased with Dr. Eschscholtz's little museum and took pains to collect from every corner of the island butterflies, beetles, birds, and marine productions, by way of showing their sense of the kindness with which he exhibited his treasures, often receiving from him in return some trifling present.[135]

Though the vice of theft has certainly greatly diminished among the Tahitians, they cannot always refrain. . . . Every theft is, however, on discovery punished without distinction of persons, and the criminal, on conviction, is generally sentenced to work on the highway. A road has been made round the island, on which those who have committed great transgressions are condemned to labour;[136] but it is probable that neglect of prayer, or any trifling offence against the missionaries, would also entail this punishment. We had an opportunity of observing the severity with which theft is punished. A complaisant husband could not resist the entreaties of his wife, who longed for one of our sheets. One day, when the sailors were washing in the river, he took an opportunity, unperceived as he thought, to snatch up one of these coveted articles and run off with it. Some of his countrymen, who had watched him, directly brought him back, bound him to a tree, and informed me and a missionary of the circumstances. On reaching the spot, I already found the judge of the district and the missionaries Wilson and Tyerman standing beside the thief, who was still bound to the tree. Mr. Tyerman, who was especially bitter, could not refrain from abuse: he called the criminal a brute who was not worthy to be treated as a human creature, and acted altogether as if the affair were his. This surprised me, as the judge of the district was present and Mr. Tyerman had no official appointment on the island, but he was a member of the Missionary Society, *et tout est dit*. I was now asked if I wished the offender to be whipped . . . I forgave him and begged that he might be dismissed with a severe admonition upon the disgrace of theft and an earnest warning for the future. This request, however, was not granted and the unfortunate offender was taken away, still tied, to work on the highway: the judge and Mr. Wilson concurred in assuring me that he was not a Tahitian but an inhabitant of another island. . . . At all events, it appears certain that thefts do not take place oftener than among civilized nations.[137]

With the chastity of the Tahitian women the case is similar; and it does not appear to me that the breaches of this virtue are more frequent on the whole than in Europe. It was with the utmost caution and secrecy, and in the most fearful anxiety lest their errors should be betrayed to the missionaries, that the females complied with the desires of our sailors.[138] An accidental occurrence proved that their terrors were not groundless. A married man who possessed a house of his own was induced to barter, according to the custom of his ancestors, the favours of his wife for some pieces of iron; he had also assisted a young man in an intrigue with a woman whose husband was not so complaisant, by lending his house as a place of rendezvous. Suddenly, the owner and his wife disappeared in the night, the house was found empty next morning, and we could never learn what had become of its proprietors. Have the missionaries already introduced the oubliettes?[139]

Having occasion one morning to visit Wilson on business, I found his door, which usually stood open, closed and fastened. I knocked several times, but the whole house seemed buried in the repose of death. At length, after loud and repeated strokes, the door was opened by Wilson, whose cheeks bedewed with tears made me apprehensive that some great calamity had befallen him. I was, however, soon satisfied that devotion alone had caused this emotion. In an ante-room I found four or five Tahitians, of the highest rank, as Wilson told me, on their knees reading the Bible. . . .

I received another visit from the royal family, accompanied this time by many of the vice-kings then in Tahiti, with their consorts. Among them was the grandfather of the little monarch Pomareh. After some preliminaries, my illustrious guests unanimously preferred a request. They wished me to get a pair of boots made for the little king. His coronation, they said, would soon take place and they did not think it decorous, on so solemn an occasion, for the sovereign of all the Society Islands to sit barefoot on his throne. I immediately ordered my shoemaker to provide for the royal necessity; the measure was taken, and my complaisance was rewarded by the gratitude of the company. At this visit, also, the guests ate and slept. I took advantage of the opportunity to observe the method of preparing the pig, always the chief dish in their feasts. A sufficiently large round hole was dug in the earth and filled with stones. A fire was then lighted in it and kept burning till the stones were red hot, when the ashes and cinders were taken out, and the stones covered with large banana leaves, upon which the pig was laid after being thoroughly cleaned and stuffed with glowing stones; and, finally, the hole was filled up with earth. . . .[140]

Matavai Bay is rich in finely flavoured fish, of various and sometimes extraordinary forms and beautiful colours. The Tahitians eat them raw or only steeped in sea water. Their fishing tackle consists of nothing more than bad angling lines and hooks; to make nets, as their forefathers did, would trespass too much upon the time they are obliged to spend in prayer. Hence fish is so great a rarity to them, that their eager desire for it sometimes prompts them to belie their good character, of which we had an example. One of our large nets having brought up a multitude of fine fish, the temptation was too strong to be resisted, and our friends would forcibly have shared our acquisition with us, had the accidental appearance of the judge of the district not restrained them. They then tried to obtain the fish by barter, and offered their most valuable tools for the smallest and worst of them. I gave them, however, so many that for once their appetite was fully satisfied with a luxurious repast.[141]

I had heard much of an institution established by the missionaries for the instruction of the people and was desirous to learn what progress the Tahitians had made in the rudiments of science. Being informed that the lessons commenced at sunrise, the first rays of that luminary found me one morning at the school house, as I conceived the simple structure before me to be. Its walls were formed of bamboo canes, erected singly at sufficient distances to admit the refreshing breeze from all sides, and supporting a good roof. The interior was one spacious quadrangular apartment, provided with benches and with raised seats for the teachers.

I had not waited long before the pupils of both sexes entered. They were neither lively children nor youths but adults and aged persons who crept slowly in with downcast looks and with prayer books under their arms. When they were all assembled and seated on the benches, a psalm was sung; a Tahitian then rose, and, placing himself on an elevated bench, he read a chapter from the Bible. After this, they sang again, and then knelt with their backs to the reader, who, also kneeling, repeated with closed eyes a long prayer. At its conclusion, the orator resigned his place to another Tahitian, when the whole ceremony commenced anew. Another psalm, another chapter, and another prayer were sung and said; again and again. . . . To pray and to obey are the only commands laid upon an oppressed people, who submissively bow to the yoke and even suffer themselves to be driven to prayers by the cudgel! A police officer is especially appointed to enforce the prescribed attendance upon the church and prayer meetings. I saw him in the execution of his functions, armed with a bamboo cane, driving his herd to the spiritual pasture.[142]

I had heard from the missionaries many wonderful accounts of Lake Wahiria [Vahiria], situated among the mountains that rise in the centre of the northern peninsula. They themselves had never seen it. . . . Mr. Hoffmann, our minerologist,[143] an active young man, resolved to undertake this expedition accompanied by three Tahitians: Maititi, who on our arrival had concluded a treaty of friendship with him and adopted the name of Hoffmann; Tauru, a respectable elderly man; and Teiraro, a brisk and lively young fellow. The latter two could write their own names. . . . Maititi, a soldier in the royal Tahitian army, bore the insignia of his rank in a musket, to which nothing but the lock was wanting, and a cartouche-box without powder. . . . They travelled on a broad fine path through forests of fruit trees and several villages, and considered the population of this district to exceed that in the neighbourhood of Matavai. In the country of Weijoride they began to climb the mountains and soon entered a charming valley stretching SSW and enclosed by high, steep rocks, basaltic, like those of Matavai.[144] A few scattered huts raised on the margin of a little river gave tokens of human habitation. In one of these, occupied by an old married pair, our travellers passed the first night. . . . Mr. Hoffmann describes the operation of lighting the fire on this occasion, in the following manner: A Tahitian took two pieces of wood of different degrees of hardness, laid the softer upon the ground, and very rapidly rubbed its length backward and forward with the harder. This made a furrow, in which the dust rubbed from the wood collected and soon became hot; it was then shaken among dry leaves and burst into flame. Before supper, the master of the house recited a prayer aloud, the family repeating it after him, but not audibly. They then ate a hearty but silent meal and prayed again before lying down to sleep. The couch offered to Mr. Hoffmann was a raised platform in the hut, thickly spread with mats, with a pair of sheets of the Tahitian manufacture, called tapa, for its covering. . . .[145]

As they proceeded, the valley became wilder but more beautiful: it opened to a greater width, and the precipices around rose to a thousand feet in height. . . . At noon the travellers reached a hut inhabited by a friend of Maititi named Tibu; the owner also of another hut some miles further up, where his wife lived with the pigs and dogs! This being the last station on the road to the Wahiria Lake, it was determined to spend the night here. At a height of 711 feet above the level of the sea, the travellers found enormous blocks of granite lying in a southeasterly direction. The way to Wahiria lay towards the SSW and they continued ascending till they reached a marsh in a rocky basin, where wild boars were running about.[146]

Another steep precipice was to be climbed before they could reach the valley of the Wahiria. This stretches from north to south and forms an oval, in the centre of which lies the lake, according to barometrical measurement 1,450 feet above the level of the sea. The surrounding rocks rise perpendicularly more than 2,000 feet. The lake is above a mile and a quarter in circumference and. . . . the depth near the shore is eleven, and in the middle not more than seventeen, *toises*.[147] After Mr. Hoffmann had satisfied his curiosity, he returned with his companion to Tibu's hut and happily reached its shelter before a heavy shower fell. . . . The following day being Sunday, Tauru, immediately on rising, repeated a long prayer and then read a chapter of the New Testament, of which at least one copy was to be found in every hut. After a good breakfast, Mr. Hoffmann wished to proceed, but his guides were not to be moved. They assured him that a continuation of the journey would be a profanation of the Sabbath, a crime for which they would be hanged should it come to the knowledge of the missionaries. This was a little too strongly expressed; and the tempting remains of the roast pig had, no doubt, as much influence in supporting their resolution as their religious scruples. The next morning at all events, they made no objection to setting out. Our travellers were joined on the road by many families laden with mountain bananas, so that they arrived in a large company at Matavai. Mr. Hoffmann made several other journeys into the interior of the island and visited Arue, the present residence of the court. . . . The houses there were built merely of perpendicular bamboo canes, standing at some distance apart to give free admission to the air. The roofs of palm leaves were strong enough to defy the heaviest rain.[148]

As curious after novelty as more civilized infants, the heads of children were thrust out from every hut he passed, and the parents hospitably asked him in. When he accepted the invitation, he was always conducted to the seat of honour, a raised bench covered with matting and tapa stuff; and after freely partaking of the best the house had to offer, he was considered to have paid handsomely for his entertainment with a knife. Bedsteads were made of bamboo canes, filled with soft matting placed along walls where they made very easy, comfortable couches. These pleasant little abodes, in which the greatest cleanliness is everywhere observable, are all surrounded by cultivated gardens. In the evenings, they are lighted by the oily nuts of the taper tree, fastened in rows on splinters.[149]

In the capital, Mr. Hoffmann found nothing remarkable. The palace inhabited by the royal family was a spacious hut, with an antechamber or outer house in which eight of the guard kept watch. Their only weapon was an old pistol fastened on a plank; this was freqently fired, probably to accustom the young king to the tumult of battle. The old king lies buried under a stone monument, in front of which three guns are kept; but, to prevent accidents, they are nailed up.[150]

We have already mentioned the trade in cocoa oil carried on by the Tahitians and the ship possessed by the queen. This is commanded by an Englishman, and a part of the crew is also English. It was just returned from a voyage among the Society Islands, where it had been to collect tribute, and was preparing to carry a cargo of cocoa-oil, stowed in thick bamboo canes, to Port Jackson.[151] From the captain, who visited me, I gained much information concerning the present state of affairs in these seas. . . .[152]

The map of Matavai, and of the bay which bounds it on the northeast, completed by us with the utmost care from trigonometrical surveys, is attached to this volume. . . . The ebb and flow of the tide in Matavai Bay differs from the ordinary rules and appears wholly uninfluenced by the moon. The rise and fall is very inconsiderable. Every noon the whole year round, the water is highest at the moment the sun touches the meridian and falls with the sinking sun until midnight. As well as the sun's motion this phenomenon serves to supply the place of clocks to the inhabitants.

Our first observation by chronometers, on our arrival at Matavai, gave the longitude of Venus Point as 149°20'30"; the true one, as given by Admiral Krusenstern on his map, is 149°27'20"; consequently, the error of our chronometers was 6'50."[153] This correction has been made in all the longitudes taken by us in the Dangerous Archipelago. From our observatory on Venus Point, we found its latitude 17°29'19" and its longitude 149°29'. The variation of the needle was 6'50"E, and its inclination 29°30'.[154] The barometer ranged from 29'80" to 29'70"; Réaumur's thermometer from 23½ to 24½°. . . .

On the morning of 24 March, we broke up our tent on Venus Point, left our dwelling, and shipped all our instruments and effects. The afternoon was appointed for our departure. The Tahitians now boarded the ship, bringing as many provisions as they could carry. They expressed great regret at losing us; and, to prove the disinterestedness of their good will, they would accept no presents in return. . . . [155]

Some months before us, the French Captain Duperré (Duperrey) had visited Tahiti upon a voyage of discovery in the corvette *Coquille*. He returned home safely, and is about to publish his travels, of which he has already had the goodness to send me some portions.[156] An important acquisition to science may be expected from this work.

THE REVEREND DANIEL TYERMAN AND OTHERS

27 March, 1824. The Russian ship *Enterprise* (Captain Kotzebue) came to anchor in Matavai Bay. The captain had commanded *Rurich* [*Riurik*], on a voyage of discovery, in 1817, etc., of which the journal has been published. His present expedition is to the northwest coast of North America. He and several officers came on shore and visited the missionaries, by whom they were hospitably entertained.

29 March. The royal family arrived from Pare to see the Russian vessel and pay their compliments to the captain, who had taken up his residence in a house near Point Venus, belonging to the late king. Some of his men having laid articles of common use on a bedstead on which Pomare was accustomed to sleep, offence was taken by his relatives, who considered that piece of furniture tabued, or in a certain fashion sacred, by the touch of the royal person, a qualm of superstition which neither the chiefs nor the people have yet been able entirely to overcome.

We paid a morning visit to Captain Kotzebue, on board his ship, where we found the young Pomare, with his mother and sister, the regent.[157] The priest who accompanies the expedition is a monk of the Greek church. Being willing to show kindness to the young king, he took him upon his knee; but the child, not less terrified at the good father's long beard than Hector's little son of old was at the "dazzling helm and nodding crest,"[158] burst into a loud fit of crying and was taken away before he could be pacified. Mr. Nott had a long conversation with the captain concerning the relation in which these islands stand towards England; Russia apparently coveting the petty, but merely nominal, distinction of adding these green specks within the tropics to the measureless deserts of snowy land which constitute her Asiatic empire. There is no disposition at all, however, on the part of the natives to acknowledge such dependence, under the pretext of alliance with the autocrat of all the Russians; whereas they would be glad to put themselves under the direct guardianship of England.[159]

Captain Kotzebue has brought his mathematical instruments on shore, and put them up in a tent at Point Venus, in order to make observations and to correct the ship's timepieces, etc. But that locality has been much changed since Captain Cook was here and witnessed the transit of Venus. The tongue of land does not extend so far into the water as it did then, by sixty feet; the ground which was covered with vegetation is now a bank of sand; while the river, which opened into the sea at some distance, has found its way close by the point. Captain Kotzebue says that he finds Point Venus to differ six to seven miles in longitude from Captain Cook's computation.

In consequence of the Russian vessel being in the harbour, the schools are forsaken, and almost every ordinary occupation suspended. The people are crowding about the strangers, both on ship-board and on shore, with their fruit, hogs, and other commodities for sale. But it was gratifying to observe that not a canoe went out yesterday, and the Sabbath was as sacredly kept by the Tahitians (both converts and half-heathens) as though there were no temptation at hand to break it for the indulgence of curiosity and the profits of commerce, eager as they are to visit the strange ships and traffic with strange people. Very differently, and very disgracefully, on the other hand, have those born-Christians, the Russians, employed *their* Sabbath which, with the exception of a formal and customary service performed on board, could not be distinguished from a day of labour and dissipation.

5 April. Captain Kotzebue dined with us. He is no doubt an able navigator, but he is not possessed of those social habits and friendly feelings which we have been in the habit of meeting within all the commanders of ships of other countries. He did not even show us the attention of inviting us to go on board his ship. His officers appear to be a number of highly respectable young men.[160]

6 April. Captain Kotzebue called upon us to take his leave. He was bound immediately to the Navigator's Islands.[161] At his request, Mrs. Wilson had provided him several articles of provision, which were to be ready by 4:00 pm; but he got under way before that time and went without them. The squally state of the weather was probably the cause of his hasty movement. The captain did not appear to think the better of these islands on account of their having renounced idolatry and embraced Christianity, though he had every reason to be satisfied with the general behaviour and conduct of the people.[162]

E.A. BERENS

2 February. By observations at noon we found ourselves in 15°59′23″S, longitude 210°46′E by the chronometers. We were now sixty miles distant from Tethuaroa and so obliged to remain under the very smallest sail during the night in order not to be less than fifteen miles distant from the island at dawn. It actually revealed itself to us at a distance of some ten miles at dawn next day. It is shown on Kruzenshtern's chart as a single island, but it appeared to us to be two fairly large and four small islets connected by a reef, part of which, as we know from Cook's *Voyage*, is submerged.[163] Tethuaroa is rich in turtles, and natives generally come over from Tahiti to get them. By 9:00 am we had left the island behind, passing it at a distance of six Italian miles. At the same time, the island of Tahiti revealed itself to us directly ahead, with the island of Eimeo off to its right.

We proceeded until noon on 3 February under a fresh following wind, making six knots. Precisely at noon, though, this wind began to die down. At 6:00 pm we were no more than six miles offshore, but we could not make out the coastline too well because of mists. More particularly, we were unable to examine a cape by the bay and so found ourselves unable to proceed further. We were thus forced to turn into the wind for the night. All the following night, we were tormented by continual squalls from various quarters of the compass, accompanied by torrential rain.[164]

4 February. From dawn until 7:00 am, the shore was concealed in a thick mist that fell in the absence of all wind. Just as soon as the horizon cleared so that the shore became visible, the captain sent Dmitrii Ivanovich [Iakovlev] in the boat to survey it. D.I. was soon back, however, having met a shore boat coming out toward him. It was the com-

mandant of Matavai Bay who had come out to us and who now showed us
the entrance into it. We could not enter even under tow, however, because
of the gentle head wind and agitated water. All morning long, heavy rain
fell and the wind blew gently from the SE.

The previous evening, we had been unable to understand why the
Tahitian natives, seeing a sloop so very near, had not come out to us.
Later, the captain remembered about the missionaries here and noted that
it was a Sunday.[165] He remarked that most likely the missionaries had not
allowed the natives to come out since it was a festival day, restraining
them from all forms of work. And this was, in fact, confirmed by the natives who came out today, bringing us a few oranges, coconuts, bread-
fruits, and bananas. The oranges were not quite ripe and were therefore
sharp and did not taste too good. As for the coconuts, they contained only
milk, with a very thin layer of meat around it. Still, the coconut milk had
an excellent taste, quite unlike that of coconuts from the Cape Verde Islands.

The commandant of the Matavai Bay settlement was wearing a short,
dark blue Chinese jacket and dyed blue breeches.[166] Other natives went
completely naked, apart from the girdle around their middle. They stayed
with us all day and so at dinner time the commandant was invited to sit at
the officers' table. He ate almost nothing, though, because there was nothing he cared for. He particularly disliked our potato sauce, which he spat
out just as soon as he had taken it into his mouth. When we asked him
why he had done so, he would not give the true reason, claiming instead
that the food was excellent and very tasty but that he could not eat any because he had a headache! They left at 3:45 pm, leaving only a pilot on the
sloop.

On the following day, 5 February, we realized that in the night we had
been carried far to the NE by the swell. And so, given the wind that prevailed, we found ourselves yet again deprived of the hope of getting into
the bay. However, a steady air that sprang up from the NW did soon bring
us to Venus Point, which, as described by Cook, serves as a very distinctive indicator of the bay's entrance, though unfortunately we who had
been coasting along the shores for two days now had hitherto failed to distinguish it from other capes that were likewise very near. Until the arrival
of the governor, in fact, we in the sloop had remained in doubt. The point
in question consists of a sandy spit that protrudes into the sea and that actually lies further north than all the other capes. On its very extremity,
many coconut palms are growing; and to the right of those palms are situated some buildings. From the side where we had been, though, these
buildings were invisible. Approaching from the east, one would find them
very useful in locating the bay, which, in truth, can easily be found on any
clear day when the hills surrounding it are visible.

As mentioned, the governor came out to us, and after him there came a great number of native craft. His arrival was the more welcome to us for the fact that the pilot who had been left on board knew his business pretty badly. The governor himself replaced the man, in fact. His first order, which was that all native canoes should position themselves at the very edge of the reef bordering the bay's entrance, obliged us to place some confidence in him; and he duly brought us, with great skill, through that extremely narrow passage no more than ten fathoms across and around its windings. Once we were in the bay, the governor pointed out the best and securest anchorage, where we at once... dropped anchor in thirty fathoms of water. Not ten minutes elapsed before the sloop was completely filled with islanders who had come out with various sorts of fruit and quantities of shellfish.

In accordance with an order from the captain, however, no one took anything from these natives, so that the necessary bartering would not be spoiled for us. The islanders were not too importunate, though: it was enough merely to utter the word "taboo" and they felt obliged to move away.[167]

V.S. ZAVOIKO, 1835

On 13 November, having rested for six days in Honolulu, we weighed anchor and set a course for the islands of Tahiti. Taking full advantage of the trade wind, we made swift progress and on 25 November crossed the equator, where we met with variable winds. By 7 December, we had come into sight of the island of Emeo [Eimeo]. As we drew near, we fired our cannon; and at that summons, a native pilot came out to us in haste. Coming on board the transport, he laughed and spoke what we afterwards discovered from the missionaries was English of a sort. Many of the natives here were convinced that they were speaking English.

Our captain did not feel able to rely on this pilot and so, not knowing the entrance into this harbour and having no charts of it, we were obliged to go in unaided. In the necessity, the captain then sent a boat ashore to a missionary, to ask if he himself would come and bring us into harbour. A missionary duly came the next day, but as it transpired we were held up for three more days by head winds and were unable to go in. Finally, on 10 January, we did so and dropped anchor.[168]

The harbour was spacious and convenient, with an entrance some two hundred and fifty fathoms wide. As we were moving in, moreover, we were surrounded by natives in little craft laden with various kinds of fruit. Having dropped anchor, the captain went ashore with the missionary, who had invited us all to call on him at any time. He was the sole European in the harbour and, to his honour, the natives loved and respected him. He was a very pious man and has behaved in such a manner that all who chance to visit that island owe him a debt of gratitude and indeed should thank God for sending down to earth a man who, sacrificing himself, has brought enlightenment to that remote spot.[169]

The people here are idle in the extreme because they can find sustenance without any effort whatever. Breadfruit grows in considerable abundance. The natives' huts are built among these trees, so placed that even when lying down the inhabitants can pick up the fruit and toss it into a fire that will bake it within half an hour! Breadfruit is extremely tasty, too, and white as though made from the best quality ground flour. We would eat it with great appetite, hot and with oil.[170] There are unlimited amounts of other fruits; whole groves of orange and lemon trees, banana plants, pineapples. On the other hand, kitchen vegetables are little cultivated because of the laziness of the natives. Only the missionaries and a few of the natives grow any.

Hens, goats, and swine are raised in large numbers. All the natives, from young to old, have a passion for money. Sometimes it happened that we would ask them if we might drink some water or coconut milk. First, they would try to get a thaler from us for it; then, seeing that we were just walking up the stream or by the trees, they would hasten to offer us their own supplies—but again extending a hand and saying, "A thaler!"[171] The missionary here watches carefully to see that rum is not brought in to the natives, so their ruin is not unhindered. Rum would certainly cause their ruin otherwise, for they are exceedingly fond of that spirit and persistently beg for it.

Yet at the same time they are very kindly people. As soon as they caught sight of us, they would immediately cry out, "*Yurona-boi!*" or "Hello!"[172] And wherever one might happen to walk on the island, one would be satiated if one had but a single thaler in one's pocket! Also, one could have anything one might wish from them. They also attend church, one should add, where the missionary instructs them in their own tongue. They have their own school, too, where they gather in order to learn psalms by heart. They all respect and fear the missionary.

I spent some time hunting on this island, roaming over the hills and around the bays, and I was very well satisfied with the pastime.[173] I should also add that I went for a fish ride! How can that be, you say! A fish ride! Yes, Venus rode on doves, and Bacchus trudged along on asses, and someone else was borne on a wooden Pegasus, and we all, in our time, rode on sticks... but I also rode fish! This is how it was. When a daring native who is crossing the bay in calm weather spots a shark in the water (sharks normally swimming two feet or so beneath the surface so they are quite easily seen in completely calm water), he lets some rope woven from coconut palm bark down from his canoe. He does it for fun, having first made loops in it. The shark, known for its gluttony, sees the rope and tries to swallow it. The native lets out more and more nooses, while the shark turns over onto its belly, wanting somehow or other to seize the rope, its jaws being under the head. At that instant, the daring fellow succeeds in passing his rope beneath the shark, tightens the noose, and pulls the creature up until its head alone is visible on the surface of the water. Having tied his rope to the prow of the canoe, the hunter no longer has any worries! He just steers from the stern, as necessary. The more the fish rushes, the faster his craft travels forward! I once had opportunity to travel in this fashion for two hours, and I believe that I covered at least fourteen versts![174]

V.S. ZAVOIKO, 1839

We left the island of Voagu [Oahu] on 5 January 1839 and steered a course for Emeo [Eimeo], one of the Tahitian Group, where we duly arrived, after a twenty-four-hour tropical passage of the most pleasant kind, on 29 January. Here I met with my old friends. They were glad to see me in hopes of getting presents, and I perceived now that friendship is everywhere and most definitely based on expectations of advantage.[175] Having passed four days with these friends, we took on stores of provisions from them and set off again on 3 February to pass around Old Man Cape Horn.

6

RUSSIAN AND RUSSO-GERMAN SCIENCE

INTRODUCTION

Comments are offered here on selected aspects of the practical ethnography, zoology, botany, hydrography, geology, and meteorology that Russian expeditions undertook in Tahiti in the early nineteenth century. Marine astronomy performed at Te-auroa at the northern end of Matavai Bay in Tahiti differed little from that performed in the Tuamotus and so is not covered here. The physics and oceanography of Emil Lenz of *Predpriiatie* have been touched on in many histories of science and Pacific exploration, and have only little bearing on Tahiti. Linguistics is also conspicuously absent from the list of Russian contributions to Tahitian studies. Adelbert von Chamisso, early student of Polynesian dialects and author of *Uber die Hawaiische Sprache* (1837, reprinted by Halcyon Antiquariaat, Amsterdam 1969), neither visited Tahiti aboard *Riurik* nor returned with *Predpriiatie* in 1824. Kotzebue's attempt to treat the subject of spoken Tahitian, published in Chapter Five ("Otaiti") of his 1830 narrative (*Novoe puteshestvie vokrug sveta*, ed. Tumarkin, 1981, pp. 123-25), is unimpressive. It scarcely bears comparison with the Polynesian word lists compiled by Aleksei P. Lazarev of *Blagonamerennyi* and Pavel Zelenoi of her sister-ship, *Otkrytie*, in 1821. (The holographs remain locked up in TsGAVMF, under reference: *fond* 213, op. 1, *delo* 43.)

Discussion of ethnography is here limited to a brief treatment of the illustrative record and of artefacts held in St. Petersburg, some of which arrived in Russia in the late 1700s but the bulk of which came from Tahiti in the sloops *Vostok* and *Mirnyi*.

THE ILLUSTRATIVE RECORD

Pavel N. Mikhailov's Tahitian drawings are today in the Drawings Division of the State Russian Museum in St. Petersburg. Few have been published, yet they are of the highest ethnographic significance as an immediate and unbiased record of the Russian sojourn at Matavai Bay in 1820. There are also other drawings and aquarelles made aboard the armed sloop *Moller*, dating from 1826-29. These drawings comprise the most important surviving record of *Moller*'s visit to Tahiti from 29 April to 15 May 1827.[1]

It was Aleksandr Varnek, a successful painter with a clientele among St. Petersburg's wealthier gentry, who sorted out Mikhailov's legacy after his death from consumption (12 September 1840) and enumerated his works with red ink. The Mikhailov Portfolio was reorganized and renumerated by the staff of the State Russian Museum in recent times, but fortunately the Soviet enumeration is complemented by the red ink pagination. The portfolio contains at least a dozen sheets with Tahitian elements on them. Three of the 1819-21 studies were worked up by Mikhailov as proposed illustrations for the Bellingshausen narrative.[2] They were lithographed at state expense and appeared in the *Atlas* as Plates 35 to 37: *Pomari, King of O-Taiti*, *The Breakfast of the King of O-Taiti*, and *A View of the Island of O-Taiti from Venus Point*. Roughs of King Pomare and his wife and two finished studies for *The Breakfast*, one in graphite and the other in water-colours, remain in the original portfolio. The original from which Mikhailov worked up his *View of the Island*, however, is not present. Some of the Tahitian pieces in the Mikhailov Portfolio are listed in Table 1.

Because Plates 35 to 37 in the 1831 *Atlas* (reproduced here as Plates 10 to 12) have been used as ethnographic records, and because roughs and sketches in the 1819-21 portfolio merit separate publication and comment, the following remarks are restricted to those Tahitian studies that Mikhailov wished to see published with the Bellingshausen text.

Mikhailov's portrait of Pomare II, then, shows the king as the Russians saw him on 22 July 1820. Mikhailov followed the letter and spirit of his instructions, as well as his romantic inclinations, by omitting the "blue spectacles" that, we learn from Midshipman Novosil'skii, the king was wearing that day.[3] "His hair was cropped short in front, but at the back it hung in a single lock, curling down." As Cook had observed, "the better sort let it grow long" in Tahiti.[4] Pomare made no use of *mono'i* (coconut oil pomade), but followed the chiefly practice noted by Forster and Bligh of keeping a tuft of chin hair and a thin moustache.[5] Pomare's shirt was evidently of European type or make, whereas his outer "white material"

TABLE 1

Tahitian pieces in the Mikhailov Portfolio

Numbering	Title	Subject matter/remarks
29071/71/obv	*Coral Island and Natives of Grand Duke Aleksandr Nikolaevich Island*, etc.	Obverse shows *Wife of the King of O-Taiti* and shorelines Teremo'emo'e shown in graphite. Unfinished
29151/150	*Native Type, Island of O-taiti*	Graphite sketch, 10.9 by 17.5 cm. 1820
29152/151	*Basket and Woven Footwear*	Graphite, 10.7 cm by 8.7 cm. Tahitian?
29220/219	*Head of a Female Native of the Island of O-taiti*	Graphite, crayon, sang on yellow paper, 22 by 14.7 cm
29221/220	*Female Native of O-taiti*	Graphite & water-colour, 26 by 19 cm
29222/221	*Native Types, Islands of the South Pacific Ocean*	Crayon & sang, 22 by 15.2 cm. Very rough
29223/222	*Native Types, Islands of the South Pacific Ocean*	Graphite & aquarelle, 27 by 19 cm
29286/284	*The Breakfast of the King of O-taiti*	Graphite, 36.7 by 45 cm, the Reverend Henry Nott, M.P. Lazarev Bellingshausen facing Pomare II et al.
1439	*The Breakfast of the King of O-taiti*	Same scene, in aquarelles
29287/285	*The Gapape [Ha'apai] River, in O-taiti*	Graphite & aquarelle, 27.7 by 38.2 cm. The Matavai River

was a bark-cloth *tiputa*. His dress reflected his position between the Tahitian and Christian worlds.

Bellingshausen reports that Mikhailov began work on *A View of the Island of O-Taiti from Venus Point* at 8:00 am on 23 July and that he was interrupted by the invitation to accompany the two ships' commanders to the royal residence. Thus work proceeded on the *View of the Island* and on *The Breakfast* almost simultaneously, and within some eighteen hours of the start of portraits of Pomare, Hitoti, and Paofai. The latter pair had arrived on *Vostok*'s quarterdeck between 3:00 pm and 4:00 pm the day before. They had been given silver medals and assorted trading goods, and had been promised more.[6]

Mikhailov positioned himself near the extremity of Te-auroa, the sandy spit known as Venus Point, facing SW and Mount Tahara ("One Tree Hill"). Because there is no sign of Dolphin Bank in his panorama, he was evidently standing parallel to it, that is, at least 400 metres from Te-auroa's tip and close to the site of Cook's Fort Venus, the strong point quickly thrown up by the British on 17-18 April 1769.[7] From the anchorages of *Vostok* and *Mirnyi* in the centre at a distance, it is clear that the water at the far left of the painting is the British and Russian watering place, where the Vaipopo'o River ran parallel to the shore. From the position of Mount Tahara (Tahara'a), the rugged hills around and beyond it can only be those southwest of the Tuauru Valley.[8] The time, indicated by shadows falling SSW, is late afternoon.

A View of the Island of O-Taiti gives a good impression of the size and layout of Matavai Bay. The distance from Venus Point to Mount Tahara is at least two miles. By their smallness, *Vostok* and *Mirnyi* indicate that distance most convincingly. Equally accurate and convincing, however, are the details of human activity ashore. Mikhailov's instructions of 1819 said: "You will pay very particular attention, so that everything that is portrayed by you is the most faithful representation of what you observe. For this reason, you will assuredly draw nothing from memory alone . . . and, insofar as it is possible, you will avoid all additions and embellishments. . . ."[9]

In an age before photography, governments relied on graphic artists for a true impression of distant lands and peoples. And there existed, for men like Mikhailov and Korneev of *Otkrytie*, also at work in Oceania in 1820, the danger of attending exclusively to the "documentary aspect of the assignment."[10] Mikhailov walked the fine line between pure documentation and true art.

Significantly, much of the activity portrayed in *A View of the Island of O-Taiti* is oriented toward the bay. Single and double canoes come and go. Figures point or walk toward the water. Even furthest from the bay, at the extreme left, stands a *fare va'a* or canoe shed; and, of course, the Russian vessels lie at anchor. Kotzebue notwithstanding, the Tahitians had retained a keen awareness of the sea and of canoes in which to cross it. Shown at right are a *pu ho'e* with a single paddler, a larger *va'a* with a sail, and a *pahi*. Most figures wear *ahu* and eyeshades. In the foreground is, apparently, a large unfinished plaitwork basket.[11]

Turning, finally, to the most celebrated of Mikhailov's three Tahitian paintings of the 1820s, *The Breakfast of the King of O-Taiti*, here certainly is an elaborate yet lively composition. The scene shows no less than thirty-two human figures, of whom only thirteen are within the courtyard surrounding Pomare's sleeping hut. There are plates in the 1831 album with even more men, such as the *View of the Coral Island of Moller* (Pl. 29), and even *A View of the Island of O-Taiti* has at least twenty figures. Still, the royal breakfast scene creates a powerful impression of crowds under control. Here, numbers do not threaten. All is orderly and the decorum of the royal breakfast party, reinforced by Henry Nott's sobering presence and the bulk of King Pomare and his wife, is further emphasized by the deliberately horizontal lines. They do not superimpose control on all the onlookers, perhaps, but they at least reflect the principle of hierarchy, embodied in Pomare and his guests, with which the visitors were comfortable and which, despite the tropical heat and the large crowd, infuses Mikhailov's study.

In the shade of two breadfruit trees, whose trunks recall Sydney Parkingson's of fifty years[12] before, two Tahitians prepare breadfruit for immediate consumption on a *papahia* block. According to William Ellis: "The *papahia* is extensively used. It is a low solid block or stool, supported by four short legs, and smoothly polished on the top. It is cut out of one piece of wood and is used instead of a mortar for pounding breadfruit, plantain, or bruising taro; which is done by beating them with a short stone pestle called a *penu*."[13]

Breadfruit lie by the tree trunk, ready for such treatment. While Pomare and his family are seated on a large, fine mat, his foreign guests have *iri* stools; and another two *iri* lean against Pomare's sleeping hut. On the ground between the host and his guests are polished coconut shells. No *umete* dish is depicted. Among other articles shown by the sleeping hut wall are a large calabash water container and an *aano*, a coconut shell for water, used in washing the feet.

Supposing the two doors of the *fare manihini* beyond the royal residence proper to be six feet high, the structure itself was not less than ninety feet long. Cook had seen others more than twice this length and had made this observation: "There are generally two or three of them in every district and they seemed not only built for the accommodation of the principal people but common to all the inhabitants of the district."[14] Later observers suggested that these houses were indeed mainly for the convenience and accommodation of *ari'i*, and that the crowds who also seemed to make use of them were, in reality, retainers.[15] In July 1820, the structure was being used by *ari'i*, "officials," in Novosil'skii's interpretation. All women of rank in Mikhailov's study wear eyeshades. The European guests facing Pomare are, from the left, Henry Nott, M.P. Lazarev, and Bellingshausen. Teremo'emo'e is at Pomare's right hand, and also present, to judge by the narrative evidence, are Pomare Vahine and Aimata.

THE PHYSICAL RECORD: TAHITIAN ARTEFACTS IN ST. PETERSBURG

The powerful grip that Tahiti held on the European imagination is reflected in the fact that St. Petersburg's small Tahitian collection had taken shape as early as 1780 and continued to grow in that decade. It is a matter of pride in the Peter the Great Museum of Ethnography that the collection originated with Cook's final voyage.

After Cook's death at Kealakekua Bay, Hawaii, on 14 February 1779, command of his expedition passed to Captain Charles Clerke. As his orders required, Clerke took *Resolution* and *Discovery* into Arctic waters in an attempt to find a navigable passage home to England. He brought his weary men down to the Russian port of Petropavlovsk-in-Kamchatka on 1 May 1779, where after tense initial probings by both sides he was welcomed by the courteous Baltic German governor, Magnus Karl von Behm (1727-1806).

Hastening up to Petropavlovsk from Bol'sheretsk, where rumours of the arrival of ill-intentioned and bellicose foreigners had caused a wave of nervousness, Behm received his unexpected guests with the greatest civility and generosity. Clerke was given victuals in unforeseen abundance, and several officers of *Resolution* and *Discovery* made the journey south to Bol'sheretsk, where they passed several happy days as guests of Behm and his wife. Behm presented his British visitors with fine fur cloaks and hats and other "liberal presents,"[16] while up in Avacha Bay *Resolution* and *Discovery* were provisioned at Crown expense. The generous governor and the consumptive Captain Clerke parted company on 26 May. "And as some return for the civilities he showed," wrote Welsh surgeon David Samwell, Behm was in turn given a number of personal gifts, including "Rum & Wine, 4 Quadrants and a spying Glass and several articles from the different Islands we had visited in the South Sea."[17] From other narratives it is clear that these gifts were intended as personal presents for the governor, not for the Court or the State; and that they were regarded by the British officers as a distinct matter from the transfer to Behm of documents and charts for forwarding to St. Petersburg and London. It had been decided by 22 May 1779 that Behm should be entrusted with these, as a decent and reliable officer and the servant of a country at peace with Great Britain.[18] Furthermore, Clerke had decided that the papers should be supplemented by "the Journal of our late Commander,"

Captain Cook, and by reports for the Board of Longitude written by Lieutenant King and Bayly the astronomer. In sum, Behm was given an assortment of Polynesian artefacts for his own use and pleasure. Not surprisingly, he was "much pleased with them."[19] Whether or not he found
the Pacific curiosities of intrinsic interest, he certainly foresaw the possibility of making an impressive contribution to the *Kunstkammer* and thus
winning the further favour of imperial authority. According to Samwell,
Behm "intended to present them to the Empress."

There are several references to the artefacts sent by Behm in the archive of the Academy of Sciences (LOAAN) in St. Petersburg. The first
is in a letter from Procurator Prince Aleksandr Viazemskii to the director
of the *Kunstkammer*:

> Doc. No. 42 Her Imperial Majesty has deigned to instruct that the var-
> ious articles brought this present year from Kamchatka,
> by Major Behm, are to be transferred to the Academy of
> Sciences for preservation in the *Kunstkammer*; in con-
> nection with which order, I have the honour to send
> them on to you, sir, together with the appended listing;
> and I remain always, Your Excellency's most obedient
> servant, etc., etc.
>
> Doc. No. 43 Inventory of Articles Brought from Kamchatka in 1780
> by Major Behm
> 1–Fifteen stamps, depicting natives of various Islands
> in the South Sea.
> 2–Wooden implements, weaponry, cloths, etc.[20]

The expeditionary artist John Webber, who had participated in Cook's
final expedition from its inception and made numerous drawings and aquarelles along the way, was almost certainly the source of the fifteen
"stamps" and made at least three dozen other drawings in Kamchatka.[21]
Among the drawings presented to Behm was one of "a lady of O'Taiti."
She was accompanied by drawings of "Caledonians" and Kamchadales,
of ceremonial dress, musical instruments, Aleut knives and clothing, and
Hawaiian *opahalo*.[22]

It is clear that the South Pacific artefacts acquired from Clerke and his
people had reached the *Kunstkammer* by June 1780. The original number
of items in the collection is not known, but thirty-three remain today as
Collection No. 505. An explicit reference to these Polynesian artefacts
occurs in the guide, *Kabinet Petra Velikago* (*Peter the Great's Cabinet of
Curiosities*), compiled in the late 1790s by Orest Beliaev and published in
1800. They are mistakenly referred to, however, as American, and a half

century was to pass before the Tongan, Tahitian, and Hawaiian objects were recognized as such.[23]

When *Resolution* and *Discovery* returned to England, King and his officers stressed Major Behm's great kindness in several reports to the Admiralty. The British government instructed that Behm should be given a piece of silver plate, suitably inscribed, and a gold medallion as marks of official British esteem. The piece was cast and engraved in Latin in the summer of 1781.[24] Behm never received his gifts, however; for the plate, if not the medallion, was treated in St. Petersburg as an official gift to the Crown. In a letter dated 20 September 1799 and written in London, Behm frankly told Joseph Banks of Prince Grigorii Potemkin's part in the diverting of the silver plate to "official" hands.[25] Now elderly and impoverished, he had gone to England that summer hoping to extract a small pension from the British government. Banks promised to help and discussed the problem with Evan Nepean and Lord Spencer.[26] Behm left England empty handed. Fortunately, however, a former colleague in Riga, General Aleksandr A. Bekleshev, had just been raised by the vagaries and whims that marked the reign of Tsar Paul I (1796-1801) to the post of procurator general of the Empire.[27] Bekleshev remembered his former colleague and secured an annual pension of 1,000 roubles for him. Behm did not live long to enjoy it; he was dead within six years. But already on display in St. Petersburg were a number of Tahitian artefacts that he had given to the Academy, including a magnificent mourner's pearl-cloth breastplate (*ahu-purau*) and two military demi-gorgets (*taumi*): wickerwork frames grandly embellished with sharks' teeth, white dog hair, and blue-black glossy feathers.[28] All three remain on permanent display in St. Petersburg.

Behm's role in fostering Pacific studies in St. Petersburg was first discussed at length in 1900, by Friedrich (in Russian, Fedor Karlovich) Russow, in the first bulletin of the series that survives to this day as *Sbornik Muzeia Antropologii i Etnografii* (*SMAE*). Russow's essay, entitled "Anfänge und Wachsthum der Sammlungen" ("Beginnings and Growth of the Collections"), dealt with the development of the *Kunstkammer*'s collections of ethnographica from the 1730s to the 1890s. As an appendix, he added "Notizen zur Cook'schen Collection, nebst biographischen Nachrichten über Major Behm" ("Notice on the Cook Collection, together with the Biographical Information on Major Behm"). That 800-word appendix contained a number of bibliographical references, without which an examination of Behm's contribution to Pacific and Northwest Coastal studies would not be practicable.[29]

Behm played a significant role in the first phase of European study of Tahiti. Through him, the St. Petersburg Academy of Sciences acquired specimens of *ahu-purau* (pearl-cloth) and martial gorgets equal in technique and historical interest to any held in other European museums at the time. Those pieces served as the basis for a small Tahitian collection to which, as documents in the Archive of the Academy of Sciences (St. Petersburg) make clear (LOAAN, *fond* 3, op. 8: "perepiska"), the German savant and traveller Johann Reinhold Forster, Captain Henry Barber of the *Unicorn*, Captain Benjamin Swift of *Hazard*, and other non-Russian fur traders then active on the Northwest Coast contributed in the late 1700s. These acquisitions and others purchased in the early part of the reign of Alexander I were placed, with assorted other artefacts from Oceania, in a "general *fond*." In 1809, the *fond* held some four dozen artefacts, of which forty-four remain today. In due course the *fond* became known as Collection No. 737. Tahitian tapa specimens (737-1, -2, -3, -21, -31) are outweighed by Hawaiian, Samoan, and Fijian artefacts, all of unspecified provenance but clearly in the Academy's possession by 1809. Taken together, Collections 505 and 737 go far toward compensating for the Russian Navy's inability, because of its belated arrival on the Tahitian scene, to provide Russian academic circles with examples of Tahitian workmanship and artistry of the pre-missionary period.

Predictably, a number of recent *SMAE* articles make reference to Behm and the Cook artefacts from Polynesia now held at MAE.[30] The first, published in 1960, was a survey of "The Hawaiian Assemblages in the MAE Collections" by the Soviet ethnographer Iuliia M. Likhtenberg. There were remarks on the original and present status of the subcollections (Nos. 505, 2520, etc.) into which went artefacts brought from Kamchatka by Behm; on the Governor's dealings with the British in 1779 and later; and on geometrically patterned Chilkat cloaks supposedly given to Behm by Clerke in 1779, but which evidently came to St. Petersburg aboard *Neva* in 1806.[31] Then, in 1964, the Soviet museologist Tat'iana V. Staniukovich published an exhaustive paper entitled "The Museum of Anthropology and Ethnography after 250 Years." It offered a 500 word passage on Behm, his various contributions to the museum in the 1770s, and the enormous interest provoked by his consignment of 1780 because it included the first set of Tahitian items ever to reach Russia.[32] Next, in 1966, came the first of three contributions to the study of the Russian Tahitian collection by L.G. Rozina-Bernstam, the leading authority on Polynesian material culture at MAE in the post-Stalinist period. This was the article "The James Cook Assemblage in the Collections of MAE," published in *SMAE*, Volume 23, pp. 234-53. It contained a full, illustrated description of Collection No. 505, paying due attention to its Tahitian component: Nos. 505-20 (*ahu-purau*, mourner's mother-of pearl breastplate), 505-10 (*taumi*, demi-gorget), and 505-14 (*taumi*, "in worse repair").[33]

Rozina's two subsequent treatments of Tahitian artefacts, in "The Collection of Objects from the Society Islands at MAE" (*SMAE*, Volume 25, pp. 317-36) and "Tapa of Oceania" (Volume 30, pp. 51-100), marked the high point of Soviet studies of Tahitian material culture. Published in 1969 and 1974 respectively, they rested on familiarity with the MAE holdings but showed the author's developing strength in the area of woven artefact description. Shortly after the appearance of "Tapa of Oceania," Dr. Rozina began the process of emigrating from the USSR and later settled in Ann Arbor, Michigan. Both articles are lightly annotated but contain solid introductions to Tahitian and other Polynesian material culture as well as descriptions of artefacts held at MAE. In the 1969 paper, descriptions are by class (Ritual Objects, Clothing, Implements of Labour and Domestic Utensils, etc.). In the 1974 paper, they are by collection number (Nos. 736, 4100).

Because it is pointless to duplicate the relatively recent work of Rozina, the following sections rest, with her consent and approval, on those pages in the aforementioned articles that bear on the Tahitian artefacts held in the Peter the Great Museum of Ethnography. Photographs of artefacts under discussion, however, were taken by me in 1985, with macro-lens equipment and with the assistance of Dr. Tamara K. Shafranovskaia of MAE's Australia and Oceania Division. Rozina's articles, translated, edited, and combined by me, are briefly discussed as well.

TAHITIAN ARTEFACTS IN COLLECTION NO. 505 (THE JAMES COOK COLLECTION) BY L.G. ROZINA

Those collections acquired by Captain James Cook are preserved with the greatest care in the museums of the world. For, assembled by the celebrated discoverer of so many peoples of the Pacific basin, they constitute an eloquent historical record of the cultures of those same peoples before their destruction under the influences of European civilization. All the artefacts here were brought to St. Petersburg and so comprised the very first such assemblage from James Cook's third voyage to reach Europe. Even in a catalogue to the *Kunstkammer* published in 1800, one finds a description of some of these items (see Orest Beliaev, *Kabinet Petra Velikago*, Part 2, p. 229). At that time, the collection consisted of thirty-eight objects. Today, the Peter the Great Museum of Ethnography of the Academy of Sciences of the USSR holds thirty-two of them in the collection known as No. 505. Brought from Polynesia, the artefacts consist of specimens of clothing, ornaments, implements of labour, everyday objects, and weaponry. More than half of the total presented to Governor Behm had been collected in the Hawaiian Islands, and the remainder had come from the islands of Tonga and Tahiti. Three items in Collection No. 505, Nos.

505-25-27 inclusive, have nothing on or with them to indicate their provenance, which has therefore yet to be established.[34] Three others, however, are unquestionably from Tahiti: a mother-of-pearl breastplate and two military breast protectors. The first was once worn by a mourner.

The ancestor cult that formerly existed in Polynesia, it may be noted in this connection, had taken various and specific forms on each of the archipelagos. On the island of Tahiti, burial rites for dead chiefs or nobles required the closest relatives of the deceased to wear very complex and sumptuous attire, known as *heva*, as they moved towards the burial place. (According to Teuira Henry, though, in *Ancient Tahiti* [Honolulu 1928; p. 293], such attire was worn by priests—GB.) The islanders valued such dresses very highly and parted with them or sold them to Europeans most unwillingly (ibid., p. 253). Peter the Great Museum holds the most precious portion of this special attire, a mother-of-pearl breastplate of *ahupurau*. The specimen measures 34 cm along its edges and is 60 cm wide.

> 505-20. Mother-of-pearl breastplate, made of fine, thin, and well-polished plates of very small dimension. They have all been tied together with threads, for which purpose a small hole has been bored through the end of each plate. Pulled tightly together, they make up twelve horizontal rows, if the uppermost corners are included. In total, the breastplate contains some 1,700 little plates. Such an article would have been attached to a light wooden arc, worn at shoulder level, and its considerable value becomes entirely comprehensible if one bears in mind the time and labour that would have been required to fashion such a piece of jewelry with a bone or a stone implement. It was the most striking part of the ancient mourner's dress, which would also have been embellished with multicoloured feathers and by large nacred shells.

As James Cook writes, the martial dress of the nobility was likewise very sumptuous and unwieldy on the island of Tahiti. On top of clothing made up of several layers of tapa, military leaders also wore a light shield of a sort, to protect the chest against spears. These Tahitian shields or protectors were of such elegant form and so smart that they were undoubtedly worn as much for embellishment as with a practical view to protection in battle. The St. Petersburg collection has two specimens.

> 505-10. *Taumi* breast protector. The base is a horse shoe shaped frame of little rods or switches, reinforced by other such rods, tied to them crosswise. This frame has been covered with broad bands of solidly woven coconut fibre; and the bands themselves are embellished

by three rows of small shark teeth and, between the rows of teeth, by blue-black feathers. Along the lower border and at the ends of the shield, there is a white dog-hair fringe. This hair has been carefully attached to little sticks, which are fastened to the shield's reverse side. In addition, both ends of the shield are decorated with three rows of mother-of-pearl round circular sticks. Overall length, 37 cm; overall width, 51 cm; length of fringe, 9 cm.

505-14. *Taumi* breastplate. This resembles the item just described, but it is less well preserved. Overall width 46 cm; overall depth, 35 cm.

OBSERVATIONS

As Rozina intimates, a significant description of the ancient costume of the mourning ceremony is contained in Teuira Henry's *Ancient Tahiti*. Henry makes plain that the St. Petersburg specimen of *ahu-purau* was classic in being "about a foot deep and covered with a brilliant network of thin chips of mother-of-pearl about one inch long." It is, however, by no means certain that the dress itself was called *heva*. The data of Morrison, Ellis, the two Forsters, and other early visitors on the subject of mourning costumes and masks, as well as on the very violent antics associated with the mourning procession, are conveniently summarized by Douglas L. Oliver in his essential study, *Ancient Tahitian Society* (1974; Volume 1, pp. 502-6).

St. Petersburg's two *tuami* gorgets, wickerwork breast coverings with shell, sharks' teeth, and feather decorations, similarly represent Maohi battle dress of pre-European and early contact times. Maohi "armour" always included fine mats or sheets of tapa and a network of sennit cords wound around the torso and limbs not quite tightly enough, as Ellis records, "to impede the circulation of the blood."[35] MAE's gorget 505-10 may usefully be compared with similar specimens held at the British Museum in London and in the Bernisches Historisches Museum.[36]

SPECIMENS OF ANCIENT TAHITIAN TAPA HELD IN THE MAE COLLECTIONS
BY L.G. ROZINA

One peculiarity of Tahitian tapa ornamentation was the use of a number of plants as stamps or dies. These plants were dipped into a colouring substance, then simply pressed onto the tapa. They were mostly fern fronds, hibiscus flowers, or the ends of sliced bamboo stems. Fern fronds were evidently touched up on occasion. It is otherwise difficult to explain the great distinctness of repeating designs on some specimens of tapa. Other plants and leaves were also used, of course, as stamps to make patterns; and sometimes the tapa background itself would be coloured and the impression of the plant or leaf left untouched, as on No. 737-21 in the collection.

Another purely Tahitian peculiarity in ornamentation was the use of appliqué, that is, of pieces of tapa that were glued into places cut out specially to receive them in the outermost or surface layer of the base tapa. Such a method of ornamentation may be seen on No. 737-2 at MAE and on the *heva-heva*, or Tahitian mourner's costume, held at the British Museum.[37] The actual manufacture of tapa, except that meant for temples and divinities, was women's work. The general or collective term for it in Tahiti was *ahu*. In addition, every sort of tapa stuff had its particular name. Men's girdles were made of thick varieties of tapa and so were women's *pareu*; but richly ornamented shawls or *ahu-fara* were of fine material. A solid, multi-layered tapa was used in capes. And besides the kinds of clothing already mentioned, both men and women used to wear cloaks called *tiputa*, whose shape resembled that of the American Indians' ponchos.

There are six specimens of ancient tapa from the Society Islands in the Museum of Anthropology and Ethnography, St. Petersburg. Five are in Collection No. 737 and one is in No. 4100, which the museum received from the Frunze Naval Institute in 1930. Besides these, MAE holds one related implement: a tapa beater, now held in collection No. 3117, that was acquired from the Stockholm Museum in 1925.

OBSERVATIONS

All the tapa specimens at MAE are of *Broussonetia papyrifera*, or *'aute*, which still grew abundantly on Tahiti when Bellingshausen arrived in 1820 and had been cultivated in large plantations in the pre-missionary days.[38] Zavadovskii of the *Vostok* saw soaked strips being felted together by beating, helped by the resinous substance in the bark, and also witnessed appliqué work, which he mistook for plain repairing of damaged tapa. Chemical analysis of the coloured impressions on several of these MAE specimens would almost certainly reveal that a red dye had been made from *Picus tinctoria* (*mati*) berries. Despite the observation of William Ellis that such flower designs did not last well, the distinctness and colour of patterns imprinted on 737-1, -2, -3, are indisputable.[39]

The *ahu* registered as No. 4100-9 is one of thirty artefacts transferred to the Peter the Great Museum in 1930 from the M.V. Frunze Naval Institute. The collection from Fiji, New Caledonia, New Zealand, Hawaii, and

Tahiti had originally been sent to that institute from the Academy of Sciences, and evidence from the artefacts themselves also points to an early nineteenth-century origin for most pieces, including the *ahu*. As for the olive brown beater, No. 3117-271, obtained from Sweden in 1925 as part of an enormous acquisitions program focused on Leningrad's need to expand Melanesian holdings,[40] its striking faces show more complicated grooving than Rozina's description suggests. A single face, moreover, has areas of small squares and areas of parallel and slightly notched lines. Such wooden mallets had been in use in Tahiti for many generations and were still visible and audible in the 1820s.[41] Zavadovskii's evidence supports Banks, Parkinson, and Ellis in indicating that bark cloth manufacture, and beating in particular, was women's work in former times.[42]

TAHITIAN RITUAL AND OTHER OBJECTS IN MAE'S COLLECTION NO. 736
BY L.G. ROZINA

The material culture of Tahiti and the Society Islands has been subject to significantly less study, hitherto, than the material cultures of the surrounding archipelagos. This may be explained largely by the fact that Tahiti was the very first island in Polynesia on which European missionaries settled (1797) and began to spread Christianity. Thus, the ancient ways of life were already being destroyed in Tahiti, and ancient cults and beliefs were already being annihilated, at a time when they were still intact in other Polynesian islands, where, indeed, they were to survive for some time. This circumstance also explains why far more objects of material culture from surrounding regions have survived to the present than have survived from Central Polynesia. Even so, by no means all the collections from Central Polynesia that are extant have been published.

In the Peter the Great Museum of Ethnography there are thirteen artefacts from the Tahitian group, besides another three, described earlier (*SMAE*, Volume 23, pp. 243, 253, Table 2), that belong to the "James Cook Collection." Almost all thirteen of the artefacts here in question are among the very oldest in the museum. Seven of them are in the large, composite collection (No. 736) into which went objects brought back from the South Pacific Islands by the first Russian circumnavigators.[43] There are, unfortunately, no indications with the assemblage as to which of the early voyagers presented particular pieces, where the latter originated, or even what the artefacts were used for. Since Tahiti was visited only by F.F. Bellingshausen and O.E. Kotzebue among the earliest Russian mariners, however, in the course of voyages of 1819-21 and 1823-26 respectively, it must be supposed that the artefacts in question were brought back by them, and that the great majority were brought by Bellingshausen. In his book *Dvukratnye izyskaniia* (*Repeated Explorations in the Icy Ocean and a Voyage Round the World*), Bellingshausen writes plainly that artefacts presented to him by islanders of Tahiti were submitted to the Admiralty Department.[44] The objects comprising collections acquired from the first Russian voyagers and held in the museum of that department were transferred to *Kunstkammer* in 1828 and went into Collection No. 736.[45] Kotzebue's own book, conversely, contains no reference whatsoever to any transfer of objects brought back from his voyage. (As noted above, several specimens of tapa clothing in the Peter the Great Museum of today are kept in an even older collection, No. 737, which dates back to 1809. On the basis of data in MAE's archive, we may say that Collection No. 737 is half made up of tapa specimens acquired by Governor Behm of Kamchatka, half from items of later provenance.)[46] The following artefacts are held in Collection No. 736, together with another 320 or so pieces from Australia, New Guinea, Fiji, Kiribati, New Zealand, Samoa, Tonga, the Marquesas Islands, Easter Island, the Hawaiian archipelago, Mangareva, Vanuatu, the Solomon and the Admiralty islands, and the Marshall Islands' Radak and Ralik chains.

11   736-226. Wooden figure of a god, standing erect on legs wide apart, with five-fingered hands resting on the belly. Round head with a broad face, small nose, large eyes and mouth with lower lip protruding. The back is flat and rectangular, and the lower part of the body protrudes sharply. The figure is polished, fashioned from a light coloured wood, covered with a light yellow lacquer. Torso and head are both seriously damaged within, by termites. Overall length, 51 cm; length of head, 18.5 cm; width at the shoulders, 18 cm.

12   736-231. Large vertical drum (*pahu nui*), fashioned from a single piece of heavy, dark brown timber. The drum is cylindrical in form and hollowed out to three-quarters of its depth. A slightly convex base is over a small, latticed stand. This stand has nine little posts, an equal number of apertures, and a broad lower ring. In the upper portion of these nine rectangular apertures there have been carved festoons or toothed designs that end with half-moons. The whole drum, including the stand, has been embellished with a carved ornamentation in high relief; and immediately by the upper, open end, across which a piece of shark skin has been stretched, has been placed a band of 45 identical, erect, anthropomorphic figurines, with eyes, mouth, and ears indicated on triangular faces. Each figurine stands on a long vertical strip of ornamentation, consisting of intersecting wavy lines and lines of rhomboids. All these vertical bands, which extend down to the stand, change at the figurines' feet into a stylized fist, which seems to support the figurines. Each post of the stand has

carved on it a row of rhomboids with broken lines between them. And on the lower ring there are merely broken lines. The half-moons of the festoons are themselves embellished with two fern leaves, bound cross wise. All the drum's carving is coloured with a pinkish ochre. The shark skin, gray, is attached to the drum by a large number of coconut fibre threads, all sewn through its edge; and these threads descend to the stand and are fixed behind its posts and festoons. In addition, the threads are reinforced by a band of twisted fibre attached to the drum above the stand. Inside the drum and by its base are two light, white wooden sticks which cross each other and rest on the internal wall of the instrument. Overall height, 145 cm; diameter, 45 cm; height of stand, 37 cm. Dimensions of the stand's apertures, 29 by 10 cm; of the half moons of the ornamentation, 8 by 2.5 cm; of the figurines, 4 by 2.5 cm. Thickness of the stand, 4 cm. Width of the threads, 0.5 cm; base thickness, 10 cm; dimensions of the openings in the drum wall, 2.7 by 3.2 cm. Length of small sticks, 45 cm; diameter, 1.5 cm and 2 cm.

13   736-232. Horizontal gong (*pahu ruturoa*), made from a single piece of light brown wood, of irregular cylindrical shape with a broad, rectangular split along its entire length. Along the entire length of the gong's wall, by this split or opening, there are rows of stylized figures, 73 on one side and 78 on the other; and triangles below the feet of these figurines have the appearance of tiny stylized heads. Below, there are broad, carved ornamental bands showing a pattern of rhomboids in series and of broken parallel lines. These bands are interrupted at the centre of the gong by smooth, unornamented areas. Here fell the blows of two hammers, which have left dents on either side of the gong. Polished and coloured with a dark brown colouring agent. External faces at both ends are smooth. Signs of working by a primitive implement within. Length of gong, 90 cm; diameter, 34 cm. Overall length of the ornamental bands, 19 cm; sizes of figurines in the upper row of the ornamentation, 1.8 by 1.3 cm. Dimensions of smooth striking surfaces of the gong, 21 cm by 19 cm. Thickness of walls, 2.5 cm. Dimensions of split or aperture for sound, 81 by 8 cm.

14   736-230. Sunshade for the eyes, made from the narrow leaves of the coconut palm; has the appearance of a wide peak, bent slightly at the centre. At the back, it becomes merely a twisted band. 16 cm in diameter. Peak length, 10 cm and 5 cm (at sides).

15   736-164. Wooden adze, of one piece, hoe-shaped and fitted with an arching, curved haft. The striking end is triangular in cross-section, the cutting edge being carved at a sharp angle. An aperture has been bored

through the haft for suspension. The adze is made from a solid piece of heavy timber, brown, and has been polished all over. The outer angle of the tool has been sliced and carved with transversal, sharp-edged grooves. Length of the striking portion, 32 cm; width of adze, 10 cm; width of the haft, 3 cm.

16   736-165. Wooden adze, similar to the preceding item, but here the outer angle lacks grooves. The end of the haft, with a bored aperture for suspension, is broken off on one side. Length of the striking portion, 12 cm; length of haft, 30 cm; width of adze, 11.5 cm; width of the haft, 2-3 cm.

17   736-248. Mat made of soft, flexible, large but very finely split straws. It consists of six narrow, elongated, strongly plaited panels that, at the meeting points, are stoutly interwoven and so form thick bands. The front of the mat is decorated with six broad stripes of light brown tone, which contain a chequered pattern. Overall length, 298 cm; width, 243 cm; width of ornamental stripes, 3.5 cm; width of the overlapping bands, 2.5 cm.

OBSERVATIONS

Bellingshausen recorded explicitly on 27 July 1820 that Tahitians at Matavai Bay "hastened out to exchange something from morning onward, bringing various artefacts that we duly took from them in barter and later presented to the museum of the Admiralty Department." He adds that on that same busy day, just before *Vostok*'s departure, Pomare II came out yet again and handed over a large mat as a personal gift for Tsar Alexander I, with the words, "Although there are many finer things in Russia, this large mat is the work of my subjects, and for this reason I am sending it."[47] There can be no doubt, as Rozina observes, that Bellingshausen here refers to the Tahitian artefacts in Collection No. 736. The mat would appear to be 736-248, a particularly soft and flexible floor mat of the sort on which Pomare II had sat while breakfasting with his Russian visitors and Henry Nott. It measures 243 cm by 298 cm. Ordinary floor mats were smaller. "Mats of this size," Ellis remarked with reference to one specimen of very unusual length, "are only made for high chiefs."[48] Like bark cloth, moreover, fine and long mats were frequently used in gift exchange. Plaitware was also employed in Tahiti as room partitioning and in canoe sails.[49] Elsewhere in his narrative, Bellingshausen mentions the "spears and other weapons, shells and hooks made of shell and coral, and other curiosities" that were stowed aboard *Vostok* in Matavai Bay.[50] Like the "skilfully woven grass mat" acquired in barter at Nihiru atoll on 13 July 1820, which the Russians had seen worn by a Tuamotuan woman working there and which was "among the rarities kept in the museum of the State Admiralty Department" in the mid-1820s,[51] these Tahitian weapons, fish-hooks, and other articles are conspicuous by their absence from the inventory of Collection No. 736. It must be borne in mind, however, that, as Rozina justly notes, a number of the pieces held in that collection cannot be confidently ascribed to a given island or area for want of documentation. Lack of documentation is as great a problem for the would-be user of St. Petersburg's "pre-1828" collection as it is for the student of Cook voyage materials held in Great Britain.[52] Analysis of items in Collection No. 736, though, might also be exhaustively conducted on the basis of technique, style, and chemical examination (wood varieties, dye bases, pollen and spore accretions, plant species employed in manufacture of, say, sennit, cloth, and threads). No such analysis has yet been undertaken by the Russian authorities, for want of funds and expertise. It is plain that practical collaboration between Russian and Western scholars would result in major benefits for Polynesian studies as a whole and for material and social culture records in particular.[53]

As for the other six Tahitian items in Collection No. 736, it may be said that the presence of a *pahu nui* drum and an *ihara* gong in St. Petersburg is somewhat surprising. Bellingshausen and Kotzebue both confirm that the missionaries in Tahiti frowned on music and that traditional music was not to be heard. It was perhaps because drums and gongs were subject to official disapproval in 1820-24, and were merely being stored unused, that Tahitians regarded them as suitable trade goods, which would hardly be missed but could be converted into desirable Russian clothing or cloth. The drum registered as 736-231 is made of extremely close grained wood and is in excellent repair after almost two centuries. One is inclined to think that the material used was *pu'a* (*Fragraea berteriana*).[54] The drum is of average height for a base instrument, to judge by Cook's evidence from his second voyage,[55] and has sennit lashing of the variety seen on many eighteenth-century drums in European museums. Such drums, often in groups of different tone or pitch, accompanied nose flutes, castanets, and dance rattles, and were invariably fixed upright on the ground.[56] MAE lacks examples of these other musical instruments and of Tahitian shell trumpets (*pu*); but its *ihara* gong is a fine specimen of the traditional gong described in some detail by the helpful Ellis.[57]

Both Tahitian adzes in Collection No. 736 are breadfruit or coconut splitters of the type seen in use by the 1820 visitors. The Maohi adze proper had a basalt or *Tridacna* shell flaked blade, hafted to a wooden handle by means of gum adhesives and cordage. MAE has no such tools from Tahiti, and the two splitters are, in any case, non-composite. No. 736-154 has an elegantly carved outer angle, as Rozina puts it, suggesting chiefly ownership. Both it and 736-165 were polished thoroughly. "All their woodwork," as Banks wrote, had "a certain neatness in the finishing, for they polished everything . . . with Coral sand . . . and ray's skin, which makes them very smooth."[58] As for the eyeshade, it is exactly like those painted by Mikhailov and evidently worn by women of rank every day.[59]

MAE's Tahitian wooden figure (736-226) bears certain resemblances to a *ti'i* held at the British Museum in London, which was once fitted with a feather wreath. Happily, the London figure was photographed in the nineteenth century and the print survives in the Haddon Collection of Cambridge University.[60] MAE's *ti'i* was most probably adorned in the same manner and created a similarly alarming impression on viewers.[61] "The overall effect is one of dynamic vitality."[62]

ZOOLOGY AND BOTANY

Staff surgeons aboard Russian ships in Oceania took an informed professional interest in the medicinal properties of plants. There are therefore passages of minor botanical interest in the journals and other writings of such men as Iakov Berkh and Nikolai A. Galkin of *Vostok* and *Mirnyi*, Petr Aleman and Petr Ogievskii of *Kreiser* and *Ladoga*, and Karl Izembek of the *Moller*. All five visited Matavai Bay in the 1820s as fully qualified physicians[63] and had explicit instructions from the Naval Ministry to keep daily records of their doings and impressions. Regrettably, only Galkin and Ogievskii succeeded in publishing sections of their original journals and reports; and Galkin's "Letters Regarding the Voyage of the Sloops *Vostok* and *Mirnyi* in the Pacific Ocean," published in 1822,[64] are eloquent about his visit to New Zealand but silent on the sojourn in Tahiti.[65] Neither Aleman's nor Izembek's journals have ever been used as source material by an historian; both remain, almost certainly, in the deep storerooms of TsGAVMF in St. Petersburg. Ogievskii's survey of the natural and physical conditions of Tahiti, published in part by the courtesy of his former commander, Andrei Petrovich Lazarev, is included in this volume. From the scientific standpoint, its botanical component is far weaker than that of his survey of Van Diemen's Land (Tasmania) of two months earlier.[66] Moreover, it is almost certain that whatever plant collection or herbarium Ogievskii took to St. Petersburg from Oceania in mid-October 1824 no longer exists.[67]

Essentially, then, only Johann Friedrich Eschscholtz, of Kotzebue's *Predpriiatie*, conducted systematic botany, studied the marine and land creatures of Matavai Bay and its environs, and published his results. However, he was not greatly interested in mammals, birds, or even fish; rather he was an ocean insects, jellyfish, and acaleph man. He therefore devoted far more time to the marine creatures of Matavai Bay's northeastern reef than to the animals and birds of the interior, which he, unlike his younger colleague Gofman, never crossed.

Eschscholtz was twenty-five years old when he first returned to Dorpat University in 1818 with specimens of flora and fauna collected in Oceania during the *Riurik* expedition.[68] In 1826, when he returned there again with collections assembled during the *Predpriiatie* venture, he was almost thirty-four, and had already been head of the university's prestigious Cabinet of Zoology. As a professor of the university, as Kotzebue's friend, and as the guardian of a major zoological collection of "2,400 kinds of animal" for which there were not adequate facilities at the St. Petersburg Academy of Sciences, he claimed the right to take his South Pacific trophies home to Dorpat. In 1826-28 he sorted out and began full descriptions of his specimens. Despite his duties at the university, he corresponded steadily with Kotzebue, who was then drafting his narrative (*Novoe puteshestvie vokrug sveta*) in Reval.[69] On 7 January 1828, he presented his friend and ex-commander with an "Übersicht der Zoologischen Ausbeute" ("Overview of the Zoological Collections") for inclusion in the German edition of Kotzebue's work. It appeared in Volume Two of the *Novoe puteshestvie* (St. Petersburg 1830) and briefly mentioned 28 mammals, 165 birds, 90 fishes, 127 crustaceans, 1,400 insects, 162 gastropods, 63 acalephs, 90 zoophytes, and assorted other creatures, most collected in the South Pacific Ocean.

Here is an extract from Eschscholtz's survey of Tahitian fauna:

> During the short space of ten days that we stayed at Tahiti, the inhabitants, who for a trifling remuneration brought us all sorts of marine animals, enabled us to make the acquaintance of all the natural productions of that much praised country. Birds are scarce in the lowlands along the coast. The little blue *Psittacus taitianus* frequents the top of the coconut palm; the *Ardea sacra* walks along coral reefs; but it is seldom that a tropical bird is seen on the wing. A gecko of the species *Hemidactylus* lives about old houses; a small lizard of the family *Scincoidea*, with a copper-coloured body and a blue tail, and a striped *Abelpharus*, are met with frequently among the rocks.
>
> Of fishes, the variety is great, many of them of splendid colours, particularly the small ones that feed on the coral and seek shelter among its branches. The same place of refuge is chosen by numbers of variegated crabs, especially the *Graspus*, *Portunas*, and *Galathea*.

Three kinds of *Canceres* already known were brought to us, the *Maculatus*, *Corallinus*, and *Floridus*; the two former move but little and their shells are as hard as stone. A small *Gelasimus* burrows under the ground and makes himself a subterranean passage from the water to the dry land. The female has very small claws, but the male has always one very large pink claw, which is sometimes the right and sometimes the left.

A large brownish *Gecarcinus* lives entirely on the land in holes of his own making; his gills accordingly are not open combs but consist of rows of bags closely pressed together and somewhat resembling bladders. *Hippa adactyla* F. is very frequent here and keeps itself concealed under sand on the seashore. It was from these that Fabricius, who was given a wrong description of their legs, formed his *Genus Hippa*; Latreille mentions them by the name of *Remipes testud*. There are six kinds of *Pagurus*. Of Crustacea already mentioned, *Palaemon longimanus*, *Alphaeus marmoratus*, and *Squilla chiragra*; the legs of the last are red and formed like clubs; it uses them as weapons of offence or defence, and inflicts wounds by striking them out by a mechanism peculiar to itself.

The number of insects collected on the low land was very small; among them were the *Staphylinus erytrocephalus*, also a native of New Holland, Australia; an *Aphodius*, hardly to be distinguished from the *Limbatus wiedem* of the Cape of Good Hope; an *Elater* of the species *monocrepis*; and of *oedemera*, are three varieties of the species *dytilus*, to which belong the *Dyrops livida* and *Lineata* F; also two small varieties of *Apate*.

No place could be more convenient for the observation of Mollusca and Radiata than Cape Venus. At a few hundred paces from the shore is a coral reef, which at low tide is completely dry. In the shoal water between the reef and the shore is to be found the greatest variety of the more brittle kinds of coral, and among their sometimes thick bushes, molluscs and echinoderms lie concealed. The rapid movements of a small *Strombus* that when taken, beats about it with its shell, formed like a thin plate of horn and armed with small teeth, were very curious. On breaking the stone formed by fragments of coral, a *Sternaspis* was found burrowing in its interior. Seven classes of *Holothuria* were examined. Three belonged to the *genus* called by Lamarck Fistularia, but which name had already been given by Linnaeus to the tobacco-pipe fish. . . . We found five small kinds of sea-leeches; and among three kinds of starfish, the *Asterias echinites*, the large radii of which easily inflict a severe wound. Another had the form of the *Asterias luna*, was eight inches in diameter, without radii, and had more the appearance of a round loaf of bread somewhat flattened.

Of corals, the variety was very great, as may be judged from the fact that we collected twenty-four kinds within so short a time. *Fungia* is quite at home here; for, independently of *F. agariciformis*, *Scutaria*, and *Limacina*, a long kind was also found, having, like the two former, only one central cavity; they are to be seen in shallow water, among other corals. . . .[70]

It is for zoologists and historians of science to discuss the significance of the assortment of land and marine creatures listed by Eschscholtz. He made an effort to couch his findings in a style that the non-specialized reader of the Kotzebue narrative would find acceptable, with reassuring references to the humour of a *Strombus* and the beauty of the beach and shallow waters. The passage makes it obvious, however, that he hardly left the "lowland" area of *Predpriiatie*'s Tahitian anchorage throughout his stay, depending heavily on native collectors for his specimens and working in his cabin, unlike Chamisso at Honolulu in 1817. The reef off Te-auroa was the focal point of his activities, as Venus Point was the focal point for Kotzebue.

Eschscholtz's collection was the jewel of the Dorpat University Zoological Museum and was always given the greatest attention and protection that the university could offer, in good times and in bad. In Tartu, as Dorpat has been known for three-quarters of a century, the bad times were particularly grim. The First World War and the Russian Revolution and its aftermath reduced the Zoological Museum's 18,000 storage items to a thousand. Rebuilt in the years of the independent Estonian Republic, the collection was again shattered in 1941-45; Tartu itself, which for months formed the front line between Nazi and Soviet forces and was shelled and burned remorselessly, was reduced to a half of its prewar size. Then came a period of Soviet neglect. In times of terror, zoological and other treasures were abandoned to the ravages of moths, mildew, and even rain. Under these circumstances, plus major fires that destroyed Cabinet holdings in the early nineteenth century,[71] one would hardly be surprised to learn that nothing had survived of Eschscholtz's Pacific Island *fond*. It is a measure of Estonian respect for him that some specimens have survived. Several starfish, including one *Asterias echinites* from Tahiti, and several small parrots, including one *Psittacus taitianus*, are today in the keeping of Dr. Kalju Poldvere at Tartu University's Zooloogiamuuseumi.[72] The museum now has 380,000 storage items and a permanent display of more than 5,000 exhibits. In size and scope it holds fourth place among zoological collections in the former USSR.

The period 1829-31 marked the high point of Eschscholtz's publishing and lecturing activity. His contribution to the Kotzebue narrative was complemented by his masterpiece, the *Zoologischer Atlas*, offering illustrations and descriptions of the creatures discovered in the course of *Predpriiatie*'s voyage.[73] He died within weeks of its appearance in Berlin. Two recent scholars have investigated Eschscholtz's place in the history of Russian exploration and science. The first, Dr. T.A. Lukina, produced the biography *Iogann Fridrikh Eshol'ts* in 1980. The second, the Estonian historian, I. Heidemaa, devoted two articles to the Zoological Museum and Faculty of Dorpat University, published in Tartu in 1975 and 1981,[74] before producing the official modern guide to the museum in its Soviet manifestation.[75] Both Lukina and Heidemaa made use of archival materials held at LOAAN, in *fond* 260, op. 2, among others, in the course of their work on Eschscholtz's connections with St. Petersburg's Academy of Sciences. Unfortunately, a study of Eschscholtz in English has yet to be produced.

Despite the lack of printed records, there can be little doubt that other zoological specimens from Tahiti reached St. Petersburg, Reval, and Dorpat in the early nineteenth century. We know, for instance, that *Kreiser*'s third lieutenant, Fedor Vishnevskii, and Captain Andrei Petrovich Lazarev of *Ladoga*, both in Tahiti in 1823, were keen amateur botanists and zoologists.[76] Such men pursued their interests, duty permitting, when they could. And the very size and volume of the "Natural Historical and Ethnographic Articles" cramming the Navy's museum by the later 1820s makes it obvious that most men followed orders and surrendered their collections to the Crown at the conclusion of their voyages. Such articles filled forty-five large boxes.[77]

Not the largest but the best Soviet survey of the growth of the St. Petersburg Academy's Zoological Museum, which attracts large crowds of visitors today, is Dmitrii V. Naumov's *Zoologicheskii Muzei Akademii Nauk SSSR* (Leningrad 1980). As Naumov notes with pride, the Great South Sea had been represented even in collections formed by Peter the Great, which had already grown to more than a thousand bird varieties and several hundred fishes when lost to fire in 1747.[78] But, of course, Tahitian specimens could not have reached St. Petersburg by then. The earliest of Russia's Tahitian acquisitions are unknown, but it is plain that early specimens, though very likely not the first, were linked with Aleksandr F. Sevast'ianov (1771-1824), a zoologist with many friends abroad. Sevast'ianov published on the major zoological results of Baudin's voyage to Australia and Oceania,[79] and he recognized the meaning of the natural historical collections made by Cook in Polynesia. Cook's companion on his second voyage, Johann Reinhold Forster, had his own links with

St. Petersburg[80] and very possibly had fauna as well as ethnographica for sale. Other Russian scientists with active interests in Polynesian fauna in this period where Georg Heinrich Langsdorf, who worked in Polynesia with *Nadezhda* in 1804, and the early taxidermist Timofei Bornovolokov, who was anxious to improve the preservation of exotic birds and insects.[81] To these, by 1817, we may add the name of Eduard I. Eikhval'd (1795-1876), who studied zoology and medicine in Prussia and then in London, where Cook exotica had long been on display in muddled fashion.[82] In 1823, he became Professor of Zoology at the youthful Kazan' University, and so became the colleague of Ivan M. Simonov, late of *Vostok*, who had successfully brought part of his Pacific Islands haul to an approving alma mater.[83] Like Sevast'ianov, Eikhval'd was particularly interested in the animals of Oceania; in 1823 it was he who, despite his tender years, was charged with the systematic study of Australian and Polynesian plants brought to St. Petersburg aboard *Vostok*.[84] Zoology and botany, twin sciences for centuries, had not yet parted company forever.[85]

It is true, as E.E. Shvede observes, that *Vostok*'s and *Mirnyi*'s officers did all they could to compensate for the absence of trained natural historians. It is also true that the cautious Bellingshausen had such specialists examine and correct his account of his Antarctic and Pacific enterprise where flora and fauna were discussed. It is wishful thinking, however, to assert that zoological or other specimens that reached St. Petersburg with Bellingshausen in 1821 hold "an honoured place" at ZIAN today. Even in 1821, we know, stuffed birds from Oceania "had to be put into boxes between display cabinets."[86] Twenty years later, all such specimens were brought into the new and larger building of the Zoological Museum, but they remained packed into drawers. They are still in trays and boxes to this day, identifiable not by correct documentation but by labels that would seem to have been tied to certain specimens in 1828-29 or shortly thereafter. I found such faded labels on the claws of birds from Sydney-Parramatta (New South Wales) and Tahiti on brief visits to ZIAN in 1985[87] and 1991.

HYDROGRAPHY, GEOLOGY, AND METEOROLOGY

Bellingshausen and Kotzebue made minor contributions to contemporary knowledge of Tahiti's geographical realities and to the area of Matavai Bay. Among other instruments of the very latest make were marine barometers, dipping needles, log and sounding machines by Massey, six thermometers, aerometers, and artificial horizons;[88] and a bathometer was constructed aboard *Vostok*, with the aid of which water samples could be raised from an ocean depth of five hundred meters.[89] No ship left

Kronstadt for Oceania without a set of new thermometers and an assortment of charts and atlases. Bellingshausen was issued with his copy of the *Tables of Positions, or of the Latitudes and Longitudes of Places* (London 1816) produced by the British hydrographer John Purdy (1773-1843). His orders from the Naval Ministry enjoined him to make accurate reckonings of anchorages used and, when necessary, to set up land observatories. The latter were "to resemble forts and to be armed positions,"[90] lest "savages" attempt to storm them. Like Kotzebue in 1815-18, Bellingshausen and Lazarev were "attentively to observe, and circumstantially to describe, every unusual phenomenon, and especially to measure everything measurable."[91] Admiralty sailing instructions for *Vostok* and *Mirnyi* included outlines of modern procedures for coast surveys. All "astronomical, mathematical, and physical instruments wanted but unavailable" in St. Petersburg were bought in London.[92]

Vostok's survey of Matavai Bay was conducted by her navigator, Iakov Poriadin, with the assistance of Midshipman Dmitrii Demidov and Naval Cadet Robert Adams. The compass work essential for such surveying was familiar to all cadets: it was taught at the Naval Cadet Corps in St. Petersburg and had been undertaken by other Russian youths since the Navy had arrived in Oceania in 1804.[93] Kotzebue left a description of V.S. Khromchenko's surveying at Honolulu, with posts that so alarmed the Hawaiians as almost to cause an attack on the visitors, in his narrative of 1821.[94] Bellingshausen's findings in Matavai Bay were never printed in chart form, no doubt because the Naval Ministry felt that the place had been sufficiently well charted by Cook and several other British voyagers of high repute.[95] Bellingshausen's and Lazarev's fixes for Cape Venus were, respectively, latitude 17°29′20″ and 17°29′19″; and they concurred in determining its longitude as 149°27′20″W. The reckonings were not among their most accurate for the voyage.[96]

Ever less generous than Bellingshausen in his acknowledgements of contributions made by his subordinates, Kotzebue leaves no clues as to who in *Predpriiatie* conducted the boat-based survey work in Matavai Bay in mid-March 1824. Normally it would have been undertaken by Assistant Navigator Fedor Grigor'ev and by one or more of the ship's eight midshipmen.[97] In any event, a chart of the bay was produced. It appeared in *Neue Reise um die Welt* (Weimar 1830) and showed Matavai Bay from Mount Tahara in the south to the reef protecting Te-auroa in the north, with depths in fathoms. Like the German text of Kotzebue's narrative of *Riurik*'s voyage, *Entdeckungs-reise in die Sud-see und nach der Beringsstrasse*, which the philologist and diplomat Hannibal Evans Lloyd (1771-1847) had translated into English with extraordinary speed at the request of London publishers, *Neue Reise um die Welt . . .* was the object of immediate negotiations between author, German publisher (Verlag Wilhelm Hoffman), and would-be British publishers and editors.[98] The British rights soon went to Henry Colburn and Richard Bentley of New Burlington Street, who in their turn looked for engravers to produce new, English plates on the basis of the Hoffmann illustrations. Bentley was famous for his treatment of woodcuts, and Colburn had made his fortune by combining publication of fashionable novels and of celebrated diaries with constant socializing.[99] Kotzebue's map of Matavai Bay went to Sidney Hall, a specialist in map engraving who in 1821 had had connections with his new employers' business rival, Richard Phillips (1767-1840), London publisher of a translation of the first of Kotzebue's major Voyages.[100] Hall's "Plan of Mattaway Bay and Village," published in Volume One of the Colburn-Bentley edition of *A New Voyage Round the World*, clearly marks "the Boatswain's House" and other structures south of the watering place to which the 1820 Russian visitors make no allusion, and clearly shows that Wilson's and Nott's houses stood a little inland, despite Russian narrative suggestions to the contrary.[101]

By *Predpriiatie*'s reckoning, Venus Point lay in latitude 17°29′22″S, with magnetic needle deviation of 6′50″E. The modern fix for the spot is latitude 17°28′57″.[102] Kotzebue's meteorological and oceanographic work of 1815-18 and 1823-26 was a development and refinement of the pioneering efforts made in 1803-6 by *Nadezhda*'s Swiss astronomer and physicist, Johann Caspar Hörner.[103] By using six thermometers, Hörner had succeeded in checking the ocean temperature at many depths in Oceania, comparing the results with those of a pre-checked regular mercury thermometer. Ably assisted by Kruzenshtern, Hörner had found that "at first the warmth diminishes imperceptibly, then more rapidly, then at a great depth, it drops more slowly again; and finally it remains constant."[104] Problems raised by these data, which bore directly on climatic conditions across the Pacific, were correctly viewed by Hörner. They later attracted the notice of pioneering oceanographers, notably Iurii M. Shokal'skii of St. Petersburg, who, in his classic work *Okeanografiia* (1917), justly stressed how Hörner had doubled the value of his data by making sets of observations at different points in the Pacific, giving "vertical" series of temperature readings.[105] Hörner had also blazed a trail for Kotzebue and his scientific staffs by determining the specific weight of water samples at thirty-three points in the Pacific, concluding that salinity varied with distance away from the equator.[106] Finally, at Kruzenshtern's suggestion, the Swiss savant had drafted Kotzebue's scientific orders, effectively ensuring that the emphases in his earlier work in Oceania would be continued by the Russian. These instructions bore on ways of countering barometric oscillation, the correct use of the Woltmann wind-gauge, depth sounding at sea, and proper measurement of ocean tides and currents.[107] In addition, Kotzebue was required to investigate salinity and to assess marine phenomena then little understood, for instance, surface fluorescence, "falling stars," and "fire-balls." He did so systematically, aided by Wormskiöld and Chamisso in *Riurik* and by Seewald and Lenz in *Predpriiatie*.

Admiralty instructions for Kotzebue in 1823 required that a minimum of three barometric readings be taken daily aboard *Predpriiatie*, at 6:00 am, midday, and 10:00 pm. Barometric pressure and air temperature were to be fixed at the same moment, an important innovation. *Predpriiatie* carried a delicate marine barometer by Peter Dolland (1730-1820) and another by a Russian maker, Samoilov.[108] Full meteorological and related data are to be found not in *Neue Reise um die Welt* or in foreign translations of it, but in Kotzebue's far briefer and persistently neglected Russian narrative of 1828.[109] *Predpriiatie* was certainly better equipped and manned for oceanographic and meteorological work in Oceania than even Bellingshausen's ships. As Kotzebue dryly put it at the expedition's end, "we were richly stored with astronomical and other scientific instruments."[110] H.R. Friis has discussed the successful use that Lenz made of the bathometer that he himself and Friedrich Parrot of Dorpat University designed for the sampling of sea water at depth and for estimating specific water weight: "These two inventions can well be regarded as the true beginning of an exact oceanographic technique.... A theory of oceanic water circulation formulated by Lenz, as an explanation of the appearance of lower water temperatures at great depth, was based on factual data observed on the *Riurik* and in his own tests on the ship *Predpriiatie*."[111]

Certain of Lenz's other conclusions, which have since been found to be correct, help to explain Tahiti's physical conditions. Lenz posited, for instance, the existence of "salinity maxima" to the north and south of the equator, and of "minimal salinity localities" between, rightly explaining the phenomenon in terms of a more intense evaporation process in the areas affected by trade winds and of calm within the lowest latitudes. Again he posited continuous but ever shrinking drops of water temperature in the latitude of the Society Islands, at least to 1,900 metres.[112] Such ocean conditions predetermined the mobility of marine fauna in general and had a bearing on the natural resources man might find. Lenz's conclusions appeared in 1830, complementing *Neue Reise um die Welt*. His work, entitled *Physikalische Beobactungen, anggestellt auf einer Reise um die Welt . . . in den Jahren 1823-1826*, was warmly received in both Russian and German learned circles and ensured that his return to Dorpat would be triumphant. By 1836, he held the chair of physics at St. Petersburg University.[113]

Meteorological records kept by Russian ships in Polynesia in the early nineteenth century remain largely unpublished. What value they have for climatology has been well demonstrated by the Russian geographer Vasilii M. Pasetskii. While preparing a monograph on the geographical interests of the Decembrist rebels of 1825-26, Pasetskii in 1975-76 consulted official nineteenth-century publications giving data on the science undertaken by the Russian Navy vessels (*Ladoga*, *Kreiser*, *Vostok*, and *Apollon*) in which future Decembrists M.K. Kiukhel'beker, D.I. Zavalishin, K.P. Torson, and F.G. Vishnevskii had arrived in Oceania in 1822-24.[114] Among these publications were *Meteorological Observations Made During the Voyage Round the World of the Frigate "Kreiser" in the Years 1822-1824* (St. Petersburg 1882). *Kreiser* stood in Matavai Bay, Tahiti, for twelve days in July 1823. Associated bulletins, offering surveys of meteorological data collected on board many Russian ships in Polynesia in the nineteenth century, are referred to by W. Wiese in Andrei Fersman's edition of *The Pacific: Russian Scientific Investigations* (Leningrad 1926). Unpublished meteorological records in the logs of such ships are still held in the Archive of the Main Hydrographic Department, at TsGAVMF in St. Petersburg.[115] It is for Slavists and climatologists with mid-Pacific interests to collaborate in using such materials. The winds of glasnost blow. They are accessible.

> Throughout the entire voyage of the sloops *Vostok* and *Mirnyi* [writes E.E. Shvede], systematic measurements were taken of air temperature, atmospheric pressure, and wind strength. And periodically, it would seem, observations were also made by means of "small aerial spheres." The resultant data were generalized and most significant scientific deductions were drawn on the basis of them. Astronomer Simonov especially occupied himself with these meteorological observations. During one sixty-one day period, he observed on an hourly basis "the state of the barometer, likewise the degree of warmth according to the thermometer and the degree of dryness of the atmosphere according to the hygrometer." And in the tropics, he made 4,000 or more entries. The result of these labours was a scientific work entitled "On Temperature Differences in the Northern and Southern Hemispheres," of 1825....[116]

That article, prepared at Kazan' University, to which Simonov had returned in 1822 and where his academic career was already blossoming,[117] was complemented by another, published in St. Petersburg in 1828, entitled "Determination of the Geographical Position of the Anchorages of the Sloops *Vostok* and *Mirnyi*."[118] One of these anchorages was, of course, Matavai Bay, Tahiti.

It would have been surprising, in view of their growing interest in the processes by which coral reefs are formed, if either Chamisso or Belling-shausen had failed to bring specimens of tropical coral to Russia. Both men later published on the subject and no less an authority than Charles Darwin was to acknowledge the basic correctness of their theories of sub-marine accretion.[119] Of Eschscholtz's awareness of the potential impor-tance of the corals that he saw off Venus Point, suffice it to note that he described their many forms and types, almost poetically, in "Ubersicht der Zoologischen Ausbeute" of 1828.[120]

Coral and rock samples brought from Oceania aboard *Vostok* and *Mirnyi* were submitted to the naval authorities together with all other ma-terials.[121] The latter handed them to the Academy of Sciences's Geological Museum, a Petrine institution that had become a chaotic, dusty storage house by the early 1800s.[122] Coral and mineral specimens brought to Rus-sia by Kotzebue in 1818 and in 1826 fared far better. Some specimens brought in *Riurik* found their way into Count Nikolai P. Rumiantsev's personal collections and, thence, went to Moscow in 1826.[123] Others, in 1818 and 1826, went with Eschscholtz, Lenz, and Gofman to Dorpat Uni-versity.

Gofman, youngest of the scientists in *Predpriiatie*, was also the one with keenest mineralogical interests. In Tahiti, he made the journey to Lake Vahiria, collecting as he went. On Hawaii Island ten months later, he climbed as far up Mauna-Roa (7,000 feet) as his native guides dared to go, again collecting minerals or lava and observing on the way.[124] It is not reasonable to suppose that Eschscholtz presented mineral and coral speci-mens collected in Tahiti to Professor Christian-Moritz Engelhardt (1779-1842), head of Dorpat University's Cabinet of Mineralogy, while Gofman kept his for private study.[125] Whether or not Gofman submitted specimens to Engelhardt, however, thereby adding to the "scoriaceous lava" that Eschscholtz had collected in a lava stream from Mount Hualalai near Kailua Bay, Hawaii,[126] he set forth his views and findings on Tahiti and many other South Pacific Islands in his study *Geognostische Beo-bachtungen auf einer Reise um die Welt* (Berlin 1828). In 1961 the Estonian historian of science, L. Sarv, discussed the Geological Museum of what is now Tartu State University in a survey of museums in that re-public. [127] Also relevant in this connection is the history of Tartu State Uni-versity (Tartu Ulikooli Ajalugu) of 1982. Unlike Eschscholtz, Engelhardt, and Kotzebue, Gofman loosened his professional and family connections with that ancient university and town, moving to the Ukraine and then St. Petersburg. His later interests revolved around the Urals, not the South Pacific Ocean.[128]

Appendix

TABLE A.1
Russian-Tuamotuan contact during the Russian naval visits of 1816-24

Date of visit	Island	Signs of occupation	Islanders observed	Landing made	Close contact established	Remarks
16 Apr. 1816	Pukapuka	no	no	no	no	*Riurik* passed within 3,000 yards of N. point
20 Apr. 1816	Tikei	yes	no	yes	no	Well-trodden paths, a small abandoned canoe, huts containing artefacts, fishing nets observed
22 Apr. 1816	Takapoto	no	no	no	no	No coconut palms; ship passed within 900 yards
23 Apr. 1816	Apataki	no	no	no	no	Swift passage; poorly inspected by Kotzebue
23 Apr. 1816	Arutua	no	no	no	no	No coconut palms; ship skirted S. coast closely
24 Apr. 1816	Rangiroa	no	no	no	no	Kotzebue was himself surprised to find nobody, in view of size and woods
25 Apr. 1816	Tikehau	no	no	no	no	Adequate inspection
5 Jul. 1820	Manuhangi	no	no	yes	no	Russians collected sea-urchins, birds, pandanus
6 Jul. 1820	Hao	yes	yes	no	yes	Armed men signalling; three canoes observed
8 Jul. 1820	Amanu	yes	yes	yes	yes	Second Russian landing in Tuamotus repulsed by 60 armed men, reinforced by armed women; no bloodshed

Date	Year	Island					Notes
10 Jul.	1820	Angatau	yes	yes	no	yes	Approach by 6 evidently predatory canoes, 20 feet long; spear thrust at a Russian officer; no trade
11 Jul.	1820	Takume	yes	no	no	no	Smoke seen in various parts, but no canoes along shoreline
12 Jul.	1820	Raroia	yes	yes	no	no	Much smoke; men and canoes seen from *Mirnyi* only
13 Jul.	1820	Nihiru	yes	yes	yes	yes	Approach by canoe holding a chief, Tatano, and a commoner; barter civilities; woman also drawn by Pavel Mikhailov
14 Jul.	1820	Taenga	yes	yes	no	no	Two canoes seen under sail, but no village site or structures
15 Jul.	1820	Makemo	yes	yes	no	no	Two men seen in a canoe, which approached *Mirnyi*; barter
15 Jul.	1820	Raevskii	no	no	no	no	Russians passed at ten miles' distance; no true examination
15 Jul.	1820	Katiu	no	no	no	no	Adequate inspection in-shore
16 Jul.	1820	Tahanea	no	no	no	no	Pass within 800 yards, good light; no evidence of mankind
16 Jul.	1820	Faaite	yes	yes	no	no	Two men seen in the distance, considered temporary visitors
16 Jul.	1820	Fakarava	yes	yes	no	no	Some 40 natives with sizeable canoes spotted in the dusk; no contact feasible, but regrets
17 Jul.	1820	Toau	no	no	no	no	No coconut palms

(continued on next page)

Table A.1 (continued)

Date of visit	Island	Signs of occupation	Islanders observed	Landing made	Close contact established	Remarks
18 Jul. 1820	Niau	yes	no	yes	no	Russians saw an abandoned canoe and fire sites; collected birds, timber samples, coral, and shells
19 Jul. 1820	Kaukura	yes	yes	no	yes	Armed men, canoes, huts, dogs observed; approach by two men; sketch by Mikhailov; barter
20 Jul. 1820	Makatea	yes	yes	yes	yes	Rescue of four youths, natives of Anaa; breadfruit and coconuts in evidence; no village seen
30 Jul. 1820	Tikehau	no	no	no	no	Vostok coasted within 800 yards, improving on Kotzebue's survey
30 Jul. 1820	Matahiva	no	no	no	no	Heavily wooded, but no trace of residents
2 Mar. 1824	Fangahina	yes	yes	no	no	Alarmed islanders flee inland; large canoes
3 Mar. 1824	Angatau	no	no	no	no	Presence of islanders in 1820 recalled with surprise by Kotzebue
8 Mar. 1824	Takaroa	no	no	no	no	Very brief inspection
9 Mar. 1824	Apataki	no	no	no	no	Approach within a mile; vast colonies of seabirds; no human structures visible

TABLE A.2
Russian ships in Matavai Bay, Tahiti, and Opunohu Bay, Mo'orea, 1820-40

Ship	Tonnage	Commander	Bay of call	Arrival	Departure
Vostok	900	F.F. Bellingshausen	Matavai	22/7/1820	27/7/1820
Mirnyi	530	M.P. Lazarev	Matavai	22/7/1820	27/7/1820
Kreiser	1100	M.P. Lazarev	Matavai	9/7/1823	20/2/1823
Ladoga	530	And. P. Lazarev	Matavai	14/7/1832	20/7/1823
Predpriiatie	?	O.E. von Kotzebue	Matavai	14/3/1824	24/3/1824
Moller	?	M.N. Staniukovich	Matavai	29/4/1827	15/5/1827
Krotkii	?	L.A. Hagemeister	Matavai	5/2/1830	11/2/1830
Amerika	655	I.I. von Schantz	Opunohu	10/12/1835	3/1/1836
Nikolai	540	E.A. Berens	Opunohu	29/1/1839	2/2/1839

Note: Arrival dates are when ships arrived at their anchorage, not off the bays in question. All European shipping was liable to lengthy delays because of calms or contrary winds offshore. *Ladoga* was in sight of Tahiti for a week before entering Matavai Bay, and *Nikolai* was becalmed off Mo'orea and Tahiti from 6-10 Dec. 1835.

As their 17-day and 24-day stays suggest, *Moller* and *Amerika* were in need of repairs when they came. The average length of call was 9 days. See Ivashint-sev 1980:139-48 on ship's companies and Montgomery 1832, 2:216 on the effects of their presence in Tahiti.

Notes

ACLS	American Council of Learned Societies
AGO	Arkhiv Vse-Soiuznogo Geograficheskogo Obshchestva (St. Petersburg)
AVPR	Arkhiv Vneshnei Politiki Rossii SSSR (Moscow)
BL	British Library
DNB	*Dictionary of National Biography* (London 1885-1912)
EB	*Encyclopaedia Britannica*, 11th ed. (Cambridge 1911)
ES	*Entsiklopedicheskii slovar'*, ed. Andreevskii (St. Petersburg 1890-1907)
GPB	Gosudarstvennaia Publichnaia Biblioteka
GSE	*Great Soviet Encyclopaedia*, 32 vols. (New York 1983)
IVGO	*Izvestiia Vsesoiuznogo Geograficheskogo Obshchestva*
JPS	*Journal of the Polynesian Society* (Wellington, NZ)
L.	Leningrad
LOAAN	Leningradskoe Otdelenie Arkhiva Akademii Nauk SSSR
M.	Moscow
MAE	Muzei Antropologii i Etnografii Akademii NAUK SSSR (St. Petersburg)
MSb	*Morskoi Sbornik*
OMS	*Obshchii morskoi spisok* (St. Petersburg 1885-1907)
ORGPB	Otdel Rukopisei Gosudarstvennoi Publichnoi Biblioteki (Saltykov-Shchedrin Public Library, St. Petersburg)
PHR	*Pacific Historical Review*
RBS	*Russkii Biograficheskii Slovar'*, St. Petersburg 1896-1913
SEER	*Slavonic and East European Review*
SMAE	*Sbornik Muzeia Antropologii i Etnografii*

St. P.   St. Petersburg
TIIET   *Trudy Instituta Istorii Estestvoznaniia i Tekhniki*
TsGADA   Tsentral'nyi Gosudarstvennyi Arkhiv Drevnikh Aktov (Moscow)
TsGAVMF   Tsentral'nyi Gosudarstvennyi Arkhiv Voenno-Morskogo Flota SSSR
TsGIAE   Tsentral'nyi Gosudarstvennyi Istoricheskii Arkhiv Estonii
TUAK   Tartu Ulikooli Ajaloo Küsimusi (Tartu)
ZADMM   *Zapiski Admiralteiskago Departamenta Morskago Ministerstva*
ZUKMS   *Zapiski Uchenogo Komiteta Morskago Shtaba*

CHAPTER ONE: A SURVEY

1 For a survey of these and related discoveries, see Sharp 1960:193-207.
2 Kotzebue 1821, 1:16-18; Kotzebue 1830, 1:3, 12; Bellingshausen 1945, 1:38-40; Friis 1967:191-93, 195.
3 Sharp 1960:73-74, 97-98.
4 Markham 1904; Stevens 1930:86-205; see also Great Britain 1931-57, 3:100.
5 Beechey 1931, 1; Duperrey 1827.
6 Ivashintsev 1980:88.
7 Ibid.:145.
8 Gough 1973:4.
9 Berg 1949:163.
10 Kotzebue 1821, 1:1-2.
11 Ibid., 1:7-9.
12 Barratt 1981:98, 108.
13 Penrose 1959:94.
14 Kotzebue 1821, 1:10-11.
15 Mahr 1932:13-14 (Chamisso and the *Quarterly Review* for Jan. 1822, etc.).
16 Kotzebue 1821, 1:23-24; on Chamisso's scientific work in Oceania in 1816-17 see Menza 1970 and my study, *The Russian View of Honolulu, 1809-1826.*
17 Lebedev and Esakov 1971:328; Friis 1967:192-93.
18 Alexander Turnbull Library, Wellington, NZ:MS journal of Samuel Wallis, HMS *Dolphin*, 20 August 1766; see also Beaglehole 1955, 1:cxxxiii, 392.
19 Beaglehole comments constructively on this: 1955, 1:119 n. 1; see also Sharp 1960:2-3.
20 *EB*, 19:290-98, on navigational technique and instruments.
21 See Vorontsov-Vel'iaminov 1956, chs. 2-3, and Varep 1981:61ff.
22 Kotzebue 1821, 1:21-24; Chamisso 1859, 3:18-19.
23 Kotzebue 1821, 1:87; Ivashintsev 1980:138.
24 Summary in Langdon 1959:105-08.
25 Perm' District State Archive, Perm', *fond* 445, op. 1, *delo* 401 (notes by A.K. Shvarts); AGO, *razr.* 99, *dela* 36, 46, etc.; TsGIAE, *fond* 2057, op. 1, *delo* 381 (Khlebnikov's diary) and 489 (letters to F.P. Vrangel', 1832-34). See also Vishnevskii 1957 on Khlebnikov's travels in Oceania and the Americas, and Ivashintsev 1980:112 (Lt. Fedor Bodisko's landing on Pitcairn, provisioning, three islanders aboard the *Amerika* overnight, etc.) Mikhlukho-Maklai discussed Pitcairn in his essay "Ostrova Rapanui, Pitkairn, i Mangareva," 1873:42-55.
26 See Rovinskii 1957 on the saga of Fletcher Christian, Bligh, and John Adams; and Chlenov 1962.
27 Kotzebue 1821, 1:144.
28 Ibid., 1:133-36; on Davis's reported sighting in latitude 27° 30'S., see Sharp 1970:5-7 and Sharp 1960:88-90.
29 Kotzebue 1821, 1:146.
30 Sharp 1970:10-11, 179; also Sharp 1960:73.
31 Sharp 1960:73-74.

32 Sharp 1970:11.
33 Kotzebue 1821, 1:10-11, 28-31.
34 Sharp 1970:7-8.
35 Kotzebue 1821, 1:146-47; also Chamisso 1936, 1:120.
36 Kotzebue 1821, 1:147; Sharp 1960:73.
37 Kotzebue 1821, 1:46-50.
38 On Hörner, See Kruzenshtern 1814, 1:5-6, 28.
39 Kotzebue 1821, 1:54-83.
40 Ibid., 1:147; Chamisso 1836, 1:120. Biographical data on Eschscholtz in Kotzebue
     1981:317 and W. Lenz 1970:199.
41 Kotzebue 1821, 1:148-49.
42 Sharp 1970:120-21 and notes; also Behrens 1739, 1:141-43.
43 Kotzebue 1821, 1:150; complementary accounts in Chamisso 1836, 1:121-22 and Choris
     1826:18-20. Choris's text accompanied his Plate X, showing the landing on Tikei
     (Rumiantsev) atoll. The Dutch had left no description of its encircling reefs: see Sharp
     1970:120. On Lt. Ivan Zakharin, described by Chamisso as "sickly, irritable, but kind-
     hearted," see Mahr 1932:12.
44 Kotzebue 1821, 1:151-52 and 3:221-22. Choris suggests that 12 men landed.
45 Kotzebue 1821, 3:223; also Choris 1826:19.
46 Sharp 1970:121-28.
47 Kotzebue 1821, 1:153-54; Chamisso 1836, 1:124-25; Gallagher 1964:100-1.
48 Beaglehole 1955, 2:380; Sharp 1960:130-31.
49 Sharp 1970:135-36.
50 Kotzebue 1821, 1:154-57; Berg 1949:162.
51 Kotzebue 1821, 1:159; Sharp 1960:193.
52 Beaglehole 1955, 2:379-80.
53 Sharp 1960:74; Sharp 1970:134.
54 Lebedev and Esakov 1971:328.
55 Kotzebue 1821, 1:145, 161; Sharp 1960:59 (Quiros's "San Pablo" as Hao).
56 Kotzebue 1821, 3:220; Kruzenshtern 1824-27 for comments on *Riurik*'s findings in rela-
     tion to others. See also Nevskii 1951:250-57 on Kruzenshtern as a comparative hydrog-
     rapher, Russian use of Aaron Arrowsmith's charts of 1790 and 1794, and Kruzenshtern's
     acquaintance with the Spanish hydrographer Espinoza.
57 Kotzebue 1821, 1:162; Choris 1826:20; Chamisso 1836, 1:123.
58 Ivashintsev 1980:34-35.
59 Hawkesworth 1773, 1:362-522; Sharp 1960:105-6.
60 Ivashintsev 1980:35.
61 Thomson 1915:244.
62 See Beechey 1831 on the British visit of Jan. 1826; Sharp 1960:163; Ivashintsev
     1980:139.
63 Sementovskii 1951, intro.; Shokal'skii 1928:55-71; Skerst 1961:85-90; Barratt 1979:13.
64 Bellingshausen 1945, 1:221-25; Sementovskii 1951:141-57.
65 Bellingshausen 1945, 1:226-27; Sementovskii 1951:142.
66 Details of Wallis's finds in the Tuamotu Archipelago are given in Hawkesworth 1773, 1,
     of which *Vostok* carried a copy in 1819-21.
67 Bellingshausen 1945, 1:228; Sementovskii 1951:144.
68 Beaglehole 1855, 1:71.
69 Ibid., 1:66 n. 3; Markham 1904:323ff.; Great Britain 1931-57, 3:100.
70 Sharp 1960:59-60.
71 Bellingshausen 1945, 1:230-31.
72 Ibid., 1:231; Sementovskii 1951:145-46.
73 Sharp 1960:125.
74 Bellingshausen 1945, 1:232.
75 Russian data on these and other Polynesian craft were, regrettably, overlooked by A.C.
     Haddon and J. Hornell in their classic study (1936). The Russian materials relating to
     Nukuhiva, Rapa, Tahiti, and Hawaii deserve more attention in the West.

76 Bellingshausen 1945, 1:235; Sementovskii 1951:147-48.
77 Bellingshausen 1945, 1:237-38.
78 Gaillot 1910, 6; Angas 1848:306-8.
79 Bellingshausen 1945, 1:240/obv (Plate 23) and 6 on Mikhailov's 1819-21 portfolio of drawings and its fate.
80 Bellingshausen 1945, 1:240-41; Berg 1949:164; Kruzenshtern 1836, 2:33 on the authenticity of these discoveries.
81 Beaglehole 1955, 2:196.
82 Bellingshausen 1945, 1:242; Sementovskii 1951:148-52.
83 The Russians compared this tattooing with that seen six weeks earlier in Queen Charlotte Sound, New Zealand. *Vostok* carried a copy of the original German edition of Georg Heinrich Langsdorf's *Voyages and Travels* (see 1:114-18 for his treatment of Nukuhivan tattooing in 1804), and Bellingshausen was also familiar with his substantial essay on that subject, "Opisanie uzorov navodimykh zhiteliami ostrova Vashingtona na ikh tele," 1810, 2:100-121.
84 Penrose 1959; 93-94; Barratt 1981:89-91.
85 Sharp 1960:185-86.
86 Bellingshausen 1945, 1:250/obv., for example, shows Takume, Raroia, and Angatau.
87 Bellinsgauzen 1831 offered 19 maps of portions of the Pacific, plus 15 views and 30 illustrations based on aquarelles by Mikhailov. As Friis notes (1967:195), the 1831 maps are "schematic cartographic representations" of Tuamotu Archipelago islands.
88 Bellingshausen 1945, 1:244-45; Beaglehole 1955, 2:380.
89 Beaglehole 1955, 2:279-80.
90 Bellingshausen 1945, 1:244.
91 Ibid., 1:247; Sementovskii, op. cit.:153-54.
92 Bellingshausen 1945, 1:249.
93 Bellingshausen 1945, 1:250; see also Lebedev and Esakov 1971:328 and Magidovich 1957:508, 513.
94 See *The World Atlas* (Moscow, Chief Administration of Geodesy and Cartography, 1967, 2d ed., in English), sheets 236-37. The dignitaries and military or naval leaders for whom Bellingshausen named coral islands in 1820 were: Aleksei A. Arakcheev (1769-1834), military figure, Chairman of the State Council, organizer of the infamous "Military Settlements" (1817); Mikhail B. Barclay de Tolly (1761-1818), hero of the Patriotic War (1812), field marshal (1814); Pavel V. Chichagov (1767-1849), naval minister (1802-9), commander of an Army Corps at Berezina River (1812), blamed for defeats and living abroad since 1814; Aleksei P. Ermolov (1777-1861), general, Commander-in-Chief of the Caucasian Corps (1816-27), Governor of the Caucasus; Aleksei S. Greig (1775-1845), son of Catherine the Great's Scottish admiral, Samuel Greig, Commander-in-Chief of the Black Sea Fleet since 1816; Mikhail I. Kutuzov (1745-1813), field marshal, victor over Napoleon in 1812; Mikhail A. Miloradovich (1771-1825), general of infantry, Military Governor of St. Petersburg since 1818, killed during the Decembrist uprising of 14 Dec. 1825; Aleksandr V. Moller (1764-1837), naval minister; Fabian Gottlieb von der Osten-Saken (1752-1837), general, Military Governor of occupied Paris, 1814, Commander-in-Chief, Third Infantry Corps; Petr Kh. Vitgenshtein (1769-1843), Commander-in-Chief of the Russian Army on Kutuzov's death (1813-14), Commander-in-Chief, First Infantry Corps since 1812, field marshal (1826); and Prince Petr M. Volkonskii (1776-1852), field marshal, Chief of the General Staff and Military Directorate (1813-25). All were linked with the Russian defeat of Napoleon's Grande Armée in 1812-13.
95 Bellingshausen 1945, 1:253.
96 Ibid., 1:255. See Sharp 1970:137-40 (the Dutch landing on Makatea, or "Verquicking," of 2-3 June 1722).
97 Bellingshausen 1945, 1:255-56.
98 Beaglehole 1955, 1:xlviii, 66.
99 Bellingshausen 1945, 2:292; Sharp 1960:198.
100 See Bellinsgauzen 1960:309.
101 Sharp 1960:196.

102 Ibid.:5-6.
103 Turnbull 1805, 1.
104 Details of the *Aguila*'s voyage in Corney 1913-19.
105 See Christie 1951:109; Shokal'skii 1928:195-97; Lebedev 1963.
106 Nevskii 1951:251-55, 261-62. For a survey of Russian cartography as it related to the Pacific in this period, see Akhmatov 1926:30-34.
107 Discussions in Nevskii 1951:252-60 and Friis 1967:195-97; also Magidovich 1957:513-14.
108 Ethnography performed from *Vostok* and *Mirnyi* in Oceania is barely touched upon by Lipshits, Berg, Shur, A.I. Andreev, or Sharp (see Bibliography for works); indeed, it is dealt with adequately only, on a strictly regional basis, in *SMAE* (e.g., N.A. Butinov and L.G. Rozina on the Maori, Iu. Likhtenberg on Hawaii).
109 Bellinsgauzen 1960:65.
110 Beaglehole 1955, 1:520-21.
111 Details in Bellinsgauzen 1960:66.
112 Bellingshausen 1945, 1:230-31.
113 Ibid., 1:233.
114 Davies 1961:94, 107 ("a cruel war among themselves . . ." in 1807, etc.).
115 Bellingshausen 1945, 2:271.
116 Davies 1961:269-70. For materials on the social and political structures on the Tuamotus in early post-contact times, see *Bulletin de la Société d'Etudes Océaniennes* (Papeete, 1917-59), pts. 1-7. On earlier and subsequent life on the coral islands examined by Bellingshausen, see Emory (1934).
117 Davies 1961:172, 207, 247.
118 See n. 92. Russian ethnographic data on the Tuamotus of 1816-24 may usefully be collated with the works of Emory and Father Honoré Laval: see the latter's *Histoire ancienne d'un peuple polynésien* (Braine-le-Comte, Belgium 1938), for example, on pre-contact Mangareva.
119 Barratt 1979:123-26.
120 Bellinsgauzen 1960:65-66.
121 Darwin 1874:115-16; Dubois-Reymond (1889) on Eschscholtz's contribution to the subject; Newell 1959, 3:120-28.
122 Bellingshausen 1945, 1:251-52. Bellingshausen incorporates then-unpublished ideas advanced by Chamisso on the basis of his observations in Oceania in 1816-17. On Chamisso's natural historical work and dealings with the Russians, see Brun 1896:141-46, 210-16; Feudel 1971; Menza 1970. In a Ph.D. dissertation (Bonn 1951), Heinz Kelm stressed Chamisso's ethnography in Polynesia in its relation to the natural sciences ("Adelbert von Chamisso als Ethnograph der Südsee").
123 Bellingshausen 1945, 1:252.
124 Kotzebue 1830, 1:2-3, 12; Kotzebue 1981:317-18; E. Lenz 1831:221ff.; Friis 1967:193.
125 Bellingshausen 1945, 1:250.
126 Ibid., 1:251.
127 See n. 121.
128 Kotzebue 1981:317 and W. Lenz 1970:199-200 on Eschscholtz's writing and career.
129 Lütke's *Voyage* appeared in two Russian editions, one with the subtitle "Historical section" and the other with the subtitle "Nautical section," as follows: (1) *Puteshestvie vokrug svieta . . . na voennom shliupe Seniavine . . . .* Otdielenie morekhodnoe s atlasom. SPB, 1835. x, 356 pp. ---*Atlas*: SPB, 1832. 34 double spread sheets containing 51 maps and plans; (2) *Puteshestvie vokrug svieta . . . na voennom shliupe Seniavine . . . .* Otdelenie istoricheskoe. S atlasom. SPB, 1834-36. 2 vols. (294 pp. and 282 pp.) + atlas (xiv, 270 pp.). This atlas includes the works of the scientists on board the *Seniavin*— Postels, Mertens, Kittlitz, and other scientific notes. It is a large folio size.

These editions were translated into French from the author's Russian: (1) *Voyage autour du monde . . . sur la Corvette Le Seniavine . . . .* Partie historique, avec un atlas, lithographie. Paris, 1835-36. 2 vols. (xxiv, 410 pp. and ii, 387 pp.) + atlas (xiv, 352 pp.).

The atlas is "Les travaux de M.M. les naturalistes"; (2) *Voyage autour du monde*. . . . Partie nautique avec un atlas, (St. P. 1936), X, 343 pp. This information was taken from V. Lada-Mocarski, *Bibliography of books on Alaska published before 1868* (New Haven, 1969). There is a very detailed explanation of the publishing history. Lütke's text was complemented by Baron Friedrich H. Kittlitz's *Denkwurdigkeiten einer Reise um die Welt* (Gotha 1858). On this expedition, see Barratt 1984 and Friis 1967:193-94; also Berg 1962:165-66.

130 Kotzebue 1981:317.
131 Ivashintsev 1980:143-44.
132 See the travel diary of Midshipman Count Loggin Geiden (Heyden) of *Predpriiatie*: TsGAVMF, *fond* 5, op. 1, *delo* 95.
133 Ferman 1926:188-89, etc.; Lukina 1975, chs. 1-3; Kotzebue 1821, 1:23-24; also Merrill 1954, no. 5-6.
134 See Kotzebue 1981:14 and Friis 1967:191-93.
135 Details of ships' movements in Ivashintsev 1980:79, 86.
136 Barratt 1979:10-12; Barratt 1984:1012; *Allgemeine Deutsche Biographie* (Leipzig 1885), 21:470.
137 See pp. 303ff. above.
138 Kotzebue 1830, 1:77-99.
139 Ibid., 1:253-55.
140 Ibid., 1:103.
141 Ibid., 1:104.
142 Ibid., 1:105.
143 Ibid., 1:107-8.
144 Sharp 1960:5-6, 206.
145 Kotzebue 1830, 1:108-9.
146 Ibid., 1:110.
147 Bellingshausen 1945, 1:39, 234-35; Kotzebue 1830, 1:12.
148 Hawkesworth 1773, 1:1-139.
149 Gallagher 1864:100-1; Sharp 1960:102; Kruzenshtern 1824-27 and 1836.
150 Kotzebue 1830, 1:112.
151 Ibid., 1:113.
152 Ibid., 1:113-14.
153 Ibid., 1:114-17.
154 Berg 1962:165; Magidovich 1957:513; Ivashintsev 1980:75.
155 Beaglehole 1955, 1:196.
156 P. Schmidt, "Zoology," in Fersman 1926:188-89; also Lukina 1975:150-52.
157 Translation ("Zoological Appendix") in Kotzebue 1830, 2:336-37. See Heidemaa 1975, 2:164-74 and 1981, 11:87-92 on zoological specimens that returned to Tartu with Eschscholtz, his Pacific notes, etc. Other materials relating to these matters are held at LOAAN in *fond* 260, op. 2. They bear particularly on Tahiti, Sitka, and Kamchatka.
158 Kotzebue 1830, 2:336.
159 Tilesius von Tilenau's album of sketches of 1803-66 is in the Lenin State Library, Moscow: Rukopisnyi otdel, *fond* 178, M. 10693a. His *Nadezhda* journal, however, is at LOAAN, *razr.* 4, op. 1, *delo* 800a.
160 The Elmer E. Rasmusen Library of the University of Alaska at Fairbanks (Shur Collection, reel 79) holds microfilm of lengthy extracts from *Nadezhda*'s 1804 journal containing meteorological and related data (original in TsGIAL, *fond* 15, op. 1, *delo* 2: fols. 33ff.). It shows the beginning of Russian meteorology in Oceania.
161 Kotzebue 1830, 1:106.
162 Ibid., and 1:116.
163 E. Lenz 1831:221-344 & 1847:65-74. For later development of Lenz's mid-Pacific research of 1824-25 see Prestwich 1974:587-674.
164 Summary in Friis 1967:193.
165 Kotzebue 1981:318.

166 Krümmell 1907, 1:371.
167 See Barratt 1981:228-39.
168 Berg 1949:163.
169 See Tumarkin 1964, chs. 4-6; Pierce 1965:26-28.
170 See Polansky 1974:77-83; also Ravva 1972:162-68.
171 Ivashintsev 1980:85-86.
172 Ibid.:93.
173 *ZGDMM* 1833, 1; Sharp 1960:214-15; Kruzenshtern 1836.
174 Ivashintsev 1980:88, 145: Bellingshausen 1945, 2:292.
175 Sharp 1960:189, 213; Lisianskii 1812, 2:224-25; Nevskii 1951:184-86; Kruzenshtern 1936:109.
176 Kotzebue 1821, 1:152; Kruzenshtern 1836:109-10, 162; Sharp 1960:209, 213.

CHAPTER TWO: THE RUSSIAN TEXTS

1 On Honden Eylandt and the observations of the *Eendracht*'s landing party there in latitude 15°12′S see Engelbrecht 1945.
2 Compare Kotzebue 1821 1:147-48, and Chamisso 1836, 1:120. The "doubts" were reinforced by Pukapuka's position as given by Aaron Arrowsmith, whose Pacific chart was in constant use aboard *Riurik*: Kotzebue 1821, 1:17.
3 This was correct at the time.
4 The Russians pardonably failed to recognize Tikei as Roggeveen's Bedrieglyke Eylandt, seen by the Dutch on 18 May 1722.
5 On Tikei's western side. Kotzebue's charts have, unfortunately, not been reprinted from the 1821 edition of his *Puteshestvie v Iuzhnyi okean i v Beringov proliv*.
6 See Sharp 1970:120-21.
7 Choris drew the "raft" or *radeau* which measured four feet square and was largely made of poles or slats, with a degree of precision missing from this word picture.
8 French: *deux vieilles cabanes*. Native structures, not European.
9 Reef-forming corals.
10 Pandanus.
11 Choris's correspondence with Kruzenshtern of 1821-22, that is, when the young artist had already left Russia for Paris, reflects his awareness of the importance of publicly recognizing indebtedness to Rumiantsev, his former patron: holographs in TsGIAE, *fond* 1414, op. 3, *delo* 42.
12 Actually, latitude 14°58′S, longitude 144°33′W. Kotzebue and Bellingshausen's tracks through the Tuamotus may conveniently be followed on a 1:1,000,000 navigational chart. I have used UK-US operational navigation charts, World Area code 1084, ONC N-20/21 (1976-77), which lend themselves to collation with the Russians' original charts as printed in 1821 and 1830.
13 Actually, Aratua's centre lies in latitude 15°19′S, longitude 146°45′W. See Sharp 1960:98 on Roggeveen's pass by Aratua on 30 May 1722.
14 Choris 1826:18-20 (accompanying text for Plate 10).
15 Kotzebue 1821, 3:331-36.
16 French: *cavités*. Choris evidently has natural depressions in mind.
17 Count Rumiantsev died in 1826. Ethnographic, botanical, and other Pacific collections in his personal museum were later sent to Moscow to form the basis of the Moscow and Rumiantsev Public Museum. See *Materialy dlia istorii Rumiantsevskago Muzeia* 1882, 1:93-95, 180-82 and Staniukovich 1978:74-75 on Rumiantsev and Polynesian objects collected by *Riurik*.
18 Chamisso headed this essay "The Low Isles Lying in Latitude 15°S, between 138° and 149°W: Romanzoff Island," but he wished to avoid entanglement in hydrographic controversy, since he entertained doubts about Kruzenshtern's findings of 1819 but lacked materials that would have allowed him to pursue the matter in Berlin.

19 Drawn for James Cook in March 1770 by Tupaia, *ari'i* of Raiatea, who was then voyaging in HMS *Endeavour*: see Beaglehole 1955, 1:293-94; Forster 1778:511-12; Burney 1802-7, 2:281-82.

20 Kruzenshtern was correct in his identification, which he based on collation of Dutch, British, and Russian reckonings of position. He did not, however, find it on Tupaia's list of atolls—despite the presence on it of both Apataki ("Oopate") and Tikehau ("Teoheow"), as transcribed by the British, among *Riurik*'s 1816 sightings.

21 The reference is to the 1821 ed. of Kotzebue's *Puteshestvie*: see n. 5.

22 For treatment of botanical data omitted here, see chap. 6 here.

23 *Rattus exulans*, eaten in Tahiti and the Tuamotus in times of famine only, but considered good food in New Zealand and the Austral Isles. It shared Tikei's insects, as Chamisso suggests, with woodcocks and curlews.

24 Actually, a gecko. The foolish bird was *Anous stolidus*, the noddy.

25 Tikei was intermittently visited by parties from "King George's Islands" to the NW.

26 This text is also available in Henry Kratz's translation of Chamisso, published as *A Voyage Around the World with the Romanzov Exploring Expedition in the Years 1815-1818 in the Brig Rurik, Captain Otto von Kotzebue* (Honolulu 1986) pp. 65, 69-71. Chamisso was evidently familiar with Jacob Le Maire's narrative and certainly knew Carl Friedrich de Behrens' 1739 *Histoire de l'Expédition de Trois Vaisseaux* as well as James Burney's early nineteenth-century compilation, *Chronological History of the Voyages and Discoveries in the South Sea*. A copy of the latter was in *Riurik*'s wardroom.

27 See Sharp 1960:73-74.

28 Text given on p. 74 above.

29 Moringuid eels are occasionally seen in these waters.

30 For the preceding passage, covering *Riurik*'s search for San Pablo Island, sea birds observed, etc., see Kotzebue 1821, 1:145-46 (from Chapter 3 of the 1821 *Puteshestvie* text).

31 Kotzebue's brig had a markedly narrower range of vision than did Bellingshausen's *Vostok*; but Pukapuka rises a mere 15' above sea level.

32 E.g., Chile around Talcaguano and Easter Island.

33 Jacob Le Maire's people had had the same impression on 10 April 1616, landing, indeed, on the shoreline seen by Kotzebue: Engelbrecht 1945, sec. 7.

34 An unoriginal opinion, derived as much from Cook's published officers as from experience: Beaglehole 1955, 2:335, 642, re frigate birds, terns, etc.

35 Pukapuka's principal inlet lies in the NNW quarter.

36 Actually, they were 7°30' too far eastward: Kruzenshtern 1836:108 and Kotzebue 1981:74-75; also Sharp 1960:2-3 on longitudinal error in earlier times.

37 Kotzebue 1821, 1:16-18 (instruments by British makers).

38 Palms did grow on Pukapuka's higher areas, but Tikei's lack of any lagoon is distinctive.

39 Plate 1 depicts the start of these operations.

40 Choris points out that all cartouches were drenched too; but Kotzebue omits this from his printed account of his efficient landing.

41 Details of Tuamotuan canoes of ancient types in Haddon and Hornell 1936, 1:50-92.

42 Presented to Count Rumiantsev in 1818, these Tuamotuan artefacts went to Moscow with other Pacific ethnographica: *Materialy dlia istorii* 1882:180ff.; Rozina 1969:317. They were lost during the Second World War, if not earlier.

43 On this, see Wagner 1938:297-326. Russia never laid any claim to Tikei or other atolls in the Tuamotu Archipelago.

44 See n. 37. The latitudinal fix was almost precisely correct.

45 Kotzebue had with him accounts of both Byron's pass by Takaroa-Takapoto of June 1765 (in Hawkesworth 1773, 1) and Cook's second voyage, during which King George's Islands were again visited: see Beaglehole 1955, 2:378-79. Although unaware of Roggeveen's precise track to "Schadelijk Eylandt" (Takapoto), therefore, he should not have presumed to name it after Spiridov. Even Cook's fix for it (latitude 14°37'S, longitude 145°10'W) adumbrated his own—given his allowance for longitudinal error—to within

3′ or 4′. But low atolls were appearing on the horizon so frequently and the dependent decisions were so pressing that Kotzebue had no time to weigh the situation. Oddly, Takaroa seems not to have been sighted from *Riurik*'s cross trees.

46 As given in the Loggin Golenishchev-Kutuzov translation. On Cook's reckonings for the positions of Apataki, Toau, and Kaukura (April 1774) see Beaglehole 1955, 2:379-80 and notes.

47 *Riurik* had approached Tehere Pass, on the NW of Apataki where Cook had never been, before sailing though to Porovaki Pass. Rightly identifying Apataki, off his port bow, as Cook's first Palliser Island, Kotzebue rechecked Cook's latitudinal fix, then coasted around his supposed discovery: Aratua (Riurik's Chain).

48 Unwittingly, the Russians were in the exact track of Roggeveen, who had skirted Aratua on the south on 28 May 1722. To the Dutch, the atoll meant merely "More Trouble" (Meerder Zorg).

49 SE Rangiroa: Dean's Island was Le Maire's Vliegen Eylandt, but the Russians passed along the southern, not northern, coast.

50 Kotzebue wished to reach Kamchatka by early June in order to spend an entire Arctic summer in exploration: Ivashintsev 1980:26-27.

51 Sharp 1960:73-74. *Riurik*'s wardroom held no copy of Le Maire's narrative, first published in 1622, and this caused slips.

52 A revised printing of the 1794 *Map of the World* on a scale of five equatorial degrees to one inch. On Aaron Arrowsmith see *DNB*, 1:595-96 and Nevskii 1951:250-51. The island "spotted to SSE" from a position off the SE of Rangiroa was, presumably, Motu Panao on the NW edge of Kaukura.

53 A severe overestimate: actually, some 54 statute miles.

54 Both Berg (1962:162) and Svet (1966:217) offer wrong data here. Kotzebue's own 1821 figures were excellent by contemporaneous standards.

55 Tikehau, or Tikahau, had not been seen by the Dutch: Sharp 1960:193.

56 *Riurik* was proceeding directly up the 148th meridian. Again, one hears in Kotzebue's reflections echoes of Cook's and his people's comments on "those drowned isles" (the Pallisers) and conditions around them: Beaglehole 1955, 1:70-72; 2:379-81.

57 Boumann's or Boumans Islands, seen by Roggeveen on 14 June 1722 in latitude 14°9′S, longitude 171°W, were the Manua Islands of the Samoa group. On Cornelis Bouman of the *Thienhoven* and these sightings see Mulert 1911:166ff. Kotzebue finally investigated the "Navigators' Isles" (Samoa) eight years later (April 1824) in *Predpriiatie*: see Kotzebue 1981:136-51.

58 In fact, the only adjacent atoll, Matahiva, was due west. It was found by Bellingshausen on 30 July 1820. Areas of smooth water were caused by counteraction of wind and surface current.

59 Text from Bellinsgauzen 1960:249-75.

60 This was Manuhangi, sighted by Captain Samuel Wallis of HMS *Swallow* on 12 June 1767 and named by him Cumberland Island.

61 The Russians were justified in their unwillingness to identify the atoll they were seeing with Wallis's Cumberland Island. Their far more accurate reckonings of position placed the work of Wallis and his master, George Robertson, in an unflattering light. (On their accounts of Manuhangi and Nengonengo, or Prince William Henry Isle, see Hawkesworth 1773, 1:362ff.) The mention of Lt. Konstantin Petrovich Torson (1796-1851) was one of several left by Bellingshausen in his narrative, despite Torson's disgrace and banishment to Siberia for involvement in the insurrection of 14 December 1825.

62 The plunging birds were *Fregata minor palmerstoni*, known to Cook and Kotzebue as man-of-war birds, and the zoological-anatomical deduction was correct. On Russian taxidermy in Oceania in 1820, see Barratt 1988, app. A. The stuffed frigate birds, treated aboard *Vostok* in accordance with procedures laid down by the Abbé Denis Joseph Manesse (1743-1820) in his 1787 treatise on taxidermy, are today in the drawers of the Ornithological Division of the Zoological Institute, Academy of Sciences. Mikhailov painted the Pandanus specimen over the next few days while *Vostok* surveyed Hao and

Amanu (Bow and Moller islands). The surf-zone echinoid was very probably *Strongylocentrotus purpuratus.*

63 Compare Beaglehole 1955, 1:69-71 (adjacent Vahitahians "of a dark Coper colour," their gestures of opposition, etc.).

64 *Vostok* rounded Hao's NW point because Cook's *Endeavour* had sailed up the atoll's eastern side on 6 April 1769 and, as usual, Bellingshausen was trying to complement Cook's surveying. Hao apparently had a permanent or quasi-permanent population.

65 Significantly, Bellingshausen again fails to mention Bougainville, of whose passage through the Tuamotus in March 1768 he is only dimly conscious. Details in Sharp 1960:114-15 (Isle des Lanciers, Isle de La Harpe, etc.).

66 Moller Island (Amanu) had been sighted in 1774 and probably even in 1606 by Spaniards. Bellingshausen did not know this: see Svet 1966:226-27; Sharp 1960:58-60, 125.

67 The village on Amanu remained on the western headland until modern times.

68 Novosil'skii gives his own account of the landing, but see Barratt 1979:22-23 on striking similarities between his narrative and Bellingshausen's of 1831.

69 These Amanuans wore the *maro*, or breech clout, and brandished both short bludgeons (*'omore*) and long spears; but the Russians saw no slings with stones here. See ch. 3 here on Russian evidence of warfare in the Tuamotus.

70 Gustav Kunze and Karl-Heinrich Mertens had literally missed the boat at Copenhagen in July 1819: see Barratt 1979:10-12. Mertens sailed for Oceania with Captain Fedor Petrovich Lütke in the *Seniavin* in 1826 and pursued various branches of natural science in Micronesia.

71 Fedor Vasil'evich Moller (1760-1828), Military Governor of Kronstadt.

72 See Bellinsgauzen 1960:19-21 on the earlier career.

73 These seafaring islanders came off the west side of Angatau.

74 See "Ethnography: Clothing and Body Ornament" in ch. 3 here.

75 The canoes were *pahi*, composite-plank keeled craft, but evidently they were single-hulled.

76 Despite the precision of the Russian terminology (*po arkanu iz spletennykh verevok,*) these "lassos" were in fact slings from which such warriors flung stones with great accuracy. For descriptions of the Maohis' use of them on Tahiti see Wilson 1799:364 and Ellis 1829, 2:490. See also Oliver 1974, 1:376-81, on Tahitian weaponry in general, which was closely allied to Tuamotuan weaponry.

77 The minimal safe distance on a lee shore (uncharted), among reefs. See Bellinsgauzen 1960:65-66 on the medallions offered and the trade goods left at Angatau.

78 A correct inference, but of course fire also covered the rear of a retreating party.

79 Aleksei Andreevich Arakcheev (1769-1834), Alexander I's principal military adviser and creator of the infamous "military colonies": *ES*, 3:7-10. Arakcheev Island (Angatau) was Bellingshausen's first true discovery, since Magellan's sighting of an atoll like it in 1521 had not—and still has not—been convincingly tied to that island.

80 Omitted here are remarks on fish behaviour; but see "Zoology" in ch. 3. The island spotted after Angatau was Takume, a particularly low-lying atoll just NE of Raroia, which the Russians saw next day.

81 This was true; but native traditions in the Takume-Raroia sector did refer to European visitors, who may tentatively be identified as Pedro Fernandez de Quiros's men in the *San Pablo* (February 1606). The Russians fired many more rockets in the Tuamotus than had any of their European predecessors—and not a few non-fatal cannonballs.

82 After Field-Marshal Prince Petr Mikhailovich Volkonskii (1776-1852), a hero of the campaigns of 1812-13. Takume had no permanent village and was a satellite of Raroia.

83 Passing down the eastern littoral of Raroia (see Map 6,) the Russians failed to spot Ngarue Pass on its NW side. Prince Mikhail Barclay de Tolly (1761-1818) was another of Kutuzov's illustrious subordinates, commanding divisions in the Napoleonic Wars: *ES*, 5:74-75.

84 This was Nihiru, lying SW of Taenga, which had been sighted a few hours earlier. The Russians approached Nihiru's NW headland, then moved slightly southward.

85 A slight underestimate. Today Nihiru has palms.

86 These were pearl-shell composite hooks, and the visitors were then engaged in seasonal fishing for species other than bonito, which had already left these waters in mid-July.

87 *Nio* signified "small sphere, pearl" in the Papahoe dialect spoken at Nihiru and had nothing to do with quantity, as the Russians thought. Tatano, as this islander was named according to Simonov, had come specifically to collect pearls and of course foodstuffs, to judge by Mikhailov's illustration (Plate 7).

88 This is difficult. Niau is the strongest candidate in view of the Russians' tendency to incorporate Polynesian nominative prefixes into nouns, such as Otaheite (Tahiti). From Simonov's rendering of his name, Eri-Tatano, it is plain that the pearl-gatherer referred to himself as *ari'i* (chief). He cannot however have been a powerful or influential one.

89 The Russians had practised this in Queen Charlotte Sound, NZ, seven weeks previously; see also n. 77.

90 Cuttlefish were captured by means of cowrie or other lures in the widespread South Pacific manner: see Ellis 1829, 2:292-93. They were and are plentiful in Nihiru's coral rocks and constitute excellent travelling rations.

91 It is apparently not among the specimens of Polynesian clothing and material at MAE in St. Petersburg: Rozina 1969:317-18. The Russian cloth was immediately treated as a potential *pareu*.

92 Plate 9 above.

93 Further on this, see Henry 1928:41-45. Bellingshausen echoed Charles Clerke of HMS *Resolution* in supposing that *Cocos nucifera* (*niu*) was the *only* fruit or foodstuff produced on these low atolls (see Beaglehole 1955, 2:194, n. 1). In fact, numerous atolls supported small "gardens" of the sort seen by the British on Takaroa on 18 April 1774 (ibid., 2:378, n. 2), and Taenga was by no means barren.

94 Taenga had been found in March 1803 by a trading captain, Buyers, in the merchantman *Margaret* and had been called Holt's Island. Of these facts, Bellingshausen could have known only from John Turnbull's *Voyage Round the World* (London 1805). But Kruzenshtern correctly collated *Margaret*'s and *Vostok*'s sightings in 1823.

95 Makemo, long the base for pearl divers in this sector.

96 Makemo had also been sighted by Buyers, but it was first surveyed from the northern coral rim by the Russians.

97 These were, respectively, Tepoto ("The Raevskiis") and Katiu, according to the generally reliable Svet 1966:226. The latter atoll, named after Count Dmitrii Erofeevich Osten-Saken, was indubitably Katiu; but Tepoto was one of Commodore John Byron's Islands of Disappointment, sighted on 7 June 1765 in latitude 14°07'S, longitude 141°25'W, and so cannot conceivably have been the Raevskii cluster. Debenham offers the solution (Bellingshausen 1945, 1:241).

98 See Bellingshausen 1945, 1:240.

99 *Mirnyi*'s encounter with these men was off NE Makemo, where a village stands today. Regrettably, Novosil'skii is silent about it. See Plate 7 for Tatano's thigh tattooing.

100 Sementovskii 1951:152.

101 Faaite. *Vostok* had already coasted past Tahanea ("Chichagov"). General Mikhail Andreevich Miloradovich (1771-1825), a hero of the Napoleonic Wars, was shot dead on 14 December 1825 by P.G. Kakhovskii; Pavel Vasil'evich Chichagov (1765-1849), minister of the marine in 1808-11, had won victories against the Swedish Fleet of Gustavus Adolphus: *ES*, 76:886-87.

102 This was Fakarava, later (1888) visited by Robert Louis Stevenson and celebrated in his *In the South Seas*.

103 *Pahi* of this size, still common in the Tuamotus, were already growing rare in Tahiti, whose government depended increasingly on Tuamotuans for maintaining contact with outlying islands. Details of craft in Haddon and Hornell 1936.

104 Count Petr Khristianovich Wittgenstein (in Russian, Vitgenshtein, 1768-1842), Field-Marshal: *ES*, 12:557.

105 Toau: Debenham (Bellingshausen 1945, 1:243) has Bellingshausen reach the Pallisers before he has even rounded Fakarava.
106 See Beaglehole 1955, 2:379-80.
107 This was Toau, seen some four leagues SE of Apataki's south.
108 All correct. For *Resolution*'s sighting of armed men and canoes on the shore of Kaukura (Palliser III) see Forster 1982, 3:495; Beaglehole 1955, 2:380.
109 See n. 52. In this period, there were four "Elizabeth Islands" in Oceania.
110 The atoll spotted but not examined was Kaukura.
111 On Torson's work aboard *Vostok*, see Pasetskii 1977 and Sheshin 1980:32-37.
112 The little island was Niau, which rises 26 feet above sea level: Great Britain 1931-57, 3:115.
113 See Barratt 1979:10-12.
114 From a point near the modern village, well in view of what was then an extensive freshwater lagoon. Hurricanes have since made that lagoon brackish.
115 See ch. 3 here.
116 Large masses of coral cast up onto the reef of Niau: see Great Britain 1931-57, 3:115.
117 On Samuel Greig of Inverkeithing see Cross 1974; on his son, Aleksei Samuilovich, see Barratt 1981:108, 160; Bellingsgauzen 1960:20-21 (Black Sea work).
118 See Beaglehole 1955, 2:380 and Forster 1982, 3:495 (Cook's passage round Palliser III).
119 See n. 64.
120 Tatano, drawn by Mikhailov (Plate 10).
121 Plate 6.
122 Bellingshausen here seems to count Toau as Palliser I. The typesetters preparing the 1831 text of *Dvukratnye izyskaniia* perhaps misread the III on the (long missing) holograph for II: Bellingsgauzen 1960:55-57; Barratt 1979:16-18.
123 Commentaries by Debenham (Bellingshausen 1945, 1:250, n. 1) and Friis 1967:195. See Kruzenshtern 1823-26, 2, sec. 24:5 on Kotzebue's improvement on Cook's data for Aratua, etc., and Kruzenshtern 1836, 2:33 on Bellingshausen's hydrography off Makemo and Katiu.
124 Details of Russian translations and use of Cook's *Voyages* in Barratt 1979 (4):227-29; see also Hotimsky 1971 (2):3-12 and T. Armstrong 1979. Bellingshausen much respected the astronomical work of William Baillie of the *Adventure* and his companion William Wales: Beaglehole 1955, 2:xl-xli, etc. But it was Simonov, *Vostok*'s astronomer, who made most consistent use of that work: Sementovskii 1951:127.
125 Makatea, the sole elevated island in the Tuamotus, was sighted by Roggeveen on 2 June 1722: Sharp 1960:97-98.
126 Kotzebue 1821, 1:156-57.
127 Kaukura: see n. 108.
128 The "matting" was probably clothing.
129 The landing was by Temao village but on the NE coast.
130 Turnbull 1805.
131 See Emory 1975:85-86 (Sandals).
132 See Bellingshausen 1945, 1:257ff. on subsequent events.
133 This was Nengonengo, sighted by Samuel Wallis in HMS *Dolphin* on 13 June 1767: data in Hawkesworth 1773, 1.
134 Hao; Bougainville's Isle de la Harpe, as Bellingshausen recognized.
135 This was Amanu.
136 In Russian, *korotkimi lopatkami* ("with short shovels"), suggesting spatular weapons rather than common truncheons.
137 For written orders regarding dealings with hostile native groups see Bellinsgauzen 1960:69. They support this comment.
138 Willem Schouten applies the term "Angry Sea" (Engelbrecht 1945, ch. 3) to waters in latitude 15°S; Bougainville refers to atolls between latitude 18° and 19°S as "L'Archipel dangereux."

139 See nn. 75-77 on this meeting with Angatauns, and Kotzebue 1981:72 on larger canoes seen in the same area in 1824.

140 "Summit" is here applied to an outcrop 26 feet above sea level. The only truly elevated non-coral island in the Tuamotus is Makatea (Roggeveen's "Verkwikking"), where the Russians landed on 20 July 1820.

141 Anaa, latitude 17°21'S, longitude 125°31'W, was Cook's Chain Island: see Beaglehole 1955, 1:73. Through an American interpreter, the boys told King Pomare of Tahiti that their cannibal enemies had come to Makatea from Tai, which Debenham identifies as Toau with unwarranted confidence (Bellingshausen 1945, 2:271, n. 1).

142 As usual, Simonov ignores the French explorers.

143 Aerial photography suggests nothing bowlike.

144 Manuhangi, sighted by Samuel Wallis in June 1767: Simonov had spent an hour or two on its northern tip on 5 July to fix the precise latitude: see Bellinsgauzen 1960:250 and Sementovskii 1951:142.

145 From the meridian of Paris. Amanu lies in 140°40'W from the Greenwich observatory, which Bellingshausen always bore in mind.

146 Remarks made after dealings with the Maori of Queen Charlotte Sound.

147 The *Coquille* visited Amanu on 26 April 1823 en route to Tahiti, and Duperrey failed to recognize it: Duperrey 1827:23, alluded to in Dumont D'Urville 1834-35, 2; see also Dunmore 1969, 2:122-23.

148 Sharp (1960:196-99) concedes six of these as genuine first sightings by a European (Angatau, Nihiru, Raevskii, Katiu, Fakarava, and Niau), and adds Matahiva—seen on 30 July 1820 and known to the Russians as Lazarev Island. Svet (1966:226-28) disputes the prior (Dutch, Spanish, or British) discoveries of several atolls unconvincingly.

149 The primary accounts of Roggeveen's expedition, *Twee Jaarige Reyze rondom de Wereld* (1728) and Carl Behrens's *Histoire de l'Expedition de Trois Vaisseaux* (1738), were known to the Russians through Alexander Dalrymple's *Historical Collection of Voyages* vol. 2. Both Simonov and Bellingshausen were also familiar with James Burney's *Chronological History of Voyages* (London 1816), the fourth volume of which discussed those primary accounts and sightings made by the Dutch in the Tuamotus (pp. 556-75). *Africaansche Galey* was lost on Takapoto's reef on 21 May 1722.

150 Incorrect: swine were absent from the Tuamotus in pre-contact and early post-contact times except for Matahiva in the far west; nor were dogs to be found on all atolls: Corney 1915, 36:189, 387. The "Mice" were, of course, rats.

151 Discussion in Emory 1975:171-72.

152 Ibid.:95-96 on thigh tattooing. Nihiru's reef sheltered the great pearl oyster (*Pinctada margaritifera*) as well as *Tridacna* clams and numerous echinoderms, and so was "harvested" by guests from other islands.

153 *Vostok* and *Mirnyi* had stood together off Nihiru on 13 July, but *Mirnyi* had left Makemo several hours later than her escort.

154 See nn. 112-17.

155 The realms of animals, plants, and rocks. These "numerous objects" were submitted to the Academy of Sciences by the Naval Ministry (Bellingsauzen 1960:49) and many are to be seen in St. Petersburg today. See Barratt 1988, app. A on zoological and botanical results of the expedition and the whereabouts of Australian and Oceanic articles.

156 The blue-crowned lory, *Vini australis* (Gmelin 1788), is a candidate. Arkadii Leskov, *Vostok*'s third lieutenant, returned to Polynesia and the Tuamotus in the *Moller* in April 1827: Ivashintsev 1980:85-88, 145.

157 Roggeveen's people had landed and been attacked on Makatea on 1-2 June 1722 (Sharp 1960:97); but its geographical position was erroneously given in *Twee Jaarige Reyze*, as on Carl Behrens's later chart of the area (Burney 1802-17, 4:571-72), so that John Buyers, whose voyage in the trader *Margaret* was recorded by Turnbull (1805), *might* have regarded himself as its first discoverer—if he had seen it. *Margaret* in fact called at Mehetia.

158 Bellingshausen does not substantiate this.

159 The Reverend Henry Nott, who had reached Tahiti in the missionary ship *Duff*.

160 Beaglehole 1955, 1:72.
161 See Kotzebue, 1981:70-71 for preceding remarks on *Predpriiatie*'s passage west from Chile.
162 The 1981 text has 129°40'W.
163 See Sharp:206.
164 Emory (1975:176) uncharacteristically confuses (F)angatau with Fangahina. Huts of "plaited reeds" were dwellings of coconut leaf and/or pandanus thatch; the canoes were evidently *pahi*. See Kotzebue 1821, 1:153 on the 1816 reckoning of Tikei's position, etc.
165 Takapoto ("Spiridov") had indeed been seen by Byron, as well as Roggeveen and others.
166 By Kruzenshtern in his *Atlas Iuzhnago Moria* (1823-26); see n. 45.
167 See n. 61.
168 Actually, it was not "Carlshof" (see Burney 1802-17, 4:566-67 and Sharp:97-98) but Aratika.
169 Kruzenshtern had, in fact, not identified Roggeveen's Bedrieglyke ("Doubtful") Island as Tikei; but the errors in the Dutch accounts made that pardonable.
170 See nn. 2, 4, and 18.
171 *Predpriiatie* thus moved up on the east of Niau.
172 On Napuka, 7 June 1765: Byron 1767:124.
173 On Takaroa, 18 April 1774: Beaglehole 1955, 2:378.
174 Kotzebue thoroughly disapproved of the manner in which Nott and the London Missionary Society were proselytizing in Tahiti in the early 1820s: Kotzebue, 1981:94-95.

CHAPTER THREE: RUSSIAN SCIENCE

1 Survey in Nevskii 1951:215ff.
2 See Bibliography under Friis, Magidovich, and Shokal'skii.
3 Krümmel 1907, 1; Makarov 1894; Prestwich 1874:462-68.
4 Fersman 1926:95-96; Friis 1967:193, etc.
5 Lazarev 1950:27, 87; Kotzebue 1981:317.
6 Kotzebue 1981:318.
7 Further on Preis, see Barratt 1988:99-101.
8 Heidemaa 1981:87-91 and 1975, 2:164-66; also Barratt 1988:378.
9 Kotzebue 1821, 1:11-15, 22-23; Bellinsgauzen 1960:77-80; Barsov 1882, 1:93-95; *Piatidesiatiletie Rumiantsevskogo Muzeia v Moskve* (M. 1912), pp. 163-66.
10 Different food sources, for example, were available: see Emory 1975:24-25 (pandanus development).
11 Friis made a useful start (1967:193ff.), but it has not been pursued in the West even to the point reached by Berg (1962:115-16).
12 See n. 121 to ch. 1 here.
13 Biographical data in Lukina 1975 and W. Lenz 1970:199-200.
14 Kotzebue's Stalinist biographer A. Dobrovol'skii followed the example of L.G. Berg (in Fersman 1926) in suggesting the contrary. D.D. Tumarkin, editor of *Novoe puteshestvie* (Kotzebue 1981), offered a far truer picture (pp. 15-20).
15 *Bolsh. Sov. Entsiklopediia* (M. 1970-78), 7:189; Ivashintsev 1980:101-3.
16 Kotzebue 1821, 1:x.
17 Mahr 1932:12-13; Chamisso 1836, 1:342.
18 Ivashintsev 1980:144; Barratt 1988:100.
19 By engaging the Munich instrument maker Georg von Reichenbach (1772-1826), Kruzenshtern showed himself aware of the most recent advances in combinations of the transit instrument and mural circle.
20 See Barratt 1981:140-41 on the Baltic German element in the Russian enterprise in Polynesia in the early 1800s; also nn. 8 and 13 above on Eschscholtz's work in Dorpat.
21 Hitzig 1842:349; Reyond 1890, ch. 2; Brun 1896:138-41.
22 Text given above: see p. 78.
23 Kotzebue 1821, 2:365-66.
24 Ibid., 2:287; Brun 1896, ch. 12.

25 For comments on the Hawaiian collection now held at BIAN in St. Petersburg, see Barratt 1988:111-15.
26 Reymond 1889, ch. 7.
27 "De Plantis . . . Labiatae," *Linnaea*, 1831, 6:78-82.
28 Kotzebue 1821, 3:221.
29 Chamisso 1836, 2:283-84.
30 Ibid., 1:345.
31 See Barratt 1988:223-29.
32 Choris 1826:19.
33 *Gentleman's Magazine* 1847, 2:324-26; *DNB*, 33:421-22; Brun 1896:212ff.
34 Friis 1967:193.
35 Bellinsgauzen 1960:254.
36 Ibid.: 49, 83; Barratt 1988:128-29.
37 Litke 1835, 3; Barratt 1979:10-12.
38 See Kotzebue 1981:342-43 and Lukina 1975, ch. 4.
39 Kotzebue 1830, 2, App.
40 Kotzebue 1821, 1:13; also Houston 1939:78-79.
41 Kotzebue 1821, 3:327 (318 plant types collected in Chile; 393 butterflies).
42 Mikhailov drew and painted a frigate bird ("or sea-eagle") that survives in his portfolio (State Russian Museum) as R-29248, and it is possible that No. 14 in the Mikhailov album in Moscow (State Historical Museum), entitled *Weather-Bird or Stormy Petrel*, was also based on a study dating from July 1820. All but these birds in Mikhailov's 1820 collection of drawings, however, may be associated with far higher latitudes or with Australia. In 1816, Choris was similarly unoccupied by bird studies in the low atolls, preferring to work on recent compositions with human figures.
43 Kotzebue 1821, 1:145.
44 Chamisso 1836, 2:284.
45 Further on these matters, see Barratt 1988:218.
46 Ibid., Plate 29.
47 Bellinsgauzen 1960:250.
48 Ibid.:251. See also n. 42 above.
49 A blue-crowned lory survives at ZIAN with its "Ex-Admiralt" label.
50 Sementovskii 1951:153.
51 Kotzebue 1821, 2:191, 3:352. For the growth of geological collections in St. Petersburg, see *Geologicheskii muzei osnovan v 1716 godu* (L. 1925). The coral specimens are, at the time of writing, most inadequately labelled and poorly displayed.
52 See n. 9 above.
53 Information from Dr. Tat'iana V. Staniukovich. On the ethnographic component of the collection that remained in St. Petersburg until Rumiantsev's death see *Piatidesiatiletie Rumiantsevskago Muzeia v Moskve, 1862-1912: istoricheskii ocherk* (M. 1912), pp. 163-66. There are annotations in "pre-1828" *opisi* at the Peter the Great Museum of Ethnography, St. Petersburg (MAE), e.g., no. 736, indicating that certain Polynesian items brought to Russia before 1828 are still in the hermitage.
54 Kotzebue 1981:74.
55 Mikhailov had painted a similar flying fish at Port Jackson, NSW, in 1820: see Barratt 1981, Plate 17.
56 Bellinsgauzen 1831:77-80.
57 LOAAN, *fond* 1, op. 2 (1827), no. 462.
58 LOAAN, *fond* K-IV, op. 1 ("Zhurnal postuplenii Otdela fondov"), no. 1; Beliaev 1800, 2:228-30 (Polynesian and other articles jumbled together); Naumov 1980:5ff.
59 Komissarov 1975:8-15; Nevskii 1951:57-58.
60 LOAAN, *razr.* 4, vol. 1, No. 800.
61 Barratt 1988:221-23.
62 Komissarov 1977:26-33.
63 A. Shtraukh 1889.

64 See n. 8.
65 I thank Dr. Kalju Leib, assistant director of TsGIAE, for establishing in August 1989 that portions of the Eschscholtz collections from Polynesia are no longer there.
66 TsGIAE, *fond* 1414, op. 3:App.
67 Barratt 1988:361-64; Goncharova 1973:67ff. and 1972:60-64.
68 Barratt 1988:100-6.
69 See Bibliography.
70 Ryden 1963:66ff.
71 Further on this, see Barratt 1979:101-3.
72 Wilkes 1845, 1:334.
73 Emory 1975:7.
74 Sementovskii 1951:153.
75 Survey in Emory 1975:7-8.
76 Kotzebue 1821, 3:222; *Linnaea: ein Journal für die Botanik* (Berlin 1829), 4:181-82, 465-66; Beechey 1831, 1:222.
77 Byron 1767:129.
78 Bellinsgauzen 1960:269.
79 Ibid.:263.
80 Ibid.:257.
81 See Emory 1975, Fig. 3.
82 Ibid.:8.
83 Ibid.:Fig. 15.
84 Bellinsgauzen 1960:259.
85 Emory 1975:199, 203-4.
86 Ibid.:21.
87 Corney 1915:188-89; see also Forster 1777, 2:40.
88 Chamisso and others vainly sought used earth ovens on Tikei and Niau: see Emory 1975:13-16.
89 Bellinsgauzen 1960:275.
90 Davies 1961:269-70; Emory 1975:149.
91 Choris 1826:19 (*des espèces de citernes creusées par la main*).
92 Sementovskii 1951:149.
93 Hawkesworth 1773, 1:103.
94 Emory 1975:72-73.
95 Ibid.:Fig. 54.
96 Bellinsgauzen 1960:256; Sementovskii 1951:241.
97 Bellinsgauzen 1960:260.
98 Barratt 1979:119-21.
99 Beechey 1831, 1:209.
100 See Emory 1975:84 (allusions to capes in chants).
101 Ibid.:4-5.
102 Kruzenshtern 1814, 1:frontispiece.
103 Sementovskii 1951:150.
104 Ivashintsev 1980:139, 145.
105 On this, see Barratt 1989:219-20 and Plate 2.
106 Bellinsgauzen 1960:250.
107 Barratt 1988:136-37.
108 Barratt 1980:77; Fedorov-Davydov 1953:219-21, 324; Petrov 1864-66, 1:327, 460, 467, 485-86.
109 Plate 5. Men paddling a canoe in the uppermost part of another of Mikhailov's 1820 sheets, which he worked up in 1823-24 as *Views of the Coral Islands of Count Arakcheev, the Eastern Tip of the Coral Island of Pallizer III, Matea [Makatea] Island . . .* are shown with their hair similarly bound and tied. The aquarelle is No. 38 in the Mikhailov album at the State Historical Museum in Moscow and is reproduced in Sementovskii 1951, facing p. 154.

110 Mikhailov twice changed his mind about the ordering of his aquarelles in 1822-24. The annotation below the right-hand male head on R-29070, "To No. 43," suggests that the head was a rough of an Austral Islands portrait set (No. 43 in Moscow's album). In fact, as the roughed-in date ("19 July") clearly shows, the two heads were certainly of two men encountered off Kaukura but were wrongly associated with Rapa—probably by the artist himself, working in haste or without concentration on the high seas—because they were on the same sheet of paper as views of the northern coastline of Rapa Island in the Austral Group. It was Mikhailov's custom to note proper names of individuals he had drawn, e.g., Toubi, Volendens, Gulanba Duby, Bourinoan, and other members of Boongaree's Cammeraigal group on the North Shore of Port Jackson in New South Wales (R-29206-12 in St. Petersburg), also met in 1820, in Latin and not Cyrillic characters.

111 By "Palliser III," Bellingshausen and the Russian Naval Ministry always meant Kaukura: see Beaglehole 1955, 2:380 and Forster 1982, 3:495. Pallisers I and II were Apataki and Toau, Palliser IV was Aratua.

112 Compare Plate 8 here with Fig. 75 in Emory 1975.

113 Ibid.:95-96.

114 Lucett 1851, 1:254.

115 Wilkes 1844:339.

116 Emory 1975:97.

117 Davies 1851:15.

118 Emory 1975:97.

119 The Russians depended on the English missionaries at Matavai Bay for information about battles.

120 Emory 1975:119.

121 Forster 1777, 2:42.

122 See Emory 1975:122ff.

123 Beechey 1831, 1:208. In his text, Bellingshausen refers to certain clubs observed on Amanu as "wooden shovels" or "spatulas" (*derzhali dereviannuiu lopatku*); and *lopatka* is applied, in his New Zealand passage, to the Maori *taiaha* staff as well as to shorter and functionally different *mere*. Together with the fact that the Maori did not make particular use of their *taiaha* to break their enemies' skulls, however, the insistence in Russian passages describing the Tuamotuan weapons on these wooden clubs' *shortness*, effectively rules out the paddle-club or oarlike club described by Wilkes at Napuka: Emory 1975:128-29.

124 Emory 1975:131.

125 Harris 1744, 1:55; Corney 1915 (36):112. The length of the sling cords led Novosil'skii to describe the weapons as *arkany*: Sementovskii 1951:241.

126 Bellinsgauzen 1831:256 (wounded officer).

127 Davies 1961:94, 107.

128 Bellinsgauzen 1960:274-75.

129 Davies 1961:269-70.

130 Kotzebue 1981:76.

131 See Emory 1975:3.

132 Davies 1961:172, 207, 247.

133 Details in Bibliography.

134 Bellinsgauzen 1831:255.

135 See Emory 1975, Fig. 145.

136 Haddon and Hornell 1974:51.

137 Markham 1904, 2:336; Forster 1777, 2:42.

138 The crude, three-boom craft lacked all decoration. The forward paddler appears to be standing in the finished effort, whereas in the draft (R-29070) he is seated.

139 Haddon and Hornell 1974:56.

140 I discuss these matters briefly in *Southern and Eastern Polynesia*, pp. 90-91.

141 The bulk of those now in the keeping of the Bernice P. Bishop Museum Library, which reflect *Riurik*'s two stays in the Hawaiian Islands (1816 and 1817), were acquired from Donald Angus of Honolulu. Examples appear in Barratt 1988 (preliminary sketch for a

portrait of Queen Kaahumanu, Hawaiian dwelling, natives in *kihei*). The Choris portfolio has received almost no scholarly attention since 1958, when Jean Charlot produced his little work *Choris and Kamehameha* (Honolulu, Bishop Museum). Yet several of the original drawings bear immediately on Polynesian ethnography and ethnohistory, and those reflecting Kotzebue's visits to Tikei and to the Cook Islands have *never* been collated with other early European and traditional oral records.

142 Haddon and Hornell 1974:56.
143 Emory 1975:180-82
144 Bellinsgauzen 1831:265.
145 Kotzebue 1981:77.
146 Bellinsgauzen 1960:261.
147 Haddon and Hornell 1938:50.
148 Hawkesworth 1773, 1:100 and 2:77; also Lesson 1839, 1:232 (Tuamotuan sails seen at Papaoa, Tahiti, in 1823).
149 Duperrey 1827, Fig. 47; Paris 1843, Plate 1; Emory 1975:183-84.
150 Wharton 1893:98.
151 Bellingshausen 1962:115; Moerenhout 1837, 1:159; Ellis 1829, 1:181.
152 Turnbull 1813:263; Emory 1975:175-76; Haddon and Hornell 1974:79-80. Bellingshausen had with him no botanist of Chamisso's excellence, as he himself recognized and deplored (Bellinsgauzen 1960:267), and so the *Dvukratnye izyskaniia* lack those botanical data provided by Chamisso for the accounts of *Riurik*'s passage of 1816 and visit to Tikei. These data, taken together with Choris's illustration of the Russians' awkward landing on the reef-flat of Tikei, indicate that *tou* (*Cordia subcordata*), the Tuamotuans' preferred wood for canoe building, was lacking on that atoll or was far from abundant. And it is significant that Chamisso himself should mention having seen on Tikei both *Tournefortia* (or *Messerchmidia*) *argentea* and *Guettarda*. These timbers, locally known as *tohunu* and *kahaia* (Emory 1975:140), were precisely the ones sought when the larger and more durable *tou* was unavailable (see Kotzebue 1821, 3:222). The wording of Choris's 1826 description of the old and deteriorated canoe found on Tikei, however (*mauvaise pirogue creusée dans un tronc d'arbre*), clearly suggests that it was a dugout, not a composite-hull craft.
153 Bellinsgauzen 1960:88. The tour of London instrument makers' workshops is also described by Novosil'skii in *Iuzhnyi polius*, p. 5. TsGAVMF, *fond* 166, op. 1, *delo* 660, pt. 1:492 on *Vostok*'s library.
154 Kotzebue 1981:74.
155 See Lebedev and Esakov 1971:328; Svet 1966:214-17 and map on p. 174 ("Routes of Navigators of the Eighteenth Century in the Tuamotu Archipelago").
156 Beaglehole 1955, 2:379-80.
157 See Lebedev and Esakov 1971:328 and Sharp 1960:74, 193.
158 Svet 1966:226.
159 Ibid., map on p. 227.
160 Lebedev and Esakov 1971:328; Svet, 1966:215-17, 226-28.
161 TsGIAE, *fond* 1414, op. 3, Nos. 31-33 (letters in German and French to and from Duperrey, Sir John Barrow, et al.). See also Nevskii 1951:250ff. and Veselago 1869, chs. 3-4, on Kruzenshtern's hydrographic studies.
162 Kotzebue 1821, 2:296. Further on Byron's "King George Islands," on "Oura," and "Tiookea" see Sharp 1960:102.
163 See Sharp 1960:97-98, 131.
164 Ibid.:193.
165 Kotzebue 1821, 2:303.
166 Notably, in the *Ob'iasneniia* (1826-27) and in the *Dopolnenie k izdannym v 1826 i 1827 godakh ob'iasneniiam, posluzhivshikh dlia sostavleniia Atlasa Iuzhnago moria* (St. P. 1836).
167 Sharp 1960:5-6, 196.
168 Turnbull 1805:1; Svet 1966:227.
169 See Corney 1913 on the track of the *Aguila* (Captain Domingo de Boenechea) in 1774 and the Spanish sighting of Tahanea.

170 Shokal'skii 1928:195-97; Lebedev 1963:166ff.; Svet 1966:226-28.
171 *Riurik* reached Petropavlovsk-in-Kamchatka on 19 June 1816 and her despatches went overland to St. Petersburg via Irkutsk. Officially, news of Kotzebue's activities in Oceania arrived only in October; in reality, reports certainly arrived in the capital by August 1816. Holographs went to Count Rumiantsev, not to the Naval Ministry, and for that reason they were never filed with the in-letters that are in TsGAVMF today.
172 *Niles' Weekly Register*, 17 May 1817, p. 11; *Boston Patriot*, 17 May, p. 17. See also Findlay 1884:621, 624.
173 Findlay 1884:960.
174 Ibid.:961; Ivashintsev 1980:26; Berg 1962:115.
175 *New England Palladium and Commercial Advertiser* (Boston), 1 Aug. 1817, p. 2. Variants appeared in the *Independent Chronicle* for 4 August (also in Boston) and in the *Salem Gazette* for 4 Nov. 1817, among other New England newspapers with strong maritime interests.
176 See Wilkes 1845, 4:265 and Belcher 1843:122ff. To these and other navigators, such a name as Golenishchev-Kutuzov-Smolenskii Island (for Makemo atoll) was tolerable only as Kutusoff.
177 See *Lippincott's Gazetteer of the World* (New York 1961), p. 1549.

CHAPTER FOUR: AN OVERVIEW

1 A.S. Wood 1957:190-208; Lovett 1899, 1:1-28; Stock, 1:58-64.
2 Haweis 1795:12-13.
3 Davies 1961:xxviii.
4 Griffin n.d.:121-36.
5 LMS Archives, Home Odds 1:1764-1829, Circulars: 21 Apr. 1796.
6 Ibid., Boards Minutes, 28 Sept. 1796.
7 Moorehead 1966:80.
8 Lovett 1899, 1:126-27; Wilson 1799, 1:155ff.; also, for an entertaining popular account, Langdon 1959:83-87.
9 Lovett 1899, 1:127-45; Ellis 1844:101-14; Davies 1961:xxx-xxxi.
10 Moorehead 1966:81.
11 Lisianskii 1814:88ff.; Shemelin 1816, 1:106-8; Barratt 1981:120-21; Dening 1974.
12 See Barratt 1987:30ff.
13 These matters are dealt with in Barratt 1979 and 1987.
14 See Barratt 1989, pt. 1.
15 Montgomery 1832:xiv-xvii.
16 Davies 1961:xxxi-xxxii.
17 Moorehead 1966:81-85.
18 Bellinsgauzen 1960:277.
19 Ibid.:282.
20 Lovett 1899, 1:172ff.
21 O'Reilly and Teissier 1962:336-37.
22 Nott had left Matavai Bay in December 1808, after the fall of Pomare II and the outbreak of violent opposition there: see Oliver 1974, 3:1314-32 and O'Reilly and Teissier 1962:336. Mo'orea had remained his base until 1816, and his return to Tahiti via Huahine had followed Pomare II's definitive victory over all rivals at the Battle of Fei Pi (Nov. 1815).
23 Bellinsgauzen 1960:287.
24 Moorehead 1966:82. Details of the military campaign and Battle of Fei Pi in Oliver 1974, 3:1342-49. The "cathedral" was at Papaoa and was used as a public meeting hall: see Davies 1961:244-45.
25 The original is at the State Russian Museum, St. Petersburg: Mikhailov Portfolio, R-29286, and the finished aquarelle of 1822-24, lithographed by I.P. Fridrits for Bellingshausen's *Atlas* (1831), is at the Russian Historical Museum in Moscow.

26 Moorehead 1966:83.
27 Moerenhout 1942, 2:504ff; Davies 1961:254-55.
28 Bellinsgauzen 1960:294-95.
29 Williamson 1924, 1; de Bovis 1863:217-301.
30 See Barratt 1988:169-95 for Russian texts reflecting approval of monarchical principles.
31 Bellinsgauzen 1960:287.
32 Davies 1961:233-34 and n. 1; also 222-28 on sugar cane, distilling of spirits, accusations of their sales by and for the missionaries, etc.; Moorehead 1966:88-90 on New England liquor and on drunkenness.
33 Herman Melville, *Omoo* (New York 1844), p. 358.
34 See n. 30.
35 Sementovskii 1951:255.
36 GPB, St. Petersburg: *Otdel rukopisei, fond* 1000, op. 2, No. 302: "Dnevnik puteshestviia na korable *Nikolae*, 1837-39 gg." (A diary of Baron Alfred Geiking, supercargo on that ship, with notes on Mo'orea.)
37 Bellinsgauzen 1960:283-85.
38 See Watson 1986:57-71.
39 Samarov 1952, 1:83; Ivashintsev 1980:57-58 (sickness in *Borodino*, 1820).
40 *Publications of the Hudson Bay Company: McLoughlin's Fort Vancouver Letters, First Series, 1825-1838* (London 1941), pp. xx-cx; also Barratt 1983, chs. 1-2 (British reluctance to guard those economic and strategic interests despite clamour from the city and the spectre of Russo-American entente.)
41 Barratt 1981:216-18.
42 Okun' 1951:224-26; Huculak 1971; Barratt 1981:218-19.
43 *The Alaska Boundary Tribunal: Appendix to the Case of Great Britain* (London 1903), pp. 6-8.
44 Ibid.: 7; Hudson's Bay Company Archives (Ottawa), A/6/20:27 Feb. 1822 (Company determination to "keep the Russians at a good distance" by pressing far NW of the Fraser River valley).
45 AVPR, *fond kantseliarii Ministerstva Vneshikh Del*, 1822, *delo* 3645, fols. 30-32.
46 Okun' 1951:224-26 and Mazour 1944:168-73.
47 AVPR, *fond kantseliarii Ministerstva Vneshnikh Del*, 1822, *delo* 3645, fol. 33.
48 TsGAVMF, *fond* 166, *delo* 666; Lazarev 1832:4-16; Ivashintsev 1980:70, 140, 143.
49 Ex-midshipman Zavalishin's dyspeptic account of this voyage, which was written in middle age on the basis of original notes and with characteristic bravura and paranoia, was ultimately published in the journal *Drevniaia i novaia Rossiia* (1877 (5):54-67; (6):115-25; (7):199-214; (10):143-58) under the title "Krugosvetnoe plavanie fregata 'Kreiser' v 1822-25 godakh, pod komandoiu Mikhaila Petrovicha Lazareva." Zavalishin is omitted from this work as an unreliable informant.
50 TsGAVMF, *fond* 212, *delo* 4093, fols. 119-20; *Historical Records of Australia: Series 3* (Sydney 1921), 4:73 (Sorell to Bathurst); *Bent's Almanac for 1823* (Hobart Town 1824: "Arrival of Vessels at Hobart Town and Their Departure," 30 May).
51 TsGAVMF, *fond* 212, *delo* 4093, fols. 126-27 (M.P. Lazarev to A.V. Moller, 23 July 1823); also Zavalishin 1904:295-96. I cover this visit in more detail in a short paper in *SEER*, 53 (1975: no. 133):566-78.
52 Ivashintsev 1980:71. Emendations by translator on the basis of the 1849 St. Petersburg original.
53 For a summary of the Tyerman-Bennet tour of inspection of 1821-29 see Montgomery 1832:x-xi and Davies 1961:232-33.
54 Montgomery 1832:188, 216-17; Davies 1961:228-31, 341.
55 Lazarev 1832:82-84; Ivashintsev 1980:71.
56 Lazarev 1832:86-87.
57 Ibid.:91.
58 Bellinsgauzen 1960:66.
59 Lazarev 1832:91.

60 Summary in Ivashintsev 1980:71.
61 See Barratt 1988:177-79 on Ogievskii's report and tour of Tasmania, and the same writer's *Russian View of Honolulu, 1809-1826*, pp. 182-83 on other Russian surgeons in Polynesia.
62 "Ofitsial'nyi otdel," pp. 456-66.
63 Lazarev 1832:98-99. Further on him, see Lazarev 1950:29ff.
64 Kotzebue 1981:90.
65 Ibid.:91; Montgomery 1832:215.
66 Kotzebue 1830, 1:168-69.
67 Ibid., 1:150-51.
68 Ibid., 1:153-54.
69 Ibid., 1:158.
70 Ibid., 1:163; also Davies 1961:234, n. 2 and Adams 1968:177.
71 Kotzebue 1830, 1:164; Davies 1961:265-76 (Code of Laws).
72 Kotzebue 1830, 1:166-67.
73 Ibid., 1:168-69, 173.
74 See Bibliography for details.
75 Sidney Hall, the London engraver, was hired by Henry Colburn, co-publisher of the 1830 edition of *New Voyage*, to produce "A Plan of Mattaway Bay and Village" on the basis of the St. Petersburg edition. It appeared facing page 201 in the London edition, uncoloured.
76 Kotzebue 1830, 1:192-93.
77 Ibid., 1:206-14; also Kotzebue 1981:318.
78 Geologicheskii Muzei Akademii Nauk. Gofman's major work resulting from his voyage with Kotzebue was *Geognostische Beobachtungen auf einer Reise um die Welt* (Berlin 1829).
79 *DNB*, 13:764-67.
80 See Holland and Everett 1854-56, Vol. 2.
81 Details in Barratt 1988:301-2.
82 Barratt 1981:13-14.
83 Montgomery 1832:xiv-xvii.
84 Kotzebue 1830, 1:169.
85 Davies 1961:59, 65; Adams 1968:88-90.
86 Kotzebue 1981:99.
87 Ibid.:106. See Barratt 1988:253-54 on Kotzebue's attitude toward the New England mission at Honolulu, led in 1824 by the Reverend Hiram Bingham, and on the difference between Kotzebue's hostile views and those shown in 1821 by Captain M.N. Vasil'ev of *Otkrytie*.
88 Kotzebue 1981:183.
89 Davies 1961:334-35.
90 Moorehead 1966:88.
91 Ibid.:89.
92 Wheeler 1839:757.
93 *Zapiski Gidrograficheskago Departamenta Morskago Ministerstva*, pt. 11 (St. P. 1843), pp. 10ff.
94 See Barratt 1988:253-54; also Ivashintsev 1980:85-91.
95 Barratt 1988:136-37.
96 Suris 1962 (7):67-68.
97 TsGAVMF, *fond* 283 (1829), op. 1, no. 948; also TsGIA, *fond* 733, op. 12 (1826), no. 308, fol. 6.
98 The original finished aquarelles remain in the State Historical Museum in Moscow, in the Mikhailov Album, as Nos. 35 (*Pomari, korol' O-Taiti*), 36 (*Zavtrak korolia O-Taitskago*), and 37 (*Vid ostrova O-Taitskago s Mysa Venusa*).
99 TsGAVMF, *fond* 238 (1829), op. 1.
100 Ivashintsev 1980:103. On Hagemeister see W. Lenz 1970:284-85 and *ZUKMS* 1835, 2:355-57.
101 Ivashintsev 1980:106; also, on *Krotkii*, *Severnyi arkhiv* 1828, pt. 36:49ff., and, on the situation in California, Bancroft 1886, p. 3, ch. 5.

102 See Barratt 1989:133-34; on Hanstein, or Hansteen (1784-1861), with whom Kruzenshtern corresponded regularly in the 1820s, see Larousse, *Grand Dictionnaire Universel du XIX siècle*, 9:65.
103 Ivashintsev 1980:108.
104 "Zapiski michmana Evgeniia Andreevicha Berensa, vedennye . . . v 1828-1830 godakh," *MSb* 1903, 1 (Jan):33-74; 5 (May):47-74.
105 Ibid., (5):71.
106 Ibid., (5):70. The comparisons were with fruit of the Cape Verde Islands and Teneriffe, where *Krotkii* had called in Nov. 1828.
107 Zavoiko 1840:57-58 on the ship and crew, 117-25 on Mo'orea; also Ivashintsev 1980:113, 147.
108 See Gibson 1976:75-85.
109 For a survey of the origins of the Russians' Pacific enterprise and the beginnings of Russian circumnavigation see Barratt 1981, chs. 5-8.
110 Ivashintsev 1980:115. *Amerika* entered the maritime extension of Mo'orea's central, northward running Opunohu Valley, anchoring a mile or so SE of the old mission station at Papetoai. The "king" in question was most probably Queen Pomare's cousin, Tenani'a (Ari'ifa'aite), whom she had married in 1834.
111 Davies 1961:239-40; also O'Reilly and Teissier 1962:208-9 and Ivashintsev 1980:119.
112 Davies 1961:223.
113 Zavoiko's account is usefully complemented by Herman Melville's *Omoo* (chs. 54-58), based on a visit to the Opunohu Valley and Afareaitu (Griffin Town) mission station in 1842, three years after the Russian. Melville also hunted wild boar and bulls in the hills around Mount Rotui and Mount Tohivea. See Zavoiko 1840:120.

CHAPTER FIVE: THE RUSSIAN TEXTS

1 Taiarapu Peninsula.
2 Ututuroa Point. *Vostok* was coasting in toward Te Aharoa and moved WNW from the locality of Tiarei or Roby Town, so that fires were visible ashore from that mission station west to Fa'aripo.
3 The Russians were off the coast of Papeno'o and looking south toward its valley; the "great mountains" visible included Toopuu, Aorai, and Orohena (at 2,241 feet).
4 Bellingshausen was familiar with *A Missionary Voyage to the Southern Pacific Ocean . . . in the Ship Duff, Commanded by Captain James Wilson* (London 1799).
5 Beaglehole 1955:73-76 and notes.
6 The Russians' anchorage lay between those of HMS *Dolphin* and HMS *Endeavour*, being a little further NE from Mount Tahara (Robertson's Skirmish Hill and Cook's One Tree Hill) than Wallis had selected in June 1767. Following Cook, as usual, Bellingshausen preferred to keep some distance between him and Dolphin Bank, and so anchored in the centre of Wallis's "Port Royal" and conveniently parallel with the British visitors' watering place (Vaipopoo River).
7 Bellingshausen here followed the precedent set by Kruzenshtern at Taio-hae Bay, Nukuhiva, in 1804: see Barratt 1981:5-7 and 1989:187-91.
8 A number of New England seamen entered the temporary service of the Russian-American Company at Sitka (Novo-Arkhangel'sk), having reached it aboard fur-trading vessels.
9 Centre of Russian activities during the Kruzenshtern-Lisianskii visit of 1804: see Kruzenshtern 1809, 1:142-224; Lisianskii 1812, chs 5-6; Shemelin 1816, 1:106-20; Rezanov 1825, 24:73-96. More recently, the centre of Captain Porter's activities at the time of the USS *Essex* visit.
10 I.e., *Piper methysticum*, or *'ava*, of which there were tidy gardens near Matavai Bay in early contact times: see Wilson 1799:193; Cook, *Voyage*, 1784:145; Forster 1777, 1:406.
11 Not the Malay apple (*Eugenia malaccensis*, *'ahi'a*), which fruited only in summer and was unavailable for the Russians, but the so-called "custard apple" (*Morinda citrifolia*, *mono*). The Russians saw its leaves used to wrap fish for baking: see Oliver 1974, 1:247, 366-67.

12 Bellingshausen knew of Henry Nott's enforced exile, as it were, on Mo'orea (1808-15): see O'Reilly and Teissier 1962:336.

13 Russian tilt-cart or covered cart. The "awning" was a matwork canopy of the kind commonly built on Tahitian *pahi* or composite-plank keeled double canoes.

14 This suggests the general unreliability of Russian recording of Tahitian proper names, difficulties of Cyrillic and transliteration apart: Bellingshausen seems here to combine an echo of Terito (Teremo'emo'e) with the name of her elder sister Teri'itar'a Vahine. As the 1820 Russian texts make plain, nobody at Matavai Bay chose (or managed) to explain to the visitors the true relationship of the two royal sisters to King Pomare II. Pomare had been intending to marry Teri'itar'a, first daughter of Tamatoa IV of Ra'iatea (1808-9), but had preferred and married instead the younger daughter, Terito-o-tera'i, who had reached Tahiti first: see Davies 1961:126, 137n, 153; and Oliver 1974, 3:1336-37.

15 P. 175. Aimata, born on 28 Feb. 1813, was seven when Bellingshausen took her for ten. The eyeshade that caught the Russians' attention was a plaited coconut-leaf protector (see Oliver 1974, 1:154). While Terito and Teri'itar'a evidently wore European dresses, their courtiers wore *pareu* with classic red *tou*-leaf (*Cordia subcordata*) and *mati* berry patterning (Oliver 1974, 1:146-47 and notes).

16 *Ho'e* (in Russian, *malymi veslami*). Bellingshausen here notes, quite inaccurately, that "paddles are the same on all the islands of the Great [Pacific] Ocean."

17 The original of the portrait of Pomare II is at the State Historical Museum in Moscow, P.N. Mikhailov Album, No. 35, and it does not show Terito, though a finished study is to be seen in the original Mikhailov Portfolio at the State Russian Museum.

18 Hitoti (Vaiturai), chief of Tiarei, had supported Pomare II and the mission since 1808 and, like his brother Paofai (Upaparu), was to play a large part in the events leading to French occupation. The "keeper of the general store of coconut-oil" in 1820 was Tati of Papara (1774?-1854), whom Pomare II would willingly have seen as his successor in 1821 but whom Nott and Wilson opposed.

19 On the silver medals struck in St. Petersburg for distribution in Oceania, and on other gifts and trade goods, see Bellinsgauzen 1831:65-67; on Pomare II and the love of grog, see Newbury 1967:226-33. The "ground coconut kernels" were balls of shredded coconut meat—a serrated blade, or *'ana*, was used—placed in plant fibres and leaves. The "mountain bananas" (Russian, *bananov gornykh*) were probably *meia* rather than the wild-growing *fe'i* from the high country; but see Beaglehole 1955, 1:81 n. 3 and Oliver 1974, 1:252.

20 I.e., false fires (in Russian, *fal'shfeiera*): Bellinsgauzen 1960:285. Both they and, especially, star rockets had been used to great effect among the Tuamotus, as seen.

21 See n. 19.

22 Specimens of tapa remain in the Peter the Great Museum of Ethnography, St. Petersburg (Collection No. 737, etc.), but they appear to predate the 1820 visit to Matavai Bay. Internal textual evidence also indicates that much Tahitian tapa never made it into the Admiralty Department Museum or the *Kunstkammer*. Like preserved Maori heads, pieces of Polynesian tapa were highly prized in Russia and elsewhere as souvenirs: see Barratt 1979:105, 179.

23 HMS *Endeavour* had not managed to stock lemons at Matavai Bay in 1769; and the Russians were also more fortunate than they recognized in acquiring large quantities of breadfruit in July, the main crop of Tahiti being in March-April: see Beaglehole 1955, 1:114, n. 2. Bellingshausen made successful use in Antarctica of his lemon juice and pickled lemons, which were issued to *Vostok*'s 119-strong company by Surgeon Iakov Berkh.

24 The former Miss Annie Turner was one of four "godly young women" sent out from England by the directors of the LMS in 1809, with missionaries in view: Davies 1961:159, and O'Reilly and Teissier 1962:336. Nott worked untiringly on his pioneering translations of the Gospels during the 1820s and '30s, saw his and John Davies's work crowned in 1838 with the publication of the Bible in Tahitian (*Te Bibilia Moa Ra iritihia ei parau Tahiti*), and died at Papara, Tahiti, on 2 May 1844. His wife survived him.

25 Bellingshausen had landed slightly north of the watering place, on the spot where the Vaipopoo River bent north to run parallel with the shoreline. Wilson's and Nott's houses

stood here, a mile and a quarter northeast of Mount Tahara; and from them, the Russians walked a mile or so north along the shoreline to Point Venus. Mikhailov and Simonov had landed there independently some time before 8:00 am, and the artist had begun work on the panorama that appeared in Bellingshausen's *Atlas* as No. 37 (*A View of the Island of O-Taiti From Point Venus*). Mikhailov evidently did not find much "worthy of his brush," as he strolled south with his commanding officer: his surviving portfolio gives little evidence of "worthy objects." Later he returned to Point Venus and continued his work there. Mount Tahara and the hills beside and beyond it along the Ururoa Valley are clearly visible in the middle distance of the finished aquarelle (see Plate 12).

26 Obviously the Vaipopoo River, which Bellingshausen now crossed from south to north near Point Venus—by 1820 it debouched into Matavai Bay considerably nearer the point than in Cook's time—in order to reach the royal residence compound (also well drawn by Mikhailov: Plate 11).

27 The main dwelling or "sleep house" (*fare ta'oto*) was evidently a very sizable, walled-in structure with two doors or more and was capacious enough to accommodate many visitors, as *fare manihini*. Pomare's own house, through which Bellingshausen was to be taken after the meal (on the extreme right in Mikhailov's illustration), measured 14 by 28 feet, an average-sized dwelling: see Oliver 1974, 1:162ff. *Fara* is pandanus.

28 Bellingshausen had served on the Black Sea station in 1811-19, so he knew its native peoples well.

29 See Oliver 1974, 1, fig. 9-2c (coconut-splitter) and p. 245 ('*ana*, the shredding tool in use for Bellingshausen's benefit, as fresh coconut was to be served with pre-cooked breadfruit, to judge by p. 289 of *Dvukratnye izyskaniia* and Mikhailov's record). The redwood box was for the storage of books, and Pomare II kept in it his copy of John Davies's elementary arithmetic, printed on Huahine in 1819: *Aritemeti: Oia Te Haapao o te Taio*. . . . Bellingshausen suggests that the king also had an English primer in geometry.

30 This church had been built close to the site of Pomare's former personal *marae*. Surgeon Ogievskii of *Ladoga* visited and described it in 1823 ("splendid yet simple"), and it remained in use as a meeting-house when Kotzebue arrived. By "Reformed church" Bellingshausen meant Lutheran.

31 This was prescient: Paofai a Manua, high chief of Tiarei, became a powerful patron of the missionaries and played a major role in events leading up to the French occupation: Davies 1961:335, 349; O'Reilly and Teissier 1962:351-52.

32 Bellinsgauzen 1960:273-75.

33 On this incident, see above, pp. 114-15.

34 This valuable service was repeated for the Russians in 1823 and, again, no payment was demanded. By 1825, writes Kotzebue, the hunger for money had grown considerably at Matavai Bay.

35 This remark reflects the author's recent experience in New Zealand rather than the fact of the matter.

36 The *marae* (temple) in question had stood on Point Utuhaihai (Robertson's or Marae Point) and had actually been more than three miles distant from Venus Point by land. *Vostok*'s launch moved to the west of Mount Tahara and Vaiamo Bay into Bounty's Channel, so that the entrance into Pare Harbour would have been visible; but the Russian party landed a little eastward of point Utuhaihai. The "royal church," also described by Surgeon Ogievskii (see above, pp. 327-8), was rather further west and inland at Papaoa. Bellingshausen had thus walked through the missionaries' "Hankey Town"; the "Royal Mission Chapel of Papoar" or "Cathedral of Papoar" caught the eye of numerous foreign tourists in the earlier 19th century, such as Herman Melville in 1842: see his *Omoo*.

37 He had not. Cook's only detailed description of a Tahitian *marae* was of the enormous and magnificent Mahaiatea, built in 1766-68: see early accounts, collected by Emory 1933:30, 72-74, etc.). Mahaiatea was perfectly intact in 1820 and, indeed, remained so until 1865: see Beaglehole 1955, 1:112, n. 2; 532-34.

38 The *marae* on Point Utuhaihai had, indeed, been destroyed on the instructions of Pomare II in 1815: Davies 1961:193-94.

39 This aged man was Manaonao, a chiefly adherent to Pomare Vahine, who had embraced

Christianity enthusiastically in July 1815 and had subsequently been of much use to Nott—who obviously exaggerated his influence and rank for Bellingshausen's benefit—and to Aimata, the future queen: see Davies 1961:188.

40 The "large shed" (*fare va'a*) was one of several around Matavai Bay in 1820, to judge by Russian evidence. Mikhailov depicts the lower edge of one at Venus Point. See Oliver 1974, 1:173-74 and 196-99 on hardwoods used in canoe building. On contributions of coconut oil and arrowroot to the LMS see Davies 1961:306, 332, 348-49. The vessel expected back from Sydney was the mission ship *Haweis*, a brig built locally in 1818: see Ellis 1829, 1:417-20.

41 *Mati* berries (*Ficus tinctoria*) and *tou* leaf (*Cordia subcordata*). Bark cloth was decorated after sun bleaching. Repairs involved careful resoaking: see Ellis 1829, 2:174ff. and Morrison 1935:160-61.

42 See Beaglehole 1955, 1:82ff.

43 This was *Queen Charlotte*, purchased by the king in 1820 but actually built in 1813 or earlier: see Davies 1961:331-32.

44 Bellinsgauzen 1831:66.

45 Ibid.:295.

46 Among the artefacts presently held in Collection No. 736 of MAE that evidently left Matavai Bay with Bellingshausen are a sun-shade (736-164), two wooden adzes (736-164-165), and a fine, flexible mat (736-248). Missing from that and from other pre-1828 St. Petersburg collections, however, are "spears and other weapons, shells, and hooks made of shell," also mentioned by Bellingshausen as having been stowed before his departure.

47 This shocked a number of Russian officers. However, the 1820 visitors or, less probably, visitors of 1823-24 did manage to acquire at least one large vertical drum (*pahu nui*: MAE 736-231) of a type seen in use by Cook, and one gong (*pahu-rutu-roa*: MAE 736-232).

48 Duperrey's people had a similar experience four years later; nor were the (increasingly sophisticated) Tahitians impressed by whistles, rattles, and flutes of Russian make.

49 By contrast, Kamehameha I of Hawaii encouraged his people to gain sea experience in New England with British merchantmen: see Barratt 1988:94-96.

50 Sharp 1960:58f.; also Corney 1913, 1, intro.

51 Oliver 1974, 1:234-45 (breadfruit & coconut) and 366-67 (use of the custard-apple or *nono* blossom by lovers and lovesick women).

52 *Aito* (*Casuarina*) was indeed extensively used in tool-making, and Bellingshausen left Matavai Bay with examples; *parau* (*Hibiscus tiliaceus*) was easily worked and used for canoe hulls as well as rafters and joists. Bellingshausen's *tao* tree was, of course, *tou*, while the trees "suitable for the gathering of cotton" were *Gossypium purpurascens* or *vavai*, still plentiful in the mesotropical zone of Tahiti in 1820 but now gone. The tree whose fruit suggested "a small pumpkin" was probably Tahitian mango (*Spondias dulcis*).

53 In Russian, *kolgan*. Aromatic ginger (genus *Alpinia*).

54 In Russian, *morskie chervi*, "marine worms." This suggests *teredo navalis*, the shipworm that troubled Russian and all other navigators in the tropics, which of course plays no role whatever in coral formation. Bellingshausen was building on Chamisso's work on the theory of coral growth but was still grasping for his basic biological terms.

55 Hook-and-line fishing and spearing: Ellis 1829, 2:297ff.; Moerenhout 1837, 2:104-5.

56 For a discussion of this matter, see Beaglehole 1955, 1:clxxiv-clxxvii.

57 See n. 50. By Buenevo, Bellingshausen doubtless meant Boenechea, who actually estimated Tahiti's total population as "about ten thousand at the lowest computation."

58 Wilson 1799:181-215; see also Forster 1777, 1:365 and 2:65-66; Forster 1778:214-21; and Morrison 1935:171.

59 Sound observations: see Beaglehole 1955, 1:clxxv.

60 Further on early population estimates, probable realities, and decline see Davies 1961:xxxix, 58. See Oliver 1974, 3:1339-49 for an excellent survey of the "conversion" of Pomare II (July 1812), the struggle between adherents of Jehovah and 'Oro, and the Battle of Fei Pi. Nott's account is naturally echoed in Davies 1961:191ff. and may usefully be compared with that of Moerenhout (1837, 2:464-68).

61 Bellingshausen's version of the institution of a Code of Laws in Tahiti and of its drafting by Nott himself (Davies 1961:220, 365-76) similarly betrays its source. *Vostok* carried Aaron Arrowsmith's map of the Pacific Ocean; and Nott was very aware of Pomare's extension of authority over "High Island" (Raivavae), if only because it had occurred a mere nine months before (Oct. 1819) despite Bellingshausen's mention of 1818.

62 *Arab* (Captain Lewis). See Davies 1961:273-74.

63 All this derives immediately from Nott and the mission. The five "parts" were, under their Cyrillic disguise, Te Porionu'u, Te Fana, Te Oropa'a, Teva-i-ta'i, and Teva-i-uta and had been named by Captain Wilson in his *Missionary Voyage* (pp. 186-215), with which Bellingshausen was familiar. But of course the Russian list serves only to reflect its author's ignorance of the complex and fluid realities of Tahitian administrative and chiefly controls. See Davies 1961:xxxix-xxv on the missionaries' relative ignorance and confused nomenclature.

64 Davies 1961:228-31 (*ti*-roots and spirits, etc.); Moorehead 1966:83-85 (Russian evidence of an almost total transformation of society); Beaglehole 1962, 1:335-36 and Oliver 1974, 1:159-60 (geometrical tattoo marks, stars and circles, etc.).

65 A correct deduction.

66 Some were printed in Bellingshausen's *Atlas* (1831), but most were submitted to the Hydrographic Department of the Naval Ministry and simply stored. See Barratt 1988:120-27 on Russian naval cartography and hydrography in Polynesia, equipment, and reckoning techniques; see also 1-8 and 182-202 on hydrography in the Tuamotus.

67 See n. 46 above and ch. 6.

68 See Oliver 1974, 1:162ff. (building types) and Ellis 1829, 2:181-84 (furniture). The "little low stools" painted by the expeditional artist Mikhailov were *papahia*, also used for the pounding of breadfruit and plantains. Yellow and red had for centuries been the colours associated by Polynesians with royal or high chiefly rank and so were preferred colours even in bedcovers.

69 In Russian, *obednia*, Mass. Novosil'skii thought in terms of Orthodox liturgy, as Bellingshausen and Kotzebue thought in German Lutheran terms.

70 A correct prediction: Pomare II died on 7 Dec. 1821 and death was certainly hastened by intemperate drinking: but see Davies 1961:233, n. 1.

71 The dramatis personae here are Amo, Purea, and Temari'i, Amo's son by a niece of Purea: see Oliver, 3:1202, 1219; Adams 1968:96-105, 118-29, etc.

72 The reference is to the Papara Debacle and the emergence of the Pomares: see Beaglehole 1962, 1:304-5 and Oliver 1974, 3:1217ff.

73 Details in Davies 1961:44-45. The sacrifices took place in the Utu'aimahurau *marae*, Atehuru: see Oliver 1974, 3:1307-8.

74 Tante is an obvious typographical slip: Pomare II's military adversary at the close of 1808 was Taute, chief of Faena (see Davies 1961:118-21 and Oliver 1974, 3:1322-23). *Venus*, a 20-ton schooner owned by John MacArthur of New South Wales, was actually taken on Mo'orea in September 1809: see Davies 1961:135.

75 Again, this is the official missionary version of events, as also given—in far more detail and colour—in Davies 1961:190-92 and in Ellis 1829, 1:250ff. Moerenhout, in his *Voyages aux Iles*, presents the story from the vantage point of Papara (2:464-68) and so renders a major service to Tahitian studies.

76 Davies 1961:193-94 (destruction of the 'Oro idol kept in Tautira, etc.); 204-8 (Ellis and the printing press on Mo'orea in 1817). On the basis of his 1819-21 naval journal Novosil'skii wrote in 1854-55.

77 Sementovskii 1951:156.

78 See Barratt 1979:35-36, 72-78.

79 Simonov was acquainted with Cook's accounts of Tahiti in Russian translation, on which see Barratt 1988:20-24. This misquote from the first (?) *Voyage* derives from *Sobranie liubopytnykh...puteshestvii* (St. P. 1795-98), which was a version of J.H. Campe's *Sammlung interessanter Reisebeschreibung für die Jugend* (1786-90, 8v.): it offered variants of the first 13 chapters of the Cook-Hawkesworth account of *Endeavour*'s voyage.

80 On Kiselev see Barratt 1979:24. These are the sole references in the 1820 Russian texts to

Pomare's receiving "bags of white sugar" from *Vostok*'s storeroom and to an abundance of wild goats on Tahiti. These must have been lately introduced stock that had multiplied around Matavai Bay.

81 *ZADMM*, 6:460ff. M.P. Lazarev was anxious to reach Novo-Arkhangel'sk (Sitka) by late summer and did so by 3 September 1823 despite the Tahitian interlude: see Ivashintsev 1980:71.

82 Mount Orohena, or Orohena, 7,321 feet. Lazarev here echoes Cook: Beaglehole 1955, 1:119.

83 Dolphin Bank. *Ladoga* was working up towards *Kreiser*, which, as Lazarev noted, stood "behind a grove of coconut palms," that is, immediately SW of Venus Point.

84 In Tahitian, *maitai*! (good!).

85 The queen in question was Terito (Terem'emo'e), Pomare II's widow, not Pomare Vahine, then regent. Papaoa was her residence in Arue, and she preferred it to Matavai Bay, whose royal residence reminded her painfully of her late husband, as Russian visitors in 1824 discovered: see Kotzebue 1830, 1:182 and Adams 1968:175.

86 Duperrey 1827, 1:202ff.

87 This was presumably Uata, head of the Pomare family and feeding-father of the little Pomare III (see Adams 1968:176-77); but he certainly did not rule absolutely. Pomare II's candidate as successor to the throne, Tati of Papara, was a power in the land in 1823 (Moerenhout 1837, 2:486 and O'Reilly and Teissier 1962:444). Despite the marriage of Aimata in Dec. 1822 to Tapoa of Taha'a, whom Kotzebue was to regard as a mountain of flesh and a pawn of the missionaries, Hitoti, Paofai, Utami, and other great chiefs were stabilizing and extending their authority. By 1823-24, when the *Kreiser*, *Ladoga*, and *Predpriiatie* arrived at Matavai Bay, these chiefs had made the missionaries practically dependent on them for their livelihood, for their congregations, and for the moral tone of their converts: see Davies 1961:334-35 on these developments.

88 I omit the conclusion of this panegyric to Nott.

89 Enigmatic: Ogievskii perhaps meant that only the southeastern edge of Matavai Bay is steep, even sheer, in places.

90 On the "royal church" of Papaoa see Melville 1847:199-202; on structures and building methods and materials see Oliver 1974, 1, ch. 7 (the churches were modelled on traditional *fare manihini*). The hill between Matavai Bay and Papaoa in Arue, over which an M-shaped road had been laid, was Faatepare, northeast of the Ururoa Valley. The "three little rivers" were the main tributaries of the Papeno'o River, which join it east of Mount Orohena; but they do not flow into Matavai Bay, so the passage is obscure. The "straight road" passing through groves of trees was the so-called Broom Road, for which *corvée* labour had been used since 1815. Pomare II had fallen prey to Sydney trader Henry Eager in 1821 and had died owing Eager six thousand pounds: on this, and on Pomare II's speculative purchase of the *Queen Charlotte*, see Davies 1961:233, n. 1 and 331-32.

91 Ogievskii's comments generally substantiate the early British data on Maohi (Tahitian) maladies, as summarized in Oliver 1974, 1:484ff. The "sores" considered by Tahitians to have been introduced by Europeans were evidently venereal in nature; but early visitors commonly confused the symptoms of these introduced diseases with yaws: see Forster 1777, 1:370-71; Morrison 1935:228-30; Bligh 1792, 1:388-89, 398. In addition, the Tahitians had certainly been suffering for centuries from coral sores. Ogievskii's "dropsy" had been noted by J.R. Forster and the "malevolent scabs" were perhaps body ulcers. *Fe'efe'e* was elephantiasis. Banks had seen the application of "vulnerary herbs" and "mild juices," such as casuarina juice, before Ogievskii's birth: see Beaglehole 1962, 1:375-76.

92 Ogievskii's little list of Tahitian edible plants and roots (*natere, iniak*, varieties of *egue*, etc.) is worthy of a separate study not as an ethnographic source but as a specimen of linguistic and textual confusion. Useful points of departure are Beaglehole's notes to Cook's scramblings of botanical terms in Banks's MS journal (1955, 1:120-22); Morrison 1935:152-53; Forster 1777, 1:341-42; and Ellis 1829, 1:357ff. Ogievskii's "egue" derives from Cook's and Forster's "eddy-root"; but the Cyrillic prism or sheer carelessness on the

writer's or typesetter's part has placed the original of *iniak* beyond reach. Cursive Russian "p" and "n" in a poor or hurried hand are easily mistaken for each other, so that *nateri* may be seen to derive from *patara*, a "wild yam" eaten by the Tahitians in times of scarcity: see Ellis 1829, 1:361 and Oliver 1974, 1:251. The "sweet-smelling oil" used as a pomade was *mono'i* (Morrison 1935:164). The Tahitians' own large seine nets (*'upea*), which had so impressed early European visitors (Oliver 1974, 1:287-89), were not in use around Matavai Bay in April–May 1823. See Oliver 1974, 1:283 on saltwater fish in the Maohi diet, etc.

93 Montgomery 1832, 2:187-88; also Barratt 1981:13-17 on the origins of British Russophobia in the South Pacific.

94 Here and elsewhere, I omit material. The Russian text (*Novoe puteshestvie*, pp. 88-89) may be collated with the 1830 London edition of *A New Voyage*, 1:144-47.

95 Another echo of Cook and Banks, on which Kotzebue expands for some ten lines here: see *Novoe puteshestvie*, p. 90.

96 Nonetheless, Kotzebue concedes that Tahitian females did grant their favours to his seamen, as other Polynesian girls had favoured Kruzenshtern's seamen twenty years before on Nukuhiva (E.E. Levenshtern, "Zhurnal," TsGIAE, *fond* 1414, op. 3, *delo* 3, fol. 93) and as others had often tried to do at Honolulu (see Barratt 1988:91-94).

97 Charles Wilson (1770-1857), bachelor, had reached Tahiti with the *Royal Admiral* party on 10 July 1801; retreated to Mo'orea and Huahine in 1808-15; married in Sydney (1810); converted Tamatoa of Ra'iatea; and settled at Matavai Bay in 1818, where his wife died almost immediately. Biographical data in O'Reilly and Teissier 1962:492. Melville clashed with his son at Matavai Bay in 1842: see *Omoo* pp. 130-32.

98 The complications of reckoning time and date had preoccupied Kotzebue since 1816, when his companion in the *Riurik*, Chamisso, had discussed them: see Chamisso 1836, 1:230-41 and Barratt 1988:146.

99 *Predpriiatie*'s thermometer stood at 24.5° Réaumur on occasion (87°F). Four years earlier, Bellingshausen had endured that degree of heat even in the shade (*Dvukratnye izyskaniia*, p. 302), despite having come to Tahiti three months later, and he had not complained!

100 This was Wilson's second wife. His two children by his first marriage were Samuel (born 1811), who became his father's assistant in 1834, and Charles Jr., interim British consul at Papeete and Melville's *bête noire*. The Reverend Daniel Tyerman and George Bennet of Sheffield had reached Tahiti in the whaler *Tuscan* in September 1821 and subsequently travelled extensively among the Societies: Davis 1961:232ff. and Montgomery 1832, 2, intro.

101 Papaoa: see Davies 1961:243.

102 Full bibliographical details in Davies 1961:xviii. The book was really John Davies's work, though Nott had assisted.

103 All Russian texts reflect this assessment, which inevitably rested on missionary and Tahitian converts' testimonies.

104 Wilson was 54 at the time of Kotzebue's visit, and was to live another 33 years in Tahiti and Samoa. He had once been a baker's apprentice: see Davies 1961:xlvi.

105 In *Puteshestvie vokrug sveta* . . . (St. P. 1809-12). This was hardly "lately," by the late 1820s! See Davies 1961:289-91 on the LMS moves to Tonga in 1826 and 1828, of which Kotzebue had learnt since his return to Russia in 1826.

106 Starting in 1821, Tuamotuans who had studied with the missionaries at Paofai on Tahiti, or on Mo'orea, took the Gospel to Anaa. Only in 1829, however, did the missionaries plan to push further east to Makatea, with Tahitian and Tuamotuan assistance; nothing was done that year by the Europeans themselves: Davies 1961:269-72.

107 See Montgomery 1832:xvi for an angry response to this species of vilification.

108 This was the "new and decent Chapel" built in 1822 a little north of Wilson's and other European houses and so midway between the main watering place and Venus Point: Davies 1961:242. It is described as a meeting-house on Kotzebue's plan of Matavai Bay, which is tolerably accurate in the Tahitian context. It had originally been 98 feet long and 42 broad.

109 This account of Polynesian adoption and adapting of European clothes and fashions closely echoes Kotzebue's scornful description of the situation at Honolulu in Dec. 1824. See my *Russian View of Honolulu*, narratives 54 and 115, and p. 75. Sheets were commonly used as exclusive *pareu* by 1824.

110 Not traditional bark cloth turbans (*taumi upo'o*) or caps, but hats modelled on those introduced very recently by Duperrey's men. *La Coquille* left a sartorial legacy of which both Russians and local missionaries disapproved.

111 French evidence confirms this.

112 I omit Kotzebue's development of this thought.

113 Omitted here is a somewhat inaccurate précis of the early activity of the LMS missionaries, dealings with Teu, etc., to which Montgomery took great exception (1832:xiv-xv).

114 On the Pomare and Tamatoa Codes of 1819-20 and the appointment of heads of extended families as judges see Davies 1961:367-69.

115 Tamatoa IV of Ra'iatea, also known as Tapoa II of Borabora; Aimata's husband since Dec. 1822.

116 Davies 1961:234 and notes.

117 This observation is echoed in Lesson 1839, 1:437ff. The French had attempted a translation of the 1819 Code, and one of *La Coquille*'s officers, Lejeune, sent a copy to the LMS agent in Paris, Mark Wilks. See also Moerenhout 1837, 2:480-88.

118 Davies 1961:xxxvii-xxxviii (the Pomares and wars of the early contact period).

119 Tamatoa IV of Ra'iatea,

120 See Davies 1961:234 on the "coronation" of the infant Pomare III; Kotzebue gives a description (1830, 1:165-66) that emphasizes the Russians' interest in such ceremonies and their predisposition to give them importance in Oceania and elsewhere.

121 Montgomery responded, not surprisingly, to this libel (1832, 2:xiv-xv).

122 Sugar had been made on Tahiti and Mo'orea on a small scale even in 1818: Davies 1961:222-24.

123 Aimata had wed Tapoa II of Taha'a, later paramount chief of Borabora, not "her uncle" of Ra'iatea. Kotzebue confuses mother and daughter.

124 Untrue: the topography had changed even in the fifty years since Charles Green, Daniel Solander, and Cook had set up their land observatory near the end of Venus Point (Teauroa). Details in Beaglehole 1955, 1:cxli-cxliii.

125 Description of "enchanting scenes" omitted: full text in Kotzebue 1981:103. I touch on Kotzebue's role as scientific intermediary and on the *Predpriiatie*'s astronomical and other scientific equipment in *Russian View of Honolulu*, 100-2, 128-31. See Oliver 1974, 1:162ff. on Maohi structures and shelters.

126 Beaglehole 1962, 1:335-36; Moerenhout 1837, 2:121ff. (tattoo); Davies 1961:252-53; 239, n. 3 (renewal of the practice in the '20s, in reaction to the Code of Laws, etc.). Full text in Kotzebue 1981:104.

127 The queen was Teremo'emo'e (Terito). Kotzebue appears to have regarded Pomare Vahine as one of her sisters, if in fact she was present at Venus Point on 17 March 1824.

128 Baked pig with yams, fruit, etc.: Kotzebue 1981:105.

129 See Montgomery 1832, 2:xvii.

130 First with Kruzenshtern aboard *Nadezhda* (1803-6), then in the brig *Riurik* accompanied by Chamisso (1815-18).

131 Beaglehole 1955, 2:422-23.

132 Details of the Tahitian Court's arrival aboard *Predpriiatie* are omitted: Kotzebue 1981:107.

133 Further on this see Davies 1961:331-32.

134 Full text in Kotzebue 1981:110-11.

135 Eschscholtz took part of his large zoological collection from Polynesia to Dorpat University, where, tragically, the specimens were destroyed by fire: see Heidemaa 1975:164-65. He succeeded in publishing his *Zoologischer Atlas* (Berlin 1829-31) just before his premature death and contributed modestly to Kotzebue's *Novoe puteshestvie*.

136 The Broom Road.
137 The "judge" was Iatoa'i for Arue: Davies 1961:368.
138 See n. 96.
139 See n. 113.
140 This method had been observed by Cook in July 1769 (Beaglehole 1955, 1:103, 122) and by Kotzebue at Honolulu. Subjective reflections on the Tahitian cuisine are omitted here.
141 Other European accounts fail to confirm this suggestion that nets and seines were scarcely in use by the mid-1820s. Possibly they were less used in Matavai Bay than elsewhere in Tahiti, but the Russian evidence reflects ignorance of the complex regulations and traditions governing fishing.
142 Fuller text in Kotzebue 1981:116.
143 Ernst Karlovich Gofman (1801-71), student and later professor at Dorpat University. His Tahitian experiences find some reflection in his *Geognostische Bobachtungen auf einer Reise um die Welt....* (Berlin 1829).
144 From Matavai Bay, the little group had moved east through Orofara to the Papenoo Valley, then south. I cannot identify "Weijoride" (Vai-orite or Veioride in the 1830 Russian text), but I suspect Tevaiiohiro, a day's march up the Papenoo Valley and facing Mt. Aramaoro. The basalt cliffs would have been the Teivimarama Ridge, to the hikers' southwest.
145 Ellis 1829, 2:66-68 and Mortimer 1791:39 (sleeping arrangements and elevated bed places).
146 Gofman had evidently been taken up to the Viriviriterai Plateau, still east of the Papenoo Valley. The next "steep precipice" was a face of Mt. Urufa, beyond which lay the Tearoa Pass—oval in shape, as Kotzebue comments.
147 In Russian, approximately two versts in circumference; Kotzebue 1981:119.
148 The place visited was Papaoa, Pomare Vahine IV's preferred seat.
149 *Tiairi* or *tutui* candlenuts, about the size of a walnut: Beaglehole 1955, 1:125, 127; also Oliver 1974, 1:170.
150 Pomare II's lay on a headland slightly NE of Papaoa, between points Iriti and Honu. The site, with its several mausoleums or tombs, remains a site for touristic pilgrimage to this day.
151 *Queen Charlotte* (Captain Samuel P. Henry, 1800-52). The elder son of the missionary William Henry (1770-1859), Samuel was known in Tahiti as Tiritahi and had been made sole agent for the sale of Pomare II's cargoes in Sydney in 1821. See Davies 1961:156, 274-75, 332n.
152 Samuel Henry spoke fluent Tahitian, had an extensive knowledge of the Society Islands and their politics, and had received a sound schooling in Sydney: see O'Reilly and Teissier 1962:207-8.
153 Actually, the error was nearer 8', the true longitude being 149°29'W. Cook had been more accurate 56 years before: see Beaglehole 1955, 1:119.
154 See above, pt. 1, ch. 3 on Russian hydrography in the Tuamotus and error margins.
155 Omitted here are Kotzebue's observations on tides, trade winds, *Predpriiatie*'s departure, and the Tahitian language. They stretch to a thousand words, almost a mini-essay; but they are superficial from the standpoint of comparative linguistics and—unlike Chamisso's work in Hawaii of 1816-17, which resulted in *Uber die Hawaiische Sprache* (1837)— contribute very little to Polynesian studies. See Barratt 1988:99-100 on Russian contributions to the study of Polynesian languages and, for the text of Kotzebue's remarks on "the Tahitian dialect...distinguished by its euphony," see *Novoe puteshestvie*, pp. 123-25.
156 In 1829-30, Duperrey corresponded extensively with both Kotzebue and Kruzenshtern: the unpublished letters remain at TsGIAE under the archival reference *fond* 1414, op. 3, Nos. 24 and 26.
157 Teremo'emo'e's and Pomare Vahine's visit to the Russian ship was, in several respects, an echo of their visit to *La Coquille*, in the course of which their portraits had been sketched: see Duperrey 1826, Plate 13.
158 *Predpriiatie*'s chaplain was Father Viktor (Kotzebue 1981:24). Kotzebue follows the

examples of Iu. F. Lisianskii and V.M. Golovnin in making almost no mention of his ex-chaplain in his published narrative—and in having merely tolerated the priest's presence aboard.

159 A tendentious remark. Tyerman and Bennet certainly knew that it was Henry Nott, acting in the name of his royal charge, Pomare III, who had proposed "guardianship" or suzerainty. The natural curiosity of such visiting foreigners as Kotzebue and Duperrey, and especially the arrival of American shipmasters, combined with local factors to induce Nott to send a request to King George IV for protection and the Union Jack on 5 Oct 1825: LMS Archives, Letters & Journals of Missionaries and Directors, South Seas 5.

160 For biographical data of Lts. Timofei Kordiukov, Nikolai Rimskii-Korsakov et al., see Ivashintsev 1980:143-44, Kotzebue 1981:317, and *OMS*. *Predpriiatie* carried no less than five future admirals.

161 This was true: Kotzebue made for Samoa and reached Tau, easternmost of the Manua Cluster, on 2 April 1824. The missionaries were as predisposed to doubt the purity of Kotzebue's scientific objects as he was hostile to their true aims.

162 These last two paragraphs, as we learn from a footnote to p. 217 of vol. 2 of the 1832 edition of the *Journal of Voyages and Travels*, are directly from the private journal of the Reverend Tyerman (under 5-6 April 1824). The lengthy footnote reads in part: "It is sufficient here to say that the circumnavigator, when he sat down, in the seat of the scornful, to write these strictures, either misunderstood or misrepresented what he saw of the moral and civilizing effects of the gospel there . . . Feb. 10, 1831."

163 *Krotkii* was approaching Tetiaroa (Tethuroa) from the east, whereas *Endeavour* had approached it from the south on 14 April 1769: see Beaglehole 1955, 1:140 and Ivashintsev 1980:108. Kruzenshtern's representation of it was rather inaccurate.

164 This was a nor'-wester, with violent veerings, of the sort noted by Kotzebue (1830, 1:215). The cape and bay in question were presumably Teauroa and Matavai.

165 By Hagemeister's Julian calendar, it was Thursday.

166 Chinese wares and silks had been brought to Tahiti in growing quantity by New England shipmasters.

167 Regrettably, the Berens text ends here (see *Morskoi sbornik* 1903, [5]:71), and subsequent events must be reconstructed principally on the basis of Hagemeister's dry contribution to the *Zapiski Gidrograficheskago Departamenta*, 8:107-10. In brief, the north wind continued to make problems and even destroyed native huts and uprooted palms. *Krotkii*'s astronomical instruments and tent were drenched and taken back on board within one day; and Hagemeister, who almost took a dip in Matavai Bay as his launch was pulling back from the village, was ashore too briefly to be affected by the mission or by the May 1826 Port Regulations, which would otherwise have been relevant to him: see Ellis 1829, 2:455-56 and Davies 1961:373.

168 *Amerika* had approached Mo'orea from the northeast and made straight for Talu or Opunohu Bay, on its north shore, but Kruzenshtern's *Atlas Iuzhnago moria* (1826) gave Captain von Schantz no help where Mo'orea's harbours were concerned, and the *Dopolnenie k izdannym v 1826 i 1827 godakh ob'iasneniiam* . . . in which the admiral focused on the problem, would not appear for another year. The missionary at Papetoai station, on the western headland of Opunohu Bay, was William Henry (1770-1859), father of master mariner Samuel (Tiritahi) Henry, who had obliged Kotzebue a decade earlier.

169 Henry's wife, born Ann Shepherd (1797-1882), was also at Papetoai: See O'Reilly and Teissier 1962:208-9 on their labours, which fully justified the young Lt. Zavoiko's encomium.

170 I.e., baked in an earth oven: see Oliver 1974, 1:236-38.

171 Dollar. On the development of local price controls and a money economy, see Moerenhout 1837, 2:505-7 and Davies 1961:332-33. Henry had managed to keep Papetoai free of the grog shops that had sprung up at Papeete by 1835.

172 *Ia orana oé*! (Good-day to you!)

173 Zavoiko and his fellow officers were followed in 1842 by Herman Melville: see *Omoo* chs. 54 and 56 (hunting wild bulls, etc.) and ch. 79 ("Taloo Chapel" and "Partoowye,"

i.e., Papetoai). Unlike Tahiti, Mo'orea had considerable herds of wild cattle, which, though they belonged to Pomare Vahine IV, planters had permission to shoot.

174 Such games with sharks were traditional in Tahiti: see Morrison 1935: 154-55 and Ellis 1829, 2:290-91.

175 Ivashintsev 1980:119 (*Nikolai*'s route); Davies 1961:238-40 (Papetoai station in the late 1820s and the growth of "a covetous and worldly spirit," tattooing, etc.).

CHAPTER SIX: RUSSIAN AND RUSSO-GERMAN SCIENCE

1 *ZGDMM*, 1 and Ivashintsev 1980:87-88.

2 TsGIAL, *fond* 789, op. 20, *delo* 7-9, 19-21, 28-30, 36, etc. These aquarelles were in private hands by the late 1800s and found their way into the collection of P.I. Shchukin. In 1912, they went from the Shchukin estate to the museum now known as the State Historical Museum in Moscow. Shelved and mislaid in the Revolutionary and Civil War period, the Mikhailov Album was "rediscovered" in 1948: see Bolotnikov 1949 and Ostrovskii 1949. See Shokal'skii 1928:197 on early Soviet plans to publish certain of Mikhailov's original pen and watercolour sketches, which passed from A. Varnek to the Academy of Arts and so (in 1926) to the State Russian Museum.

3 Sementovskii 1951:246.

4 Beaglehole 1955, 1:123-24.

5 Bligh 1792, 1:404; Forster 1777, 2:111.

6 Bellinsgauzen 1960:248.

7 See Beaglehole 1955, 1:81-83.

8 Modern maps indicate that Mikhailov was depicting the Faatepare range, lying between the Tuauru and Ururoa depressions.

9 TsGIAL, *fond* 789, op. 20, *delo* 28b, fol. 26.

10 On this, see Fedorov-Davydov 1953:219-20, 324.

11 Oliver 1974, 1:149.

12 Beaglehole 1955, 1, fig. 29.

13 Ellis 1829, 2:183.

14 Beaglehole 1955, 1:129. Beaglehole states flatly that the sort of large building seen by the Russians at Point Venus and drawn by Mikhailov was an *arioi* house, a place "of general, but especially *arioi*, entertainment" (n. 4). By 1820, as the Russians remind us on every page of their accounts, the influence of the mission had made the *arioi* a thing of the past.

15 See Ellis 1829, 1:388; also Wilson 1799:206.

16 Holmes 1972:133.

17 Beaglehole 1967, 3, pt. 2: 1248.

18 Ibid., pt. 2:671-72.

19 Ibid., pt. 2:1249; also Staniukovich 1978:59.

20 LOAAN, *fond* 3, op. 3, Nos. 42-43. The list makes terse references to Polynesian, Kamchatkan, Aleut, and Koniag artefacts. Among the 50 or so items were at least 20 from the Hawaiian Islands (see Likhtenberg 1960:168-205 and Rozina 1966:235ff.), listed as Nos. 20-42, and several from Unimak in the Aleutian chain (Nos. 43-44, etc.).

21 Some appeared as plates in Cook 1784: Plates 70, 74, 78. Details and full discussion in Joppien 1987.

22 Staniukovich 1978:59; Likhtenberg 1960:168ff.; Barratt 1987:171-78.

23 Arkhiv MAE, *Zhurnal postuplenii: Koll. 505*, fol. 1; Beliaev 1800, pt. 2: 13.

24 Golenishchev-Kutuzov 1805, 2:54; Rozina 1966, 23:234.

25 Dawson 1958:43-44.

26 BL Add. MSS 8098, ff. 416-24. Behm wrote four times to Banks, on 21 July, 12 Aug., 10 Sept., and 20 Sept. 1799; but the urgency of the Napoleonic War left the latter's powerful friends with neither time nor inclination to reflect on obscure Baltic petitioners and South Seas exotica.

27 *RBS*, 2:354-55 and Russow 1900:36. Behm had been president of the Riga Magistracy (1783-90) during Bekleshev's term as governor-general of Livonia.

28 Rozina 1966:243, 253; Henry 1928:253, 293-94; Oliver 1974, 1:380, 505-5.
29 Russow drew attention to such Baltic German news-sheets and journals as *Ostsee-Provinzen-Blatt vom Jahre 1823* (nos. 15-16) and *Neues St-Petersburgisches Journal für 1782* (Bd. 2); also to *Sibirskii vestnik* 1823, pt. 1, containing a silhouette of Behm to supplement the portrait by John Webber done on 23 May 1779 (see Beaglehole 1967, 3, pt. 2:1246-47 and Ellis 1782, 2:225) and now held in the Dixson Library, State Library of NSW, Sydney (Thomas Pennant copy of King-Cook *Voyage*, 2d ed., 1785:Q. 77/37).
30 See *SMAE* 1960, 19:168; 1964, 22:34; and 1966, 23:234-35.
31 MAE Collection No. 2520-4, -5, -7. These Chilkat cloaks were collected by Iu.F. Lisianskii in Sitka Sound in 1804-05: see La Pérouse 1799, 1:406-7; Vancouver 1798, 3:249-50; Langsdorf 1814, 22:112.
32 "Muzei Antropologii i Etnografii za 250 let," *SMAE* 1964, 22:5-150.
33 Pp. 243-44, 253.
34 *SMAE* 1966, 23:253.
35 Ellis 1829, 2:500.
36 See Oliver 1974, 1, fig. 12-7.
37 Rozina here refers her readers to Cranstone and Gewers 1968 (3-4):138-44.
38 Forster 1777, 1:118-19; Morrison 1935:159-61.
39 Ellis 1829, 2:178-79.
40 See Shafranovskaia and Azarov 1984:20.
41 Ellis 1829, 2:179.
42 Beaglehole 1962, 1:355-56; Ellis 1829, 2:178; Oliver 1974, 1, figs. 5-13, 5-14.
43 Inaccurate. For instance, a number of Polynesian artefacts collected by Lisianskii and Povalishin of *Neva* in 1804 went into Collection No. 750; and Vanuatuan pieces collected in 1809 by V.M. Golovnin of *Diana* were never in the Academy's hands.
44 Bellinsgauzen 1960:295. Among the papers at LOAAN recording the nature of the Oceanic collections submitted by *Vostok* and *Mirnyi* to the Admiralty Department Museum, and by the latter to the Academy, are those in *fond* 1, op. 2 (1827), no. 462 and in *fond* 2, op. 1 (1827), no. 3, fols. 11-12. See also Staniukovich 1978:64 and Berg 1949 (2):33ff.
45 The transfers of the Admiralty collections of ethnographica went on over a four-year period, ending in 1831. Further on these matters, see my *Russians and Australia*, p. 219.
46 The writer does not accept this bare statement by Rozina (*SMAE* 25:317-18). Links between Captain Henry Barber and Russian officials in the Pacific settlements deserve investigation, however.
47 Bellinsgauzen 1960:295.
48 Ellis 1829, 2:181.
49 Oliver 1974, 1:149.
50 Bellinsgauzen 1831:260. In view of his instructions and his captain's having shown interest in the clothing, it is reasonable to suppose that Mikhailov depicted the mat in his study of the Nihiru-based Tuamotuan party: see Plate 7.
51 Bellinsgauzen 1831:303.
52 See Kaeppler 1979:167-68.
53 Some indication of the benefits to be expected may be seen in the results of a working visit to the Peter the Great Museum by the Maori authority on New Zealand's ancient material culture, David R. Simmons of Auckland. A fine Maori carving, 736-120 at MAE, identified by the museum authorities merely as "a carved phallic group," was recognized by Simmons as one of four bier stays used to steady the corpse of a high chief of South Island (Kai Tahu) on her final voyage south from the Bay of Islands. Oral tradition enabled Simmons then to give the MAE authorities the name of the chief, her tribal affiliations, and final resting place. See my *Southern and Eastern Polynesia*, pp. 163 and 166. In a similar spirit, macro-lens photographs of objects taken from Hawaii's Kona coast in 1804 by Lisianskii went from St. Petersburg in 1987 to Dr. Roger Rose, Hawaiian material culture authority at the Bernice P. Bishop Museum in Honolulu. Findings were reflected in my *Russian Discovery of Hawaii*, pt. 4.

54 See Ellis 1829, 1:282.
55 Beaglehole 1955, 2:804.
56 Ibid., 2:805; Beaglehole 1962, 1:350; Ellis 1829, 1:283.
57 Ellis 1829, 1:284; also Henry 1928:275.
58 Beaglehole 1962, 1:364; also Oliver 1974, 1:134-37 (adzes) and fig. 9-2c (coconut splitter in Bern).
59 See Plate 11 and Beaglehole 1962, 1:338.
60 Barrow 1979:20-21 and Plate 17.
61 Compare, for instance, with the tame effect created by the *ti'i* shown as Plate 5.5 in Gathercole 1979:147.
62 Barrow 1979:44. Despite the inclusion of the MAE *ti'i* in collection No. 736, its true provenance is mysterious. No Russian narrative makes even passing mention of any Tahitian image obtained from Nott, Wilson, or other LMS missionaries based in Tahiti or Mo'orea in the 1820s, and such an acquisition would have merited allusions. After all, both Bellingshausen and Kotzebue strove for comprehensive coverage of their visits. On the other hand, we know that J.R. Forster was the source of certain Polynesian articles in the former *Kunstkammer*, of a whole collection of Tahitian tapa specimens at the Estonian Historical Museum in Tallin (Coll. no. 4330-51, 52, 56, 57, 149), and of at least one of the British Museum's Tahitian *ti'i* (which he had personally collected in the course of Cook's second voyage: see Barrow 1979, Plate 46). MAE documentation of provenance leaves much to be desired, as I show in *The Russian Discovery of Hawaii*, pp. 171ff. And 736-226 was worked with stone tools, which does *not* suggest that it had been made shortly before the arrival of the Russians in Matavai Bay.
63 Ivashintsev 1980:40-45; Barratt 1979:15.
64 "Pis'ma g. Galkina o plavanii shliupov 'Vostok' i 'Mirnyi' v Tikhom okeane," *Syn otechestva* 1822 (49):100-15.
65 See Barratt 1979:63-70.
66 Survey in Barratt 1988:177-79.
67 A search conducted in 1985 at the V.L. Komarov Institute of Botany (BIAN), Academy of Sciences, in St. Petersburg by Dr. E.A. Bobrov was unsuccessful. On the other hand, Chamisso's Hawaiian herbarium of 1816-17 was found: see my *Russian View of Honolulu, 1809-1826*, pp. 107-15.
68 See Lukina 1980, ch. 4; also Heidemaa 1975, 2:164-174 and 1981, 11:87-92.
69 *OMS* 1893, 7:320. Kotzebue was living in Reval until late Nov. 1827, in contact with Kruzenshtern, Eschscholtz, Dr. Karl Espenberg of *Nadezhda*, Major Karl von Nolken of *Apollon*, and Lenz, Gofman, and Seewald (Russian: Zival'd) of *Predpriiatie*. Estonia (Estliandiia) was home to a veritable Baltic-German South Pacific club in the 1820s.
70 *Ubersicht der Zoologischen Ausbeute* (Weimar 1830), pt. 4.
71 See Heidemaa 1975:164-65; also Rosenberg 1988:71-72. In the 1950s, great damage was done to materials from the Kruzenshtern and Kotzebue expeditions both at the Zoological Museum and at TsGIAE. Roofs leaked, and paper being in very short supply, even first editions and lithographic originals were put to primary, functional use.
72 Heidemaa 1981:33ff.; also Ling 1961:157-59. I thank Dr. I. Kusik and especially Dr. Kalju Leib of TsGIAE in Tartu for assisting me there and at TRU Zoological Museum in 1989 and 1991, and for providing microfilm.
73 See n. 68; also Lukina 1975, ch. 6.
74 See n. 68.
75 That guide (n. 72 above) may be used in conjunction with reference works listed by Rosenberg 1988:126-27.
76 The Lazarev brothers, on whom see Lazarev 1950:26ff., all had interests in natural history. Aleksei Petrovich was presented with a collection of Australian birds and insects by Lt. Phillip Parker King, RN, in 1820 (ibid., p. 154). Vishnevskii shared the palaeontological interests of Staff-Surgeon Grigorii A. Zaozerskii of *Blagonamerennyi*, who conducted a dig on Sydney's North Shore that same year: TsGAVMF, *fond* 215, op. 1, *delo* 1203; also Kuznetsova 1968:244-45.

77 TsGAVMF, *fond* 213, op. 1, *delo* 52.
78 Trenov 1742, pt. 2; Naumov 1980:6-7 (Dr. Seva, items from the East Indies, etc.).
79 "Izvestie o nekotorykh zhivotnykh," *Tekhnologicheskii zhurnal* 1805, 2 (2):159-61.
80 On the Forsters' earlier links with Catherine II and Russia see Hoare 1976:26-36.
81 Bornovolokov 1809, 6 (2):96-110; also Barratt 1988:217-18 (Abbé Manesse and the intro-
    duction of taxidermy to St. Petersburg).
82 See Kaeppler 1979, 3:167-68.
83 Details in Barratt 1990:150-53; also Vorob'ev 1949:497-504.
84 Bellingshausen 1945, 2:348; *ES*, 79:209-10; Barratt 1979:131, 224-25 on Eikhval'd's (or
    Eichenwald's) collaboration with Ferdinand Ernst Fischer of the St. Petersburg Imperial
    Botanical Garden on analysis of the botanical results of the Bellingshausen-Lazarev ex-
    pedition.
85 Bellinsgauzen 1960:49.
86 Naumov 1980:13.
87 See Barratt 1988:218-21 and Plate 30; also my *Russian View of Honolulu*, pp. 102-3, for a
    survey of Eschscholtz's zoology while in the Hawaiian Islands in 1816-17.
88 Barratt 1980:24-25 (Aboriginal Australians' reactions to instruments); Kotzebue 1821,
    1:16.
89 Bellinsgauzen 1960:47.
90 Ibid.:70 and Barratt 1988:123-24.
91 Kotzebue 1821, 1:41.
92 Bellinsgauzen 1960:75.
93 Barratt 1988:124-25.
94 Kotzebue 1821, 1:341.
95 No chart of Matavai Bay is mentioned in *Opisanie starinnykh atlasov, kart, i planov,
    khraniashchikhsia v Arkhive Tsentral'nogo Kartograficheskogo Proizvodstva VMF* (Mos-
    cow 1958); nor does a detailed chart appear in the 1831 *Atlas*.
96 For comments on the 1820 hydrography among the Tuamotu atolls see above, pp. 191-97.
97 Personalia in Ivashintsev 1980:144 and Kotzebue 1981:24.
98 *Gentleman's Magazine* 1847, 2:324-26; *DNB*, 33:421-22; Barratt 1988:300-1.
99 *DNB*, 2:316.
100 See Hunnisett 1980:16.
101 The "boatswain" in 1824 was evidently still the New England beachcomber, Williams,
     whom the Russians had met there in 1820.
102 French charts give latitude 17°28′ 55″S, longitude 149°29′ 30″W.
103 Nevskii 1951:57-58; Kruzenshtern 1814, 1:1-2.
104 Kruzenshtern 1812, 3:277 (from "The Degrees of Sea Water Temperature at Various
     Depths").
105 Discussion in Rudovits 1954, 27:5-7; also Shokal'skii 1917:33.
106 Kruzenshtern 1812, 3:333-41 (Hörner's paper, "Udel'naia tiazhest' morskoi vody").
107 Kotzebue 1821, 1:67-75.
108 Kotzebue 1828:7; on Dollond, see *DNB*, 5:1102-4; also Nevskii 1951:42 (barometer selec-
     tion).
109 See Kotzebue 1981:2-3 for remarks by D.D. Tumarkin on confusion between the 1828 and
     1830 texts.
110 Kotzebue 1981:24.
111 Friis 1967:193.
112 Lenz 1831, 1:221-44; see also Prestwich 1874, 165:587-674.
113 Kotzebue 1981:318.
114 Pasetskii 1977:71-73, 176; also Ivashintsev 1980:71-73, 67.
115 For surveys of archival holdings and access conditions in the last phase of Soviet power
     see Grimsted 1972.
116 Bellinsgauzen 1960:48.
117 See Barratt 1989:132-34.
118 *Zhurnal Ministerstva Narodnogo Prosveshcheniia* 1828, 22:44-68.

119 Darwin 1874:115-16; see also Newell 1959, 68 (3):120-28.
120 Kotzebue 1830, 2:338.
121 Bellinsgauzen 1960:77-78 (Admiralty Dept. Instructions, Article 15).
122 See *Geologicheskii muzei, osnovan v 1816 godu* (Leningrad 1925), ch 3.
123 *Materialy dlia istorii Rumiantsevskago Muzeia* (Moscow 1882), bk. 1 and *Piatidesiatiletie Rumiantsevskago Muzeia v Moskve, 1862-1912: istoricheskii ocherk* (Moscow 1912).
124 Kotzebue 1821, 2:246-47;
125 Kotzebue 1821, 3:377-52, Larousse, *Grand Dict. Universel*, 7:570.
126 See Barratt 1988:102.
127 Sarv 1961:168-82.
128 Kotzebue 1981:318.

Bibliography

ARCHIVAL MATERIALS

Archives in Russia and Estonia

(a) *Tsentral'nyi Gosudarstvennyi Arkhiv Voenno-Morskogo Flota SSSR* (TsGAVMF, St. Petersburg)

fond   14 (I.F. Kruzenshterna), op. 1, *delo* 12-13 (Kruzenshtern's earlier naval service); *delo* 200 (letters inward, Bellingshausen to Kruzenshtern, 1841-43, re extractions of data on longitudinal readings from ships' logs). This *fond* contains 529 items, many bearing on the South Pacific Islands; *delo* 192 (Otto E. Kotzebue, account of voyage of *Predpriiatie*).

fond   5, op. 1, *delo* 95 (*Putevoi zhurnal* or service journal kept by Midshipman Count Loggin Ivanovich Geiden [Heiden] during his voyage in Kotzebue's sloop *Predpriiatie*, 1823-26: passage on Matavai Bay, Tahiti).

fond   166, op. 1, *delo* 660, pt. 1 (printed works and charts taken to Polynesia aboard *Vostok*, many of British publication); *delo* 666 (appointments to *Kreiser* and *Ladoga* and service arrangements); *delo* 691 (correspondence with Academy of Arts re secondment of Pavel N. Mikhailov and the use of his drawings); *delo* 2596 (despatches from Lt. Arkadii Leskov, ex *Vostok*, to A.V. Moller, chief of Naval Staff, 1823; re achievements and prospects in the far South Pacific); *delo* 2698, fols. 1-3 (report to A.V. Moller from L.I. Golenishchev-Kutuzov, head of Naval Scientific Committee, 17 March 1825, re materials submitted to the Admiralty Department prior to Oct. 1824 by Bellingshausen, including 59 notebooks and a collection of 19 charts).

fond   212 (*Gosudarstvennoi Admiralteistv-Kollegii*), op. 3, *delo* 4093 (1823 correspondence from the *Kreiser* and *Ladoga*, especially despatches to A.V. Moller from Mikhail P. Lazarev re stay in Van Diemen's Land, movement onward to Matavai Bay, Tahiti); op. 9, *delo* 477, 479 (official responses to *Vostok*'s successful voyage, annual pensions for lieutenants, etc.; plans to have Lt. K.P. Torson work in St. Petersburg and "complete matters with regard to the voyage to the South Pole"); op. 9, *delo* 1252 (Torson's orders of 30 Oct. 1822 to prepare an official account of *Vostok*'s and *Mirnyi*'s activities in Oceania).

fond   215, op. 1, *delo* 1203 (natural historical and ethnographic materials from Polynesia and Australia, brought aboard the *Otkrytie* and *Blagonamerennyi* to St. Petersburg in 1822).

fond   283 (1829), op. 1, no. 948 ("Report Concerning the Refusal of the Crew of the Armed Sloop *Moller* to Take to Bed on the Orders of the Duty Officer").

fond   406, op. 7, *delo* 62 (Iurii F. Lisianskii aboard the Indiaman *Royalist*, 1799, and his passage from Madras to London).

fond   870, op. 1 *delo* 3599 (log of *Kreiser*, 1822-24, with meteorological and other data in the hands of F. Vishnevskii and D.I. Zavalishin).

fond   1166, op. 1, *delo* 9 (Pavel S. Nakhimov on *Kreiser*'s 1823 voyage across Oceania: Tahiti, arrival in Sitka Sound).

(b) *Tsentral'nyi Gosudarstvennyi Istoricheskii Arkhiv* (TsGIAL: St. Petersburg)

fond   733, op. 12 (1826), no. 308 (Pavel N. Mikhailov's selection by Captain M.N. Staniukovich as artist aboard *Moller*, terms of his appointments, duties in Oceania); op. 91 (1819), no. 17, fols. 6-7 (A.N. Olenin's formal recommendation of Mikhailov to the Naval Ministry, to serve as artist on a "far from danger-free voyage").

fond   789 (*Akademii Khudozhestv*), op. 1, *delo* 1854, 1949, 2460 (materials re the qualifications and release of the artists P.N. Mikhailov and E.M. Korneev); op. 2, *delo* 28 (same); op. 20, *dela* 7, 9, 17, 21 (Mikhailov and the 1819-21 expedition, his procedures, results); op. 20 (1819), *delo* 28b, fols. 26-28 ("Artistic Instructions" for Mikhailov from A.N. Olenin).

(c) *Arkhiv Vneshnei Politiki Rossii* (AVPR, Moscow)

fond   *Kantseliarii Ministerstva Vneshnikh Del* (1822), *delo* 3645 (*Apollon* to proceed at once to Northwest Coast of North America, patrol there until relieved; Russian trading and strategic interests).

(d) *Leningradskoe Otdelenie Arkhiva Akademii Nauk* (LOAAN, St. Petersburg)

fond   1, op. 2 (1802), *delo* 345 (Special instruction for *Nadezhda* and *Neva* re pursuit of physics, geology, zoology in Oceania from Academicians V.M. Severgin and A.F. Sevast'ianov).

fond   1, op. 2 (1827), *delo* 462 (ethnographica from Polynesia collected in 1820 by Bellingshausen, Lazarev, and their people; objects from Tahiti sent to the Admiralty Department to be transferred to *Kunstkammer*; duplicates, administrative procedures, etc.).

fond   3, op. 8, *dela* 42, 43 (correspondence between Prince A. Viazemskii and the *Kunstkammer*, March 1780, re artefacts received from Major Karl Magnus von Behm of Kamchatka being sent on to the Academy; with list of articles obtained in 1779 from Capt. Charles Clerke, including 15 "stamps" [by John Webber, of Polynesians, etc.] and 48 Polynesian and Aleutian artefacts).

razr.   4, op. 1, *delo* 800a (travel journal of W.G. Tilesius von Tilenau, kept aboard *Nadezhda* in 1803-6; zoological and botanical emphases, early patterns for other savants with Russian ships in Oceania).

(e) *Muzei Antropologii i Etnografii Akademii Nauk imeni Petra Velikogo* (MAE, St. Petersburg)

Arkhiv Muzeia, Zhurnal postuplenii: Kollektsiia No. 505 (accession of the Tahitian, Tongan, Hawaiian, and Aleut/Koniag artefacts obtained via Behm from Clerke and other officers of HMS *Resolution* and *Discovery*; origins of the so-called "James Cook Collection" of MAE).

(f) *Gosudarstvennyi Russkii Muzei, Otdel Risunka* (St. Petersburg)

R-29001-308 (Pavel Nikolaevich Mikhailov Portfolio). A collection of pen, ink, sepia wash, and water-colour illustrations, most from Mikhailov's two voyages around the world with *Vostok*, 1819-21, and *Moller*, 1826-29; but some later pieces were included, evidently by A. Varnek, in the 1840s. Tahitian items include Nos. 29151/150, 29152/151, 29221/219, 29221/220, 29286/284, 29287/285, and 29196/194.

R-9750 (Mikhailov, P.) "Attestat," formal letter of recommendation for the artist, signed by F.F. Bellingshausen, 15 Aug. 1821. Mikhailov's willingness to fulfil all his instructions, and competence.

(g) *Tsentral'nyi Voenno-Morskoi Muzei* (TsVMM, St. Petersburg)

No. 41820/2 ("Vakhtennyi zhurnal leitenanta Iuriia Fedorovicha Lisianskago," holograph journal kept by Lisianskii in 1797-1800 in HMS *Raisonnable*, *Sceptre*, and *Loyalist*. Journal contains long extracts from the observations made by Admiral Sir Erasmus Gower [1742-1814], who had visited Tahiti as master's mate of HMS *Dolphin* [Captain Samuel Wallis] in 1767).

No. 9170-8/1938 ("Zhurnal korablia *Nevy*, 1803-1806 godov," the log of *Neva*, kept by Navigator Danilo Kalinin).

No. 9170-3/1938 ("Chernoviki pisem Lisianskago k raznym litsam s 1803 po 1832 god": originals of Lisianskii's letters to relatives and service colleagues, later interests).

(h) *Arkhiv Geograficheskogo Obshchestva SSSR* (AGO, St. Petersburg)

razr.   99 (Rossiisko-Amerikanskoi Kompanii), *dela* 36, 46 (travel notes of Kiril T. Khlebnikov, director and annalist of the Company, taken during voyages and travels of 1830-31; California and Pacific Islands).

(i) *Saltykov-Shchedrin Public Library* (Manuscripts Dept. [ORGPB], St. Petersburg) *fond*   1000, op. 2, no. 302 ("Dnevnik puteshestviia na korable *Nikolai* v 1837-1838 godakh," anon.). Internal textual evidence clearly indicates that the author was Baron Alfred Geiking, supercargo aboard the *Nikolai* and an acquaintance of her commander, Evgenii A. Berens. Pp. 85-95 on Honolulu, pp. 98ff on Talu Bay, Mo'orea. This same collection of MS journals and travel diaries contains "Zhurnal M.I. Ratmanova," No. 1146, i.e., the 1803-6 journal of Lt. Makar' Ivanovich Ratmanov of *Nadezhda*, a variant of which is held in the Département des Manuscrits, Bibliothèque Nationale, Paris, under ref: Slav, NN 103(1), 104.

(i) *Tsentral'nyi Gosudarstvennyi Istoricheskii Arkhiv Estonii* (TsGIAE, Tartu)

fond   1414 (I.F. Kruzenshterna), op. 3, *delo* 23 (Count Nikolai Petrovich Rumiantsev's letters to Kruzenshtern, 1815-25; many re Kotzebue's undertakings and scientific observations); *dela* 42-43 (L. Choris: letters to St. Petersburg from Paris, 1822, re publication of his *Voyage pittoresque autour du monde*, plates, etc.); *delo* 22 (Kruzenshtern-Hörner correspondence, 1807-34); *delo* 38 (hydrographic studies, 1813-17, in French and German).

fond   2057 (F.P. Vrangelia), op. 1, *delo* 381 (diary of K.T. Khlebnikov, to 1838: many materials on Russian America and activities in the Pacific basin, the voyages to the colonies of the ship *Elena*, 1824-25 and 1828-29).

   (k) *Perm' District State Archive* (Perm')

fond   445 (K.T. Khlebnikova), op. 1, *delo* 43 (Khlebnikov's unpublished and incomplete biographical sketch of Captain Leontii A. Hagemeister); *delo* 401 (A.K. Shvarts, holograph of a sketch of Khlebnikov's life and work for the Russian-American Company, travels, etc.).

Western Archives

(l) *Public Record Office* (PRO, London)

Admiralty 1 (In-letters and despatches), 1/498, cap. 370 (George Murray to Stephen, 17 May 1794, re HMS *Thetis* sailing for North America with Kruzenshtern as a volunteer).

(m) *British Library* (London)

Additional Manuscripts Collection, Add MS 8098, fols. 416-424 (Major Karl Magnus von Behm–Joseph Banks correspondence, July–Sept. 1799. Banks' efforts to secure a small pension).

(n) *London Missionary Society Archives* (London)

Home Odds, 1 (1764-1829), Circulars, April 1796–May 1803. Board Minutes, September 1795–May 1803.

(o) *Elmer E. Rasmusen Research Library*, University of Alaska at Fairbanks

Shur Collection, Microfilm Reels. Most important collection of materials from TsGIAL,

TsGAVMF, AGO, and other major Russian archives. Many reels contain extracts from documents that bear on Russian expeditionary activity in Polynesia.

(p) *Alexander Turnbull Library* (Wellington, NZ)

MS Journal, Samuel Wallis, in HMS *Dolphin*: 1766-67.

PRIMARY PRINTED MATERIAL

Adams, H.B., ed. *Tahiti: Memoirs of Arii Taimai*. Ridgewood, NJ 1968
Alaska Boundary Tribunal: Appendix to the Case of Great Britain. London 1903
Angas, G. *Polynesia: A Popular Description*. London 1848
Beaglehole, J.C., ed. *The Journals of Captain James Cook: The Voyage of the Endeavour, 1768-1771*. Cambridge 1955; *The Voyage of Resolution and Endeavour, 1772-1775*. Cambridge 1961
—— *The Endeavour Journal of Joseph Banks*. Sydney 1962
Beechey, F.W. *Narrative of a Voyage to the Pacific and Bering's Strait . . . in the Years 1825, 1826, 1827 and 1828*. 2d ed. London 1831
Behrens, C.F. *Histoire de l'Expédition de trois Vaisseaux, envoyés par la Compagnie des Indes Occidentales*. La Haye 1739
Belcher, E. *Narrative of a Voyage Round the World Performed in HMS Sulphur*. London 1843
Beliaev, Orest. *Kabinet Petra Velikago*. St. P. 1800
Bellingshausen, F.F. *Atlas k puteshestviiu kapitana Bellinsgauzena*. St. P. 1831
—— *Dvukratnye izyskaniia v Iuzhnom ledovitom okeane i plavanie vokrug sveta v prodolzhenie 1819, 1820, i 1821 godov*. St. P. 1831, 2 ed. intro. & annot. by A.I. Andreev, M. 1949; 3d ed. intro. & annot. by E.E. Shvede, M. 1960. Large parts of the 1831 text were presented in English by Frank Debenham as *The Voyage of Captain Bellingshausen to the Antarctic Seas, 1819-21*. Cambridge, Hakluyt Society, 2d ser., no. XCI, 1945.
Bent's Almanack for 1823. Hobart Town 1824
Berens, E.A. "Zapiski, vedennye v krugosvetnom plavanii na shliupe 'Krotkii' v 1828-1830 godakh," *Morskoi sbornik*. St. P. 1903: no. 1:33-54; no. 5:68-74
Bligh, W. *A Voyage to the South Sea*. London 1792
—— (I. Lee., ed.). *Second Voyage to the South Sea*. London 1920
Bornovolokov, T.A. "O sokhranenii ptichnykh chuchel' i nasekomykh," *Tekhnologicheskii zhurnal*, 6 1809: no. 2:96-110
Bougainville, L.A. *Voyage autour du monde*. Paris 1771
Burney, J. *A Chronological History of the Discoveries in the South Sea*. 6 vols. London 1802-17
Byron, J. *A Voyage Round the World in the "Dolphin."* London 1767
Campe, J.H. *Sammlung interessanter Reisebeschreibungen für die Jungend*. 8 vols. Berlin 1786-90
Chamisso, A. von. "Bemerkungen und Ansichten auf einer Entdeckungs Reise unternommen in den Jahren 1815-1818 . . . von dem Naturforscher der Expedition," in O. von Kotzebue, *Reise um die Welt*, vol 3. Weimar 1821

—— *Reise um die Welt mit der Romanzoffischen Entdeckungs expedition in den Jahren 1815-1818, auf der Brigg Riurik: Erster Theil: Tagebuch.* in *Werke*, Bd. 1, ed. J.E. Hitzig. Leipzig 1836; translated by Henry Kratz as *A Voyage around the world with the Romanzov exploring expedition in the years 1815-1818 in the brig Rurik, Captain Otto von Kotzebue.* Honolulu 1986

—— *Uber die Hawaiische Sprache.* Berlin 1937. Edited by S.E. Elbert and reprinted by Halcyon Antiquariaat, Amsterdam 1969

Choris, L. *Voyage pittoresque autour du monde.* Paris 1822

—— *Vues et paysages des régions équinoxiales.* Paris 1826

Cook, J. *A Voyage towards the South Pole and Around the World.* London 1777. See also Wharton, W.J.

—— *A Voyage to the Pacific Ocean...for Making Discoveries in the Northern Hemisphere.* 3 vols. London 1784 (vol. 3 by James King)

Corney, B.G., ed. *The Quest and Occupation of Tahiti by Emissaries of Spain during the Years 1772-1776.* London Hakluyt Society, 2d ser., nos. 32 (1913), 36 (1915), 43 (1919)

Crozet, J. *Nouveau Voyage à la Mer du Sud.* Paris 1783

Dalrymple, A. *Historical Collection of the Several Voyages and Discoveries in the South Pacific Ocean.* 2 vols. London 1770-21

Darwin, C.R. *The Structure and Distribution of Coral Reefs.* London 1874

Davies, J. *Aritemeti: Oia te Haapao o te Taio.* Huahine 1819

—— *E Parau Faatoito i te Tamarii rii....* Tahiti 1822

—— *Grammar of the Tahitian Dialect of the Polynesian Language.* Tahiti 1823

—— *Te Bibilia Moa Ra iritihia ei parau Tahiti.* London 1838 (compiled with aid from Henry Nott *et al.*)

—— *A Tahitian and English Dictionary.* Papeete 1851

—— (C.W. Newbury, ed.). *A History of the Tahitian Mission, 1799-1830.* Cambridge 1961

Dening, G., ed. *The Marquesan Journals of Edward Robarts, 1797-1824.* Canberra 1974

Dumont D'Urville, J.S. *Voyage pittoresque autour du monde.* 2 vols. Paris 1834-35

—— *Voyage au Pôle sud et dans l'Océanie.* Paris 1841

Duperrey, L.I. *Voyage autour du monde...pendant les années 1822, 1823, 1824 et 1825. Hydrographie, atlas.* Paris 1827

—— *Mémoire sur les Opérations géographiques...dans la Coquille.* Paris 1827

Ellis, W. (Surgeon) *An Authentic Narrative of a Voyage performed by Captain Cook and Captain Clerke.* London 1782

Ellis, W., Rev. *Polynesian Researches.* 2 vols. London 1829

—— *The History of the London Missionary Society Compiled from Original Documents.* London 1844

Engelbrecht, W.A., ed. *De Ontdeckkingsreis van Jacob le Maire en Willem Corneliszoon Schouten.* The Hague 1945

Erman, G. *Reise um die Erde durch Nord-Asien und beide Oceane.* 3 vols. Berlin 1833-48

Eschscholtz, J.F. *Zoologischer Atlas, enthaltend Abbildungen und Beschreibungen neuer Thierarten, während des Flottecapitains von Kotzebue zweiter Reise um die Welt beobachtet.* Berlin 1829-31

Findlay, A.G. *Directory of the North Pacific Ocean for Navigation.* London 1851; 3d ed., 1884

Forster, G.A. *A Voyage Round the World in His Britannic Majesty's Sloop Resolution . . . during the Years 1772, 3, 4, & 5.* London 1777

Forster, J.R. *Observations Made During a Voyage Round the World.* London 1778

—— (M.E. Hoare. ed). *The Resolution Journal of Johann Reinhold Forster, 1772-1775.* 4 vols. London 1982

Galkin, N.A. "Pis'ma g. Galkina o plavanii shliupov 'Vostok' i 'Mirnyi' v Tikhom okeane," *Syn otechestva* (1822): no. 49:100-15

Gamaleia, P.Ia. *Vyshniaia teoriia morskago iskusstva.* St. P. 1801-4

Gofman, E.K. *Geognostische Beobachtungen auf einer Reise um die Welt in den Jahren 1823-1826.* Berlin 1829

Golenishchev-Kutuzov, L.I., ed. and trans. *Puteshestvie v Severnyi Tikhii okean . . . Dzhemsa Kuka.* St. P. 1805

Gough, B.M., ed. *To the Pacific and Arctic with Beechey.* Cambridge 1973

Greig, A.S. "Otzyv ob Atlase Iuzhnago moria i Gidrograficheskikh Zapiskakh Vitse-Admirala Kruzenshterna," *Shestoe Prisuzhdenie Uchrezhdennykh P.N. Demidovym Nagrad.* (1837):97-105

Harris, J. *A Complete Collection of Voyages and Travels.* London 1744

Haweis, T. *Sermons Preached in London, at the Formation of the Missionary Society*, 22, 23, 24 September 1795, London 1795

Hawkesworth, J. *An Account of the Voyages Undertaken for Making Discoveries in the Southern Hemisphere.* 3 vols. London 1773

Henry, T. "More on the Ari'is of Tahiti," *Journal of the Polynesian Society*, 20 (1911):4-9

—— *Ancient Tahiti.* Bernice P. Bishop Museum Bulletin no. 48. Honolulu 1928

Hitzig, J.E., ed. "Leben und Briefe von Adelbert von Chamisso," in *Chamissos werke*, Bd. V/VI. ed. Hitzig. Leipzig 1842

Holmes, C., ed. *Captain Cook's Final Voyage: the Journal of Midshipman George Gilbert.* Honolulu 1972

Kiselev, E. "Pamiatnik prinadlezhit matrozu pervoi stat'i Egoru Kiselevu, nakhodivshemusia v dal'nem voiazhe na shliupe 'Vostok' v 1819-1821 godakh," *Vokrug sveta* (1940):no. 4:40-43. See also under Sementovskii, V

Kittlitz, F.H. *Denkwürdigkeiten einer Reise um die Welt.* Gotha 1858

Kotzebue, O.E. *Puteshestvie v Iuzhnyi okean i Beringov proliv v 1815-1818 godakh.* 3 vols. St. P. 1821. German edition published as *Reise um die Welt.* Weimar 1821. H.E. Lloyd's translation of the German text given as *A Voyage of Discovery into the South Sea and Beering's Straits, Undertaken in the Years 1815-1818.* London 1821. Volume 3 is Chamisso's "Observations and Remarks" ("Bermerkungen und Ansichten")

—— *Puteshestvie vokrug sveta, sovershennoe . . . na voennom shliupe Predpriiatii.* St. P. 1828

—— *Neue Reise um die Welt, in den Jahren 1823, 24, 25 und 26.* Weimar 1830. English trans. as *A New Voyage Round the World in the Years 1823, 24, 25 and 26.* London 1830. Translated and introduced by D.D. Tumarkin as *Novoe puteshestvie vokrug sveta v 1823-1826 godakh.* Moscow 1981

Kruzenshtern, I.F. "Prodolzhenie ob otkrytiiakh Tasmana," *Tekhnologich zhurnal*, 3 (1806): pt. 4:126ff.

—— "Puteshestvie ot Mysa Dobroi Nadezhdy k Madrasu v 1797 godu," *Zapiski Admiralteiskago Departamenta Morskago Ministerstva*, 3 (1815):55ff

—— *Puteshestvie vokrug sveta v 1803, 4, 5 i 1806 godakh na korabliakh "Nadezhda" i "Neva."* St. P. 1809-12. Translated by R.B. Hoppner as *A Voyage Round the World.* 2 vols. London 1814

—— *Beiträge zur Hydrographie der Grösseren Ozeane, als Erläuterungen zu einer Charte des ganzen Erdkreises nach Mercator's Projection.* Leipzig 1819

—— *Atlas Iuzhnago moria.* 2 pts. St. P. 1823-26

—— *Sobranie sochinenii, sluzhashchikh razborom i iz'iasneniem Atlasa Iuzhnago moria.* St. P. 1823-26. French text printed in St. Petersburg as *Receuil de Mémoires hydrographiques, pour servir d'analyse et d'explication....* St. P. 1824-27

—— *Dopolnenie k izdannym v 1826 i 1827 godakh ob'iasneniiam osnovanii.* St. P. 1836

Langsdorf, G.H. "Opisanie uzorov, navodimykh zhiteliami ostrova Vashingtona na ikh tele," *Tekhnologicheskii zhurnal,* 7 (1810):pt. 2

—— *Bemerkungen auf einer Reise um die Welt in den Jahren 1803 bis 1807.* 2 vols. Frankfurt 1812. Translated anonymously and indifferently as *Voyages and Travels in Various Parts of the World.* 2 vols. London 1814

La Pérouse, J.F. de. *Voyage autour du monde.* 4 vols. Paris 1797. English version: *Voyage Round the World.* London 1799. Russian version, by L.I. Golenishchev-Kutuzov: *Puteshestvie La Peruza v Iuzhnom i Severnom Tikhom Okeane.* St. P. 1800

Lazarev, Aleksei P. (A.I. Solov'ev, ed.). *Zapiski o plavanii voennogo shliupa Blagonamerennogo v Beringov proliv i vokrug sveta dlia otkrytii v 1819-21 godakh.* M. 1950

Lazarev, Aleksei P. "Plavanie shliupa Ladogi v 1822, 1823 i 1824 godakh...," *Zapiski Izdannye Gosudarst. Admiralteiskim Departamentom.* (1826) ch. 11, sect. II, pp. 57-93

—— *Meteorologicheskie nabliudeniia, proizvodivshiiasia vo vremia krugosvetnago plavaniia shliupa "Ladoga."* ...St. P. 1882

Lazarev, Andrei P. *Plavanie vokrug sveta na shliupe "Ladoga" v 1822, 1823, i 1824 godakh.* St. P 1832

Lazarev, Mikhail P. (A.A. Samarov,ed.). *Russkie flotovodtsy: M.P. Lazarev: sbornik dokumentov* 2 vols. M. 1952

Lenz, E. *Physikalische Beobachtungen, angestellt auf einer Reise um die Welt unter dem Commando des Capitains Otto von Kotzebue.* St. P. 1830. Partially reprinted in *Académie des Sciences: Mémoires.* St. P. 1831, pp. 221-344

—— "Bemerkungen über die Temperatur des Weltmeeres in Verschiedenen Tiefen," *Académie des Sciences: Classe Physico-Mathématique* (1847):65-74

Lesson, R.P. *Voyage autour du monde, entrepris par ordre du gouvernement sur la corvette la Coquille.* 2 vols. Paris 1839

Lisianskii, Iu. F. *Puteshestvie vokrug sveta v 1803, 1804, 1805, i 1806 godakh, na korable "Neva."* St. P. 1812. Translated by the author as *Urey Lisiansky: A Voyage Round the World in the Years 1803, 4, 5 & 6.* London 1814. 2d ed. M. 1947

Litke (Lütke), F.P. *Puteshestvie vokrug sveta na voennom shliupe "Seniavin" v 1826-1829 godakh.* St. P. 1835. French translation as *Voyage autour du monde.* Paris 1835-36. 2d ed. M. 1938

—— "Soobshchenie o smerti admirala I.F. Kruzenshterna," *Zapiski Russkogo Geograficheskago Obshchestva* (1847):bk. 2:13-20

Lucett, E. *Rovings in the Pacific, from 1837 to 1849 ...by a Merchant Long Resident in Tahiti.* London 1851

Markham, A.H. *The Cruise of the "Rosario" among the New Hebrides and Santa Cruz Islands*. London 1873

Materialy dlia istorii Rumiantsevskago i Moskovskago Publichago Muzeia. 2 vols. M. 1882

Melville, H. *Omoo: A Narrative of Adventures in the South Seas*. NY 1847. 7th ed. NY 1963

Miklukho-Maklai, N.N. "Ostrova Rapanui, Pitkairn, i Mangareva," in *Izvestiia Imperatorskago Russkago Geograficheskogo Obshchestva*, 8 (1873):42-55

Moerenhout, J.-A. *Voyages aux Iles du Grand Océan, contenant des documents nouveaux sur la géographie physique et politique*. 2 vols. Paris 1837; 3d ed. 1942

Montgomery, J., ed. *Journal of Voyages and Travels by the Reverends Daniel Tyerman and George Bennet, Esq., Deputed from the London Missionary Society to Visit their Various Stations*. London 1830. Boston ed. 1832

Montiton, A. "Les Paumotus," *Bulletin Hébdomadaire Illustré de l'Oeuvre de la Propagation de la Foi*, 6. Lyons 1874

Morrison, J. (O. Rutter, ed.). *The Journal of James Morrison, Boatswain's Mate of the Bounty, Describing the Mutiny and Subsequent Misfortunes of the Mutineers*. London 1935

Mortimer, G. *Observations and Remarks Made During a Voyage to the Islands of Tenerife . . . in the Brig Mercury, Commanded by John Cox, Esq*. London 1791

Mulert, F.E., ed. *De Reis van Mr Jacob Roggeveen*. The Hague 1911

Novosil'skii, P.M. *Iuzhnyi polius: iz zapisok byvshago morskago ofitsera*. St. P. 1853

Paris, F.E. *Essai sur la construction navale des peuples extra-Européens*. 2 vols. Paris 1834

Prestwich, J. "Tables of Temperature," *Proceedings of the Royal Society*, 22 (1874):462-68

Purdy, J. *The Oriental Navigator*. London 1816

Rezanov, N.P. "Pervoe puteshestvie Rossiian vokrug sveta, opisannoe N. Riazanovym," *Otechestvennye zapiski*, 24 (1825):246-53

Samarov, A.A., ed. See Lazarev, M.P.

Sarychev, G.A. *Pravila, prinadlezhashchie k morskoi geodezii*. St. P. 1804

Sementovskii, V.N., ed. *Russkie otkrytiia v Antarktike v 1819-1821 godakh*. M. 1951. Contains extracts from the writings of E. Kiselev and P.M. Novosil'skii as well as I.M. Simonov's "Slovo o uspekhakh puteshestviia shliupov 'Vostok' i 'Mirnyi'" and passages from his unfinished MS (No. 4533 at Kazan' State University Library), "Shliupy, 'Vostok' i 'Mirnyi,' ili plavanie Rossiian v Iuzhnom ledovitom okeane i vokrug sveta"

Severgin, M.V. "Instruktsiia dlia puteshestviia okolo sveta," *Severnyi vestnik* (1804): no. 2-3

Shemelin, F.I. *Zhurnal pervogo puteshestviia Rossiian vokrug zemnago shara*. 2 vols. St. P. 1816-18

―――― "Istoricheskoe izvestie o pervom puteshestvii Rossiian vokrug sveta," *Russkii invalid*, 146 (1823):nos. 23-28, 31-36

Simonov, I.M. "Précis du Voyage de découvertes, fait par ordre du gouvernement russe, en 1819, 1820 et 1821, par le Capitaine Bellingshausen," *Journal des Voyages*, 23 (1824):no. 69:12ff.

―――― "Opredelenie geograficheskogo polozheniia mest iakornogo stoianiia shliupov 'Vostok' i 'Mirnyi'" *Zapiski Ministerstva Narodnogo Prosveshcheniia* (1828):pt. 22:44-68. See also Sementovskii, V., above

Skelton, R.A., ed. *The Voyages of Captain Cook: Charts and Views Drawn by Cook and His Officers*. Cambridge 1955

Trenov, B.V. *Katalog Zoologicheskogo Razdela Akademii Nauk*. St. P. 1742

Turnbull, J. *A Voyage Round the World in the Years 1800 to 1804*. 3 vols. London 1805

Vancouver, G. *A Voyage of Discovery to the North Pacific Ocean and Around the World . . . performed in the Years 1790-1795*. 3 vols. London 1798

Wharton, W.J., ed. *Captain Cook's Journal during His First Voyage*. London 1893

Wheeler, D. *Extracts from the Letters and Journal of Daniel Wheeler, Now Engaged in a Religious Visit*. London 1839

Wilkes, C. *Narrative of the United States Exploring Expedition, during the Years 1838 to 1842*. 5 vols. Philadelphia 1845

Wilson, J. *A Missionary Voyage to the Southern Pacific Ocean, Performed in the Years 1796, 1797, 1798, in the Ship Duff*. London 1799

Zavalishin, D.I. "Krugosvetnoe plavanie fregata 'Kreiser' v 1822-25 godakh, pod komandoiu Mikhaila Petrovicha Lazareva," *Drevniaia i novaia Rossiia* (1877):no. 5:54-67; no. 6:11-25; no. 7:199-214; no. 10:143-58

—— *Zapiski dekabrista*. Munich 1904

Zavoiko, V.S. *Vpechatleniia moriaka, vo vremia dvukh puteshestvii krugom sveta*. 2 pts. St. P. 1840

SECONDARY PRINTED MATERIAL

Akhmatov, V.M. "Cartography," in A. Fersman, ed., *The Pacific: Russian Scientific Investigations*. L. 1926, pp. 30-34

Alekseev, A.I. "Russkaia morskaia gidrograficheskaia nauka v XIX-nachale XX vekov," *Trudy Instituta Istorii Estestvoznaniia i Tekhniki*, 42 (1962):bk. 3:86-89

Armstrong, T. "Cook's Reputation in Russia," in R. Fisher and H. Johnston, eds., *Captain James Cook and His Times*. Vancouver 1979, pp. 121-28

Bancroft, H.H. *A History of Alaska, 1730-1885*. San Francisco 1886

Barratt, G.R. "Russian Warships in Van Diemen's Land: the *Kreiser* and *Ladoga* by Hobart Town, 1823," *Slavonic and East European Review* 53 (1975):no. 133:566-78

—— "The Russian Navy and New Holland: Part 1, 1705-1814," *Journal of the Royal Australian Historical Society*, 64 (1979):no. 4:217-34

—— *Bellingshausen: A visit to New Zealand, 1820*. Palmerston North, NZ, 1979

—— *The Russians at Port Jackson, 1814-1822*. Canberra 1980

—— *Russia in Pacific Waters, 1715-1825: A Survey of the Origins of Russia's Naval Presence in the North and South Pacific*. Vancouver 1981

—— *Russophobia in New Zealand, 1838-1908*. Palmerston North, NZ, 1981

—— *Russian Shadows on the British Northwest Coast of North America, 1810-1890*. Vancouver 1983

—— *Russian Exploration in the Mariana Islands 1816-1828*. Micronesian Archaeological Series, No. 17. Saipan 1984

—— *The Russian Discovery of Hawaii, 1804: The Journals of Eight Russian Explorers*. Honolulu 1987

—— *The Russian View of Honolulu, 1809-1826*. Ottawa 1988

—— *Queen Charlotte Sound, New Zealand: The Traditional and European Records*. Ottawa 1987

——— *Russia and the South Pacific, 1696-1840:* vol. 1: *The Russians and Australia*, Vancouver 1988; vol. 2: *Southern and Eastern Polynesia*, Vancouver 1989; vol. 3: *Melanesia and the Western Polynesian Fringe*, Vancouver 1990

Barrow, T. *The Art of Tahiti and the Neighbouring Society, Austral and Cook Islands*. London 1979

Barsov, E.V. "O znachenii grafa N.P. Rumiantseva v etnograficheskoi nauke," *Materialy dlia istorii Rumiantsevskago Muzeia*, M. 1882, bk. 1:93-95

Berg, L.S. *Ocherki po istorii russkikh geograficheskikh otkrytii*. M.-L. 1949. 3d ed. 1962

——— "Russkie otkrytiia v Antarktike i sovremennyi interes k nei," *IVGO*, 81 (1949):no. 2

Bolotnikov, N.I. "Al'bom khudozhnika Pavla Mikhailova," *Krasnyi flot*. 2 Mar. 1949

Bovis, E. de. "L'Etat de la Société tahitienne à l'arrivée des Européens," *Annuaire de Tahiti* (1863):217-301

Brun, X. *Adelbert de Chamisso de Boncourt*. Lyon 1896

Caillot, A.C.E. *Histoire de la Polynésie Orientale*. Paris 1910

Charlot, J. *Choris and Kamehameha*. Honolulu 1958

Chlenov, M.A. ed. E.M. Marzaeva. "A. Ross o toponimike ostrova Pitkern," *Toponimika Vostoka: trudy soveshchaniia*. M. 1962

Christie, E.W.H. *The Antarctic Problem: An historical and Political study*. London 1951

Churkin, V.G. "Atlas Cartography in Pre-Revolutionary Russia," translated by J.R. Gibson, *Canadian Cartographer*, 12 (1975):1-20

Craig, R.D. "The 1780 Russian Inventory of Cook Artifacts," *Pacific Studies*, 2 (1978):no. 1:94-97

Cranstone, B.A. and & Gewers, H.J. "The Tahitian Mourner's Dress," *British Museum Quarterly*, 32 (1968):no. 3-4:138-44

Cross, A.G. "Catherine the Great's Scottish Admiral, Samuel Greig," *M.M.*, 60 (1974):no. 3, pp. 251-65

Dawson, W.R. *The Banks Letters*. London 1958

Day, A. *The Admiralty Hydrographic Service, 1795-1919*. London 1967

Dobrovol'skii, A.D. *Otto fon Kotsebu*. M. 1953

Dubois-Reymond, E.H. *Adelbert von Chamisso als Naturforscher*. Leipzig 1889

Dunmore, J. *French Explorers in the Pacific: Eighteenth Century*. Oxford 1969

Emory, K.P. *Stone Remains in the Society Islands*. Bishop Museum Bulletin 116. Honolulu 1933

——— *Tuamotuan Stone Structures*. Bishop Museum Bulletin 188. Honolulu 1934

——— *Material Culture of the Tuamotu Archipelago*. Pacific Anthropological Records No. 22. Honolulu 1975

Escher, E.K. *Hörners Leben und Wirken*. Zurich 1834

Fedorov-Davydov, A.A. *Russkii pei-sazh XVIII-nachala XIX veka*. M. 1953

Fersman, A., ed. *Tikhii okean: russkie nauchnye issledovaniia*. L. 1926. Also published in a Soviet translation as *The Pacific: Russian Scientific Investigations*. L. 1926. Reprinted by Greenwood Press. NY 1969

Feudel, W. *Adelbert von Chamisso. Leben und Werke*. Leipzig 1971

Friederici, G. "Ein Beitrag zur Kenntnis der Tuamotu-Inseln," *Mitt der Vereins für Erdkunde zu 1910*. (1911):97-176

Friis, H.R. ed. *The Pacific Basin: A History of Its Geographical Exploration*. NY 1967

Gallagher, R.E., ed. *Byron's Journal of his Circumnavigation, 1764-1766*. Cambridge 1964

Gathercole, P. et al. *The Art of the Pacific Islands*. Washington, DC, 1979

Gibson, J.R. *Imperial Russia in Frontier America: The Changing Geography of Supply of Russian America*. NY 1976

Golson, J., ed. *Polynesian Navigation: A Symposium on Andrew Sharp's Theory of Accidental Voyages. JPS*, 71(1962): suppl.

Goncharova, N.N. "Vidopisets E. Korneev," *Iskusstvo* (1972):no. 6:60-64

—— "Khudozhnik krugosvetnoi ekspeditsii 1819-1821 godov E. Korneev," *IVGO*, 105 (1973):67-72

Griffin, J. *Memoirs of Captain James Wilson, Containing an Account of his Enterprises*. London, n.d

Griffiths, R.L. *Y Bara Gwell John Davies, Tahiti, 1772-1855*. London 1955

Grimsted, P.K. *Archives and Manuscript Repositories in the USSR: Leningrad and Moscow*. Princeton 1972

Gunson, N. "A Note on Difficulties of Ethnohistorical Writing with Special Reference to Tahiti," *JPS*, 72 (1963):415-19

Haddon, A.C. & Hornell, J. *Canoes of Oceania. Volume One: the Canoes of Polynesia, Fiji, and Micronesia*. Bishop Museum Special Publication. Honolulu 1936. All volumes of this set were reprinted as one volume by the Bishop Museum in 1974

Handy, E.S.C. *History and Culture in the Society Islands*. Bishop Museum Bulletin 79. Honolulu 1930

—— *Houses, Boats, and Fishing in the Society Islands*. Bishop Museum Bulletin 90. Honolulu 1932

Harding G.L. & Kropelien, B. *The Tahitian Imprints of the London Missionary Society*. Oslo 1950

Heidemaa, I. "Zooloogia kateedri ja Zooloogiamuuseumi Ajaloost," *TUAK*, 2 (1975):164-74

—— "Zooloogiamuuseumi Fondidest," *TUAK*, 11 (1981):87-92

—— *TRU Zooloogiamuuseumi ekskursioonijuht*. Tartu 1981

Hill, S. *Travels in the Sandwich and Society Islands*. London 1856

Hoare, M.E. *The Tactless Philosopher: Johann Reinhold Forster, 1729-1798*. Melbourne 1976

Holland, J. & Everett, J. *Memoirs of the Life and Writings of James Montgomery*. 2 vols. London 1854-56

Horne, C.S. *The Story of the London Missionary Society, 1795-1895*. London 1895

Hotimsky, C.M. "A Bibliography of Captain James Cook in Russian, 1772-1810," *Biblionews and Australian Notes and Queries*, 5 (1971):no. 2:3-12

Houston, S.K. "Chamisso in Hawaii," *Hawaiian Historical Society 48th Annual Report* (1939):55-82

Howay, F.W. ed. R.A. Pierce. *A List of Trading Vessels in the Maritime Fur Trade, 1785-1825*. Kingston, ON, 1973

Howse, D.K. *Greenwich Time*. London 1980

Huculak, M. *When Russia Was in America: The Alaska Boundary Treaty Negotiations, 1824-25, and the Role of Pierre de Poletica*. Vancouver 1971

Huguenin, P. "Raiatea la sacrée, Iles Sous-le-Vent de Tahiti, Océanie française," *Bulletin de la Société Neuchâteloise de Géographie*, (1903):no. 14:1-256

Hunnisett, B. *Steel Engraved Book Illustrations in England*. London 1980

Ivashintsev, N.A. *Russkie krugosvetnye puteshestviia s 1803 po 1849 god*. St.P. 1872. Translated by Glynn Barratt as *Russian Round-the-World Voyages from 1803 to 1849*. Kingston, ON, 1980

Joppien, R. *The Art of Captain Cook's Voyages*. 3 vols. Melbourne 1985-87, Joppien collaborated with Bernard Smith

Kaeppler, A. *Cook Voyage Artifacts in Leningrad, Berne, and Florence Museums*. Bishop Museum Special Publication 66. Honolulu 1978

—— "Tracing the History of Hawaiian Cook Voyage Artifacts in the Museum of Mankind," in T.C. Mitchell, ed., *Captain Cook and the South Pacific*. British Museum Yearbook, 3 (1979):167-97

Kissell, M.L. "The Early Geometric Patterned Chilkat," *American Anthropologist*, 30 (1928):113ff.

Komissarov, B.N. *Grigorii Ivanovich Langsdorf, 1774-1852*. L. 1975

—— *Russkie istochniki po istorii Brazilii pervoi chetverti XIX veka*. L. 1977

Kooijman, S. "Ancient Tahitian God-figures," *JPS*, 73 (1964):110-25

Krümmel, O. *Handbuch der Ozeanographie*. Stuttgart 1907

Kuznetsova, V.V. "Novye dokumenty o russkoi ekspeditsii k Severnomu poliusu," *IVGO*, 100 (1968):no. 3:237-45

Langdon, R. *Island of Love*. London 1959

Laval, H. *Histoire ancienne d'un peuple polynésien*. Braine-le-Comte 1938

Lebedev, D.M. & Esakov, V.A., eds. *Russkie geograficheskie otkrytiia i issledovaniia*. M. 1971

Lebedev, V.L. "Reshenie spornykh voprosov antarkticheskoi istorii na novoi osnove," in *Antarktika: doklady kommissii, 1962 god*. M. 1963

Lenz, W., ed. *Deutsch-Baltisches Biographisches Lexikon, 1710-1960*. Köln-Wien 1970

Liapunova, R.G., ed. *Russkaia Amerika v neopublikovannykh zapiskakh K.T. Khlebnikova*. L. 1979

Likhtenberg, Iu.M. "Gavaiskie kollektsii v sobraniiakh Muzeia Antropologii i etnografii," *SMAE*, 19 (1960):168-205

Ling, H. *Eesti NSV Teaduste Akadeemia Zooloogia ja Botaanika Instituudi Zooloogiamuuseum: NSV Muuseumid*. Tallin 1961

Lovett, R.K. *History of the London Missionary Society, 1795-1895*. 2 vols. London 1899

Lukina, T.A. *Iogann Fridrikh Eshchol'ts*. L. 1975

Lurie, N.O. "Ethnohistory: An Ethnological Point of View," *Ethnohistory*, 8 (1961):78-92

Lysaght, A.M. "Banks's Artists and His 'Endeavour' Collections," in T.C. Mitchell, ed. *Captain Cook and the South Pacific*. British Museum Yearbook, 3 (1979):9-80

Mackaness, G. *The Life of Vice-Admiral William Bligh, RN, FRS*. 2d ed. Sydney 1951

McArthur, N. *Island Populations of the Pacific*. Honolulu 1968

Magidovich, I.P. *Ocherki po istorii geograficheskikh otkrytii*. M. 1957

Mahr, A.C. *The Visit of the "Rurik" to San Francisco in 1816*. Stanford 1932

Makarov, S.O. *"Vitiaz" i Tikhii okean*. St. P. 1894

Markham, C., ed. *The Voyages of Pedro Fernandez de Quiros, 1595-1606*. London 1904

Mazour, A.G. "The Russian-American Company: Private or Government Enterprise," *Pacific Historical Review*, 13 (1944):168-73

Menza, G. *Adelbert von Chamissos Reise um die Welt mit der Romanzoffischen Entdeckungs-Expedition in den Jahren 1815-1818*. Frankfurt 1970

Merrill, E.D. "The Botany of Cook's Voyages," *Chronica Botanica*, 14 (1954):nos. 5-6:52ff.

Miller, E. *That Noble Cabinet*. London 1973

Moorehead, A. *The Fatal Impact: An Account of the Invasion of the South Pacific, 1767-1840*. London 1966

Morison, S.E. *Maritime History of Massachusetts, 1783-1860*. Boston 1921

Naumov, D.V. *Zoologicheskii muzei Akademii Nauk SSSR*. L. 1980

Nevskii, V.V. *Pervoe puteshestvie Rossiian vokrug sveta*. M. 1951

Newbury, C.W. "Te Hau Pahu Rahi: Pomare II and the Concept of Inter-Island Government in Eastern Polynesia," *JPS*, 76 (1967):477-514

Newell, N. "Questions of the Coral Reefs," *Natural History*, 68 (1959):no. 3:120-28

Novikov, P.A. "Zoologicheskie issledovaniia Shamisso i I. Eshchol'tsa vo vremia krugosvetnoi ekspeditsii O.E. Kotsebu na Riurike," *TIIE*, 40 (1962):248-82

Okun', S.B. *Rossiisko-Amerikanskaia Kompaniia*. M. 1939. Translated by C. Ginsburg as *The Russian-American Company*. Cambridge, MA, 1951

Oliver, D.L. *Ancient Tahitian Society*. 3 vols. Honolulu 1974

O'Reilly, P. & Teissier, R. *Tahitiens: Répertoire bio-bibliographique de la Polynésie française*. Paris 1962

—— *Bibliographie de Tahiti et de la Polynésie française*. Paris 1967

Orme, W. *A Defence of the Missions in the South Sea*. London 1827

Ostrovskii, B.G. "O pozabytykh istochnikakh i uchastnikakh ekspeditsii Bellinsgausena-Lazareva," *IVGO*, 81 (1949):no. 2

Pasetskii, V.M. *Geograficheskie issledovaniia dekabristov*. M. 1977

Penrose, C.V. ed. R.C. Anderson and C. Lloyd. *A Memoir of James Trevenen, 1760-1790*. London 1959

Perel', Iu.G. "Vikentii Karlovich Vishnevskii," *Istoriko-astronomicheskie issledovaniia*, 1 (1955):133-48

Petrov, P.N. *Sbornik materialov dlia istorii Imperatorskoi St. P. Akademii Khudozhestv za sto let eio sushchestvovaniia*. 2 vols. St. P. 1864-66

Pierce, R.A. *Russia's Hawaiian Adventure, 1815-1817*. Berkeley 1965

Polansky, P. *Russian Writings on the South Pacific*. Honolulu 1974

Pypin, A.N. *Istoriia russkoi etnografii*. 4 vols. St. P. 1890-92

Ravva, N.P. "Missionery i kolonial'naia ekspansiia na Taiti (Konets XVII–30e gody XIX veka)", in V.A. Tiurin, ed., *Ocherki iz istorii Iugo-Vostochnoi Azii*. M. 1965

—— "Obshchestvennyi stroi Taiti (konets XVIII-nachalo XIX v)," *Narody Azii i Afriki*, (1966):no. 1:59-66

—— *Polineziia: ocherk istorii frantsuzskikh kolonii*. M. 1972

Rosenberg1, I. *Museums of Tartu*. Tallin 1988

Roth, H. Ling. "Tatu in the Society Islands," *Journal of the Anthropological Institute*, 35 (1905):283-94

Rovinskii, V.I. *Miatezhnyi korabl'*. M. 1957

Rozina, L.G. "Kollektsiia Dzhemsa Kuka v sobraniiakh Muzeia Antropologii i Etnografii," *SMAE*, 23 (1966):234-57. Translated by Ella Wiswell and included in Adrienne Kaeppler's *Cook Voyage Artifacts in Leningrad*...(1978), pp. 596ff.

—— "Kollektsiia predmetov s ostrovov Obshchestva v sobraniiakh MAE," *SMAE*, 25 (1969):317-36

—— "Tapa Okeanii (po materialam Muzeia Antropologii i Etnografii," *SMAE*, 30 (1974):51-100

Rudovits, L.F. "Pervoe russkoe krugosvetnoe plavanie, 1803-1806: obzor nauchnykh rabot," *Trudy Gosudarstvennogo Okeanograficheskogo Instituta*, 27 (1954):3-12

Russow, F. "Beiträge zur Geschichte der etnographischen und antropologischen Sammlungen der Kaiserlichen Akademie der Wissenschaften zu St Petersburg," *Sbornik Muzeia po Antropologii i Etnografii pri Imperatorskoi Akademii Nauk* (1900):no. 1

Ryden, S. *The Banks Collection: An Episode in Eighteenth-century Anglo-Swedish Relations.* Stockholm 1965

Sahlins, M. *Social Stratification in Polynesia.* Seattle 1958

Salmon, Tati. "On Ari'is in Tahiti," *JPS*, 19 (1910):40-46

Sarv, I. *Eesti NSV Teaduste Akadeemia Geoloogia Instituudi Eesti NSV Muuseumid.* Tallin 1961

Shafranovskaia, T.K. & Azarov, A.I. "Katalog kollektsii otdela Avstralii i Okeanii MAE," *SMAE*, 39 (1984):5-25

Sharp, A. *The Discovery of the Pacific Islands.* Oxford 1960

⸻ *The Journal of Jacob Roggeveen.* Oxford 1970

Sheshin, A.B. *Dekabrist Konstantin Petrovich Torson.* Ulan-Ude 1980

Shokal'skii, Iu.M. *Okeanografiia.* Petrograd 1917

⸻ "Stoletie so vremeni otpravleniia russkoi antarkticheskoi ekspeditsii," *IVGO*, 60 (1928):bk. 2:55-71

Shtraukh, A.K. "Akademik Fedor Fedorovich Brandt, osnovatel' i pervyi direktor Zoologicheskogo Muzeia," *Zoologicheskii Muzei Akademii Nauk*, (1889):10ff.

Shur, L.A. "Dnevniki i zapiski russkikh puteshestvennikov kak istochnik po istorii i etnografii stran Tikhogo okeana," *Avstraliia i Okeaniia*, (1970):201-12. This is also available in English as "Russian Sources for the Writing of Pacific History," translated by Ella Wiswell, prepared for publication by Robert Langdon, *Journal of Pacific History*, 17 (1982):no. 3:218-21

⸻& Pierce, R.A. "Pavel Mikhailov, Artist in Russian America," *Alaska Journal*, 8 (1978):no. 4:360-63

Skerst, L. von. "Admiral Fabian von Bellingshausen und seine Expedition in die Antarktis," *Jahrbuch des Baltischen Deutschtums*, 8 (1961):85-90

Smith, B.W. *European Vision and the South Pacific, 1768-1850: A Study of the History of Art and Ideas.* Oxford 1960

Smith, E. *The Life of Sir Joseph Banks, President of the Royal Society.* London 1911

Smith, S.P. "The Genealogy of the Pomare Family of Tahiti, from the Papers of the Rev. J.M. Orsmond," *JPS*, 19 (1910):40-46

Staniukovich, T.V. *Etnograficheskaia nauka i muzei.* L. 1978

Stevens, H.N., ed. *New Light on the Discovery of Australia.* London 1930

Stimson, J.F. *Dictionary of Some Tuamotuan Dialects of the Polynesian Language.* The Hague 1964

Stock, E. *The History of the Church Missionary Society.* London 1899

Suris, B.N. "P.N. Mikhailov—khudozhnik i puteshestvennik," *Iskusstvo* (1962):no. 7:66-70

Svet, Ia.M. *Istoriia otkrytiia i issledovaniia Avstralii i Okeanii.* M. 1966

⸻ "Novye dannye o prebyvanii na Kamchatke tretei ekspeditsii Dzhemsa Kuka v 1779 gody," in K.V. Malakhovskii, ed., *Novoe v izuchenii Avstralii i Okeanii.* M. 1972

Thomson, B., ed. *The Voyage of HMS Pandora.* London 1915

Tumarkin, D.D. *Vtorzhenie kolonizatorov v "krai vechnoi vesny": Gavaiskii narod v bor'be protiv chuzhezemnykh zakhvatchikov*. M. 1964

—— "A Russian View of Hawaii in 1804," *Pacific Studies*, 2 (1979):109-31

—— "Materialy ekspeditsii M.N. Vasil'eva—tsennyi istochnik po istorii i etnografii Gavaiskikh ostrovov," *Sovetskaia etnografiia*, (1983):no. 6:48-61

Varep, E.T. "O prepodavanii fizicheskoi geografii v Tartuskom universitete v 1802-1917 godakh," *TUAK*, 9 (1981):61-86

Veselago, F.F. *Admiral Ivan Fedorovich Kruzenshtern*. St. P. 1869

Vishnevskii, B.N. *Puteshestvennik Kirill Khlebnikov*. Perm' 1957

Vorob'ev, N.I. et al. "Etnograficheskie nabliudeniia I.M. Simonova na ostravakh Tikhogo okeana," *IVGO*, 81 (1949):bk. 5:497-504

Vorontsov-Vel'iaminov, V. *Ocherki istorii astronomii v Rossii*. M. 1956

Vucinich, A. *Science in Russian Culture: A History to 1860*. Stanford 1963, 1970

Wagner, H.R. "The Creation of Rights of Sovereignty through Symbolic Acts," *PHR*, 7 (1938):297-326

Ward, J.M. *British Policy in the South Pacific, 1786-1893*. Sydney 1948

Ward, T.G., ed. *American Activities in the Central Pacific, 1790-1870*. 8 vols. Ridgewood, NJ 1966-67

Watson, B.W., ed. *The Soviet Navy: Strengths and Liabilities*. London 1986

Wilder, G.P. *The Breadfruit of Tahiti*. Bishop Museum Bulletin No. 50. Honolulu 1928

Williamson, R.W. *The Social and Political Systems of Central Polynesia*. Cambridge 1924

—— ed. R. Piddington. *Religion and Social Organization in Central Polynesia*. Cambridge 1937

Wood, A.S. *Thomas Haweis, 1734-1820*. London 1957

Zagoskin, N.P. *Istoriia Imperatorskogo Kazanskogo Universiteta za pervye sto let ego sushchestvovaniia, 1804-1904*. 4 vols. Kazan' 1906

Zubov, N.N. *Otechestvennye moreplavateli-issledovateli morei i okeanov*. M. 1954

Name Index

Place Index

Ship Index